ECONOMIC DEVELOPMENT IN AFRICA

ECONOMIC DEVELOPMENT IN AFRICA

PAPERS PRESENTED TO THE

NYASALAND ECONOMIC SYMPOSIUM

HELD IN BLANTYRE 18 TO 28 JULY 1962

EDITED BY E. F. JACKSON

BASIL BLACKWELL, OXFORD

PRINTED IN GREAT BRITAIN
BY ADLARD & SON LTD., DORKING, ENGLAND

CONTENTS

266651

CONTENTS

INTRODUCTION

This Symposium was held from July 18 to 28, 1962 in Blantyre, Nyasaland under the sponsorship of the Government of Nyasaland. It was conceived, organized and chaired by the late D. K. Chisiza, at that time Parliamentary Secretary to the Ministry of Finance and Secretary-General of the Malawi Congress Party. His untimely death in a motor accident is a great loss to his country, to Africa, and to the world.

The Symposium consisted of 23 experts on development from India, Western Europe and the United States, and over 50 African experts and observers concerned with economic and social development. The purpose was to relate the general principles of economic development specifically to the development problems of the African countries. Each of the foreign experts prepared a paper—distributed to the participants prior to the Symposium—in response to a question on an important aspect of African economic development. These papers were summarized at the sessions by their authors and then discussed by the participants. Subjects covered include agriculture, industry, education, manpower, commerce, fiscal and monetary policies, cooperatives, and planning.

In an address at the Symposium, Mr. Chisiza discussed some of the major political and social problems facing the new African nations, and eloquently explained the traditional values of African society which they are striving to realize in ways consistent with modern needs and limitations. Mr. Chisiza asserted that 'an insight into these problems and emotions is essential if foreign experts are to give effective and acceptable advice.' He concluded:

'If we do not accept the good advice of foreign experts, if we are lackadaisical towards some of their brilliant ideas, and if we do not get on well with some of them, it may be because of some of the things which have been mentioned above. The experts do not stand to lose anything if their advice is not acted upon. We would be the losers'.

From *Development Research Digest*.

THE TEMPER, ASPIRATIONS AND PROBLEMS OF CONTEMPORARY AFRICA

BY D. K. CHISIZA†

This paper sets out to provide the background against which the attempt to relate principles of economic development to African economic development should be made. It portrays the mood, the aspirations, the determination and the problems of contemporary Africa. An insight into these emotions and problems is essential if foreign experts are to give effective and acceptable advice.

For the purpose of the present exercise the Continent is divided into two parts: Colonial Africa and free Africa.

REVOLT AGAINST COLONIAL RULE

In Colonial Africa (which comprises South Africa, South West Africa, Bechuanaland, Swaziland, Basutoland, Southern Rhodesia, Northern Rhodesia, Nyasaland, Mozambique, Angola, Kenya, Uganda, Algeria and Rio de Oro) the dominant sentiment is the urge to be free. It is no exaggeration to say that the African in this part of Africa is in a state of general revolt. He is revolting against Colonial rule; more specifically:

> He is rebelling against the imperialist treachery of trapping him into signing treaties which are subsequently unilaterally violated by the metropolitan powers.
> He is rebelling against rule without the consent of the governed.
> He is rebelling against the practice of packing colonial legislatures with nominated stooges who are responsible not to the people they are supposed to represent but to the administrators who nominate them.
> He is rebelling against the practice of granting settlers political representation which is out of all proportion to their numerical strength.

He is rebelling against the denial of freedom of speech, assembly, association, movement and publication.

He is rebelling against the subtle conspiracy of imperialist powers to reduce our traditional chiefs to the status of paid messengers who are used as whipping boys against their own people (while they 'behave') but who are fired at will if they identify themselves with nationalist forces.

He is rebelling against the failure of imperialist powers to extend the principle of 'the rule of law' to their colonial territories.

He is rebelling against the semidictatorial regimes of colonial administrators who joined the colonial civil service with no love for politics and who have spent half their lives carrying out other people's orders but who have ironically been turned into decision makers, politicians and administrators all in one — a role which cannot but call forth the despots in them.

He is rebelling against the hypocritical policies of some imperial powers, which claim that their objective is 'to prepare Africans for ultimate self-rule', when in point of fact they do absolutely nothing of the kind.

He is rebelling against the deliberate failure of colonial powers to train African administrators and technicians to shoulder the responsibilities of self-rule.

He is rebelling against the concept of land purchase which dispossesses us of the mainstay of our lives.

He is rebelling against those iniquitous imperialistic agricultural policies which are designed to victimize rather than to educate the peasants, e.g. the 'Malimidwe' policy in Nyasaland, which Dr Banda has just put an end to.

He is rebelling against industrial colour-bar practised by the capitalists and condoned by imperialist powers.

He is rebelling against the economic neglect into which our countries are relegated by imperialist powers.

He is rebelling against the fact that Mother Africa is dispossessed of her mineral rights.

He is rebelling against the imperialistic device of 'imperial preference' which guarantees imperial products markets in the colonies while it does not guarantee markets for the primary products of the colonies.

He is rebelling against the low wages and the poor housing conditions to which we are condemned.

He is rebelling against the tenancy and squatter system introduced in some of the colonies.

He is rebelling against the slave labour system under which some of our brethren are groaning.

He is rebelling against the imperialist hypocrisy of condoning racial discrimination practised in their own dependencies while condemning that which is indulged in in South Africa.

He is rebelling against the abstract kind of education (which bears no relationship to the practical problems of our lives) we are given by the imperialist powers.

He is rebelling against the unnecessarily high cost of colonial administration and the resultant waste of public funds.

He is rebelling against the imperialist concept that the duty of a colonial police force is to protect settlers and to victimize African nationalists.

He is rebelling against arbitrary searches, arrests and seizures.

He is rebelling against detention and imprisonment without trial in a court of law.

He is rebelling against the colonial judiciary systems which are deliberately designed to be financially dependent upon the Government with the result that they fail to be impartial.

DETERMINATION TO BUILD NEW NATIONS

In free Africa the dominant sentiment is different. Here the main desire is to found modern nations, modern states —

in which respect for the dignity of 'the human individual and the sanctity of his personality' shall be recognized to be the sacred fountain of democratic principles;

in which basic human rights shall be guaranteed;

that will ensure religious, political, social and economic justice to every citizen;

in which indigenous people will have the freedom to choose what they want to adopt from foreign cultures;

in which the ordinary man will enjoy a sense of participation;

in which the indigenous people will have the right to manage or mismanage their own affairs;

in which the individual will be afforded opportunities to develop his talents;

in which everyone will enjoy freedom from want and fear; and a sense of security and belonging;

which will charge their citizens with a sense of mission in life;

that will foster the spirit of self-help and promote creative activities among the masses;

that will accord economic modernization the primacy it deserves;
which will be guided by the realization that we are living in an
economically interdependent world;
whose relationship with other states will be guided by the principle
of co-existence;
whose citizens will stifle dictatorial tendencies and refuse to be the
slaves of any dictator;
whose leaders will ever strive to preserve the hard-won independence.

SOME PROBLEMS OF NATION BUILDING

The drive to found modern states is bringing in its wake problems which
will require unprecedented resourcefulness and originality of thought for
their solution. The following is a brief enumeration of some of the
problems which Africans in independent African states are grappling with.
A.   On the Pan African level one of the main problems is that of reconciling divergent views on the best method of unifying Africa. There are
those who seem to believe in the dictum: 'Seek ye first political Unity
and economic union will be added thereunto.' There are others who
seem to hold the converse of this view, namely, 'Seek ye first economic
union and political union will follow.' While it is true that in the fight for
freedom the valid and efficacious slogan is 'seek ye first the political kingdom and all other things shall be added unto it', it is highly doubtful
whether the slogan also holds good in relation to the problem of unifying
Africa.

For one thing, nationals of various countries will not be favourably
disposed towards the idea of surrendering national sovereignty to a Pan
African political body unless and until the novelty of Self-Government
and Independence has been given reasonably sufficient time to wear off.
The marginal utility of Independence and national sovereignty is
infinitely higher in a country which has just become independent than in
a country which has been independent for a longer time.

For another, if the unification of Africa is not to be merely a federation of political intellectuals; if, that is to say, the unification of Africa is to
have meaningful content for the ordinary Africans (and it is these who
matter), an effort must be made to inculcate a political loyalty which is
higher than nationalism. A deliberate campaign by nationalist movements
to instil regional consciousness, and subsequently Pan Africanism, in the
minds of the masses must be undertaken immediately.

So far the nationalist movements have not initiated such a campaign.

Among the educated the inculcation of regional consciousness and Pan Africanism can be undertaken simultaneously. But to adopt a similar approach towards the masses would be to reveal a gross lack of understanding of mass behaviour.

Regional political federations and the ultimate 'United nations of Africa' can be successful only if they are superimposed on solid foundations of regional consciousness and Pan Africanism.

In this connection, it is pertinent to mention that the enemies of Pan African unity are those individuals who, driven by excessive ambition, attempt to pose as the leaders of the rest of Africa. The unification of Africa can only be based on absolute equality and not on pride that apes humility.

B.   The problem of forming regional economic unions is also engaging the minds of most African leaders. The first task in this respect seems to be that of regrouping the territories of Africa into larger economic units. But this regrouping exercise can only be partial until the whole of Africa is free; for an economic union between a dependent territory and an independent state is conceivable only on paper. Assuming, however, that the whole continent is free, what criteria must guide the selection of countries which must be grouped together?

There are several factors to take into consideration, such as: (a) geographical contiguity; (b) manageability in terms of sheer size; (c) past economic association; (d) similarity in the level of industrial development; (e) similarity in political ideas; (f) similarity in the level of political advancement; (g) personal friendship between leaders; (h) past association with metropolitan powers; (i) cultural affinity; (j) ethnic similarity; and (k) linguistic considerations. Apart from these there are a number of economic conditions which must be fulfilled if the unions are to be successful and advantageous to member countries.

Looking at the problem from the angle of geographical contiguity alone, it would appear at first sight that a free Africa would have to be divided up into ten regions. One would hope that these economic regions would later become political federations which together would eventually form the 'United nations of Africa'.

C.   Then there is the debate on whether the Pan African Trade Union Organization should be affiliated to any of the International Trade Union Organizations. There seems to be a concensus of opinion that the P.T.O. should be independent of the international organizations. But opinion is divided on whether or not the national trade union organizations should be free to associate themselves with international organizations.

It seems peculiar logic to argue that the P.T.O. should be independent of either the I.C.F.T.U. or W.F.T.U. but that the national organizations should be free to affiliate to either of the international organizations. For, if it is assumed — for the sake of argument — that all national organizations which form the P.T.O. choose to affiliate to the international organizations, a most ridiculous situation would arise where member organizations of the P.T.O. would be for affiliation to international organizations but where the P.T.O. itself would be against the idea. It would be similar to a situation in which individual M.P.s in their capacity as representatives of their constituencies profess communism, but where in their capacity as members of a legislative assembly, they advocate capitalism.

If it has been decided that the P.T.O. must be independent of any organization, it must needs follow that national organizations must be affiliated only to the P.T.O. Those who advocate a rival policy to this are people who, having failed to translate such trade union support as they claim to have in their respective countries into funds, are financially dependent on one or another of the international trade union organizations. For such people to sever connections with international organizations is looked upon as being tantamount to cutting the financial lifeline which exists between them and international organizations.

D. A similar problem to the foregoing is that which relates to the independence of a national trade union organization from political control. There is a certain amount of undetected confusion here. There is such a thing as political control of a trade union movement, and there is voluntary subordination of a trade union movement to the nationalist movement. The two are not synonymous. The former means the manipulation of a trade union movement for the personal benefit of the people in power; the latter signifies the desire of the trade union leaders to minimize the causes of disunity, misunderstanding and bickering, and to promote unity of action and loyalty to a single leader so that independence and national reconstruction are achieved in the minimum of time. Political control as defined here cannot be condoned by any right thinking person. But it would be wrong, utterly wrong, to condemn 'the voluntary subordination of the trade union movement to the nationalist movement' in the erroneous belief that it is the same thing as political control. Those who indulge in this condemnation are probably not aware, as they should be, of the strategies which a nationalist movement must adopt to achieve the goal of independence.

In a colonial territory it is a big mistake to allow a situation to develop in which the strength of the trade union movement is equal to or more than that of the nationalist movement. The fight against colonialism demands unity of action, loyalty and submissiveness to a single leader. The existence of a trade union movement of equal strength to that of the nationalist movement tempts trade union leaders into vying with, and challenging the leadership of, the top nationalist leader. Further, it divides the loyalty of the masses when the exigency of the time requires undivided loyalty.

If the trade union movement is to contribute to the achievement of independence, it seems necessary during the struggle for freedom that it should be a minor organization. After independence the trade union movement could come into its own. But here again, it is important to bear in mind that singleness of purpose, unity of action, undivided loyalty, a sense of participation, and a feeling of oneness among the masses are absolutely essential to the success and stability of a young government. It would seem, therefore, that to be useful in post independence days, the trade union movement must either be manned by people who will pledge loyalty to political leaders so long as the latter do not indulge in dictatorial activities or there must be such a community of interest between the two movements that they should stand or fall together.

E.   In some independent African States, another problem is to define the term 'African Socialism'. Many African leaders profess to be socialists of one sort or another. The danger of muddled thinking on this subject is that the masses — if not the leaders themselves — may be toying with the concept of socialism when in point of fact they have got hold of the wrong end of the stick of either communism or capitalism. Are we talking about guided capitalism and the parody of communism? Or are we trying to draw inspiration from *Das Kapital* to enable us to evolve an 'African Economic Ideology'?

F.   Then there is the problem of initiative. If a nationalist movement is to achieve the goal of independence, it is vitally important that one of the leaders should be elevated well above the others; that his former equals should look upon themselves as his juniors; that they should accept his decision as final; and that they should pledge loyalty to his leadership. But once independence has been achieved, the problem of reconciling submissiveness to the top leader and individual initiative on the part of second-level leaders arises. To a man who has been surrounded by submissive associates for a long time, the exercise of initiative by his associates is easily misconstrued as a sign of rivalry and disloyalty.

G.   Another issue currently engaging the minds of some Africans is that which relates to the participation or non-participation of African ministers in business activities. Since the most educated and the most influential Africans will be Government ministers, is it realistic to import the convention that ministers should not participate in business? If ministers set the example of frittering away their incomes on conspicuous consumption, there can be little hope that people will learn to save and invest; for the masses tend to imitate the attitude and behaviour of their leaders.

H. Further, all over Africa nationalist ministers face the problem of striking a balance between shunning their counterparts in the U.K. and the U.S. and having these counterparts pat them on the back. To be praised by western ministers is a kiss of political death in a nationalist country. But for nationalist ministers to get foreign aid they must command the respect and win approbation of western leaders.

J. The question has also been asked: how should a nationalist leader behave when he is a minister? Should he continue to behave like a nationalist and hob-nob with former party colleagues in the old hide-outs or should he begin to behave like a ruler? If the latter is to be the case, how does a ruler behave? And will such behaviour not remind the masses of the detestable colonial days?

K. It is generally agreed these days that strong man governments are needed in Africa and in other underdeveloped parts of the world. But the question must be asked: where do we draw the line between a strong man and a dictator? Professor William O. Jones has described a strong man government as a dictatorship which the citizens choose to put up with. There seems to be a great deal of truth in his statement. The danger of a strong man government is that if it is successful, its very success seems to convince the strong man of the need to have a really strong government which may be just a synonym for benevolent despotism.

L. Assuming a strong man has lapsed into a dictator, backed by the police and the army, how can his clutch be dislodged? The mind of a dictator is obviously not open to persuasion. Constitutional methods, therefore, are out of the question. In the circumstances we are left with nothing short of assassination and violent take-over as possible antidotes.

Assassination is a most dangerous method to use, because it has a built-in tendency to become habitual. Once assassination has been used it may at a later stage be used even against a legitimate and democratic government — if the assassins have personal grudges against the people in power.

Violent take-over presupposes that the people who are plotting the take-over have access to arms. This is far from being the case in most countries in Africa.

There is, of course, the possibility that the army can revolt against the dictator. Indeed this is what has happened in many countries which have fallen under the rule of a dictator. But an army that has revolted once establishes a precedent of revolt which is more often than not followed by similar revolts in subsequent years. A concatenation of revolts cannot be to the good of any country.

In the light of the foregoing, one hesitates to suggest a remedy for the problem of dictatorship. But if nothing else is clear, one thing is, and that is that no effort should be spared to prevent the establishment of a dictatorship. Salvation seems to lie not in 'cure' but in 'prevention'.

M. An allied problem to the foregoing is that there seems to be an alarming pattern of violent seizures of power in Arab and Asian countries. The problem for Africa is how to insulate herself from this trend.

N. One major problem which party leaders face is how to maintain the cohesion of their parties after independence. The sense of mission and dedication seems to vanish with the advent of independence. Full-time party workers give up party organization and take up paid employment. This withdrawal of able young men from party work cannot fail to have an effect on the strength of the party in power. This weakening of the governing party constitutes a problem in the sense that if party members are disorganized there is the possibility of disillusionment and bickering setting in on a mass scale.

O. Another problem relates to the role of the nationalist movement after independence. What should be the role of a political party that has formed a government in the economic development of the country?

P. In a country where the tentacles of the nationalist movement have pervaded every village and where the nationalist fervour has been very high, finding interesting and useful things to do for the freedom fighters becomes an exigency of the first order after independence.

Q. After independence nationalist leaders must canalize the nationalist sentiment of their followers into constructive channels, but if the switch from political agitation to national reconstruction is too sudden, it results in a psychological anticlimax. Here again the problem is how to strike a balance that will lead to a smooth transition from political agitation to nation building.

R. In the final analysis the nationalist struggle boils down to one long chapter of complaints and criticism. Towards the end of this struggle this attitude of mind becomes a habit. After independence the question is how to break this habit of fault finding. For if it is not broken, new criticism will be trained on the new governments. If the criticism is genuine and constructive, it will do the new governments a lot of good. But the chances are that it will be the type of criticism which succeeds only in undermining the confidence which the people may have in the governments.

S. Most nationalist leaders are men without professions. Once they become M.P.s or ministers they tend to look upon their public offices as sources of income. To that extent it can be said that their personal interests become identified with the national interests. Such men find it very difficult to welcome the possibility of losing office. Furthermore,

2

they do everything to hang on to their posts and to suppress the emergence of young men who might pose as possible rivals. The result is that the political system lacks new blood and is more often than not strewn with dead wood. One possible answer to this problem seems to be that politicians in Africa should be pensionable after, say, five years of holding public office. The need to hang on to a post which is looked upon as a source of income might thereby be obviated.

T. Unless measures are taken to prevent and guard against it, official corruption may also become a problem in some parts of Africa. Many people who are basically men of integrity may lapse into a certain amount of corruption unconsciously. Among people who have spent the greater part of their lives fighting for freedom and subsisting on less than the bare necessities of life, the marginal utility of a certain amount of comfort after independence is very high. Post-independence days are looked upon as days of some rest and relaxation when they too can lead normal lives and attend to the fancies of their families. Herein lies a weakness which may or may not result in corruption, depending upon the strength of an individual's character.

U. Another problem is that when independence is won, the academicians endeavour to supplant the leadership of the non-academicians who fought and struggled for freedom. The trouble is that academicians have neither interest in, nor a hold on, the masses. But stable government can be maintained only if mass support is actively maintained.

V. On the west coast of Africa we are witnessing the problem of how American negroes who elect to return to Mother Africa are accepted among their African confreres.

W. In yet other countries we also have the problem of those Europeans and Asians who have thrown in their lot with the nationalists, who have sacrificed everything to further the cause of freedom, but who — maybe because of the colour of their skin — cannot enjoy a sense of belonging and participation in the ranks of the nationalists.

DETERMINATION TO PRESERVE AFRICAN OUTLOOK

Different as the two parts of Africa may appear to be in temper, in immediate objectives, and in some of the problems which they face, they have one thing in common, and that is their determination to preserve the substance of the African outlook. It is true that there is no uniform outlook in Africa. But it is possible to single out certain features which are always present in almost every African community. What follows is a description of those features.

A.   Unlike easterners who are given to meditation or westerners who
have an inquisitive turn of mind we of Africa, belonging neither to the
east nor to the west, are fundamentally observers, penetrating observers,
relying more on intuition than on the process of reasoning.

B.   Our field is not that of spiritualism which is the domain of the east
nor that of science and technology which is the hobby-horse of the west,
but that of human relations. This is where we excel and where we shall
set an example for the rest of the world.

C.   Since time immemorial we have never claimed that we have arrested
the orb of truth. As a result we believe that there is a lot to be learned
from other cultures. That is why novelty has such a great pull for us and
that is why we do not impose our beliefs on other people.

D.   There is a tendency in the west, whether the westerners themselves
know it or not, for people to assume that man lives to work. We believe
that man works to live. This view of life gives rise to our high preference
for leisure.

E.   With us, life has always meant the pursuit of happiness rather than
the pursuit of beauty or truth. We pursue happiness by suppressing
isolationism, individualism, negative emotions, and tension on the one
hand; and by laying emphasis on a communal way of life, by encouraging
positive emotions and habitual relaxation, and by restraining our desires
on the other.

F.   We live our lives in the present. To us the past is neither a source of
pride nor the cause for bitterness. The 'Hereafter', we realize, must be
given thought but we fail to revel in its mysteries.

G.   Our attitude to religion has more often than not been determined by
our habitual desire for change. We adhere to a religious faith only so long
as it is the only faith we know. If some other faith comes our way we do
not insulate ourselves against its influence. The result is that often we are
reconverted to the dismay of those who converted us first. Sometimes we
linger undecided between two faiths while at other times we just marvel
at the claims of various religious persuasions. That we behave in this way
is no indication that we are fickle; rather it is an indication of the fact that
in each one of the religious faiths which we encounter there is an element
of divine truth whose fascination we fail to resist. And this is as it should
be for religion is one. Iqbal has told us: 'There is only one religion but
there are many versions of it.' Putting it figuratively Rumi, on the other
hand, has said, 'There are many lamps but the light is one.'

H.   In Africa, we believe in strong family relations. We have been urged
by well meaning foreigners to break these ties for one reason or another.
No advice could be more dangerous to the fabric of our society. Charity
begins at home. So does love of our fellow human beings. By loving our

parents, our brothers, our sisters, cousins, aunts, uncles, nephews and nieces and by regarding them as members of our families, we cultivate the habit of loving lavishly, of exuding human warmth, of compassion and of giving and helping. But once conditioned in this way one behaves in this way not only to one's family, but also to the clan, the tribe, the nation and to humanity as a whole.

If independent African states succeed in subordinating national loyalties to international loyalty they will do so because they have a solid foundation of lesser loyalties on which to superimpose international loyalty. To foster international loyalty among people who are steeped in individualism is to attempt to build a pyramid upside down. It cannot stand, it has no base and will topple over.

How can a person who has no real affection for his brothers or sisters have any love for a poor Congolese or Chinese peasant? When we talk about international peace, understanding and goodwill, we are actually talking about international love. But universal love does not grow from nothing; its root is family love and unless this root is there it cannot grow. The unification of mankind ultimately depends on the cultivation of family love. It would seem, therefore, that in this respect we in Africa have started towards that noble goal from the right end.

J.   Although hitherto we in Africa have been the least involved in the strains and stresses of international wars, the threat of a nuclear war has the same perturbing effects on us as it has on the rest of mankind. In the past we have lagged behind in various walks of life. We have now rolled up our sleeves; we are bending down to do a good job of work, to develop our countries and to make up for lost time. But it is at this very moment in history that the threat of the indiscriminate annihilation of the human race looms on the horizon.

We condemn war because it interferes with man's development, because it causes untold yet avoidable human suffering and because it is unnatural to man.

We believe that in the final analysis war is a habit. Those people who engage in wars are people who, on the one hand, have conditioned themselves to answer provocation with guns and bombs and who, on the other, have become unconsciously addicted to the rhythm: war-peace-war-peace. When peace goes on for a considerable period they get bored with it; they unconsciously want a change, they want something exciting, sensational — war.

Wars are not usually waged when the politicians are busy building the nations. They are indulged in when the party in power has run out of useful development ideas. They are possible because there is no higher authority above the nation-state dedicated to the maintenance of international peace, law and order. In Africa tribal wars were possible only in the absence of a higher authority above the tribe-state. As soon as colonial powers set up national governments 'to maintain peace, law and order' tribal warfare bade us goodbye. It is an irony of fate that those who prescribed this antidote for the ills of Africa hesitate to treat their own ills with it.

To effect the outbreak of peace on our planet we must: (a) uncondition ourselves; we must learn to answer provocation not with bombs but with tolerance, forgiveness, and love; (b) change our governments just before they have finished executing their major projects, and (c) form an international government charged with the duty of only maintaining international peace, law and order.

K. In human relations, we like to slur over the 'I', 'mine', etc., and to lay emphasis instead on the 'we', 'our', etc. Put differently, this means the suppression of individualism. Ours is a society where if you found seven men and one woman amongst them you would never know, unless told, whose wife the lady is. There just isn't that forwardness in us to declare our 'personal' ownership of anything. If I happen to have some heads of cattle, a car, a house, a daughter, a fishing net or a farm, it is 'our' net, it is my car just as it is my brother's, my father's, my cousin's, my uncle's or my friend's car. He or she has got as much say over it as I have. Individualism is foreign to us and we are horrified at its sight. We are by nature extroverts.

L. Love for communal activities is another feature of our outlook. Look at any African game or pastime and you notice right away that its performance calls for more than one person. Our dances are *party* dances demanding drummers, singers and dancers. Game hunting is done in *parties*. (Even those Africans who own guns cannot abandon the habit of taking some friends along with them when going out for a hunt!) The telling of fables and stories with us calls for a *group* of boys and girls not just one or two. Draw-net fishing is done by a *group* of people. Fishing with hooks is also done in *canoe parties* of two, three or four; each canoe taking at least two people. The preparation of fields, the weeding, the sowing of seeds, the harvesting, the pounding of grains — all these activities are done in parties of either men or women. Even looking after cattle is not a one-man affair. A boy might start out alone from his cattle kraal but he is sure to take his cattle to where his fellow cattle herders are with their cattle. Beer drinking is not only a group affair but also an affair that calls for drinking from the same pot and from the same drinking stick (holy communion at its best!). Above all, to see Africans mourn the death of someone is to believe that few things are done individually here.

Such an outlook can only emanate from genuine love for each other —

an unconscious love which has existed in our society since time immemorial. Here is that selfless love which all the prophets of God have
preached. It isn't something that has just been inculcated into us nor
something that has been imported from without us; it is something
springing from within us. Instead of foreign missionaries teaching
Africans how to love each other, they would do well to sit back and
observe with amazement that the very relationship they would like to
bring about is as a matter of fact already existing among Africans. Foreign
missionaries should come to Africa not so much to teach love to the
indigenous people but to see living examples of selfless love manifested in
the African way of life.

M. We are also famous for our sense of humour and dislike for melancholy. Gloom on the face of an African is a sure sign that the wearer of
that expression has been to a 'school' of some kind where he might have
got it into his head that joy and melancholy can be bed fellows in his
heart. Otherwise our conception of life precludes, as far as possible, the
accommodation of dejection. An African will not hesitate to leave a job if
he sees that he does not get a kick out of it. For him quitting a dull place
for a more lively one, even if he has a stake in the former, is nothing to
blink at. Many times I have observed people avoid the 'intellectual', the
reticent type of African as much as they avoid rattlesnakes if only by so
doing they can escape from the melancholy of the intellectual.

Even if there are real causes for sorrow somehow our people manage to
make molehills of these and mountains of the causes for happiness. The
mainstay of our life is humour. So characteristic of Africa is this that most
foreigners know this continent as 'The Land of Laughter'. What they
probably do not know is that 'laughter relieves tension. People who laugh
easily are relaxed persons'; that people with the ability to relax possess one
of the most prized qualities in this wearisome world and that a habitual
sense of humour in a person is synonymous with a 'positive outlook on
life so desperately needed in the present negative conditioning world'.

N. Our society stifles malice, revenge and hate with the result that we
are free from these cankers. Were we disposed to avenge the wrongs that
have been meted out to us by foreigners down through the ages the
course of human events would have taken a different turn altogether.
Were we addicts of hate, the Gospel of Jesus would have met its Waterloo
on the shores of the seas that border this troubled continent. Were we to
harbour malice the African empires that flourished on this continent —
empires like that of Monomotapa, Songhai, Mali and Ghana — would
have extended beyond the confines of Africa to the detriment of the
human race. But God spared us all that. As a result we tolerate on our soil
even neurotic crowds of foreigners who could not be tolerated in their

own countries; we waste love on foreign elements which are inveterately selfish, individualistic and ungrateful. Above all, we do not look forward to a day when we shall have nefarious schemes against any race.

O.   Among those who have studied Africa closely we have a reputation for taking delight in generosity, kindness and forgiveness. It has been said, with great truth, by some foreigners that few Africans will ever get rich 'for the simple reason that the African tends to be too generous'. Well, we do not want to be rich at the cost of being mean! Our society hinges on the practice of 'mutual aid and co-operation' whose corollary is generosity. When our chiefs, kings and emperors gave out acres and acres of land to foreigners they weren't prompted by bribes or stupidity but by this selfsame relishable habit of generosity. Generosity is the life-blood of our society. But even more precious, I think, is our spirit of kindness. For me to be able to walk into the home of any African between Khartoum and Durban and be certain to be accorded the utmost hospitality is to my mind a pulsating example of what quality of human relationship our society is capable of producing. It exhibits kindness at its best.

Nor is the scope of our kindness limited to our own race. Many are the days when we have preserved the life of one foreigner or another. Times without number we've gone out of our way to hunt for water, eggs, milk, chicken, fish, meat, fruit, vegetables, etc., for a choosey stranger. We've carried literally thousands of foreigners on our heads and shoulders; we've washed their clothes; we've reared their children; we've looked after their homes; we've stood by their sides in peril; we've defended them in times of war; we've given them land, we've given them our precious minerals, nay, we've given them our all. But all the gratitude we get for all that is ridicule, contempt, ill-treatment and the belief on their part that created us to be 'hewers of wood and drawers of water'. No. God knows our kindness does not stem from a feeling of inferiority. God knows we are not kind because we are fools, but because He had it that we should be kindness drunk and not pride drunk.

P.   And yet, in spite of all this ingratitude, we are still capable of forgiving and forgetting. We are in a position to do this because in our society forgiveness is the rule rather than the exception. Professor Richard A. Brown of Bluefield State College (U.S.A.) has this to say about this quality of forgiveness in us:

'The simple spirituality of the Negro and his African brother, their deep rooted belief in God, their matchless capacity to love and forgive even those who mistreat them, their natural humanity; all these characteristics of these people, tempered and refined in the furnace of trials and tribulations down through the years, are qualities the world stands most in need of in these difficult times.'

But an American Negro poet, Langston Hughes has uttered a timely
warning:

> Because my mouth
> is wide with laughter
> and my throat
> is deep with song,
> You do not think
> I suffer after
> I have held my pain so long.

Q. Another outstanding characteristic of our outlook is our love for
music, dance and rhythm. Our throats are deep with music, our legs full
of dance while our bodies tremor with rhythm. The proper sub-title
for Africa should have been 'Land of music, dance and rhythm'. This
three pronged phenomenon is indeed the spice of our life. We sing while
we hoe. We sing while we paddle our canoes. Our mourning is in the
form of dirges. We sing as we pound food grains in mortars. We sing in
bereavement just as on festive occasions. Our fables always include a
singing part. We sing to while away the monotonous hours of travel. We
sing to the strains of our musical instruments. The pulses of our drums
evoke in us song responses. We sing under moonlit nights. We sing under
the canopy of the blue sky. Gramophone record music entrances us not
because it's foreign or something out of the way, but just because it's
music. With us music, as also dance and rhythm, is a relishable obsession.

We have war dances, victory dances, stag dances, remedial dances,
marriage dances, dances for women only, mixed dances, dances for the
initiated only, dances for the youth — but all indulged in with ecstatic
abandon. We nod our heads, rock our necks, tilt our heads and pause.
We shake our shoulders, throw them back and forth, bounce breasts and
halt to intone our thanks to Him who ordained that we be alive. We
rhythmically hefty shake our rear ends, our tummies duck and peer,
our legs quick march, slow march, tap dribble, quiver and tremble while
our feet perform feats. 'Dance!' What a world of emotions that word calls
forth in us!

But dance and music by themselves are crude art, rough hewn and
devoid of sublimity. So to these we unconsciously add rhythm for a blend
that possesses both charm and grace. Rhythm is our second nature.

There is rhythm in the winnowing and pounding of grains, there is
rhythm in the gait of our women folk; there is highly developed rhythm
in coition, there is rhythm in the groan of a sick person, there is complex
rhythm in the milking of a cow, there is rhythm in pulling a drawnet
to the shore, there is rhythm that beggars description in the beats of our

tom-toms, there is rhythm that defies analysis in 'marimba', there is rhythm in almost everything we do.

R. Finally, we have a strong dislike for imposing our beliefs on other people. British people established themselves in their erstwhile and present day dependencies with the self-assuredness of angels. They believed with puritanical fervour — that the British way is the God-vouchsafed way of doing things. Their way of living is what mankind was destined to evolve up to; their ideas the gospel truth; their beliefs the paragons of man's triumph over 'superstition'. No other way — least of all the colonial people's way — could measure up to it still less be better than it. So they believed there was nothing for them to learn from their colonial subjects while the colonial indigenes had to be recast into the British mould of life, thought and belief.

That mode of thinking was all very well for purposes of empire building. To rule a people successfully you've got to drill it into their heads that you are in every way superior to them and that, therefore, it is the right thing for them to be under you. But for purposes of progress, the preoccupation of man, that way of thinking actually stops short of arresting progress itself. The advancement of man uncompromisingly demands a ceaseless synthesis of ideas, a blending of ways of living, a come and go of beliefs and above all a willingness to believe that the best is yet to come.

If persisted in this attitude of finality, superiority and self-deception can only promote hate and racial discord. When other peoples do not assert themselves it isn't that they haven't got something to be proud of, something that they believe is unrivalled, but just that they haven't got the same vulgarity of throwing their weight about and imposing themselves and their beliefs on other people. They are willing to live and let live. Further they have the sense of knowing that the part of a listener and an open mind are the 'open sesame' to the fortune of knowledge and wisdom. There is a great deal that foreigners, here as well as abroad, have to learn from the colonial peoples.

CONCLUSION

Such are currents and cross-currents of the emotions which determine the shape of things in Africa. If we do not accept the good advice of foreign experts, if we are lackadaisical towards some of their brilliant ideas and if we do not get on well with some of them, it may be because of some of the things which have been mentioned above. The experts do not stand to lose anything if their advice is not acted upon. We would be the losers.

However, since most experts want to feel, as we would expect them to, that their efforts to help fellow human beings are bearing fruit, they might do a lot worse than take off time to gain insight into our aspirations, outlook and problems so that they might be better equipped to render advice which will be readily acceptable.

INCREASING AGRICULTURAL PRODUCTIVITY IN TROPICAL AFRICA

BY WILLIAM O. JONES

Director, Food Research Institute, Stanford University, Stanford, Calif., USA

Governmental policies specifically directed at that part of the nation's population which is engaged in the production of food, feed, and fibre are the continuing subject of earnest and frequently heated debate in nearly every nation of the world today. They arouse discussion and disagreement in the industrialized countries of Western Europe and North America and in the agrarian economies of tropical Africa and Asia; they agitate the Kremlin and the White House and have direct influence on the international policies of London and Peiping.

That major questions about the most satisfactory procedures for dealing with the agricultural sector of a nation's economy should go so long unresolved may be taken to imply ignorance or uncertainty on the part of economists about the measures necessary for agricultural achievement. In fact, the conditions for high productivity in agriculture are known, and experience in many parts of the western world attests their efficacy. The reason why they have not been achieved more generally is their real or apparent conflict with other social, political, or imaginary goals of political leaders. In the United States, Canada, and most countries of Western Europe, optimum efficiency in agriculture is inhibited by humanitarian concern about the economic well-being of all members of the society, by a nostalgic desire to perpetuate characteristics of pre-industrial, even of pre-market agriculture, and by a practical concern for the political power of rural electorates. In the communist countries of eastern Europe agricultural efficiency has suffered from doctrinaire attempts to treat farms like factories, from attempts to make farm people bear too much of the cost of modernizing the economy, and perhaps from a persisting fear and dislike of the peasantry.

Agriculture differs technically from manufacturing because its characteristic input, land, is necessarily immobile, heterogeneous, and extensive, and because the supply of three other essential inputs — water, sunlight, and warmth — are usually uncertain and uncontrollable. It differs also because of special safeguards that have historically been accorded to the individual's rights in land in many societies, and because it is possible for farmers to achieve a measure of self-sufficiency, though at high cost, that is not possible for craftsmen, merchants, or labourers. Probably because of the special character of the natural inputs, economies of scale are realized in agriculture by firms much smaller in size than in manufacturing, transport, and construction. The considerable variation in soil and relief, even on relatively small farms, and the need to react promptly and appropriately to unpredictable changes in temperature and moisture greatly complicate the number and kind of day-to-day decisions that must be made in most types of farming. Costs of management therefore rise rapidly as farm size increases beyond the point where the farm manager can himself take part in work in the field. Traditions of security of tenure, and the farm's potential ability to feed the farm family, have made it possible for inefficient small operators to resist effectively economic pressures which in other occupations would either have forced them to work more productively or to seek less demanding employment. Moreover, large owners, because each tract of land is unique in site if not in quality, have enjoyed various monopoly advantages which permit and sometimes encourage uneconomic use of their properties.

Technical differences between agricultural production and other kinds of economic activity, and the dominant economic position agriculture has occupied over most of human history and that it still occupies for most of the present population of the world, are sufficient reasons why it should receive special attention in national economic decisions. The general conditions for agriculture to prosper are relatively simple, but they can be implemented only by taking into account the complex reality of each specific geographical and cultural environment. In the present paper an attempt is made to set forth these general conditions for economic progress in agriculture, and to call attention to some of the restraints under which they may have to labour and some of the conflicts with other social objectives which may arise. No attempt will be made to lay down a specific development programme for the agriculture of any particular country, but attention will be directed to some general characteristics of tropical African agriculture which must influence development plans. Specific national decisions can only be made in the light of each nation's resources, both natural and human, and of its political, social, and economic aspirations.

I. Agriculture in the National Economy

Before turning directly to a consideration of measures necessary to increase the net product from agriculture, it will be useful to survey briefly the contributions that this sector can be expected to make to the economy as a whole. These are of two general kinds, one passive, the other active. Agriculture's passive role is to supply those raw materials which are demanded from it by the rest of the society, and in particular to supply so far as economic the population's requirements in foodstuffs. To the extent that it can do so it permits economic growth without extra demands on the world economy. Agriculture's active role is actually to stimulate growth, to assist in leading or driving the society to higher levels of economic achievement.

Agriculture as provisioner. No matter what may be said about the crudeness of tropical African farming methods, they have been effective enough to enable a population of more than 150 million inhabitants to feed itself with very little supplementation from abroad. When diets are deficient in vitamins, minerals, or proteins the cause usually is to be found not in shortages of supplies but in ignorance of good feeding practices. Local shortages in foodstuffs still occur, but as long as transport and marketing services continue to operate they can be made good by supplies brought in from fairly nearby without having to call on shipments from overseas. If transport and marketing services break down, however, drought, pests, disease or civil strife can still expose sizeable populations to hunger and famine, as has been made clear by recent events in the Kasai. And inhabitants of thousands of villages all across tropical Africa that are not near all-weather roads or rail lines still find it extremely costly to bring in staple foodstuffs in quantity, with the consequence that total intake may episodically be less than needed.

It should be a primary concern of development agencies, particularly in the period when a full exchange economy is only imperfectly established, not to adopt unwittingly measures which may, by altering the existing organization of farm production, reduce the capacity of the population to feed itself. Wise planning for African agriculture requires careful attention both to foodcrop farming, including animal husbandry, and the production of industrial crops and products for sale abroad. (The question of the extent to which a nation should try to feed itself is discussed further in section 6.)

Traditional agriculture, assisted by improved transportation and communication, has done a remarkably good job of provisioning the growing population of tropical Africa during the decades of rapid increase in economic product since World War I. It will almost certainly have to achieve major alterations in its organization if it is to continue to supply as large a part of food requirements during the period of rapid growth which it is hoped will follow independence. In the years ahead, population will continue to increase unless existing medical and hygienic activities are

reduced, and the movement from country to town will probably accelerate. African farmers will have more mouths to feed and fewer hands to
work with. At the same time, increased urbanization and rising incomes
will result in increased demand for higher-value foods and for exotic
foods. The number of calories consumed per person may not increase, but
the source of these calories can be expected increasingly to be the more
costly foods. Although the amount of food and beverages consumed, in
the nutritional sense, may change little, in economic terms it can be
expected to rise steadily. To the extent that domestic agriculture can
supply these increased amounts of food economically, it will ease the
process of growth. Every reason exists for believing that the total output of foodstuffs by African farmers can be increased greatly — perhaps
fivefold or more — but not without some changes in farm organization.

Agriculture as generator. Although agriculture's first function historically
has been to feed the local population, it can also be a major source of that
increased productivity which is necessary if members of a society are to
enjoy more than the bare necessities for survival. In tropical Africa today
agricultural production, in addition to its direct contribution to domestic
consumption, is the principal source of exports, the proceeds of which are
used to obtain manufactured goods from abroad. The flow of African
agricultural products into world markets will surely continue to increase,
and to provide the foreign exchange required both for capital investment
and for raising consumers' levels of living. But beyond this first obvious
contribution of agriculture to economic growth, four others need to be
recognized.

Agriculture affords opportunity for productive investment of funds in
excess of those immediately needed for consumption. More than this,
where land is relatively plentiful as it is in most of tropical Africa and was
in the United States a hundred years ago, ambitious and industrious young
men with little or no money find in farming a kind of production where
an investment of their own labour and foresight pays off well. A very
great deal of the capital in farms, in the form of perennial orchards, of
cleared and developed land, of terraces and drains, has been built up
simply by the labour of the cultivator, frequently by labour that could
find no other employment because of the seasonal rhythm of farming.
This is as true of the farms of western Europe and the United States as it
is of the cocoa and coffee groves of tropical Africa.

Linked with the opportunities agriculture affords for productive investment are the training it can offer in management and entrepreneurship.
Because the optimum size of farm firms tends to be much smaller than in
industry, many more persons can become farm operators and learn by

experience habits of organization, risk-assumption, innovation, decision-making, and responsibility. Farm management thus serves as an important training ground and supplier of skilled manpower to the rest of the economy. It can only do so, of course, so long as farmers are left free themselves to seek the most economic use of the resources at their command under government rules that enforce fair competition to protect the rights of others.

As agriculture is the principal employment of most of the population, and the principal source of wealth, so is it also the largest potential market for most goods and services produced in the towns. But it is a difficult market to cultivate because of its dispersion and because so many of its members are in only imperfect communication with the urban economies. As farm people are increasingly integrated with the exchange economy, they can, however, provide for many African countries the large home market that domestic industries need if they are to achieve a volume of sales and size of plant large enough to make them competitors with foreign suppliers.

Finally, of course, agriculture must be looked to as a principal domestic source of investible funds for the rest of the economy. Unfortunately this contribution from the agricultural sector is not necessarily compatible with all of the others, and overemphasis on agriculture as a source of general capital can easily reduce its total contribution. A little more is involved, too, than perhaps killing the goose that lays the golden eggs. If levies on increases in farm incomes are high they may, of course, stifle any expansion in farm production and restrict the supply of savings for investment elsewhere. They may also inhibit the development of managerial and entrepreneurial skills which are a vital need of all African countries. More than this, any tendency to think of agriculture as the capital-supplying subsistence sector of the economy and of non-agriculture as the capital-using sector can blind planners to the great potential returns to be got by investment in farm enterprises. The heavy levies imposed on Japanese agriculture during that country's period of rapid industrialization have frequently been cited as a model for others. It may be a dangerous model to emulate. Japan differs from the African countries in its high density of population and in the very large capital investment which had been made in Japanese agriculture before industrialization began. More than this, the Japanese were an extremely disciplined people, and Japanese farmers were accustomed to detailed supervision and regulation by the ruling class. Under these circumstances, heavy taxation of agriculture for the benefit of industry succeeded. Could it do so in an African country?

II. EFFICIENT AGRICULTURAL PRODUCTION

The most efficient agricultural production might, under special circumstances, simply be the largest possible output, however measured, that could possibly be achieved with existing resources. The special conditions that would make optimum production identical with maximum production are unlikely to be found in fact. If a society, for example, found itself with insufficient food calories to permit its population to survive, and with no source outside the society from which food calories could be obtained, it might set as its highest goal to raise the supply of food calories to a survival level, regardless of the cost in terms of effort, of natural resources, or of capital. Such peculiar isolation is unlikely in the modern world, and poverty to the extent of a persisting absolute shortage in calories is unknown in Africa and probably elsewhere.

In fact, it is probably not possible any place to find the peculiar combination of circumstances which would dictate the maximizing of farm output regardless of cost. Even in the unlikely event that food were the only consumption goods wanted, the demand for labour to be used in raising crops and animals would have to compete with the demand for leisure. In most realistic situations the objective will be to maximize net output rather than total output; this will be achieved if the factors of production are employed in agriculture only up to the point where they yield the same increase in product as they could in alternative employment.

To call attention to the difference between maximum and optimum production may seem unnecessary, but it has happened that agricultural experts have become so enamoured of increased output per acre or per tree that they have ignored output per man-day. It has also happened that administrators who have learned their trade in the peculiar kind of non-economy of wartime have tried to transfer their costless 'economics' to peacetime.

If the goal of agricultural policy is to make production more efficient, it is probably necessary to consider 'efficiency' from three points of view — that of the firm or farm enterprise, that of the sector or community, and that of the state. Each requires something a little different, and the final objectives need to be formulated in terms of all three.

Efficiency in terms of the firm — and this is the way in which it is most often viewed by extension workers and farm management specialists — is simply a matter of combining inputs in such a way as to yield the largest possible net return to the farm operator. It is most easily achieved when all inputs can be purchased as they are needed, but it also may serve as a guide to management on the family farm where both land and labour inputs are taken as fixed. It usually involves some notion of minimum farm size necessary to realize economies of scale. In discussions of farm management the principal concerns are use of the most efficient techniques and the most economical combination of inputs. Under African conditions, efficiency solely in terms of the farm enterprise implies larger, but not absolutely large farms, and fewer farmers.

In terms of the agricultural sector — or of the agricultural community because membership in the sector also implies membership in the community — efficient operation of each firm is also desired, but this efficiency may have to be sacrificed if it leads to unemployment or displacement of a considerable part of the farm population prior to the time that such off-farm migration can be absorbed in other rural or urban occupations. Persons who think primarily in terms of the sector may assign high priority to full employment of all resources now in agriculture, even to maximum output with these resources. They may go beyond this, and assert a claim on capital resources from outside the sector in order to maintain full employment of the farm population and to increase their output. This parochial point of view seems to be held frequently by political spokesmen for farming areas, and it can be carried to the extreme, as it has been in the United States, Britain, and France, of demanding and obtaining subsidization of agriculture by the rest of the economy.

Concern over employment of farm people is reasonable and may properly serve as a restraint on too rapid changes in farm organization; sacrifice of the welfare of other members of the society to maintain or raise that of farmers may sometimes be desirable on humane considerations, but can only be achieved at the cost of efficiency in national production.

When efficiency in agricultural production is viewed in terms of the whole national economy, full employment of labour continues to be an important concern, although 'full employment' of other resources employed in farming, if this term can be given meaning, is not. Instead, the objective must be to encourage the use of each factor up to the point where its marginal productivity is no less than it is elsewhere in the economy. In terms of the whole economy, agriculture also becomes a user of goods and services provided outside the sector, and a supplier to other sectors. Agriculture can lay no special claims to improved roads and communications, to better schooling, or to subsidized credit beyond that justified by purely economic considerations or generally accepted social goals.

Maximum efficiency of farm enterprises in terms of the national economy (probably also of the sector) requires not only that the farm managers bring all inputs into their most effective employment, but also

3

that only the most effective persons shall find employment as farm managers. In this regard, too, the objectives of the state may be in conflict with those of the existing farm community.

III. CONDITIONS FOR EFFICIENT PRODUCTION

Efficient production can be achieved in agriculture to the extent that the following conditions are met:

A. Farmers are motivated by a desire to increase their command over goods and services, including leisure activities, and are able rationally to perceive the means to this end.

B. Producers are assured of access to the factors of production — land, labour, and capital — on the same terms.

C. Farmers have unrestricted access to markets for their produce and for consumer goods.

D. All persons have equal access to knowledge of production techniques, of costs and prices, and of forces determining them.

E. Some group, whether family, lineage, village, or larger political entity stands ready to protect the individual from misfortunes beyond his control; and

F. A similar group is in a position to preserve long-term economic values that otherwise might be sacrificed because some individuals are concerned only with income of the moment.

The implications of these conditions for efficiency are discussed in more detail in the following paragraphs.

It is much easier to set down these conditions than it is to realize them, but the countries of tropical Africa can go considerably further toward meeting them than they do now. The first condition, of course, is largely outside the control of group action, although it may be markedly influenced by general customs and attitudes of the community. But the other five conditions all depend on group intervention, presumably intervention by the state.

Economic motivation.—If producers and consumers are not interested in increasing their real incomes, if their economic activities are uninfluenced by changes in cost and price, if they are unable rationally to relate present effort to future reward, and if they are concerned only with immediate satisfaction with no care for what may come tomorrow, then any attempts to organize an economy by the constraints of the market will be in vain, whether the market is one in which all prices are arrived at by the free play of economic forces or by decision of the state. The allegations sometimes made, more frequently a few years ago than now, that African farmers and labourers and African consumers are unresponsive to price changes, or are content with their economic lot and desire no improvement in it, or that their time horizon is extremely near, or that their behaviour is irrational and whimsical, strike at the first foundation of economic order.

Fortunately for the economist, this description of African producers is not borne out by the facts. Ample evidence all around us demonstrates that subsistence farmers, even those remote from markets and urban centres, display in their economic activities attitudes of the same sort as are postulated by the economic theorists. Of course no man is ruled by economic drives alone, and of course the relative influence of the various determinants of human behaviour varies from one individual to another and from one population group to another. This does not impair the theory, for all that it requires is that some individuals experience some degree of economic motivation.

It is interesting to speculate about how this notion of the economic inertness of subsistence farmers came into being. It is not peculiar to Africa; for that matter it is not peculiarly attached to subsistence agriculture. It has been asserted that some of the most highly commercialized agriculture in the world, that of the Prairie Provinces of Canada, is carried on by farmers who produce less when prices rise, more when prices fall. This is not in fact the way Canadian farmers behave, but the demonstrably false idea persists in certain circles. The primary reason for its persistence may lie in the notion that farming is a peculiar sort of production in which all costs are fixed, i.e., that land, labour, fertilizer, feed, and all other inputs are supplied by the farm itself, and that there is no way for the farmer to receive income from the inputs except by employing them on his own farm. Under such circumstances, and assuming also that farmers' wants are fixed and satisfied, we might get the sort of behaviour that is said to occur. But people who know farming recognize that all costs are not fixed, that alternative employment frequently exists for farm inputs (if not for presently used inputs, at least for replacement equivalents), and that farmers rarely are able to have and to consume all they want.

Whether this romantically naive notion of farm organization is at the root of the fairly widespread belief in the irrationality of African producers, or whether the belief is compounded of misunderstanding, of differing cultural values, and of frustration of plans and programmes is probably of little importance. To many who know African farming well it may seem strange that the issue is raised at all. Yet the notion still persists and colours the interpretation of events and the direction of economic plans, even in the minds of men who would stoutly affirm the high economic rationality of producer responses in more highly developed countries.

Although the state cannot bring economic motivation into being when it does not already exist, it can heighten the degree to which economic considerations affect individual decisions. This can be done in two ways, by maintenance of a system in which economic rewards are more nearly proportional to economic contribution, and by familiarizing consumers with the various kinds of economic satisfaction in the form of goods and services that may be available to them. Rewards commensurate with contributions will follow if the access conditions discussed below are met; these conditions will also increase the consumers' familiarity with the full range of satisfactions possible to them by the widening of consumer choice which broader access to consumer goods implies.

Access to the factors.— The condition that all members of the economy be able to acquire or use factors of production on practically the same economic terms is necessary in order to permit continuing rearrangements of inputs into more efficient combinations, and to assure that their use is directed by individuals best able to do so. It is specifically directed against systems in which some individuals, by reason of race, birth, religion, or other non-economic condition are afforded priority in the use of land and capital and in the employment of labour, or special concessions in payment for their use. It is intended to make ownership and use dependent in large measure on the individual's economic contribution as this is measured by the market or by the state.

Equal access does not imply that access is free, nor does it carry the implication that every member of the society shall be endowed permanently with equal shares of the factors. In particular, it is not to be confused with the idea that every man has a right to land of the same amount and quality, or, in fact, that he has a right to land at all except as he acquires this right through performance. And it denies the individual's right to hold land in uneconomic use. It does not necessarily imply private, individual ownership of land, although this may be the easiest way to achieve equal access to this factor. The basic condition with regard to the use of land could, in fact, be met in other ways, such as, for example, by investing ownership in all land in the state but granting its use to individuals at rents determined by competitive bidding. Nor does it imply owner-operation, for in some situations considerable gains in flexibility are to be achieved by separating these two functions, either through a system of share-tenancy under which both owner and farm operator share the risks of farming, or through cash rents determined in the same way as other prices. The condition of equal access to the factors of production does of course imply that persons who employ their land in uneconomic ways may lose it to others who bid higher for its use, of through bankruptcy, and is the antithesis of systems which insure tenancy for life or in other ways tie the farmer to a particular piece of land.

Access to financial resources should be determined by the ptospects of the enterprise and the reliability of the prospective borrower. Production credit should be available to farmers on the same terms as it is to other borrowers. If monopoly control of credit or ignorance on the part of lenders of the economics of farming causes interest charges to be above a freely determined market rate, farm operators will be forced to forego the most efficient organization of the firm in order to conserve financial capital. If credit is made available to farmers at subsidized rates below the market, farms will tend to waste capital and in this way adopt a less efficient organization of production.

A special problem of farm financing is to protect the farm against random disaster beyond its capacity to meet, such as may be caused by successive years of abnormally bad weather, or by sudden large declines in prices of farm products. Involved here is more than concern over the welfare of the farm family. Risks too big to be borne by the individual enterprise may destroy an otherwise efficient operation and thus present society with an avoidable cost of reorganization. When such risks can be borne more broadly, perhaps by the entire society, their cost can be reduced. This is an argument for so-called 'disaster insurance'; it is not an argument for continued support of farm prices or for subsidy to agriculture.

If terms of access to the factors of production are to be the same to all, it may be necessary to permit collective bargaining over wages, possibly over rents. But when associations of workers, employers, traders, or lenders, whether labour unions, co-operatives, or cartels, are permitted to restrict entry to production or marketing they are in fact making access to the factors conditional on non-economic criteria. Under these circumstances the state has an obligation to intervene in order to preserve the openness of markets. Monopoly is most often thought of as a burden imposed on farmers by their suppliers and by their customers, but it can also be imposed by farmers through co-operative marketing organizations, agreements about wage levels, and through privileged control of land. Monopoly power used by farm operators against others reduces efficiency of production in just the same way as does monopoly power which is used against farmers.

If farm managers should be free to employ the factors of production in the amount and at the time that they wish, the owners of the factors should have the same freedom. For labour this means that employment should be entered into freely, and that no one should be kept in employment if he wishes to leave it. Contract and indentured labour are just as inconsistent with efficient combination of the factors in production as are other restraints.

Access to markets.— In most countries, the principal restraint on individual access to markets is imposed by market traders themselves through the agency of trade associations, rings, or monopolies. In parts of tropical Africa, and elsewhere in the world where the races receive differential treatment, restraints may be imposed by custom, even by law. This impedes the functioning of the entire market system. Markets open to all, and prices freely determined by the customary bidding and offering of the open market are a necessary condition for optimum use of resources. Perfect markets and perfect market pricing can be approximated only under very special circumstances, such as appear now to prevail in some of the organized markets for grain futures in the United States, but the state can greatly improve the functioning of markets for agricultural commodities in tropical Africa by measures that are relatively simple and not very costly.

First priority should probably be given to collection and dissemination of current and accurate information about market prices. This alone will go some distance to combat monopolistic price-fixing and restraint of trade which thrives on the suppression of market information. Measures to insure enforceability of contracts and provision of reliable government grading and inspection services will reduce the cost of long-distance trade if only because they can eliminate the need for the seller to accompany his merchandise to the point of delivery. These measures, too, will weaken the control of traders associations. Direct action to prevent and destroy monopoly in restraint of trade is more difficult — as American experience has shown — but aggressive action by the state can end the most flagrant abuses.[1]

Access to knowledge.— A man does not have to be able to read and write in order to operate a farm successfully. He does need to know intimately the details of his business, including the various techniques of production, the costs and prices of alternative inputs and outputs, and the forces that are likely to cause them to change over the course of the planning period.

There are many ways in which this kind of knowledge is acquired. A great deal is learned from doing and from watching others, hence the effectiveness of demonstration farms and the influence in some African countries of European estates.

[1] Monopolies which arise because the production function permits full economies of scale to be realized only with very large size of plant or firm must of course be dealt with directly by government. This sort of monopoly is not likely to arise in agriculture, but may in industries which sell to or buy from agriculture.

The present cultivators of African farms and gardens possess a great store of knowledge that has been handed down through the generations. Its utility has been proven by the achievement in feeding the population well enough to permit its increase. New crops have been incorporated into the agricultural cycle as they became known, and new techniques adopted when they seemed suitable. In any plans for the improvement of African agriculture it is of the first importance to build on this existing knowledge. The new techniques now required will be most effective if they are combined with the older methods rather than being substituted for them.

Knowledge of new and better methods requires continued research by agronomists and agricultural economists, and this research will be most fruitful if there is constant communication between the research worker and the man on the farm. An active and conscientious agricultural extension service, staffed by workers who understand existing farming practices as well as those being developed at the experiment stations, is probably the best means for propagating knowledge and for guiding research along productive lines.

Information about prices and markets is almost as important to the farmer as knowledge about production techniques. Except for export crops, this sort of information is scarce and unreliable in tropical Africa; in some places it is even suppressed. Yet it could be collected at not too great cost if the aid of traders were enlisted, and it could be disseminated fairly cheaply by means of daily radio broadcasts. Regular market reporting not only helps farmers to make more accurate production and marketing decisions; it also steadily increases their awareness of the market economy and of the opportunities which it offers.

Knowledge about kinds and prices of available consumer goods will assist in integrating farm people into the national economy, and will provide them with incentives for increasing their own economic production. Aggressive merchandising on the part of wholesalers to acquaint shopkeepers with the wide range of goods which can be provided is perhaps the principal way of disseminating this kind of information, but radio advertising can help and is the counterpart of news about commodity markets. Local agricultural exhibits, or fairs, held primarily to induce competitiveness in farming techniques, can also provide space for display of a wide variety of consumer and producer goods.

Knowledge of new crops and new farming methods, knowledge of market prices and of the commodities offered for sale, do not depend on formal education nor on the ability to read and write. Literacy and 'general education' are not a prerequisite for economic achievement. They bring values and satisfactions of their own, but in many circumstances they should not be set ahead of the kind of practical education that enables people to earn a living. It is extremely doubtful whether the goal of mass literacy should be set ahead of education in productive techniques and in the workings of the market.

Group responsibilities.— Increased reliance on the exchange economy and lessening of non-economic claims on the factors of production inevitably requires that new social arrangements be devised in order to provide for individuals who are by nature unproductive or improvident, or whose incomes are cut off by illness or natural disaster. In the traditional society, where membership in the society itself establishes a claim on income, this situation is taken care of by sharing within a relatively small group. In the exchange economy, with its increased emphasis on individual performance, the unfortunate can best be cared for by some larger community, usually the state, but possibly a social or religious fellowship or some political unit smaller than the state.

The traditional communal society may lessen the incentive to individual productive activity by the security it affords the indolent and by the extra demands it makes on the more productive. Because assistance from a larger entity is more impersonal, it can be more equitable, both in the conditions on which help is provided and in the way in which the cost of assistance is borne.

Group concern over the misfortunes of its members need not reduce the economic efficiency of the system significantly as long as it is limited to individuals in real distress, and as long as minimum income requirements are set realistically. Unfortunately, when this burden is assumed by the state, pressures are apt to be strong to revise upward notions of minimum income, and to extend state aid to an ever-increasing part of the population.

Vesting control over a country's natural resources in the hands of individuals may, under certain circumstances, lead to their uneconomic depletion, either because the individual puts a much lower value on future production than society would, or because provision for future economic returns requires planning for larger areas than individual owners can achieve. Reserves of underground water, for example, may be drawn on so heavily that they are exhausted and the land they had irrigated fallen into disuse before roads built by the state to make possible its economic use have been paid for. Again, erosion which could be curbed economically by group action may be beyond the control of an individual farmer unless he obtains the co-operation of farmers who live on the watershed above him. Under these circumstances, the state has an obligation to intervene, even though intervention entails some restriction of individual rights and curtails short-term production. When the state finds it necessary to act in this manner to conserve resources, it is especially necessary not to conserve simply for the sake of conserving, but only when there is clear economic advantage in doing so. It may be much better to destroy a forest today to provide lumber for railroads and buildings essential for economic growth than to restrict this growth in order to conserve the forest for a posterity that may not need it as badly.

IV. Some Reflections on Farm Organization

Two aspects of farm organization have been the subject of special attention by students of tropical African agriculture: the relative merits of smallholders and of estates, and of the various ways in which capital can be substituted for labour or land. Questions of the appropriate size of the farm enterprise and of the best way to employ capital must depend on particular circumstances of geography, climate, crop, and social and economic organization, but some general principles can be advanced tentatively for most of tropical Africa.

Farm size.— The history of cocoa and coffee production in West Africa should provide sufficient evidence of the ability of smallholders to compete effectively with plantations or estates, at least in the production of these major tree crops. Cocoa production in Ghana and Nigeria, entirely in the hands of smallholders, dominates the world cocoa market. In the Ivory Coast, African producers of cocoa and coffee have been in direct competition for labour and markets with expatriate plantations that were until recent years favoured by government in recruitment of labour and aided financially by direct government subsidies. Nevertheless, African producers now account for much the greater part of production of these crops. Certainly the advantages of estates are not as overwhelming as some of their apologists maintain.

The plantation clearly enjoys advantages in mobilization of capital, in assuring a sizeable flow of raw product, and in hiring scientific and managerial skills. These advantages would seem to favour plantation production of crops which require fairly elaborate processing or manufacturing immediately after harvest. Historically this has been true of black (fermented) tea and of sisal. Other crops with somewhat similar requirements — rubber, palm oil, sugar, and bananas — have been grown by a combination of smallholders and estates, with the estate taking responsibility for processing the crop both from its own fields or groves and from those of smallholders. Estates have also proved effective in introducing the cultivation of new crops into areas where production for market was unfamiliar, and where large volume production at the outset was necessary if a market was to be developed. But once the production of a cash crop is well established, this 'volume' advantage disappears, and if other organizations can be developed to provide processing, research, and disease control, the plantation may present no greater efficiency than production by many independent farmers. In areas where supporting industries are lacking, the estate may itself be able to provide the supporting services that in a more industrialized country would be supplied by others, but volume of output sufficient to justify an estate in performing these activities presumably would justify an outside supplier in furnishing them just as well. The estate may still enjoy advantages in bargaining power and political influence, but these are hardly advantages that can be defended on grounds of efficiency.

Estate operation also has its drawbacks, chief of them being the costs of management and the inflexibility of the farm organization when faced with changing costs and prices. Economies of scale are quickly realized, except those caused by the indivisibility of farm machinery and processing plants, and management problems are apt to beset the operation as its size grows. More serious is the resistance to change which is likely to be induced by the size of the firm relative to the market, and by the absolute magnitude of its investment. These may cause necessary changes to be long deferred because of the considerable costs of redeploying the investment; when change does come it is likely to be abrupt and to disrupt the economic fabric of the industry. Industries dominated by production from smallholders, on the other hand, may be expected to adjust to changing economic conditions more smoothly, as first one farmer and then another responds to pressures of cost and price. Each smallholder is likely also to be more sensitive to these pressures simply because his financial reserves are small. A major inefficiency of an industry made up of a few large firms as opposed to one made up of many small ones may simply be a function of numbers. Where there are many small enterprises, each making its own production decisions, constant changes in allocation of resources will lead gradually to the appropriate allocation, if only by process of trial and error. When only a few firms are involved, fewer decisions of this sort are made each year so that there is much less experimentation. When a change is made a large part of total output will be affected. If it is a wise change, all well and good, but if it is not, the cost to the industry may be heavy.

What has been said so far of smallholders should properly be taken as applying to small farms operating according to ordinary commercial principles and able to express most costs in terms of market prices. Small farms in tropical Africa typically are not so operated. Instead, they are enterprises in which the labour supply and the amount of land under cultivation are determined by the size of the family. Typically, too, the farm family, even though it is engaged in production of crops for market, also grows a large part of its own food supply. Under these circumstances it may possess further advantages over estate production for export. First, of course, is its ability to slack off on production for market when prices fall without jeopardizing its income for basic maintenance. On the other hand, with labour costs fixed, it may find it worthwhile to maintain output in the face of lower prices if alternative activities are economically unattractive.

Large processing plants that may be required for certain export crops need not be considered as a part of farming or of the farm enterprise. If they are economically sound, they can be operated in the same fashion as cotton gins (or ginneries), buying the raw produce from the farmer or processing it for him at a set charge. It is perhaps better to divorce processing from farming; where a large estate-owned factory draws both from estate production and from independent producers it can, under different circumstances, uneconomically favour its own produce or that of the outside growers. Neither sort of favouritism is desirable.

It has already been pointed out that in most kinds of farming, optimum size is relatively small when compared with other industries. If any use is to be made of mechanical equipment, however, or of animal or machine draft power, the size and capacity of the machines may indicate a size considerably bigger than that now worked by African farmers. Some of the advantages of mechanization can nevertheless be achieved by quite small farms through co-operative ownership of large machines, or by hiring the services of such machines from private or public owners. Machine tractor stations as established in the Soviet Union received a bad name in some quarters because they were used as an instrument of state control over farm operators. They need not be so used, however, and if operated on a commercial basis can serve agriculture effectively. Co-operative ownership of large harvesting machines, or the hire of such machines from individual owners, has a long tradition of success in the United States and may sometimes be appropriate in tropical Africa. In the United States this practice has frequently been associated with communal participation in harvest and processing, the so-called threshing rings and husking bees, and has thus simplified the problem of labour recruitment at times of peak labour demand.

Another kind of communal activity to enable farmers to deal with problems beyond their individual control without having to transfer all responsibility to the state are the soil conservation districts and irrigation districts most common in the American West. These are local bodies, frequently assisted during their early years by government loans, but intended eventually to be self-financed and locally governed. They have the advantage over government-controlled schemes of better preserving local self-reliance and of closer proximity to the problems with which they are intended to deal. Frequently, too, some of the labour and management required for their operation can be provided by farmers themselves when regular farm work is slack.

Use of capital.— Under existing methods of production in traditional Africa the limiting factor is labour, a fact that sets African farming off sharply from that of southern and eastern Asia. Over most of tropical Africa, land is relatively plentiful, but without animal or mechanical draft power it is in general not possible for African farmers to bring much more land under cultivation than they have now. Few estimates have been made of the amount of labour required to produce foodcrops on African farms, but these seem to show in most regions a labour force working close to the limit of its ability. A striking feature of these studies is the large proportion of total labour inputs that go into processing of the product before it leaves the farm. Shelling and grinding maize may require five times as many man-days as do all field operations, and peeling, drying, and grinding manioc (cassava) as much as ten times as many hours as it takes to grow and harvest the crop. The principal cost of land in areas where population density is still low enough to permit fairly complete regeneration of a natural cover is the cost of clearing; because land loses fertility so rapidly under tropical conditions, labour cost of clearing is also an important part of the total labour cost of growing up to harvest. If capital could be substituted for labour in land clearing, in field operations, including harvesting, or in the so-called 'barnyard operations' — drying, husking, shelling, threshing, and grinding — it should be possible to increase total output rapidly.

In areas where animal or mechanical draft power can be used, the total area under cultivation could be expanded without much other change in methods of cultivation. The problems associated with expansion of extensive cultivation in this way are, however, considerable. Over large parts of the subcontinent, animal power cannot be used until the tsetse fly is eliminated or freed of infection. Use of tractors introduces problems of maintenance which can be dealt with only if service and parts stores can be provided. When heavy tractor-drawn machinery is introduced it is also necessary to clear the land much more thoroughly than under hoe cultivation, and in forested and wooded areas such thorough clearing is extremely costly. Even assuming that the technical and financial problems of mechanical cultivation can be solved, this form of substitution of capital for labour cannot by itself present a very attractive way of expanding agricultural production. In most parts of the African tropics the soils are relatively poor in plant nutrients, and the high average temperatures and torrential rainfall quickly remove these nutrients from the soil once it is exposed to the elements. The consequence for traditional agriculture has been that yields fall so rapidly as to make it more economic, after a period of three or four years, to clear new land rather than to continue to cultivate the old. When the amount of land that can be cultivated by each farmer is limited to a few acres, there usually remains enough land in bush fallow so that this system of continual clearing, and cultivating only for a short period, can still be carried on. If the area under cultivation were to be rapidly expanded by mechanical means, resources of land could be quickly used up. High costs of clearing land and servicing machines, and the possibility of rapid exhaustion of natural fertility combine to make expansion of output by large-scale mechanization of field operations relatively unattractive in the immediate future.

The difficulties encountered in mechanization of barnyard operations are much less troublesome. Labour costs can be reduced quickly by such simple devices as hand-operated grinders and graters; introduction of grinders and mills driven by small electric motors or internal-combustion engines can reduce them much more. Where transport is available at the farm, these processing activities may easily be transferred to a location off the farm and handled by private or co-operative enterprise. Some of the labour freed by mechanization of barnyard operations will probably be used to increase the area under cultivation or to cultivate it more intensively, but it is unlikely that this will lead to a very great increase in the total amount of land in crops primarily because it does not provide much additional labour at times of peak requirements. Undoubtedly some of the time freed by this kind of mechanization would be devoted to housekeeping, child care, and education. Mechanization of the preliminary processing activities is attractive also because it can be achieved with minimum disruption of the existing farm organization. But although it can free a great deal of labour time for other employment, it is not at all certain that it will lead to much increase in total farm output, except in those instances where processing capacity puts a limit on the amount of a crop that can be grown and harvested. This seems to be true now of manioc in some localities; it may be true of other crops.

Capital can also be substituted for labour more indirectly by measures to increase the yield of farm products per acre. Because the only cost of land under traditional cultivation is the labour cost of clearing, methods that can keep land under cultivation longer or increase its output per year will reduce the amount of labour needed to open new land and free it for other purposes. Among the measures to increase yields — and

increasing yield is, of course, economically equivalent to keeping the
land in cultivation longer — is the application of commercial fertilizers.
Experiments with African soils since World War II have demonstrated
that crops grown on these soils respond to the addition of plant nutrients
through fertilizers in the same way as they do elsewhere. With the
addition of commercial fertilizers land can be kept under economic crops
for much longer periods of time, perhaps indefinitely. The principal
barrier to their increased use at the present time is economic; high costs
of transport and marketing make fertilizers too expensive and farm
products too cheap at the farm to permit their profitable employment.
As these distributive costs are reduced, however, the use of fertilizers can
be expected to rise and with it the total output of farm products.

Increased use of fertilizers is a move in the direction of intensification of
agriculture, as opposed to extensification under machine cultivation.
Other intensive measures also are available, and at relatively low cost.
They include the use of pesticides and fungicides, the planting of improved varieties of plants that have been bred specifically for the areas
where they are to be grown, and the determination and adoption of
optimum planting dates, timely weeding, crop sequences, and plant
spacing in the field. Wider use of these measures depends primarily on
agricultural research and agricultural extension programmes.

Perhaps the simplest way of all to increase agricultural production and
the one most often overlooked by persons who are preoccupied with
physical output, is by shifting to crops with higher value per acre. This
has undoubtedly been a principal contributor to increased farm output in
the United States, and it is beginning to increase output in tropical
Africa. As incomes rise and appetites become more catholic, the market
for more costly foodstuffs will expand. Near most towns of Africa today
some ground will be found under lettuce, onions, perhaps tomatoes and
green beans. These crops yield much more in economic terms than do the
traditional cereals and roots which are grown primarily as suppliers of
food calories. Increased production of livestock for market is a similar way
of increasing output by changing agriculture's product mix. In many
parts of tropical Africa the starchy roots, notably manioc, are in over-
supply and could well be used in rations for cattle, pigs, and goats.
Wherever oil seeds are produced, a potential supply of high-protein feed
supplement exists in the form of oil-seed cake, whether from peanuts,
cotton seed, or palm kernels. Increased demand for meat will undoubtedly
characterize the food economies of African countries over the decades
ahead if aspirations for increased economic well-being are realized, and
domestic agriculture should be encouraged to respond to this demand.

V. GENERATORS OF GROWTH

Sustained rapid growth of the economic product of a society cannot be achieved simply by providing the circumstances under which it is possible. Some individuals must be able to recognize and to take advantage of opportunities for development; furthermore, such opportunities must exist. Some may arise from chance circumstances essentially outside the economy, some from shifts within the economy itself, and some may be induced or created by governmental planners.

It is essential, of course, that the economy be so organized that its members can employ their capacities for enterprise and organization to good advantage, and they will be better able to do so to the extent that the conditions of equality of access to factors, markets, and knowledge are achieved. As the countries of tropical Africa move from colonial dependencies to independent self-governing states, perhaps the most important problem they must solve in their task of creating modern national economies is to identify and employ the potentialities for economic leadership of their own populations. To borrow a phrase from the political scientists, the nations must construct a kind of society in which the 'economically relevant men' can function most effectively. Bankers and traders, farmers and processors, if allowed freedom to pursue their own economic ends under a society of law and order, will serve as catalysts to set in more rapid motion the economic processes of the system. Fertilizer salesmen who persuade the farmer of advantages of particular kinds of crop dressings (and who are kept honest by their competitors and government regulations) can be just as effective in educating farmers to the uses of nitrogen, potash, and phosphate as can governmental agricultural workers. Produce dealers seeking supplies for a market they have identified and developed can be persuasive teachers of farmers who could not find the market opportunity themselves. Processors who offer premiums for standards of product that can be handled more economically in their plants, and bankers who carefully scrutinize production plans and share their experience with prospective borrowers also contribute forcefully to the education of the farm operator.

The process of improving access to markets may in itself serve as a powerful generator of increased output in agriculture and set in motion a train of changes all of which are directed at increasing output and lowering costs. The reduction in transport costs and consequent increase in prices farmers can obtain for their products that result from the building of a road linking them with central markets can completely change the orientation of a community's farming. The history of modern agriculture is filled with stories of the impact of roads, canals, and railroads on hitherto isolated communities. The part played by motor trucks in the countries of Africa today is too well-known to require elaboration here. What has been achieved to date, however, is probably no more than the barest beginning on the task ahead. Cheaper transport has an impact on almost every aspect of society, and is the principal device which will knit the new national economies together. The part played by other forms of communication and by the development of better-organized markets for raw produce and finished goods reinforces and complements the work of improved transportation. Knowledge of better ways of farming and of better crops to grow are also a part of the communication process. Any and all can spark the kind of chain reaction which will sustain economic growth.

For maximum effect on organization of the factors of production, change in the economic environment should be large enough to be easily perceived. In the same way, demonstrations of new techniques are effective when their consequences are obvious, that is, when they are large enough to be seen at once. Gradual changes, even though persistent over time, may be unrecognized long after their total effect has been relatively great; if the same change were achieved in a short period of time, its effect would be observed promptly. Economic organization has an inertia that makes it resistant to small disturbances, and fairly abrupt shocks may be necessary to provoke obviously desirable rearrangements. Harvesting machines, for example, may exist in prototype form for years yet not be adopted in practice even though they present obvious savings in cost. Their general adoption may have to wait until war or other disruption leads to a sudden curtailment of labour supply, when the new machine will suddenly be demanded by everyone. Departures from expected or customary behaviour, like the increase in birth rate in the United States beginning in World War II, may go unrecognized long after they have become the customary behaviour. This characteristic of human response argues strongly for crash programmes over limited areas rather than gradual change over a much larger territory. It supports those who advocate turning one agricultural community or enterprise into a model rather than using the same funds for small improvements throughout the agricultural sector.

Rising incomes themselves stimulate economic growth by providing both the means for increasing economic output and the will to do so. Acquaintance with new consumer goods and with new ways of life raises the standard of living or standard of consumption, in the strict sense, above the level of living currently enjoyed, and thus increases the incentive for economic production and income. (Danger lurks here, too, if standards are raised too high above level, or if the means to achieve higher standards are frustrated or made too onerous.) At the same time that rising incomes lead to rising expectations, they provide the means to realize them in the form of earnings in excess of customary requirements. The successive patterns of income, saving, and standard of consumption which characterize the economic life of the individual in industrialized societies may also be followed by entire economies.

Beyond the control of society, yet sometimes most important of all, are potential generators of growth in the form of adventitious discoveries of new resources, invention of new products and methods or of new uses for familiar products, or shifts in consumer tastes. These bring most benefit to those individuals who are alert to the new possibilities they open, and to those societies in which information is disseminated rapidly and change is easy. Their impact is inhibited by overplanning, by centralization of decision-making, and by monopoly. They are most likely to be seized by an agriculture made up of many small commercial farms that are in constant contact with the market and that are not hampered in their planning by ponderous management and single-minded investors.

VI. CONFLICTING GOALS

When the conditions necessary for achievement of increased efficiency in agriculture run counter to other goals of society or government, the economist is ill-equipped to choose between them. At most he can call attention to the nature of the conflict and suggest the costs in terms of economic achievement which other social goals entail, and sometimes he can expose the fallacy of economic arguments advanced in support of essentially non-economic proposals. Some of the possible restraints on agricultural efficiency arising from conflicting goals are listed here; it is up to others to decide whether they are worth in terms of social well-being what they may cost in economic product.

Consumer well-being.— Mention has already been made of society's responsibility to succour its members who are in distress, even though the causes of distress are of their own doing. This humanitarian concern must be felt by all societies that are worthy of the name; it is a principal reason why men live in communities and why man has survived. Before the bringing together of populations in large nation states, care for the needy was the responsibility of the family or the village. It seems inevitable that in the large political and economic groupings characteristic of the modern world the responsibility should be borne by the state.

The economic costs of welfare programmes are probably more than offset by the economic benefits of preserving distressed individuals as

4

productive members of the community, but only so long as distress is conceived of as a degree of hardship sufficient to bring an individual's level of living markedly below that of most members of the society. Minimum standards of living which should be available to all can only be determined in relationship to the economy's aggregate consumption. The hazard exists in all welfare programmes, however, that standards may be set according to some absolute criterion unrelated to the general level of living, thereby imposing a burden that impairs the total economic achievement of the state. Standards calling for universal literacy, or for achievement of a 'minimum adequate diet', or for running water in every farm dwelling may be of this sort. These are laudable goals, but they should be thought of as things to be achieved when total income permits, not as something to which every member of the state has a right.

Related to programmes for relief of actual distress are those based on egalitarian principles which call for reducing the inequalities in income distribution among individuals and groups. Farmers have frequently been the beneficiaries of such programmes, but not to the benefit of agriculture. When greater equality in incomes is considered to be a prime goal by the state, its realization will be least costly if divorced entirely from the kind of work a man does. Transfer of income from city dwellers to farmers can too easily encourage them to continue producing things which are neither needed nor wanted.

National security or prestige.— Other sectors of the economy are more likely to obtain extra funds for reasons of security and prestige than is agriculture, although one of the most popular monuments erected by rulers of modern states, the great hydroelectric dam, is frequently justified in part at least by its potential contribution to irrigated farming. Most often a realistic appraisal of the costs and benefits of such proposed structures reveals that they cannot be justified on economic grounds alone, although political leaders may consider them to be desirable for other reasons. Unfortunately, these great edifices may absorb funds that could have been more effectively employed to increase farm output, by building roads from farm to market, for example, or in supporting an agricultural extension service. Part of the reason, of course, may be the bureaucratic one that it is much easier to spend the same amount of money on one large project than on many small ones.

Agriculture is frequently the recipient of governmental attention of another sort, stemming primarily from concern over national security. Fear that supplies of foodstuffs from abroad might be cut off by war, blockade, or embargo may lead government to encourage stockpiling of food at home, or in extreme instances to try for self-sufficiency in essential foodstuffs. The preoccupation with self-sufficiency in food supplies that characterized the administration of most African territories under British colonial rule after World War II must spring primarily from this fear, a fear that was not without grounds during wartime. There can be no other reason for a country to try to grow all the food it needs, even at the cost of reducing production for export and diverting land, labour, and capital into less productive uses. On the other hand, if internal transportation is so poor as to make difficult the movement of foodstuffs to deficit areas, a limited policy of community or district self-sufficiency in staple foods may have to be adopted as a stopgap until transportation is available.

The argument sometimes advanced, that large home production of foodstuffs is necessary in order to avoid inflation induced by high food prices, must also reflect the memory of wartime when shortage of shipping and congestion of ports made it difficult to relieve unanticipated shortfalls in home production with shipments from overseas. Expenditure on food does make up a large part of urban budgets in tropical Africa, and the wage labourer is likely therefore to be disturbed by increases in food costs. Self-sufficiency schemes, however, by raising the costs of food, may foster the upward pressure on wages they are intended to relieve.

Preservation of traditional values.— The traditional organization of agricultural production in tropical Africa reflects a society in which major controls derive from kinship relationships and reciprocal obligations, seniority, magical and religious considerations, conservativeness, and strong identification of the individual with the group, frequently accompanied by distrust of strangers, sometimes outright hostility toward them. Transformation to commercial agriculture in which production decisions are made increasingly on economic considerations alone requires a weakening, perhaps elimination of the traditional controls. But these determinants are the warp and woof of the old society; when they are weakened or broken that society itself is likely to be profoundly altered. Wise leaders therefore will take into account the disruptive effect of an expanding market economy; they may consider it necessary to restrain this expansion when it does not seem feasible to accelerate compensating changes elsewhere in the social structure. But it is just as misguided to attempt to restrain changes which spring from the desires of the population itself as it is rashly to undertake to impose radically new arrangements of economic affairs against its will. The only unchanging cultures are dead ones, and attempts to freeze social patterns in any particular configuration, if they succeed, are almost certain to sterilize and eventually to destroy the society's ability to perpetuate itself. For this reason, attempts to enforce traditional systems of land tenure on a farming population already busily evolving new arrangements may be just as harmful as attempts to impose notions of land tenure derived from the

alien cultures of Europe. In these circumstances, the state can be most
helpful by easing the change to new property concepts and by providing
a legal structure sufficiently flexible to permit economic and psychological
forces to establish appropriate relationships.

It is in the general area of property rights that conflict between the old
and the new is most likely to affect the economic organization of farming.
The right to buy and sell land, to determine how it shall be used, and who
shall inherit; the right to control personal income and to determine who
shall and shall not share it; the right to adopt new methods of cultivation
without prior approval from village elders; the right to have a better
house, finer clothing, or better food than one's neighbours — all of these
characteristics of the modern exchange economies may disturb and erode
traditional values which leaders of the society wish to preserve. If so, they
can be postponed, qualified, or denied, but in doing so the state may find
that it must pay a heavy cost in diminished efficiency of production.

Consolidating political power.— Less easy to defend than intervention in
the agriculture economy for welfare considerations or in order to protect
traditional values, intervention for political reasons alone may nevertheless
sometimes be necessary. Obviously economic power so great as to
threaten that of the state must be restrained, both on political and economic
grounds. But it may also be necessary for the new states of tropical
Africa occasionally to play politics with economics in order to preserve
their integrity as nations. All of the present African states trace their
ancestry back to agglomerations of diverse peoples which the European
powers brought together under one jurisdiction in order to simplify
problems of colonial administration. The major problem of the new
governments, which must be solved if the states are to survive, is to weld
the diverse communities within their boundaries into a co-operating
national society. This does not mean that local traditions and loyalties
need be erased and all reduced to a dull mediocrity of conformity; it does
mean that the state must quell the disruptive forces of traditional rivalry
and hostility. In doing so, it may be necessary to restrict the economic
freedom of hostile groups, and build up the economic activities of other
groups to preserve some sort of balance of forces. Such policies may well
entail some restraint on the processes of economic growth, but if they
succeed in breaking down the compartments that prevent formation of a
national economy, this interference may in the long run be justified on
economic grounds as well.

Problems of transition.— New national governments won support from
their followers in part by promising that independence would bring a
rapid improvement in levels of living and in income. To make good on
these promises with the limited financial resources available to the new

states will be difficult, especially when costs of independence are taken into account. The new governments customarily assume greater expenses in the conduct of their international relations than had to be borne under colonial rule. Many of them also find their productive capacity reduced because rapid withdrawal of skilled and experienced foreign personnel must be made good by recruitment of nationals who are poorly prepared for the jobs that have been left vacant. Under these circumstances, it is too much to expect that satisfactorily large improvements in income can be registered throughout the economy. It is possible, however, to show conspicuous increases in income and well-being in smaller communities selected for intensive development. The economy will benefit from the demonstration effect of such projects, and the political structure will benefit from this proof that independence can indeed bring increased prosperity. Agriculture is an especially good place to undertake such concentrated programmes in countries like those of tropical Africa where nearly everyone has some interest in farming and many can relate achievements in the model communities to their own daily lives. It is important, of course, that when this sort of venture is undertaken it be in a district more or less like other districts in the country and that the methods used and investments made be of a sort that is generally appropriate. This may be an argument against the unique irrigation project, which, although worthwhile in itself, cannot be duplicated.

An economy is particularly vulnerable when it is changing from primary dependence on subsistence production to dependence on the market. Changes in world markets to which a fully developed exchange economy would adjust easily may be sufficient to discourage newly established industries and to stall them indefinitely. New commercial ventures may run into difficulties because complementary industries are unable to supply them with needed materials for production or unable to absorb their final product. Production for sale may be hampered simply because markets are not large enough or do not meet often enough so that the grower can rely on ready sale, or because processing, transport, and warehousing facilities are inadequate. Furthermore, farmers who are just beginning to experiment with production for market, or with improved methods of production, may easily be discouraged from further experimentation if the methods they are induced to try out are ineffective, or if the crops they are persuaded to grow cannot be sold at a remunerative price. Some mistakes must inevitably be made if there is to be any economic progress at all; one function of the entrepreneur is to test out schemes that are uncertain and to accept the costs of failures in exchange for the chance of success. But farmers should not be urged to adopt schemes fostered by the state until these have been carefully tested, both on experimental farms and under actual farming conditions, and farmers' judgements should be taken fully into account in evaluating them.

Subsistence production will continue to be an important, though diminishing, part of total output for many years to come. It provides a measure of insurance against misfortunes which may be frequent in an immature and imperfect exchange economy, and a refuge for those who cannot or will not alter their behaviour to fit the requirements of the new economic order. It also provides employment for workers who are no longer needed in commercial farming and not yet needed in other industries.

Most industrialized countries have experienced a relative decline in employment in agriculture, a decline frequently interpreted as a movement of labour out of agriculture, and it is sometimes said that movement of labour from farming to other industries is prerequisite to increases in productivity, both in farming and elsewhere. But it is not necessarily true that the most profitable opportunities for employment of labour and capital are to be found in manufacturing, transport, and services, and a decline in farm labour inputs unaccompanied by improved techniques or greater use of capital is unlikely to result in increased productivity. Frequently what appears to be an absolute or relative decline in farm employment is in fact no more than specialization and division among butchers, millers, creameries, and other processors of the tasks formerly performed by farmers. When grain is ground, butter is churned, and livestock are slaughtered on the farm, the men and women who perform these tasks are considered to be engaged in farming; when they perform the same tasks in the town they become a part of the industrial labour force. The problem of deciding what is and what is not an agricultural enterprise becomes increasingly difficult as more and more jobs that were once done by the farm resident are taken over by specialists in the towns.

Under present conditions and techniques in tropical Africa, agriculture could employ many more people than it does now; if this added population were properly distributed, it could be employed without any decline in productivity, and even when better methods of production are employed, agricultural employment may nevertheless expand profitably for some time to come.

In fact the problem in many places in Africa is not to encourage people to leave the country, but to devise ways of sustaining agricultural production after they have gone. The cities have a great attraction, partly associated with the excitement of political events which are centred there, and the movement of young men out of rural areas which results may place a heavy transitory burden on farming. It can probably only be countered by increasing labour productivity, and earnings, in agriculture.

On the other hand, introduction of improved farming methods, especially if these include the use of machines in extensive cultivation, might free labour from farm employment before alternative employment opens elsewhere, and make it necessary for the state to adopt measures to ease this transition and avoid extensive rural unemployment. Some protection of small farmers engaged in subsistence production might be one of the devices adopted.

VII. Specific Recommendations

In this final section an attempt is made to set down very briefly some specific recommendations which come out of the various considerations examined in the body of the paper. Most, but not all, have been discussed in the earlier sections.

Improvement of the marketing system.— The dominating characteristic of the new African national economies is their disjointedness, their lack of internal links and connections. The first step to increase the production of agriculture and to bring the subsistence sector more fully into the exchange economy should be expansion of the internal transportation system, followed by improvement of the marketing system generally.

A. In particular, the road net needs to be extended into every part of the country before much attention is paid to improvement of existing roads.

B. Detailed studies should be made of the existing marketing system to locate restraints on free movement of commodities and imperfections in the process of price formation.

C. Information about prices of farm products in the major markets should be collected and disseminated frequently and regularly, preferably by radio.

D. Produce inspection and certification services should be provided at the larger markets, but their use should be voluntary.

E. Enforceability of contracts and accountability of commission merchants to their principals should be insured by law.

F. The market should be relied on as the primary guide for production.

G. The state should intervene in price-making for farm products only to

    a. prevent monopolistic pricing, or
    b. insure farmers against abrupt decline in prices.

H. Licensing of traders should be required only in order to insure their financial responsibility and to control unethical behaviour, not to limit their number.

Education.— Improvement of market connections will make farmers more receptive to information about improved techniques of production and processing, and will increase their interest in consumer education. Much remains to be learned about the most effective methods of agricultural production in the countries of the tropics, but existing knowledge, if put into practice, could nevertheless result in significant increases in productivity.

A. Primary reliance in agricultural education should be placed on instruction by word of mouth and by example. The principal instruments should be extension workers, farm institutes, demonstration plots and farms, and the radio.

B. Only those techniques which have been thoroughly tested in the field should be advocated in the general agricultural education programme.

C. Companies which sell fertilizers, improved seeds, pesticides, and farm tools should be permitted and encouraged to assist in the task of introducing improved techniques to farmers, so long as they do not misrepresent the product which they sell.

D. Consumer education, including nutrition, hygiene, housekeeping, and homecrafts, should be a part of the task of the farm extension workers, supported by radio broadcasts. Conservative radio advertising can help the consumer to know what products are available, what they cost, and what their uses are.

E. Wholesalers and retailers should be encouraged to acquaint consumers with the range of goods that can be obtained. If low total volume of sales makes it uneconomic for shops to stock a wide variety of merchandise, the device of ordering from catalogues can greatly expand consumer choice. Here the state can assist by facilitating the transmission of orders, payments, and merchandise.

F. Agricultural fairs and exhibits can be an effective device in fostering technological competition in production and housekeeping, and in instruction. They can also be a place where consumers become acquainted with new products.

G. In the educational programme, as in the development of marketing and transportation, results probably can best be obtained by concentrating successively on limited areas where conditions are more or less like those of the entire country.

Research.— Despite the considerable amount of agricultural research that has been carried on in tropical Africa since World War II, and the wealth of knowledge about agriculture in the temperate zone, much needs to be learned about African conditions, particularly about the technology and economics of production of food crops by smallholders. A programme of agricultural education cannot be expected to proceed very far without support from a vigorous programme of agricultural, farm management, and farm marketing research.

A.   An agricultural research programme cannot accomplish as much as it should unless there is continuing communication between research workers and practising farmers. Extension workers, therefore, must be able to listen to farmers as well as to talk to them, and they must also be able to tell the research workers what they have learned.

B.   Efficient farm production involves both application of effective techniques and economic combination of resources. Economists and farm management and marketing specialists should work closely with the natural scientists in research and in education.

C.   The most promising directions for research effort directly related to production at present appear to be:

    a.   Mechanization of barnyard activities;

    b.   Methods for increasing yield per acre, including use of fertilizers, pesticides, improved varieties, better plant spacing, better crop sequences, and better timing of field operations;

    c.   Concentration on the problems of relatively small farms, rather than of estates;

    d.   Specialized production rather than mixed farming; and

    e.   Ways of increasing total output by altering the product mix in favour of higher-value crops, livestock feeding, and dairying.

Land.— One of the more difficult problems faced by African agriculture is redefinition of rights to land use. The preferable solution from the standpoint of economic efficiency is probably some form of individual freehold, although rights of ownership are likely to be defined differently and to be somewhat more restricted than under traditional Anglo-Saxon law. Although individual ownership may be accepted as the eventual form of land tenure, the state should not attempt to introduce it abruptly, nor to press heavily against strong opposition for its adoption.

A.   The state should facilitate the change from traditional land tenures to individual ownership as economic forces make this change appear desirable. In particular, it can make it easier for individuals or groups to register title without requiring it of those who are reluctant.

B.   No legal restrictions should be imposed on the sale or mortgaging of land, nor upon the form of tenancy agreements so long as they are freely entered into and terminable by either party.

C.   The state should proceed with topographical surveys and with mapping of soils and land use.

D.   Problems of soil and water conservation can best be dealt with by local or regional conservation districts, sponsored by the state, but controlled and financed eventually by their members.

Capital.— Although capital required for needed reorganization of the

farm enterprises will be forthcoming in part from private sources, especially from the saving of farmers (as in the cocoa farms of West Africa, for
example), it will undoubtedly also be necessary for the state to assist in the
establishment of lending institutions and sometimes to assume this function
directly.

A. Farm credit, both for production and for long-term development,
requires financial agencies especially intended to serve farmers and staffed
by officers who are familiar with the problems of agriculture. These
agencies may be divisions of general lending institutions; they are more
apt themselves to be institutions concerned almost exclusively with
agriculture.

B. The state should supervise the operation of farm credit agencies in
order to prevent monopolistic exploitation of farmers, and it may have to
regulate their lending policies. Licensing of banks and mortgage companies, as of traders and processors, should be solely to prevent unethical
practices and to assure financial responsibility, not to limit competition.

C. If the state can avoid the administrative burden of itself providing
farm financing, it probably should do so. But when private investors or
co-operatives are unable or unwilling to engage in this kind of banking
at economically reasonable rates of interest, it may be necessary for the
state to establish its own farm credit banks.

D. Group purchase or rental of heavy equipment, including tractors and
harvesting machines, is one way to enable the small operator to remain
competitive with large-scale farmers.

E. Plants for primary processing of farm products need not be owned
and operated by large plantations.

Relief of distress, and aid in transition.— The state has an obligation to
come to the aid of its members who may be in distress. It may also be
obliged to render to individuals in the process of change from a traditional
to a modern economy assistance beyond that involved in providing the
economic conditions which make this change possible.

A. Direct assistance should not be perverted into an instrument of
control.

B. Minimum standards of living should not be conceived of in absolute
terms, but relative to the level of the living of the mass of the population.

C. Devices for raising or supporting incomes in agriculture should be
completely divorced from price supports, which typically give added
income to those who need it least.

D. Subsidies to assist farmers in transforming their farms, or in changing
their occupations, should be offered only when the new organization or
the new occupation is, or soon will be, economic without subsidy.

THE ROLE OF ADULT EDUCATION IN ECONOMIC DEVELOPMENT

BY P. G. H. HOPKINS

Warden, Fircroft College, Birmingham, UK

This symposium is primarily concerned with the problems of economic growth — and rightly so: but developing countries have other, perhaps larger, problems. I suspect and hope that the conference planners included the theme of adult education in order to remind us of the close relationship between educational levels and economic growth, and to ensure that other larger problems are not overlooked, to make it possible for economic issues to be viewed in the wider context of the cognate social and political developments — so that we may be concerned with Man and not just Economic Man.

As I interpret it, our basic aim here is to enable participants to hear and discuss a variety of considered opinions about economic development in emergent countries, in the hope that more conscious and more informed choices may consequently be made by their governments. But education is more than a capital investment and, therefore, this paper on adult education and that on the principles of education must inevitably force consideration of choices about society as a whole rather than just about economics — choices which the governments of developing countries will ignore, or make unconsciously, at their peril.

In the first place, the maximization of the national income is not a sufficient end in itself: educationists and politicians should be concerned with the quality of life as well as the quantity of goods. Secondly, the very pursuit of this end of maximum incomes, especially its rigorous pursuit, inevitably creates social, political and psychological stresses which can not only diminish the satisfactions of living for large numbers of people but also jeopardise economic growth itself. The report of the I.L.O. African Regional Conference in 1960 describes the 'triple impact of economic advance, political independence and social development' and stresses what change pervades the life of the African worker 'whether he is the docker in Mombasa, the miner in the Copperbelt, the textile worker in the mills of Dakar' or any of the millions getting a living from the land. Rapid industrialization and urbanization, a sudden switch from a subsistence to a money economy, a revolution in agrarian techniques, the whole attempt to telescope the Industrial Revolution into a few years — all this could spell disaster to the social fabric of African communities, disrupting the system of tribal reciprocities and traditional mutual aid and substituting a crude mercenary individualism. Thus, below the technical questions of this conference, lie the deeper issues of individual and social adjustment to new pressures, of individual and social acceptance (or rejection) of these all-pervasive changes.

In such conditions of social change, the insight of the anthropologist is often valuable. Professor Margaret Read has spoken of the dual role of education in any society. Education should first provide an element of continuity, of respect for and adherence to tradition — i.e. we should accept our cultural heritage. This must be a very powerful element in all educational systems. But, secondly, education should also prepare the way for and sometimes induce social change, helping to incorporate it within the social fabric — i.e. we should improve our cultural heritage.

Here is the core of the answer to the question: what role should education (including adult education) play in the process of economic development? Education must keep the balance between desirable economic and political change and necessary social stability. As the 1960 UNESCO Montreal Declaration on Adult Education expressed it: *'people should be encouraged to feel pride and dignity in their own cultural heritage . . .* People must be encouraged to understand and promote change.' For such a difficult balancing operation, it is clear that school education is not enough. Unless the process is to be solely manipulation of the masses by an intellectual élite, the conscious and willing co-operation of large sections of the adult population is necessary.

It is my contention, therefore, that adult education has a supremely important role to play in the immediate future of the new African states. Together with school education, *it has the task of 'building the new African'* — the man and woman who can meet the challenge of new opportunities; who can blend the good and reject the bad of the new and the old societies; who will produce more efficiently more goods and services, but who will also consume them wisely. Certainly foundations for these constructive responses to challenge can be laid in the schooling of the young during the next few years, although so far very little positive action or thinking has been done along these lines. But school education on its own could never be enough.

I. The Importance of Adult Education

Resources should be concentrated on adult education for eight overwhelming reasons:

A. Even the best school education will be inadequate for a lifetime to be spent in the modern technical world. The changes will be so rapid and the consequent necessary adjustments so great that no once-and-for-all school education, however good, can hope to carry a man effectively through his working life.

B. The dismal fact is that the school educational provision over all of Africa has been woefully deficient in the past. If we take the statistics for our host country, Nyasaland, we find that, in the 1945 census, under 7 per cent claimed literacy in their vernacular and under 1 per cent in English. More recently, very rough estimates in the Hadlow Report on 'African Education in Nyasaland' (published 1958) indicated that illiteracy or 'very near illiteracy' was the lot of about half the adult population of Nyasaland and suggested that 'it may be another generation before even the primary school system is enough for the needs'. The Hadlow Committee therefore reached and voiced strongly the same general conclusion as the Cambridge Conference of 1952 — a conference of African leaders and British administrators called to assess the reports of the Jeffery Mission to West Africa and the Binns Mission to East and Central Africa.

The discussion at Cambridge of Group E on 'Education and the Adult' evoked 'the most revolutionary sentence spoken during the conference' — viz. 'At least for the short term there should be a quite novel concentration of energy and resources upon the tasks of informal education.' The Jeffery Report had previously defined 'informal education' as including all forms of education of adults — mass education, welfare education, literacy campaigns, community development as well as what is normally termed 'adult education' in Western Europe or the U.S.A. The Cambridge Conference Report then continues:

> 'If education departments acted upon this and concentrated for the time being upon adult and informal education rather than upon schools, the education pattern of Africa would soon look very different and incidentally the efficiency of the schools would be greatly increased. In the discussion eight speakers (seven of them African) explicitly endorsed this. No one opposed it.'

Thus we need adult education to remedy the weaknesses of the present and past school systems.

C. Further, even in areas where schooling has been efficient, the effects of this childhood instruction can evaporate in an adult community which has no respect for education. The Pakistan Commission on National Educations put this forcibly in their report (1959):

> 'It is common experience that once pupils leave the village school, they become assimilated by the community rather than function as

progressive forces for its enlightenment. Many forget in a short time even the skills of reading and writing. The reason is not only that the atmosphere of the village discourages reading, but also that little reading material is available to sustain a positive interest. In spite of their schooling, children tend to retain the old prejudices, attitudes and way of life. The education of the adult is clearly important even to ensure the continued literacy of the children.'

We need adult education so that we do not lose what benefits schooling provides and in order to create an atmosphere which will encourage our children to pursue their studies with keen interest.

D. The Jeffery Report commented on the flexibility of informal adult education in contrast to the rigidity of most school systems, especially those modelled on western lines. Here is a field where there are few western prototypes because adult education has never been a mass-movement before. Here is a field where the new African States can work out their own salvation. It is true that a few excellent schemes have been started in recent years and these can be useful guides, as can equally the abortive projects in a negative way. But those states emerging from their national struggle for independence should be in a particularly strong position to call upon tremendous stores of enthusiasm and goodwill. Fourthly, therefore, many developing countries should concentrate resources on adult education because of their unique position to make a break with cramping traditional frameworks and to harness their adult potential for large scale experiments in this field.

E. Further, if the vital function of education is, as we have said, to keep the balance between desirable politico-economic change and necessary social stability, then much of education must be concerned with the problems of real life — not with compartmentalized school subjects. Many of the issues require from the students a wide experience of life and from the teachers a complete abrogation of superior authority for a role of partnership in the search for solutions. Such issues require adult students, as Erich Fromm pointed out in 'The Sane Society':

> 'Undoubtedly the understanding of history, philosophy, religion and literature, psychology etc, is limited at this early age (i.e. up to 18) . . . For many people, the age of 30 to 40 is more appropriate for learning, in the sense of understanding rather than of memorising.'

If this is true of America with its well developed high-school system, how much more true it must be of emergent countries. Our fifth reason for concentrating upon adult education therefore is that there will be many issues in the new Africa which require adult minds and adult study-methods.

F.   Moreover, if these vital subjects are never discussed by adults and are taken only in the schools, the inevitable tensions between children and parents will become even greater. It would be disastrous for Africa if only the young were grappling with these subjects which raise the fundamental issues of living and provide the means for adjusting mentally to new conditions. As Joyce Cary said: 'Prejudice, superstition, fear, and ignorance must be attacked in their strongholds — the adult mind.' This attack must be made simultaneously with the expansion of the school system, for the only hope of bringing about a reconciliation between tradition and the new influences is through adult education — especially of women. Sixthly, therefore, adult education is necessary to help bridge the gap between traditional elders and adventurous youth

G.   From the purely economic viewpoint, too, adult education has good claims for priority. School education is usually compulsory, either by law or by parental order; adult education is voluntary — and 'a willing horse can drag a heavy load'. Holger Begtrup, the principal of a Danish Folk High School, concluded after many years of experience: 'The same amount of information which it takes a half-grown youth dozing on the school benches three to five years to learn, can be acquired in the space of three to five months by adults who are keen on learning and who have done practical work.' Many experiments in informal education have corroborated the essence (if not the mathematics) of this.

For example, ten years ago in Dar-es-Salaam an effort was made to take literacy classes to the illiterates on the fringes of the city. At Kinondoni, thirty-six adults, whilst continuing with their normal work, passed their literacy test in Kiswahili after four months of voluntary part-time classes. A group of sixty students, all eighteen years of age and from twenty-three different tribes, then built themselves the Kinondoni Adult School in the space of three weeks. Not only was literacy attained very rapidly at low cost, but creative energies had clearly been released and transmuted into constructive work.

What entrepreneur could afford to ignore Begtrup's estimate of a cutting to one-twelfth of his production time? How can emergent governments afford to neglect the time-saving and cost-reducing nature of adult education?

H.   We shall contend later that attempts at precise evaluation of the 'returns on educational investment' are misguided and inevitably doomed to failure; but this does not mean that broad comparisons and general assessments cannot be made. To illustrate, it is undeniable that in most developing countries education has been grossly neglected and that, so far, investment in physical resources has been much heavier than 'investment in human resources'. Diminishing marginal returns are, therefore, not likely to be imminent as far as educational investment is concerned; and Professor Arthur Lewis has pointed out that this is especially true of adult education. 'Investment in practical forms of education for illiterate adults in the countryside is likely to be more productive than similar expenditure for illiterate children', he says in his paper at the Addis Ababa 1961 Conference on 'Education in Africa'. He asserts that adult education shows high returns per unit of expenditure; and we have just stressed that the time-saving and cost-reducing properties of adult education will keep real expenditure low. Further, the 'opportunity-costs' of adult education are virtually negligible, both to the individual and to the nation.

If Alfred Marshall was right that 'the most valuable of all capital is that invested in human beings', then the most lucrative investment of all for new African states must be in the field of adult education.

II. The Meaning of Adult Education

Much time could be spent (and wasted) on discussing the many different definitions of 'adult education', ranging from the ultra-broad 'all living is learning' approach to the nice distinctions which permit the Ministry of Education in England to rule that a class on French Literature is 'adult education' whilst one on French Language is 'further education'.

Such differentiation is unfortunate at the best of times; in the African situation it is tragic. Surely it is simpler to avoid the type of distinction made in Para. 556 of the 1962 Phillips Report on 'Education in Nyasaland':

> 'We have deliberately separated Adult Education from Mass Literacy or Fundamental Education. In Mass Education we think of those adult persons who have missed education entirely and who are now seeking help so as to achieve literacy. In Adult Education, however, we have in mind those adult persons who have had some schooling up to either the full primary or secondary level. The aim here is to increase the student's knowledge and understanding and sharpen his critical judgement: he has tasted the fruit of learning and wishes to enjoy more of it.'

The implications of this passage are insidious and misleading. First, there is a suggestion that adult education is a superior article to mass education; secondly, there is also an assumption that all adults who have had full primary education are still literate; and lastly an equation of 'learning' and 'schooling' which most adult educationists would reject is detectable. The consequences of the definitions are unfortunate, for the section on 'Adult Education' which follows then deals almost exclusively with classes of an examination-preparation type (implying that adult education is for overgrown school-children) and culminates with Recommendation No. 1 (Para. 566): 'We are unable to recommend any material increase in government expenditure on adult education.' This is not quite as outrageous as it sounds, since help for an Adult Education Centre in Blantyre is anticipated from the AID, and since there are separate sections on leadership courses, on mass-education, and on community development. Is it unfair, however, to suggest that the splitting up of what is so patently one related field produces an inability to see the problem whole and to sense its true significance?

For this paper, we shall take as our working definition the eminently practical phrase coined by Edward Hutchinson: '*organised provision to enable men and women to enlarge and interpret their own living experience.*'

This phrase has the advantages that:

A. By stipulating 'organised provision' it excludes the purely casual or individual ways of acquiring knowledge which governments can influence only very indirectly. Such ways are impossible to evaluate and it would be pointless for us to discuss them.

B. A Gaon-Sathi's conversation with an Indian peasant, a university extension lecture in Nova Scotia, tribal initiation rites in New Guinea, a fruit-bottling demonstration under the Jamaican 3-F Scheme, a workers' class in the 'Red Corner' of a Russian factory, a five-months residential course at a Danish Folk High School, a Women's Club one-day visit to Washington, a radio-listening group in Malaya, an ILO technical training programme for Haiti leather-workers—all are 'adult education'.

C. It makes it clear that we embrace all that is called, in various settings, mass education; social education; fundamental education; literacy campaigns; agricultural and industrial development; agricultural and co-operative extension work; and vocational training for adults.

D. It ends on the keynote which distinguishes all good adult education — the fact that the experience of life which the participants bring adds a relevance and significance to the studies which are often missing in school education.

The very looseness of our definition underlines the fact that those planning adult education campaigns will have to make use of a wide variety of individuals and organizations. These will range from international agencies to individual well-wishers who assist in the teaching and organizing. They will often form small, local, *ad hoc* groups; but perhaps even more often, already existing organizations such as trade unions, co-operative associations, churches, youth groups, women's clubs and political parties will prove the spearhead of an attack in some field of adult education. Schools and/or parent-teacher associations can play a leading

5

part, as can local industrial firms and agricultural or teacher-training colleges which are willing to recognize their obligation to the wider community. On a regional or national scale, universities (with their extra-mural departments, if any) and voluntary adult associations such as WEAs can provide more formal education, and regional long-term adult residential colleges can cater for specially selected groups.

In this paper it is not proposed to give a description of the organization and techniques of adult education. A comprehensive survey will be available shortly from the ILO in their new 'Manual of Workers' Education'; and in the meantime those interested are referred to 'Methods and Techniques of Workers' Education' — ILO Geneva 1957.

III. The Content of Adult Education

Before embarking on the process of subdivision which we have already condemned, let us remind ourselves that, although the immediate objective and therefore the content of adult education will vary with circumstances, all education should aim at the development of the individual adult's capacity to live a fuller personal and social life. This may be achieved in a number of ways, but in this paper only occasional illustrations of method and organization can be included.

A. *Literacy and Basic Education.*— Opinions differ greatly as to whether literacy should be the paramount educational objective of adult education in developing countries. A. K. Coomaraswamy in 'The Bugbear of Literacy' expresses one extreme by attacking literacy for destroying 'the racial memory', breeding a reliance on the written word and bringing people into contact with an alien culture without sufficient preparation. At the other extreme are such champions of literacy programmes as J. L. McGairl, who wrote in 'Community Development Bulletin' (Sept. 1953):

> 'Becoming literate as an adult in this African society is a spiritual experience in some way related to the emergence and growth of personality. People are uplifted by it and are made aware of their power to alter their environment by individual and group action.'

Other writers concede the value of literacy but deny its necessity. 'It is not reasonable to make a fetish of literacy,' says Professor Arthur Lewis, reminding us that illiterate Japanese farmers doubled their production rapidly before World War I (Addis Ababa 1961 UNESCO Conference Report, Annex IV, p. 78). Similarly, the I.C.F.T.U. International Seminar at Calcutta in 1954 stressed that 'Nearly all the subjects taught in general and trade union courses can be included in a course for illiterate workers.'

Certainly, illiteracy does not rule out educational advance (especially in these days of radio) and adult education must not ignore illiterates. Obviously, however, literacy is a most useful tool. It can give an individual new confidence and enthusiasm; it can allow parents to share the experiences of their school-age children; it can promote political interest and civic awareness; and it can provide economic benefits for the individual and the community.

It is not surprising, therefore, that many countries with new governments after revolutions or attainment of independence, have inaugurated all-out literacy campaigns, often supported by national decree — as in USSR in 1919 and Turkey under Kemal Ataturk. Ghana provides good illustrations of concentrated literacy campaigns in which full use was and is made of the upsurge of nationalist enthusiasm, of ceremonies and celebrations, and of a special cheap literacy kit, including a badge of honour. But schemes can be much less ambitious. Indeed the Addis Ababa UNESCO Conference recommended that campaigns should generally start with smaller pilot projects until such time as an adequate and continuing output of reading matter is available for the new-literates.

The last point is vital. *Literacy campaigns should certainly loom large in adult education programmes; but they should be treated as a means rather than the end.* Literacy is a tool, a very useful and often an essential tool. It is a tool which, nowadays, can be very quickly put into the hands of ordinary adults, but it can be stopped from rusting only by constant use in some of the forms of adult education.

B.   Technical and Vocational Education.—A second major objective of adult education, and one in which literacy can assist greatly, is the training of special technical and vocational skills. The economic value of such training seems so patent that one might have expected to find adequate provision already in many developing countries. Yet investigation reveals a pathetic lack of this type of functional education. Wilbert E. Moore commented, in 'Labor Attitudes towards Industrialization in Under-developed Countries' (American Economic Review, May 1955):

> 'Education in many colonial areas has encouraged anything but the development of mechanical and technical skills, and the opportunities for use of any such skills have not been made available.'

This may be partly because of policies of reserving posts for expatriates and partly because these fields have traditionally not been the province of the Ministry of Education.

This shortcoming must be remedied, though careful co-ordination with the economic planning department will clearly be required. Planners of technical and vocational education cannot afford to ignore the economic pressures of the market and the 'prestige pressures' of society.

C. *Social and Political Education.*— The third major objective of adult education is less tangible and definite, but is, nevertheless, perhaps the most important for developing countries. *It is the task of enabling adults 'to meet the obligations and sustain the rights that belong to responsible citizens', the task of fitting men and women for their life in the local community, in the nation, in the new Africa, and in the United Nations.* This task is difficult enough in a comparatively static society; it seems well-nigh impossible in countries where the rate of economic and political change is now breath-taking. Yet there is a chance that the enthusiasm now being generated may be directed into constructive channels, making people conscious of the problems of change and eventually able to solve them. 'With the sense of national unity . . . community development can turn into a popular movement sweeping through the country and effecting over a very short period a radical transformation in the attitude and way of life of large numbers of people.'

Much excellent work in this field can be done by small groups studying subjects at depth, for example in university extra-mural classes. But the problems are so widespread and deep-seated that one must inevitably think in terms of large-scale programmes catering not for a small élite but for whole villages and districts. This has been the basis of most schemes of agricultural extension, community development, or social education. This last term, now adopted by the Indian Government and by the New Delhi Second Commonwealth Education Conference (January 1962), has the advantage of being all-embracing as far as adult education is concerned. It includes health, infant and maternity welfare, recreation and cultural activities, home life, training in citizenship, and in economic efficiency. Common factors to all programmes of community development or social education are:

a. the involvement as far as possible of a whole community, since citizenship begins in the realization and expression of common interests and common loyalty in daily activities.
b. the stress on informal and practical as against formal and theoretical education.
c. The insistence on a very large element of local initiative, co-operation and self-help.

This last feature highlights the cardinal importance of selecting the right 'animateurs' for this type of work — the right village-level workers or Gaon-Sathi (villagers' companion) as they are called in India. They need not be specialists, but they should have wide theoretical and practical knowledge; they must be tough and resourceful without showing it too much, since their task is to develop the resourcefulness of the community; they must be able to enlist the support of local leaders, being prepared to work with and not for, to help rather than direct. It is not surprising that those countries taking this work seriously have been forced to develop very careful recruitment processes, often including preliminary practical work in the field.

One must beware of expecting any panacea or short-cut solution. But there is good evidence from many parts of the world to support the U.N. secretary-general's report to the Trusteeship Council in 1956 that '. . . The people who practice Community Development are beginning to discover in it a power to effect a total transformation of their lives by gradual strengthening of their capacity to grow.' This has certainly been true in West Africa, India, Pakistan, Jamaica, in several Central and South American schemes and a host of other places.

Apart from the economic repercussions, which we shall discuss in our next section, one can hope that such education will promote social cohesion in the period of dislocatory change, bridging the gaps between literate and illiterate, between old and young, between country and town; and will also promote a sense of political responsibility. The very process of social participation is the basis for civic awareness and makes specific instruction for both electors and elected much more intelligible, for the real education in democracy is in the actual development of one's own community.

There are perhaps certain groups liable to require special attention and to derive particular benefits. These would include women, who have been so grossly neglected educationally in most of the world and who can initially be reached by homecraft and health instruction. Dr Aggrey's aphorism is still true, 'If you educate a woman, you educate a family.'

The increasing numbers of migrants into towns also present a challenge, as they are particularly in need of the sense of community: they can be helped by 'adjustment classes' (including urban health and hygiene) and by informal group activities. In some towns, very interesting experiments are being made with 'educational hostels' for young migrants. Youth tend in most societies to be worst hit by the tensions resulting from change and special provision should certainly be made for them in urban and rural programmes.

At the same time, one would hope for special citizenship education for new voters in local and national elections and for the elected representatives so that both electors and elected may understand their political rights and duties.

In all these fields there are dangers which could result from too much governmental control. The whole spirit underlying social education should be one of willing but critical and conditional co-operation which will require considerable restraint on the part of governments. As the second Commonwealth Conference Report expresses it: 'Social education cannot be carried out by Governments alone without losing its identity and force. Although Governments may and should foster social education as a matter of policy . . . the demand . . . must derive from the people themselves. Hence the importance of the principle of voluntary service and the vital role of voluntary organisations in social education.' *Co-operative bodies, trade unions, women's institutes and clubs, religious bodies, political parties, workers' educational associations — all must take their share, with the governments, in this vital task,* even if in many cases they have to be created initially with the help of the social education workers.

Good growing-points for such voluntary groups may often be found in the traditional cultural and recreational activities — songs, dances, drums, plays and so on. These can be used to make people 'feel a pride and dignity in their own cultural heritage' and such pride and dignity may be a help to new countries in their uneasy transitional periods — thus indirectly producing economic benefits.

IV. ECONOMIC BENEFITS OF ADULT EDUCATION

It should be clear by now that its very diversity makes it difficult to specify precisely the economic roles which adult education can play in a developing society.

Direct economic benefits.— Certain branches, such as technical training, bring clear and almost assessable benefits, but since these will also come within another's terms of reference, we will merely emphasize a few general points.

Two United Nations Reports in 1951 both stressed that farming was the sector where economic progress was most urgently needed. 'Measures for the Economic Development of Underdeveloped Countries' suggested that 1 per cent of the national income should be allocated to the agricultural extension services, adding that 'no other investment is likely to yield bigger returns in the immediate future.' *Such services must obviously form an important part of any adult education provision.*

There will, of course, be a similar economic return for instruction resulting in greater productivity in industry: and here we must think of the whole range, from family fishing to colossal textile mills. Professor Lewis's comments apply particularly to this field. 'Education for children is fine, but its potential contribution to output over ten years is small compared with the potential contribution of efforts devoted to improving adult skills. . . . The quickest way to increase productivity in the less-developed countries is to train the adults who are already on the job.' (Social and Economic Studies. June 1961.) This is true whether 'the job' is that of factory hand, foreman, manager, trade union officer or even entrepreneur; and particularly true of the 'middle-range of administrative, executive and technical posts', where the qualities and skills are not those which can be learned by children or adolescents, since the learning process must be based on wide experience. In all these cases it will be quicker and more economic to instruct an experienced adult than to try to train a school-child from scratch.

The economic role of this type of technical training is self-evident: but there can be benefits, only slightly less direct, from the more general forms of adult education. The acquisition of literacy can in itself affect the general confidence and productivity of a worker, even if he makes no direct use of his new skills: and the effect of community development schemes can revolutionize the economy of a whole district, producing new schools, clinics and roads and a determination to achieve further advances. Most new countries will have to rely to a large extent upon these processes of capital formation at the village level: and the changed psychological attitudes are a *sine qua non* for economic progress.

The recent researches of Professor Aukrust suggest that previous attempts to relate growth to the level of investment of physical capital have failed because of their neglect of the 'third factor'. Economists have measured physical capital and labour units but have ignored the 'human factors' — a mixture of labour skills, organization and general human efficiency. This leads Aukrust to the view that 'the rate of progress can be increased not only by increasing real capital, but also by a conscious effort to improve man himself.' His mathematical calculations are already under fire, but his broad conclusions can be substantiated by most reports of recent community development schemes and indeed of two pioneer programmes of popular adult education.

Nobody can estimate exactly what contribution to the Danish economy was made by the Danish Folk High Schools; but all who have studied these adult education colleges and have seen them in action are agreed that they revolutionized the Danish rural scene. In rapid succession in the mid-nineteenth century Denmark lost land and national prestige in the wars against Prussia and then grain markets and prosperity as the New World prairies were opened up and the Atlantic freight rates were slashed. Yet in this period the Danish residential colleges were started and thrived and the Danish peasant, who had been described as 'unprogressive, sullen, suspicious, averse from experiment and incapable of associated enterprise' became 'forward-looking, cheerful, scientifically minded, resourceful and co-operative.' A Danish Education Inspector remarked in the early days how quickly the young men and women learned: he was impressed not so much by the knowledge they acquired as by the fact that 'they leave the schools different people, having learned to hear, to see, to think and use their powers.' These became the young peasant farmers who, within a generation, transformed Danish agriculture into the most efficient butter and bacon producing economy in the world. 'The peasant helped himself. He adapted his methods to the new circumstances. . . . He was open to the new ideas and willing to apply them. The mobility, the capacity and the culture that such a radical change calls for, when it is to be made by voluntary effort, the Danish peasantry then possessed; and this fact is certainly due to the influence of the Danish Folk High School.' (Hans Lund.)

The Danish example is perhaps the best known and most striking, but adult residential colleges were also a prominent feature in the development of Norway, while a Finnish writer says, 'They were indispensable for strengthening the spiritual backbone and the powers of resistance of the people (against Tsarism) . . . the idea swept like a storm across the land.' (Viljo Kosonen.) There are certainly tremendous advantages in residence and it is interesting to note the spread of residential colleges on Scandinavian lines in the new African countries.

The other famous pioneer programme — at Antigonish, Nova Scotia — indicates, however, that residence is not an essential element. Here the stress was on study clubs and co-operative associations, and the driving forces were the Department of Extension of the St Francis Xavier University and the dormant energies of the farmers and fishermen of the locality. Many observers have noted the new positive and progressive approach to economic problems evoked by this adult education venture. It is such pioneer schemes, with their tangible economic and intangible psychological success, which inspired the community development experiments after World War II.

Other benefits.— The move into the realm of psychological attitudes obviously leads to greater difficulties in assessing effects, but all experience shows that rapid economic change is dependent on the right psychological climate and not just upon 'technical know-how'. The most rapid progress will occur (as in Denmark and Antigonish) where education has encouraged an experimental outlook and where people are able to identify their wants and to plan how to attain them. As Malinowski has said, 'The real agencies of change are organised bodies of human beings working for a definite purpose,' so that the problem for the economic planner is to discover how best to use education for stimulating people to work for certain definite purposes. The problem is not easy; and the most obvious solution may not be the best.

In many societies, the traditional family and kinship arrangements, land-tenure and ownership, tribal customs, religious beliefs and customary values all act as obstacles to rapid material advancement. In addition, to many people the marginal utility of leisure may be high, higher than that of the commodities available. Given such a situation, and if we agree to exclude the use of force, the economist's first solution will be to create and multiply conscious wants so that work becomes more attractive and output will increase. The whole pressure of modern advertising backed by the mass media could probably break through any accustomed inertia quite rapidly, releasing productive energies (and also riding roughshod over worthwhile traditional values). This is to equate 'economic growth at any price' with 'progress'. It also creates fresh problems, for if greater output can be achieved only by satisfying greater consumer-demand, valuable resources will be diverted from the producer- to the consumer-sector and the rate of capital investment will be held down.

Is it too naive to see in adult education a possible middle road? In the first place education itself, as Galbraith has said, 'has a marked influence in widening the span of the individual's wants', and it is a widening and not just an intensification. Some of the new wants will be for immediate consumption goods, but some will be for cultural and recreational satisfactions (which do not drain the economic resources) and other wants again will be in the field of investment. The villagers who are spurred on by a community development project into wanting a new road or a school will promote economic growth more effectively than the villagers who all want gramophones and bicycles.

D. K. Chisiza's booklet 'Realities of African Independence' places the dilemma clearly before us (pp. 23–24): 'As economic development proceeds the incomes of those people who are engaged in economic activities rise. Should this additional purchasing power be channelled into the purchase of cars, liquor, more wives, land, gaudy clothes, mansions, betting coupons and trinkets? Or should it be spent on better and more varied food, good but modest houses . . . educative entertainment and travel, better education for children as well as parents, good health services and future security? Most people would agree that the second alternative is preferable . . . but what guarantee is there that the new incomes will in fact be channelled into that direction? None.'

One must agree that there is no guarantee: but one can augment his solutions of advertising and propaganda and 'the identification of prestige with the consumption of the second group of goods' with the suggestion of an all-out social education campaign. In this way the new code of values and the new spending patterns become a conscious creation with reasoned participation by the people: and a sound national economic policy can expect a constructive response from them. Indeed, social education properly administered in a newly-developing country should be able to evoke a sense of patriotic enthusiasm for collective economic goals and to extend the typical African co-operative mutuality and family security into the national scene. Wilbert E. Moore has pointed out that 'a sense of social participation has been consistently neglected even in advanced industrial countries.' Here again is a field where the developing countries can learn from the mistakes of their forerunners.

V. THE EVALUATION OF ADULT EDUCATION

Any entrepreneur contemplating capital investment naturally wants accurate estimates of expenditure and of anticipated returns. This must equally be the attitude of governments and planners in developing countries, where resources are severely limited and where much of the capital will have to come from foreign sources. Further, since education is a field in which aid can be expected from international agencies and from large charitable foundations, it would be very pleasant to be able to attract large grants by guaranteeing high returns.

Certainly the expenditure can be costed fairly accurately, even on such wide projects as social education programmes. The Indian Government, for example, is prepared to assess its 'total needs for social education' in the Third Five Year Plan (1961–66) as being 750 million rupees; and its total resources available for such work as 253 million rupees. But they do not attempt any monetary estimates of the economic benefits likely to accrue. Should they be expected to do so — and if so, how?

It must be admitted that until very recently estimates were always excessively vague or, when more precise, were unsupported by evidence: so interest must be strong in two recent developments in writings about the economics of education, both of which might appear to hold out hopes of more accurate assessments. The first 'school of thought' (expressed, for example in articles by Dr H. F. Miller, Dr T. W. Schultz and Professor G. S. Becker) admits the existence of indirect benefits from education ('external economies') but then concentrates on the direct returns. These they measure by assessing the extra earnings of individuals which can reasonably be attributed to their superior or specific education (as compared with the average earnings of people without special education). Attempts are then made to aggregate the samples taken and such estimates are produced as Professor Becker's for the U.S. Bureau of

National Research — that in 1950 the U.S. male population was earning nearly 15 per cent return on what had been privately invested (in cost of education plus income foregone) in their high school, college and university education; and that when adjustments were made for the public funds also invested, the rate of return was still 11 per cent.

Such calculations are intriguing and might well tempt the government planners in developing countries, who feel a need to justify in mathematical terms their proposed educational expenditure. They certainly seem to exert a strange temptation over some very sound writers on education — such as H. M. Phillips of the UNESCO Department of Social Sciences, who discusses the ideas in his paper presented to the Addis Ababa Conference (Annex IV, pp. 100–101). Phillips very rightly comments that such figures are available only for a limited number of countries, all in an advanced stage of development and that their application to underdeveloped countries needs caution. He makes two further criticisms — that such estimates are based on long-term, and perhaps unjustifiable, assumptions of a continuance of the present income-differentiation pattern of a country; and that 'it does not follow that the sum of the differentials where added would represent the total national gain. . . . Moreover all of the gain cannot be attributed to education as there are important correlations between education and parental income.'

One would have assumed that the last two points in themselves would have refuted any idea of applying such calculations to developing countries, yet Phillips's next sentence is 'None the less these figures have their value, particularly when set against cost.' This peculiarly ambivalent attitude on the part of a UNESCO speaker might further tempt planners to embark upon similar statistical exercises in developing countries.

Surely this must be avoided at all costs. It should be stated clearly and categorically that any such criterion of increased individual earning power has no relevance at all to educational planning in the new countries. If it had, then this paper would be pointless, for adult education would be a bottom priority, since it frequently brings little *direct* results in increased individual earning capacity.

In the first place, there is no justification for assuming that the existing income differentials will persist indefinitely in the developing economies: in fact, there is every reason for hoping that they do not, as they have already distorted the educational–occupational pattern in a number of new countries. If there is a narrowing of differentials, are we seriously to accept that the direct economic benefits of education are thereby reduced? Or that if a country adopts the opposite policy and increases income inequality it will thereby increase the economic value of education? Or that if a nation adopts the extreme policy of equalizing all incomes, then its education will immediately cease to be of economic benefit?

These are the ridiculous situations we are led to if we accept a criterion which treats education as a private matter instead of a public, social matter: and further, which applies a quite indefensible measuring-rod — the money-income results. Was the benefit to the world of Einstein's education measurable in terms of his salary-differential?

This approach has the further fallacy that in its attempt to 'monetise' benefits, it ignores the indirect and intangible results. The strange fact is that Phillips, having stated that 'these figures have their value, particularly when set against cost', then goes on to point this out and to discuss the indirect effects on the economic environment. He lists 'research, inventiveness, organisation, entrepreneurship, social coherence and political performance, the flexibility of the labour force and psychological factors affecting achievement' — factors with which we had to concern ourselves in the last section. Even if these 'external economies' can be equated to Professor Aukrust's 'residual third factor', any attempt to set a monetary value upon them must be highly suspect.

Finally, their whole mathematical approach (rather like this symposium) forces one into a position of assessing education in purely economic terms. *Education, as we suggested in the Introduction, is concerned with mental and spiritual values as well as with material satisfactions; and it is difficult to see how these can be related to income differentials or indeed how they can be allotted monetary values at all.*

But the search for mathematical precision then leads Phillips and also John Vaizey in his 'Economics of Education' (pp. 47–49) into comparisons between education and other public works. Vaizey analyses an attempt made in Britain to study the cost/benefit ratio of the new Birmingham–London motorway, M1. This entailed assumptions about the future flow of traffic, its rate of growth, time-saving, accidents, etc., etc., which were then transmuted into money figures, with such ranges as '£80,000 to £227,000 on time-saving' and '£18,000 to £117,000' [sic] on fuel-saving. After another series of inspired guesses, we are told that: 'This gave a measurable rate of return on the motorway between 3·8 per cent and 4·8 per cent and a rough guess of the "immeasured" savings raised these rates of return between 10 and 15 per cent.'

One might have thought that the point of this exercise was to show the absurdity first of arriving at figures like 3·8 per cent on the basis of assumptions leading to statistical estimates with ranges like '£18,000 to £117,000'; and second, of swamping these assumed figures with a 'rough guess of immeasured savings' about three times as large as the original quotient. But Vaizey then adds: 'Now the application of this kind of reasoning to education is obviously both possible and desirable'; and later: 'It is already clear, however, that this is the most realistic procedure for calculating the returns to investment in education.'

Yet, like Phillips, Vaizey shows a strange ambivalence, for he does state that the calculation of individual benefits (on the Schultz–Becker basis) is 'subject to severe limitations and it is difficult to think of calculations of the indirect benefits'. He goes on: 'It is clear that the crucial difficulty is assigning a meaning to the indirect productive value of education and of the indirect rise in satisfactions; and later the assignment of a notional monetary value to these benefits is an arbitrary but not an intellectually arduous procedure.' (He sees the follies, yet persists in supporting them.)

One wonders what figure could be generally agreed upon as the right arbitrary, notional monetary value for the benefits to the individuals and to the community of the Indian social education or the Pakistan Village AID programme, or even of a single village literacy course. What is the economic value of education which creates a responsible democracy? What monetary value has a youth club or a film show on hygiene to an illiterate village audience, or a folk-dance festival? Such questions are quite unanswerable.

There is indeed some point in the comparison of education with other public investments like motorways or hydro-electric dams — but it lies in the way such a comparison emphasizes that these are all social activities, producing widespread and totally unassessable indirect benefits to society and to individuals.

Both these attempts at precise evaluation of the economic role of education are not only a waste of scarce time and scarce statistical skill: they appear so scientific that they could well be taken seriously instead of being treated as intellectual gymnastics. It would be a disaster if this occurred, for it could cause serious distortions in national investment programmes, as between other public works and education and as between the different types of education. *There is no mathematical basis on which to found an education-priority policy and we must therefore rely on the evidence of observed experiments from all over the world. The evidence is continually piling up to confirm Marshall's assertion that 'the most valuable capital is that invested in human beings'.* Certainly the proofs will not be mathematical, but they will be convincing — like Albert Mayer's statement in 'Pilot Project, India': 'It is now seen to be continuously and increasingly true that government investment in intensive rural development work is paid for over and over again in tangible economic returns. . . . This tangible return must be added, of course, to the important and indispensable intangibles which make this improvement possible and are the guarantee of its "built-in" continuity and permanence.'

Even if we cannot assign 'notional monetary values', we can declare confidently that adult education pays dividends and big ones; and that it must be given high priority by any nation interested in its economic, social and political development.

VI. CONCLUSION.

In conclusion, then, we may summarize the possible economic roles of adult education as:

a. instruction in basic skills capable of general application (e.g., literacy and arithmetic).
b. training in technical and vocational skills (e.g., agricultural, industrial, managerial, administrative, commercial and entrepreneurial).
c. creation of a more dynamic psychological climate — affecting individual motivation, labour mobility and willingness to save.
d. development of confidence, initiative, willingness to experiment and to co-operate in practical planning for progress.
e. creation of an awareness of national economic goals and of the role of the individual in fulfilling them.

If adult education fulfils these roles, the economic benefits can be immense though immeasurable: but they cannot be separated from the social, political, cultural and spiritual advancements which will also ensue. It is therefore not possible to assign monetary values to programmes, or even to make *general* pronouncements about the right level of educational investment or correct distribution as between adult and children's education.

It is, however, reasonable to assert that there is no country in the world yet allocating sufficient of its capital investment to the education of its adult population and that the amounts which the developing countries have been able to allot so far are pitiful. They must do much more: they must be helped to do it and do it quickly.

We began this paper by suggesting that the purpose of this conference was to help African leaders to make more considered choices in economic matters. This is its immediate goal. Its distant goal should be to help the African people as a whole to make considered choices. Adult education is the only road to this goal.

THE DEVELOPMENT OF
HUMAN RESOURCES

An Analytical Outline

BY DR. F. HARBISON

Princeton University, New Jersey, USA

I. HUMAN RESOURCES AND ECONOMIC GROWTH

A. The wealth of a country is dependent upon more than its natural resources and material capital; it is determined in significant degree by the *knowledge, skills and motivation* of its people — i.e. its stock of human capital.

B. Indeed, the proportion of high-level manpower to the total labour force (or to the total population) of a country is one of the best measures of that country's stage of economic advancement.

C. Thus, *investment in man* and his development is fully as important as material investment in dams, roads, harbours, irrigation systems, factories or communications.

D. Most newly developing countries, characteristically, are confronted simultaneously with two persistent manpower problems:

  1. *The shortage of persons with critical* skills — i.e. shortage of strategic human capital.
  2. *Surplus labour*, unemployment and underemployment.

E. An essential part of any plan for economic growth, therefore, is a broad *strategy of human resource development*. This should be a key element in every well-designed programme of economic development.

F. The objective of this outline is to set forth the major factors which should be considered in formulating a strategy for human resource development in a country such as Nyasaland.

This outline attempts to present, in skeleton form, both a 'framework' and a 'check-list' for devising a human resource development plan in a country which is committed to accelerated economic growth.

For a fuller description of some of the concepts presented, see Frederick Harbison, 'Human Resource Development Planning in Modernizing Economies,' *International Labour Review*, May 1962.

II. Definitions of Terms

A.   Human capital is the stock of knowledge and skills possessed by the people in an economy.

B.   High-level manpower is a term used to designate the most critical or strategic human resources for economic and political development. In countries such as Nyasaland, these include:

1.   Managerial and administrative personnel in both the public and private sectors.
2.   Teachers, particularly in secondary and higher education.
3.   Highly educated professional manpower such as scientists, engineers, agronomists, doctors, veterinarians, economists, accountants, etc.
4.   Sub-professional technical personnel such as agricultural assistants, nurses, engineering assistants, technicians and technical supervisors.
5.   Craftsmen and senior clerical workers.

Another way of designating high-level manpower is to assume that it consists of all persons who would be expected to have at least twelve years of formal education, *or its equivalent* in experience, etc.

C.   Strategic human capital formation refers to the accumulation of high-level manpower as defined above.

1.   The *stock* of strategic human capital is the sum total of a country's high-level manpower.
2.   The *rate* of strategic human capital formation is the annual increase (whether net or gross) in the stock. The rate may also be calculated for particular categories of occupations.

D.   Unskilled or semi-skilled manpower refers to the members of the labour force not included in high-level manpower.

1.   The acquisition of knowledge and skills by this group does represent human capital formation.
2.   But, for the purpose of this outline, it is excluded from our analysis which is confined to that part of human capital formation represented by high-level manpower.

III. The Process of Strategic Human Capital Formation

A.   Strategic human capital is acquired by several means or combinations of means:

1.   By formal education at all levels.

2. By training-on-the-job of all kinds.
3. By individual self-improvement and acquisition of skills and knowledge.
4. By importation from abroad through:
   a. Immigration.
   b. Expatriate firms.
   c. Technical assistance.
   d. Other.
5. By improvement in management of people, organization of work, and creation of appropriate attitudes and incentives.
6. By improvement in the labour force.

B. The rate of strategic capital formation is dependent primarily on the following factors:

1. The *existing stock* and utilization of high-level manpower.
2. The *rate of accumulation* of high-level manpower made necessary by:
   a. The extent of required change from a static or traditional society — i.e., pace of *innovation*.
   b. The types and levels of technology employed in various sectors of the economy.
   c. Existence of particular bottlenecks in high-level manpower.
3. The *effective utilization* of high-level manpower in productive activities.

C. In growing economies, the rate of strategic human capital formation normally must exceed the rate of increase in the labour force as a whole.

1. For example, if a country such as Nyasaland has an annual increase in its labour force of 3 per cent per year and hopes to increase its national income by 6 per cent annually, the rate of increase of high-level manpower in agriculture may need to exceed 20 per cent; the rates of increase for teachers and other particularly critical occupations may need to be even higher.
2. The necessary increases in various categories of high-level manpower may be determined through manpower analysis (see below).

D. In most cases also, the rate of increase in strategic human capital will need to exceed the rate of growth in national income.

1. It may be as high as 3–1 in newly developing societies experiencing rapid growth.
2. It may be even higher where expatriates are to be replaced by citizens of the developing countries.

6

IV. Labour Surpluses

A. The overabundance of labour is in most countries as serious a problem as the shortage of skills. Its more common manifestations are the following:

1. Unemployment in overcrowded urban areas.
2. Underemployment and disguised unemployment in rural areas.
3. Existence of unemployed educated persons, who are either unwilling or unable to work in productive activities.

B. The essential causes of labour surpluses are:

1. High rates of population growth.
2. Excessive rural–urban migration.
3. Educational facilities which are 'out-of-balance' with manpower needs of the developing countries.
4. Inadequate incentives for productive activity.
5. Slow rate of economic growth and modernization.

V. Manpower Assessments

A. Objectives:

1. To identify (by major occupational categories) the principal skill shortages in the major sectors of the economy.
2. To identify (by major occupational categories) the principal *surpluses of manpower.*
3. To ascertain the *underlying reasons* for both skill shortages and manpower shortages, including specific consideration of labour market forces, wage and salary structures, and non-financial as well as monetary rewards.
4. To construct *forward targets* for manpower development based upon a country's expectations for formal plans for general economic growth.
5. To identify and generally to appraise the present and expected *role of the principal institutions of manpower development,* including specifically:
    a. Formal educational institutions at all levels (primary, secondary, higher, etc.).
    b. Programmes and procedures for development of employed manpower (apprenticeship, on-the-job-training, manager training courses, public administration training, community development projects, etc.) in all sectors of the economy and in public as well as private activity.

6. To recommend appropriate machinery for implementation of a comprehensive programme of human resource development as part of a country's more general programme for implementing economic growth.

7. Thus, to develop the outlines of a 'strategy' of human resource development.

B. Scope:

1. A manpower assessment goes *far beyond* a statistical analysis of present or future supply and demand of human resources; it is a general judgement, in qualitative as well as quantitative terms, of the broad spectrum of problems of human resource development in an economy.

2. A manpower assessment, therefore, should be comprehensive rather than specialized in scope.

   a. It is more of an outline of interrelated problems than a definitative analysis of a particular problem (such as a forecast of requirements for high-level manpower).

   b. It sets forth, of necessity, tentative rather than definitive judgements.

3. A manpower assessment in essence is more of a *blueprint for the operation* of a human resource development programme than a survey of requirements.

   a. It is therefore more 'programme-oriented' than 'research-oriented'.

   b. One of its functions, however, is in part to determine the order of priority of urgently needed surveys, research or investigation.

4. The major parts (or chapters) of a manpower assessment thus are the following:

   a. A brief description of the economy of a country, and a brief analysis of its possible, expected, or officially planned development.

   b. A manpower inventory setting forth by occupational category within each sector the major skill shortages and manpower surpluses.

   c. A series of projections or 'targets' of manpower requirements for the future on the basis of alternative sets of assumptions.

   d. Where applicable, an analysis of the present and expected role of expatriate manpower in the economy, including a general appraisal of problems of replacing expatriates with local nationals.

e. A brief appraisal of existing capabilities of institutions (formal education as well as training-in-employment) to develop the human resources required in the future.

f. A general statement of the order of magnitude of expansion or change required in human resource development institutions if forward targets are to be reached.

g. An analysis of incentives, both monetary and non-financial, and a general statement of changes in the incentive structure which may be advisable or necessary.

h. A description of machinery necessary to achieve integration in human resource development planning and operation.

i. A concluding section setting forth priorities for critically needed research and investigations, together with appropriate recommendations for their implementation.

VI. The Strategy of Human Resource Development

A. The essential elements of the strategy are as follows:

1. Objective manpower assessments.

2. The development of adequate incentives to encourage men and women to engage in the kinds of productive activities which are needed to accelerate the modernization process.

3. The development and encouragement of effective on-the-job training problems, in both public and private activity, in all sectors of the economy.

4. Investment in and development of formal education in accordance with priorities as determined by social, political, and economic objectives.

5. A plan for rational utilization of imported manpower in critical occupations, coupled with a programme for training of local replacements.

6. The integration of all of the above factors into a country's general economic development plan.

B. *Implementing Machinery: The Human Resources Development Board*

1. *Composition:* Representation from principal ministries such as education, labour, agriculture, commerce and industry, natural resources, etc.

2. *Staff:* A small, but high-level staff capable of integrating work of the various ministries involved.

3. *Functions:* Among the more important are the following:

   a. The making of periodic manpower assessments.
   b. The integration of human resource development strategy with other components of the country's plans of economic and political development.
   c. The promotion and stimulation of planning activity on the part of the ministries represented on the board, as well as on the part of employer and labour organization.
   d. The co-ordination of the above planning activities.
   e. The determination of priorities in the strategy of human resource development, and the continuous reassessment of priorities as the programme progresses.
   f. The selection and design of research projects which may be useful for the formulation, implementation, and evaluation of the strategy of human resource development.
   g. Co-ordination and approval at the country-level of *all requests* for external and technical assistance involving manpower and human resource development.
   h. The general review of all activity connected with human resource development, and periodic evaluation of the work of the various agencies which assume responsibility for it.

4. *Major Criteria for Success:* Formal machinery such as that suggested above is not difficult to establish. Its effectiveness, however, will depend upon the people who provide its leadership and the kinds of personnel recruited for its secretariat. Its success will be related also to the effective use of the right kind of foreign experts as consultants.

NOTES ON UNDER-EMPLOYMENT

BY ANDREW M. KAMARCK[1]

*Director, Economics Dept., International Bank for
Reconstruction and Development, Washington*

The topic Mr Chisiza assigned to me to discuss is 'In the context of an underdeveloped country, what quick measures can be taken to minimize under-employment'. The first point to make, of course, is that the answer depends on the particular underdeveloped country, its particular circumstances and the kind of under-employment we are concerned with. But this does not help very much.

To begin with, then, I will define 'under-employment' generally as the labour position where without a change in the production techniques used or in the capital endowment, one can subtract people from the labour force without a loss of output. Within this definition, there are several major possible kinds of under-employment. One cannot begin to suggest the appropriate lines of policy action for a government to take to deal with the problem of under-employment until one discovers what particular kind of under-employment is involved (and what its magnitude is).

One fairly obvious type of under-employment is seasonal. This may be due to the changes in the seasons over the year, due to consumer habits (Christmas and Easter buying) or it may be due to the habits of the industry, for example, the American automobile industry's insistence on introducing new models every year at a particular time. Under-employment in agricultural countries due to the impact of the seasons can sometimes be cured by the farmer himself. Dr Jones in his excellent paper pointed out that farming is an activity where young men can put in an investment 'consisting almost entirely of their own labour and foresight'. 'A very great deal of the capital in farms, in the form of perennial orchards, of cleared and developed land, of terraces and drains, has been built up simply by the labour of the cultivator, frequently by labor that could find no other employment because of the seasonal rhythm of farming.' If existing under-employment is due to the fact that the farmer does not know enough or is not sufficiently motivated to take advantage of the

---

[1] The views expressed are those of the author and do not necessarily represent those of any institution with which he may be associated.

slack seasons to invest his labour in his farm, the government policy answer may lie in agricultural research and extension work to persuade the farmer to invest his spare labour in building up his farm. In many countries, where the weather may not permit this, the answer has been the provision of work on the roads or other public works which are scheduled for the slack season. There is a case in these circumstances for using a different and lower scale of pay than is applicable to workers whose sole occupation is wage labour. In many countries of Africa, such work traditionally was not paid for at all, but regarded as a social obligation or kind of tax paid in services, this was also often true on the American frontier. In some countries such as Guinea that have reintroduced this technique, it is now dignified by a new name 'investissment humain' or human investment. In Tunisia, work has been provided for the agriculturally under-employed in a vast well-worked out programme of conservation and afforestation. Here, the workers receive a small payment in money and the rest in the form of food provided through the American surplus food disposal programme. In some countries, farmers combine farm work with a complementary occupation — working as woodcutters in the forests in winter, for example. Agricultural processing industries may also help in this regard if their peak needs for labour in these plants can be set to coincide with the period after the harvest.

Then there is what might be called 'sociological' under-employment, which may be particularly important in parts of Africa. This may arise from a rigid division of labour between the sexes. If men, for example, regard only the clearing of new land in preparation for cultivation as man's work and the actual work of cultivation as women's work, then the men may be under-employed in the periods when no new land has to be cleared. This may be one of the economic reasons for the widespread practice of migrant labour in Africa. As Walter Elkan has pointed out, a man can maximize his income by going to work in industry or the mines as a migrant labourer, leaving his family to cultivate the land he has cleared and returning home to clear new land when this is necessary. Migrant labour, in essence, is a solution to this sociological kind of under-employment that the average African has worked out for himself. Of course, under this solution there may not be sufficient jobs in industry or mining to absorb all of the men who would want jobs and this sociological under-employment may persist for this reason. The costs and time involved in the men getting from their farms to the job opportunities in industry or mining may also be very high or the men may not know of the jobs available hundreds of miles away and this may result in inhibiting the movement and preventing this cure to under-employment. But, except in the early period when industry and mining were first beginning in Africa, and except in very special circumstances today, this does not appear to be a factor in Africa; on the contrary, it is remarkable the obstacles and the distance the average African man will overcome to get to a job that is available.

An alternative solution to the 'sociological' under-employment is to change the kind of farming that is done and to involve the men in the farming work more intensively. Dr. Jones has spelled out in his paper ways in which agricultural output could be raised. Many of these would involve employing the men more fully. The very fact of introducing new tools or equipment into agriculture would make it possible for men to participate in what before had been considered women's work. Dr. Jones has also suggested the organization of conservation or irrigation districts run by the farmers themselves with government assistance. And, he points out, 'Frequently, too, some of the labor and management required for their operation can be provided by the farmers themselves when regular farm work is slack.'

Then there is the kind of under-employment that is due to over-population: so many people on the land that farms are smaller than the area a man and his wife could cultivate, for example. This is, probably, not a widespread problem in Africa. There are instances of it in particular areas, perhaps here in the southern province of Nyasaland. In part, it is due to the fact that traditional or tribal attitudes may inhibit moves to under-utilized land. When I say 'tribal' in this context I am referring not only to Africans: the barring of African settlement from the White Highlands of Kenya until recently was also due to this sort of tribal feeling by the Europeans, for example. (I am sure the audience can think of other examples.) Where the barrier to movement may not be sociological it may be due to difficulties in using the available land because of the lack of the necessary roads or wells or because of tsetse fly or other infestation. In these cases, the solution may be one of public investment to eliminate the barriers to movement. An alternative which also has to be studied and weighed against resettlement, of course, is to take measures to improve the productivity of the existing land through capital, improvement of techniques, etc.

Still another solution to this type of under-employment is that adopted by many of the European countries — the emigration of surplus popula-tion to growing industrial centres. Much of the southern Italian problem is being solved in this way — by emigration to north Italy, to other European countries and overseas. Spain, Greece and Turkey are also trying this same solution. In some cases the governments of the emigrants' countries concerned have directly or indirectly facilitated this solution — by subsidizing the emigration or by working out agreements designed to improve the living and working conditions of the emigrants in their new homes. A country like Scotland by providing superior educational facilities for its children turns out more trained people than the country can absorb but the same education gives the Scots the skills by which they can make their way in the world.

Emigration is also a technique of development as Dr. Gaarlund has brought out in his illuminating paper on the Swedish economic development. It makes it possible to reduce population growth within the country and so to devote more of the limited capital available to improving the standard of living and less to taking care of more and more people at the same low or decreasing standard of living.

The possibilities of emigration in Africa in the future from one African country to another may in some cases be quite bright. Countries like Liberia and Gabon, for example, with extraordinarily rich deposits of minerals and very small populations may well need large numbers of immigrants if the full benefits of their resources are to be taken in Africa. Action such as that recently taken in Tunisia to introduce family planning is also important as a means of reducing under-employment.

So far I have not touched on industry or industrialization as a solution to under-employment. I believe that African countries should encourage industrialization as much as is reasonably possible and that this should be a top economic priority. The reasons for doing so are not mainly connected with under-employment, however. They are connected rather with the attempt to get economic growth ultimately faster than would come from pure reliance on growth in export earnings, etc. The possibilities of setting up economic industries in most countries in Africa are still very limited, no matter how far one stretches the concept of 'shadow prices' etc. There have been a number of contributions this week that have demonstrated this, notably by Dr. Brown and by Mr. D. S. Pearson. The industrial possibilities should be exploited to the utmost. But it would be foolhardy to imagine that these industries can possibly provide a massive amount of employment in a hurry. While doing all that is economically justifiable in this direction, the best use of the bulk of available government resources in most cases would lie in other directions.

There is a particular aspect of this general problem that I have been asked to discuss which is of growing importance in Africa. I do not know whether it has yet appeared in Nyasaland but if it has not it will. Strictly speaking, it does not fit into my definition of under-employment. However, since this has not been discussed by anyone so far in this symposium, it seems to me it is worth considering since it can be a major economic and social problem for a newly-independent country. What I am talking about is the growing number of young men without regular work in many African towns and cities. These are usually young men from rural areas who have acquired a certain minimum of education and, consequently, feel themselves above the occupation of farmer. In some countries, this is called the problem of the 'school leavers'. This is a complex problem and I am far from qualified to discuss it properly. But there are some remarks I can make about it and about what to do about it which may be of some help in at least getting some thinking started on this subject.

In part, one of the causes of this phenomenon is a wage and salary structure that has got out of line with the economic facts. At this point in time this particularly applies in some countries to the lower clerical jobs. The wages paid in these jobs were established when there were very few people who had the small amount of education necessary to fill them and, consequently, compared to the average *per capita* income in the country the wages were high. Now that there are a large number of primary school graduates qualified to fill these posts the salary structure is too high compared to the supply of people available. The result is that a primary school leaver who may have gone to school with the expectation of getting a clerical position will prefer to stay in a town without a job for months or years waiting for an opening to turn up rather than resign himself to going back to farm work and missing the glittering prize of work in a white collar. Moreover, his family, who has sacrificed to send him to school, would regard him as a failure if after all that education he becomes a farmer like his uneducated brothers.

This type of phenomenon is not unique to Africa: Italy experienced a somewhat similar 'unemployment' during the post-war period as the peasants, principally from the south, moved from the country into the cities ahead of the time that regular jobs could be provided for them. The reason they moved was that the chance of eventually getting a much higher income, even at the cost of months of difficult existence in the city, was much more attractive to them than the continuation of the poverty-stricken life their fathers had led. Somewhat as in Africa, the city earnings were kept up above the real market price by trade union and government action. In the Italian case, the number of men in the cities searching for jobs remained almost constant for many years in spite of the fact that the expansion of the economy was continually absorbing them into new jobs. As fast as one peasant got himself systematized in a regular job, another peasant would come to the city to take his place. The number of men seeking jobs was determined mainly by the opportunities there were in the city to carry on a hand-to-mouth existence — such as the men you encountered when you drove in Rome who insisted on watching your car when you parked, whether you wanted it watched or not.

In Africa, the number of men who can live in town without regular work is, in part, determined by the number of opportunities there are for picking up odd bits of money as in the Italian parallel. In Africa, another factor, perhaps much more important is also at work. This is the nature of African society.

There is a recent book of Romain Gary's that takes as its theme a quotation from a Russian poet, Sacha Tsipotchkine. This quotation freely translated runs somewhat as follows:

> 'Man — certainly. We are perfectly in agreement — one day Man will appear. There is still needed a little patience, a little perseverance — he cannot be more than 10,000 years away in the future. At the moment, there are only a few traces, a few presentiments, a few dreams. At this instant, the being who exists is only a pioneer of Man himself.'

One part of the problem in Africa, as I see it, is that human beings have evolved here somewhat farther along the road to becoming 'man' than is economically desirable.

The relevance of all this is that one of the important reasons why it is possible for so many men without jobs to continue to live in African towns is the responsibility Africans feel for their 'brothers' in the widest sense of the word. A man in town with what is regarded as good income by his relatives in the country often finds himself having to support these relatives who come and live off him. I have not seen any economic study of this but I imagine that the impact must tend to be somewhat as follows: A man with a good income in town may continue to acquire dependents until the average standard of living of himself and his immediate family sinks to something like the average standard of living of his rural relatives and there is, then, no further inducement for them to come to town and give up working.

This human feeling of responsibility for one's extended family is also, of course, an important factor in inhibiting the development of African entrepreneurs. It is very difficult for an African entrepreneur to build up his capital since any success tends to attract more and more dependents to him. John D. Rockefeller was once asked the secret of business success. He replied, 'Never let your wife know how much money you are making.' And, as a matter of fact, he did just this: his wife thought he was still a relatively poor man when he was already many times over a millionaire. In Africa, perhaps, the secret of economic development will turn out to be: 'Never let your relatives know that you are making any money.'

This is, of course, advice that does not help us move towards the poet's goal of developing 'Man' but this is an economic symposium and it may help in the goal of developing the economy.

I know these remarks may worry many of our African friends in the audience. But I hope that they are tolerant enough to realize that the kind of development of certain personalities that I am talking about was also very worrying to many people in Europe when industrialization first started there. I would like to recall to you the many hostile references in English literature of the period to the 'New Men' when they appeared. Dickens's *Hard Times* is just one example that comes to mind. As one consolation, it may be that this may be an instance where it is necessary for human beings to fall one step back to leap forward farther. The original John D. Rockefeller made possible the current generation of Rockefellers, a family of whose social and human contribution any country would be proud.

Aside from this somewhat dubious philosophical excursion, what can governments do about the problem of the unemployed young men we are talking about? There are a number of possibilities. One is to attempt to gear education more closely to the real needs of the country. Another is to take measures to narrow the great discrepancy in incomes between town and country. This can be done from the two sides of the gap. Measures need to be taken to improve agricultural productivity and raise agricultural incomes, from the one side. On the other, as a minimum, governments must be careful not to raise the incomes of those groups in urban areas where there is an over-supply of applicants still further. There is a tendency for governments to invest too much in towns and make them still more attractive through building subsidized housing, TV, etc., and not invest enough in developing the rural areas. One might suggest also that, as recently in Nigeria, the incomes of the appropriate urban groups might be cut. To some extent, the process of inflation in India, Pakistan, and now Ghana is serving a similar purpose — to bring the wage and salary structure, which earlier had been appropriate when it was necessary to rely on expatriates, back into line with the new conditions of the country.

Another solution might be the one that is being explored by several countries at the present time — the formation of Civilian Conservation Corps, Workers Brigades, Development Service Corps, etc. That is, the school leavers who refuse to go back to the farms and congregate in the towns are taken into a semi-military organization but one devoted to peaceful ends. Such a development service corps could be used to open up new areas through the building of roads, wells, public buildings, housing and laying out farms using the best agricultural knowledge available. They could then be settled on the farms that they had carved out.

Nigeria, at present, is experimenting with agricultural settlement areas. The idea is to lay out farms in new areas in such conditions that the school leavers could put to work their presumably greater willingness to apply new techniques and so earn higher incomes than the farmers in the old areas. I understand that this work is being done by the governments of the regions themselves rather than by any development service corps and, consequently, is very costly. It may be too costly to be really economic.

The general measures to help economic development that we have been discussing all week will also of course serve to meet this problem of movement from rural to urban areas. But, as the Italian experience shows, it may take many, many years before the problem becomes fully manageable. In the meantime, it is worth considering special measures to mitigate the situation.

THE DEVELOPMENT OF AFRICAN
ENTREPRENEURS

BY BERT F. HOSELITZ[1]

*Professor, Research Centre in Economic Development and
Cultural Change, University of Chicago, USA*

This paper is concerned with the problem of providing some tentative and preliminary answers to the question of what can be done to promote the emergence of a corps of African entrepreneurs and what training and facilities they must be given. The answer to this question is not easy, especially for someone who — like this writer — is not very familiar with Africa. It may, therefore, be preferable if, rather than beginning with detailed prescriptions, I first present some points relating to the role of entrepreneurs in economic development, in general, then discuss some already existing forms of entrepreneurial performance in Africa by Africans, and finally conclude with some more specific remarks on the provision of environmental conditions favourable to the development of entrepreneurship and on the training and other facilities which must be provided for newly emerging entrepreneurs.

The definition of entrepreneurship, like that of many other crucial concepts in economics, is not undisputed. Some think of entrepreneurs primarily as innovators, others think of them chiefly as managers of enterprises, others again place major emphasis on their function as mobilizers and allocators of capital. Moreover, there is some uncertainty as to whether the term entrepreneur only applies to individuals who operate a privately owned business or whether entrepreneurship is also exercised by public or semi-public officials who manage government-owned plants or enterprises. In this paper we shall be concerned primarily with private entrepreneurship. This does not mean that we stipulate that developing countries must institute a system of completely free enterprise. Many developing countries in Asia and Africa are drawing up elaborate development plans in which they make provision for elaborate public investments not only in the form of social overhead capital but also in various forms of productive establishments. Hence the developmental

[1] This paper was written while I was the holder of a John Simon Guggenheim Memorial Fellowship. I wish to express my gratitude to the officers of the Foundation for having afforded me through their generous grant the time for reflection and research for this paper.

patterns in these countries are clearly moving towards the institution of a mixed economy. But in all these countries — and this is at the core of a mixed economy — we have a sizeable sphere of economic decision-making left to private individuals, who are expected to make these decisions, particularly decisions on investment of capital and allocation of productive resources, in their own interest and with the intention of meeting their own objectives. The persons who are the major actors in this private decision-making process are the entrepreneurs and it is with them and their formation that this paper will deal.

I

If one uses the concept of entrepreneurship as described in the preceding paragraph, several things may at once be noted:

A. Entrepreneurship is not necessarily confined to innovating activity in Schumpeter's sense. Anyone who is a business leader, who guides the actions of a private productive enterprise and who makes the crucial decisions on the use of productive factors, on their remuneration, on the nature and style of commodities or services to be produced, and on the timing and other aspects of the production and marketing process, is an entrepreneur. He may imitate others, or he may innovate. For our purposes we shall not distinguish between them, since in all entrepreneurial activity — even that which appears most blatantly imitative — there is an element of innovation.

B. Though industrial development is of great interest to the new nations of Africa, entrepreneurship is exercised also in other fields. Entrepreneurs are certainly found in trade and finance, in the supply of various personal and professional services, and also in agricultural and other forms of primary production. The literature on entrepreneurship often omits consideration of the agricultural entrepreneur, though surely the leaders of the Agricultural Revolution in western countries were as truly entrepreneurs — even in the classical Schumpeterian sense — as those who pioneered in industry, mining, and similar activities. But the consideration of entrepreneurial activity in agriculture is of special importance for developing countries, and particularly for Africa, since there such a large proportion of total gross national output is produced in agriculture. And as we shall see later, without the application of entrepreneurial principles to farm production, industrial development suffers a serious setback.

C. Since we extend the concept of entrepreneurship to include also activity which is typically exercised in rural areas, we must, in discussing the external conditions, as well as the training of entrepreneurs, distinguish between two very different environments. For it cannot be denied that in underdeveloped countries, in general, and in many countries of Africa, in particular, the social, psychological, and cultural distance between urban and rural areas is wide. It is certainly wider than in economically more advanced countries and, with respect to the introduction of entrepreneurship, the rural areas are clearly at a disadvantage. On the one hand, they are much less well endowed with social overhead capital than urban areas, and on the other, they have undergone less change in general cultural standards than urban centres, especially large urban centres. In the latter we find some Africans already engaging in entrepreneurial activity; we find more people who are literate; and we find more persons who have become familiar with the economic processes and forms of economic attitudes conducive to action in a modern economy. Because of these differences between urban and rural regions and the overall disadvantage of rural areas, any programme of fostering entrepreneurship which is not extended to include agriculturalists would only widen the gap between city and countryside and would, therefore, make the developmental process much more difficult.

II

Let us now look at some of the manifestations of entrepreneurial action which have been displayed by Africans. The literature is not very rich on this subject, though a number of studies, notably on entrepreneurship in trade and commerce, have been published.[1] In fact, it appears that Africans have so far not displayed entrepreneurial talent in any fields — other than commerce — with a few possible exceptions. The most outstanding cases of African entrepreneurship are reported from various parts of West Africa, and we have some rather interesting descriptions of African traders in Nigeria and Ghana.[2] We also have some relatively brief and not too exhaustive studies on African traders in East Africa.[3]

[1] My discussion of African entrepreneurship in trade is influenced greatly by a published study by Margaret Katzin, 'The Role of the Small Entrepreneur,' submitted to the Conference on Indigenous and Induced Elements in the Economics of Subsaharan Africa, held at Northwestern University, 16th to 18th November 1961 in Economic Transition in Africa, Melville J. Herkesvits and Mitchell Harwitz (Editors), pp. 179–98.

[2] See the following studies: M. G. Smith, The Economy of Hausa Communities of Zaria, London, Her Majesty's Stationery Office, 1955; Peter C. Garlick, African Traders in Kumasi, Accra: University College of Ghana, 1959; Astrid Nypan, Market Trade: A Sample Survey of Market Trends in Accra, Accra: University College of Ghana, 1960.

[3] See the following studies: Uganda Protectorate, The Advancement of Africans in Trade Entebbe: Government Printer, 1955; J. C. Champion, 'Labour and Managerial Skill in East African Industrial Development,' The East African Economics Review, Vol. IV, No. 1 (July, 1957), pp. 24–32; A. A. Nyirenda, 'African Market Vendors in Lusaka,' Rhodes-Livingstone Journal, No. 22 (September, 1957), pp. 31–55; Walter Elkan, 'The East African Trade in Woodcarvings,' Africa, Vol. XXVIII, No. 4 (1958), pp. 314–23.

The value of these reports and studies consists mainly in showing that in several communities African entrepreneurship in trade has been practised with varying success for many years, and, above all, in exhibiting some of the main problems faced by African entrepreneurs, as regards the environmental conditions, as well as the human factors which impinge upon the successful exercise of entrepreneurial action. Several of these studies, particularly the essay by Peter C. Garlick, contain summaries of impediments to, and facilities for, the successful exercise of entrepreneurship by Africans as seen by these African traders themselves. These opinions, therefore, provide important material for the points to be raised in this paper, for here we may build upon the actual experience of persons who have tried, and many who have succeeded, in exercising entrepreneurial functions in the African context.

It may be argued that these experiences derived from interviews with traders may not be fully applicable to industrial entrepreneurship and, above all, entrepreneurship in agriculture. It may, moreover, be argued that quite a few of the persons interviewed in the markets of Zaria, Accra, Kumasi, Kampala and other places operate very small businesses, and that the capital invested in many of these businesses is so meagre as to have little significance. Hence the problems of these tiny traders and market-women are far removed from those which genuine entrepreneurs encounter who engage in industrial, transport, and mining undertakings. There is some truth in this, but it should be remembered that the development of industry and related enterprises in Africa will also result in many small and perhaps at best medium-scale plants. Though it is customary, when we think of industrial development, to evoke the picture of a large steel or cement plant, the existing markets, demand patterns, and conditions of comparative advantage in African countries are such as to make the establishment of small plants mainly producing light consumer goods most attractive.[4] Hence, industrialization must be thought of not as the growth of new Pittsburghs and Birminghams in Africa, but rather as a process in which small amounts of capital are allocated to various industrial branches, which gradually grow in size, but nevertheless still consist — from a world point of view — in fairly small and medium-scale industrial plants, rather than in industrial giants.

If this is granted, then some of the findings of Garlick, for example, are applicable, since he found some African trading firms in Kumasi whose original investment was over £1,000 and whose annual turnover ranged from £17,000 to £75,000. Similarly Mrs. Nypan found that roughly 10 per cent of the traders in Accra whom she studied had daily turnovers

---

[4] See the very interesting paper by Walter Elkan, 'Criteria for Industrial Development in Uganda,' *East African Economics Review*, Vol. V, No. 2 (January, 1959), pp. 50–57.

of more than Ł12, which would come to an annual turnover in excess of Ł3,500. These are, to be sure, not very large sums, but if they are compared with the annual per capita income of the average African agriculturalist, they take on a new significance. For the United Nations have estimated that the average annual *per capita* money income in 1950 of indigenous agriculturalists ranged from $6.00 to $16.00 in different African territories, and only in what was then the Gold Coast did it reach an average of $45.00. To be sure, in the concentrated cocoa areas of Ghana it was found that some farmers earned an average net income of Ł450 per year (after expenses) and similarly some coffee growers in Uganda had average annual net incomes of between Ł200 and Ł400.[5] But these are precisely the instances in which entrepreneurship has taken hold of some agriculturalists and these persons are rather the exception than the rule among African farmers. These figures show, however, how important it is, in terms of actual average income, for entrepreneurial behaviour to be introduced and accepted among agriculturalists as well as in other fields of productive and distributive activity in Africa.

III

Let us now turn to the problem of more specific interest, the nature of the social and economic 'environment' and the personal characteristics that are needed in order to produce a corps of adequate entrepreneurs in Africa. In a recent paper on the development of entrepreneurship in Pakistan, G. F. Papanek has pointed out that it is generally agreed in the literature that for entrepreneurs to become active in a society certain psychological conditions among the potential entrepreneurs must be present.[6] We shall discuss these psychological factors later. From the works of Garlick and others which were cited earlier, we note, however, that, quite apart from the psychological characteristics of those who reach entrepreneurial positions, we must also look for certain conditions in the economy and society which will make possible the successful exercise of entrepreneurial functions, regardless of the relative abundance of certain psychological types.

These conditions of the economy may be subdivided as consisting, on the one hand, of certain forms of social overhead capital and, on the other, as being composed of certain governmental services which are or may

[5] These data may be found in Garlick, op. cit., pp. 29–30 and 37–38, Nypan, op. cit., p. 42, and United Nations, Department of Economic Affairs, *Enlargement of the Exchange Economy in Tropical Africa*, New York: United Nations, 1954, pp. 26–27.
[6] See Gustav F. Papanek, 'The Development of Entrepreneurship,' *American Economic Review*, Vol. LII, No. 2 (May 1962), pp. 46–58.

be put at the disposal of entrepreneurs. Two of the major forms of social overhead which are required are the availability of power and the existence of convenient and relatively cheap means of transport and communication.[7] Power, it has been pointed out, is in relatively short supply in Africa. As a consequence there are few 'basic' industries, such as metallurgical industries, found in Africa. Apart from some zinc, lead, and copper foundries in the Congo, Rhodesia, and Morocco, no metals are produced in Africa. Africa also does not yet have machine building industries, chemical industries and industries producing other types of 'heavy' capital goods. As a consequence the capital goods needed for industrialization, machines and even building materials of many kinds must be imported and this makes the establishment of many industrial plants more expensive in Africa than elsewhere. The absence of many of these heavy industries is the result of several factors. One of them is the narrow market that as yet exists in Africa for these goods. But another is the relative shortage of power, either from hydro-electric or from coal or oil burning electric plants. Yet the total hydro-electric potential of Africa is larger in *per capita* terms than that of almost any other region of underdeveloped countries. This potential power must be exploited to a greater degree to facilitate the setting up of industrial, commercial, and other types of new establishments.

Analogous to the need for more power is that for more and better transport facilities. The sparsity of railways and roads in Africa, as compared with more highly developed countries, need not be pointed out. Unfortunately a large part of the African territories is criss-crossed by mountains, by jungles, or by desert areas, all of which militate against the easy and cheap extension of transport networks. Yet this is an imperative step in the policy of furthering entrepreneurship. For two of the main features of a new orientation are the wider extension of the exchange economy and the conscious production for the market. As long as a market is confined to a small territory, because — as a result of the absence of adequate transport facilities — the cost of shipping to outlying areas is too expensive, the incentives making for entrepreneurial experiments will be weak. Only if the producer of new industrial or new agricultural products can count upon shipping them relatively easily and cheaply to a wide area, only if he can be assured of a fairly wide circle of potential customers will he have the necessary incentive to undertake the establishment of a new industrial enterprise or to introduce a new cash crop on his farm. Hence it may be said that the extension of power producing facilities and the building up of a convenient, safe and extended

[7] See Jean Chardonnet, *Une Oeuvre necessaire: L'industrialisation de l'Afrique*, Geneva: Librairie E. Droz, 1956, *passim*, but esp. pp. 28–38.

transport network are two of the underlying conditions for entrepreneurship to be forthcoming in industry, agriculture, and even the supply of
many services.

IV

In addition to these aspects of the 'physical' economic environment,
certain political conditions must hold and governments must be prepared
to render certain services which at present may not be available. Papanek
found in Pakistan that among these conditions were the following:
A. A government and civil service able to maintain law and order, to
prevent excessive flight of capital, and to enforce on a reasonable basis
import and export controls, as well as to establish and maintain social
overhead capital roughly commensurate with the needs of a growing
industrial economy.
B. A political system which is geared to withstand various expressions
of dissatisfaction on the part of consumers with occasional high prices,
high profits for industrialists, and the presence in many responsible positions of foreign technicians and advisors.[8]
    There is no question that the first of these conditions would also have to
apply in African societies, though the second probably has much less
applicability. If we consider the establishment of certain large scale
industrial plants, then high prices to consumers, high profits — at least
temporarily — and the presence of many foreign technicians may be
required. But what we are concerned with here is the development of
indigenous African entrepreneurs, and although it may be argued that
these need training and education, it is not clear why this training must
take the form of their tutelage, except for a short period of time, under
foreign technical experts.
    But in view of the relatively limited skills of African entrepreneurs and
potential entrepreneurs, African governments must provide other services
which within the African context appear very necessary — and which,
incidentally, would also prove useful in Pakistan, if they were applied
there. These services have been cited by African entrepreneurs themselves
as features which they would desire and which they feel would be of great
aid to them. First of all actual or potential entrepreneurs need more information about trading and production opportunities, about technologies
and about market conditions. They cannot obtain this information on
their own, partly because of the limited or poor communications existing
at present.

[8] Papanek, op. cit., p. 56.

Secondly, in order to make possible a more rational exercise of their businesses, merchants as well as industrialists — and also farmers who turn to modern rational methods of agricultural production, mainly oriented towards the market — will need aid in accounting and the maintenance of related records. In his report on Kumasi, Garlick reports, for example, that the following complaint was voiced by his informants:

> 'There was one complaint about the cost of having to use an accountant to prepare the figures required by the Government Statistician's Office. "I don't see the use of government statistics," said the trader. "If there is a use it should be explained to us. If details are required of my business, I must know why before I tell them. What benefit do I derive?" This feeling was later found to be much more widespread.'[9]

Garlick only reports the complaints voiced by Kumasi traders on their need to obtain aid to maintain better accounts. But the main reason why centralized accounting services should be supplied by governments to new enterprises is not merely for statistical or tax purposes, but in order that the new enterprises should be helped to become established on a much sounder financial basis than they otherwise would. For there is, even among present entrepreneurs, very little understanding of different kinds of costs and of the total amount of their genuine net profits. The difficulties which many African entrepreneurs experience in this matter are well summarized by Margaret Katzin. Talking about traders, mainly in West Africa, she shows that many of them engage in trading only as a part-time occupation, but that, at the same time they are limited by law in the amount of credit they can receive. Moreover, she shows that many traders spend an extraordinary amount of their initial capital for fixed expenses, e.g., building of premises, and can, therefore, stock their shelves only inadequately. But most importantly, 'Africans often fail to evaluate properly their costs and some do not distinguish between gross and net profits. For example, a farmer-trader invests the money realized from his crops in stock and sets himself up as a trader. As he sells the goods, he regards the cash received as income to be spent as he likes, making no provision for replenishing his stock.'[10]

Now it is, of course, granted that one way of remedying this would be by education in some elementary forms of accounting and business

[9] Garlick, op. cit., p. 90.
[10] Katzin, op. cit. It should be noted, however, that information of the proper accounts of market trade can be obtained by careful investigation of a skilled researcher. See, for example, A. A. Nyirenda, 'The Blantyre-Limbe Markets, Nyasaland: the Adjustment of the Individual to an Urban Cash Economy,' in R. J. Apthorpe, ed., *Present Interrelations in Central African Rural and Urban Life* (Proceedings of the 11th Conference of the Rhodes-Livingstone Institute), Lusaka: Rhodes-Livingstone Institute, 1958, pp. 119–32.

management. But it should be remembered that however necessary education is — and we will discuss this point in a subsequent section of this paper — the provision of certain generally available accounting services would be very helpful to many entrepreneurs. These services need not be rendered freely, but if they are available at relatively low fees, it is likely that many entrepreneurs will make use of them and will, thereby, not only provide more accurate data for the statistical and revenue needs of the government, but will be induced to operate on a more economical level than without this service.

The suggestion that governmental agencies provide aid in accounting, costing, and other administrative and managerial tasks to African small and medium entrepreneurs is not new. W. A. Lewis suggested that the government of Ghana provide technical and managerial assistance to small entrepreneurs and an analogous recommendation was made by the mission of the World Bank to Nigeria. It was even suggested by R. I. Fleming that American firms should, as a form of technical assistance, establish small enterprises in Africa in order to train Africans for the responsibilities of management, and that these foreign owned firms should establish contacts with the emerging indigenous entrepreneurs on equal and friendly terms.[11]

A third and most important service is the development of suitable credit institutions and credit services for new industrialists and other entrepreneurs. There are two kinds of credit that are needed. New entrepreneurs need financial support for their more permanent investment as well as for their inventories and other short-term needs. The latter can be and are, in some cases, supplied by commercial banks, though even there many new entrepreneurs have difficulty, since they control few assets which they can use as security. Hence they are driven to borrow from relatives or small money lenders who often charge extremely high interest rates. This greatly increases the cost of doing business, or even makes it impossible for new entrepreneurs to accumulate large enough inventories for an economical operation of their enterprises.

Long-term capital is, however, much more difficult to obtain than short-term loans. In many African countries there do not exist for the African population the kind of institutions which are and were available in western countries and which made possible the collection of sizeable amounts of capital for investment in industry, mining, or transport enter-

[11] See the opinion of W. A. Lewis cited in Hugh Fearn, 'Marketing and Distribution,' *East African Economics Review*, Vol. II, No. 2 (January 1956), p. 129; see also International Bank for Reconstruction and Development, *The Economic Development of Nigeria*, Baltimore: Johns Hopkins University Press, 1955, p. 51; and R. I. Fleming, 'Africa's Challenge on the New Frontier,' in *Activities of Private United States Organizations in Africa*, Washington; Government Printing Office, 1961, p. 242.

prises. Long-term investment in industry and trade, and even in some kinds of farm equipment, often cannot be made out of the resources or on the basis of the credit rating of a new African entrepreneur. In fact, commercial banks are not equipped to provide long-term credit, and mortgages are in many instances impracticable because of the confused and imperfect land registers and the lack of firm rules surrounding real estate property. Hence credit for long-term investment must be provided by special institutions, preferably institutions which are set up under governmental auspices. Such institutions, which are often referred to as development banks or development corporations, are not uncommon in developing countries. In fact, their utility and potential general applicability are so widely recognized that the International Bank for Reconstruction and Development asked one of its senior officers to write a pamphlet outlining the principles and practices upon which such institutions may be established and their business carried on.[12] It would take too long to enter into a detailed discussion of the utility of development banks for African countries, but it should be mentioned that if it is intended to provide aid towards the emergence of an African corps of entrepreneurs, some preferential treatment should be given to Africans, as compared with Europeans, Asians, or others who might establish industrial, transport and other enterprises in African countries. However, at the same time the banks should not totally discriminate against non-Africans since their establishments clearly contribute to the overall economic development of the countries in which they are founded.

It should be remembered, however, that the activities of such a development bank, especially within the African context, may be enlarged beyond its role as a mere lender of investment funds. In particular, it should have a department of economic education in which information subsidiary to the extension of loans is provided. We have already seen earlier that African businessmen complain about being imperfectly or sometimes even falsely informed. We also know from the operation of co-operative credit institutions among Indian peasants, that the mere extension of low-interest loans, without additional information on better cropping practices, the improved use of water and fertilizer, and other types of technical information, was insufficient. It is suggested that a development bank established in an African country for the support of African entrepreneurs should perform similar information and educational tasks. In more concrete terms, when it does provide financing for new industrial or related investment by African entrepreneurs, the bank should

[12] See William Diamond, *Development Banks*, Baltimore: The Johns Hopkins Press, 1957; see also the essay by J. D. Nyhart, 'The Uganda Development Corporation and Agriculture,' *East African Economics Review*, Vol. VI, No. 2 (December 1959), pp. 104–16.

provide also all the technical and economic information which would be helpful to the new entrepreneur in the early phases of his activity. The bank will have better facilities for finding out where the most suitable machinery can be bought, and indeed, what is the most suitable machinery for a given type of productive enterprise. It will have more and better information on markets, freight charges, insurance costs, and other expenses incurred in establishing and running a business than many a trader or peasant who wishes to become an industrial entrepreneur. It is not suggested that the bank should insure a new entrepreneur against failure, nor that it should not provide him with as much freedom of action in his own productive enterprise as possible. The informational and educational services which have been proposed have rather the purpose of providing the entrepreneur with a level of information and skill which will put him into a roughly competitive position with a European or Asian who might establish a new industrial firm, or a foreign company which might establish a branch or an assembly or finishing plant in an African country.

In the preceding paragraph we have discussed, among other matters, the supply of machinery to be used in industrial enterprises. Let us remember that we are concerned primarily with small and medium scale enterprises, i.e., with firms which employ fewer than 100, and often fewer than ten workers. Machinery for these establishments is not too easy to find, since the major industrial countries, who are the chief producers of machinery, market primarily equipment for much larger scale industrial enterprises. Many small industrial entrepreneurs in India have had difficulty in obtaining adequate information on the various sorts of machines they could purchase, and in order to aid in this search, the National Small Industries Corporation has been established. This organization offers manifold services to entrepreneurs in small industrial establishments, particularly by aiding in the design of a new enterprise, by market surveys, by the allotment of factory space in industrial estates, and above all, by the operation of a hire-purchase system for the acquisition of industrial machinery.[13] The National Small Industries Corporation is a government owned enterprise which operates with public funds. Of special interest is its machinery hire-purchase system. Briefly the system works as follows: the Corporation ascertains what needs for machinery exist in Indian small industry, attempts to purchase suitable models of these machines — often on the second-hand market — and resells the machines to their prospective users on an instalment or hire-purchase plan. This procedure may be regarded as a supplement to the operations

---

[13] On the operations of the National Small Industries Corporation see Small Industries Corporation, New Delhi: Small Industries Corporation, 1957.

of a development bank, and there is no reason why such a scheme cannot be associated with the activities of a development bank. Let us note again that in this case, the National Small Industries Corporation implicitly exercises an informative and educational function. For in purchasing and disposing of machinery it studies the needs of the entrepreneurs whom it supplies and since it also has a market research division, a design division, and other related departments, it can provide a substantial amount of additional information which will strengthen the overall position of new industrial entrepreneurs.

Finally, a word may be said about using the fiscal mechanism as an incentive for the development of entrepreneurship. This is also a very common device and experience in its operation is widespread in many developing countries. The number of ways of using the tax system as a tool to enhance incentives for investment are manifold, though exemption of taxation of profits in new enterprises and reduction or exemption from paying duties on imported capital goods are the two most widely known and widely practised devices. Some developing countries have evolved extensive and refined methods of using the fiscal powers of the government for purposes of industrial development. A good example is provided by the policies of Puerto Rico, though this island was aided greatly in its efforts at economic development by other factors, notably its free access to the markets of the United States. However, depending upon the general level of economic advancement and the overall nature of fiscal systems, various methods can and should be developed which would provide greater incentives for new entrepreneurs to set up industries and related establishments and to modernize farms and agricultural enterprises.

V

In the preceding sections of this paper we have discussed some of the features of the external environment, particularly the availability of power, transport facilities, and other forms of social overhead, and some of the services supplied by government and government owned or sponsored institutions which create a generally more favourable climate for the exercise of entrepreneurship. But in the last resort the appearance of entrepreneurs is a matter of redirecting human effort and human action, and hence we must look at the more narrowly human aspects of recruiting and promoting a corps of African entrepreneurs.

In dealing with this problem we are in one of the most uncertain and disputed areas of social research relating to developing countries. For opinions on what can be done on the human level to create a corps of

98   BERT F. HOSELITZ

native entrepreneurs range from an expression of utter helplessness to elaborate educational training schemes, involving the entire school system of a developing country, its vocational training institutions, and its professional schools. Clearly with regard to the human factors involved entrepreneurship has several dimensions. As we have already pointed out several times, information and education are important aspects of a programme of training entrepreneurs. But there is also the purely psychological aspect and this must be constantly borne in mind. For if it does have the influence which some writers attribute to it, all the changes in environment, and all the adjustments in education and related public services are of only secondary importance.

The psychological aspects of entrepreneurial action have been stressed primarily by E. E. Hagen and D. C. McClelland, though each of these men has pointed to somewhat different characteristics.[14] The generally accepted view on the psychological dimension in entrepreneurship may be briefly summarized as follows: the industrial entrepreneur, and in fact the innovating entrepreneur, in general, is a distinct personality type. He must be convinced that change can occur and that it can be brought about by individual action. He must also desire to bring about this change himself. Within all societies there exists probably a limited number of persons with these beliefs and motivations, but though they will act in part from pecuniary motives, they have usually also other ambitions and objectives. For example, they may employ the acquisition of gain in order to enhance their prestige or in order to gain political influence or social recognition. For this reason the general rules of a society in which they operate must be such as to allow persons with newly acquired wealth some access to power and prestige. In other words, if the obstacles to entrepreneurship are overwhelming, persons with the right kind of personality will either be failures, will attempt to emigrate, or will turn their energies to fields other than economic entrepreneurship and business leadership.

So far our sketch of the psychological underpinnings of entrepreneurship has followed largely in the footsteps of Schumpeter and those influenced by his view on the role of innovating entrepreneurs in economic development.[15] The contribution of Hagen and McClelland has consisted

[14] See Everett E. Hagen, *On the Theory of Social Change*, Homewood, Ill.: The Dorsey Press, 1962, esp. part II; and David C. McClelland, *The Achieving Society*, Princeton: D. Van Nostrand Co., 1961, *passim*.

[15] Perhaps the best exposition of entrepreneurial psychology derived from Schumpeter's views may be found in the essay by Leland H. Jenks, 'The Role Structure of Entrepreneurial Personality,' in Research Center in Entrepreneurial History at Harvard University, *Change and the Entrepreneur*, Cambridge, Mass.: Harvard University Press, 1949, pp. 108–52. But see also Arthur H. Cole, *Business Enterprise in its Social Setting*, Cambridge, Mass.: Harvard University Press, 1959, *passim*.

in pointing to the fact that economic growth only occurs if individuals with characteristic entrepreneurial personalities appear in sufficient numbers, if the change in motivation affects not only a handful of persons, but penetrates more deeply all layers of society, and if the individuals who do perform entrepreneurial roles belong to some social group or class which has had a higher level of prestige and power in the past, has lost it, and cannot regain it by more traditional channels of upward social mobility and hence chooses the acquisition of gain and of wealth as the most appropriate and potentially most effective alternative.

According to this theory the appearance of entrepreneurship on a mass basis can be explained as a result of two factors. First it flows from a special historical situation in which new paths to higher social status are sought through economic gain. Secondly, it is the result of the appearance in a society with more than average frequency of persons with special personality traits, i.e., persons with unusually high 'achievement orientation'. Whether there is a connection between these two developments is of relatively little interest to us in the context of this paper, for we are not concerned here with historical interpretations but questions of social engineering. Hence, whatever may be said of the change in values and motivations as a precondition for entrepreneurship, the relationship between successful business leadership and certain patterns of personality appears plausible, and even substantially confirmed on the basis of empirical research in western countries. A timid person will not become an entrepreneur. A person who has a great need for cordial and friendly affiliations with others will not become an entrepreneur, for he will be too 'soft' for such a career. But a person who has a high achievement orientation, i.e., who constantly sets himself a goal which he strives to attain, who is willing to take a calculated risk, and who is eager to exploit any occasion that offers itself and use it to his best advantage — this is a man who may become an entrepreneur and who may be quite successful in this career.

McClelland has shown that such persons existed at various periods in history when societies did undergo rapid economic development. He also has shown that the appearance of persons with this disposition is a result of the way in which they have been brought up as children and raised by their parents. But the very fact that substantial numbers of entrepreneurs have appeared in countries in which little or no such talent appeared to be available a short time ago, makes one suspect that persons with the appropriate achievement motivation exist in all human societies, though they appear openly in varying numbers in different societies. If industrial and general economic development is planned and fostered as a goal of the society as a whole; if it is one of the main objectives of the public policy of a newly developing country, the environment into which entrepreneurs tend to step is quite different from that which existed in those historical instances which McClelland and Hagen — and even Schumpeter — had in mind. They were concerned with the appearance of entrepreneurs as an autonomous social process; with the development of economic achievement as an alternative path to upward social mobility in an environment in which the acquisition of wealth was not an accepted means to rise in the social scale. In such situations a more than average frequency of achievement oriented persons may be a necessary condition of economic advancement.

But we are confronted with nations in Africa which have placed the slogan of rapid economic growth on their banners and which presumably are prepared to provide the most extensive accommodation to persons who would step into positions of entrepreneurship. Moreover from the ubiquity of traders — to be sure small ones, but traders nevertheless — we may deduce that individuals of suitable personality are already available in sufficient quantity in African societies and that what is needed is not so much the creation of new personality types, but rather the opening up of opportunities in the external environment, in the type and scale of government services, and in the intellectual equipment of the persons concerned to push them into successful entrepreneurial roles.

It may well be that those concerned with the growth of a corps of entrepreneurs in Africa should study the work of McClelland and his students and should try to influence — subtly, of course — child rearing practices which will make it more likely for achievement oriented persons to appear in greater numbers. But before such policies could have an effect — and since they have as a crucial phase child rearing practices, they could not have an effect before the next generation — persons will have to be recruited for entrepreneurial positions whose achievement orientation has been acquired in the past. The experience recorded by G. Papanek from Pakistan is encouraging. For the Moslem population of British India showed very little entrepreneurial talent. But with the development of the new state of Pakistan and the opening up of new opportunities, a sufficient number of persons with the appropriate personality were coming forward to accept the challenge which the emerging situation presented. Entrepreneurs emerged in a population which half a generation ago appeared to have no persons with talent for business leadership. It is not subject to doubt that a similar 'restructuring' of opportunities in African nations will be an important, if not the most important, factor in calling forth a similar rise in entrepreneurial activity in these countries.

VI

But, obviously, the appearance of persons with the appropriate personality disposition is not quite enough. Individuals who are to fill entrepreneurial roles adequately must possess also other qualities, and outstanding among these is the possession of information and knowledge, i.e., the attainment of a reasonably advanced level of education. A good text for this section of this paper is a quotation from a book by G. B. Stapleton, who has taught for many years at different institutions of higher learning in Ibadan. Mr. Stapleton says:

> 'Where individual Nigerian businesses are concerned, if a father has £3,000 to invest in a new business, he will be well advised to spend at least half of it on the training of his son overseas and the other half on equipment, rather than to give his son the money and attempt to set up a small industrial enterprise without a trained manager.'[16]

The body of ideas behind this statement, if not the manner of its implementation, is supported by Frederick Harbison's contribution to the Ashby Report, by many papers submitted at the UNESCO-United Nations Conference on African Education, and by numerous other spokesmen.[17] This view has become so generally accepted that there is little danger that education of managerial personnel will be neglected in Africa. If there is a danger, it is more likely the opposite, that the education of other persons — whose skills are supplementary to those of entrepreneurs — will not receive sufficient attention.

In view of the extensive literature on the development of a managerial class, it is not necessary to provide a lengthy analysis of it in this paper. But I should like to offer a few observations on this point which are intended to suggest that one should not consider the question of training in entrepreneurial techniques and in sophisticated managerial methods as necessarily the same problem. As already pointed out several times in this paper, we should not imagine that industry in African nations will consist mainly of a few giant plants producing heavy goods. This would be contrary both to the historical experience of economically advanced countries and even more to existing social and economic tendencies in African countries. The highly trained managers who are required for the

---

[16] G. Brian Stapleton, *The Wealth of Nigeria*, London: Oxford University Press, 1958, p. 173.
[17] See Frederick Harbison, 'High Level Manpower for Nigeria's Future,' in Nigeria, Ministry of Education, *Investment in Education: The Report of the Commission on Post-School Certificate and Higher Education in Nigeria*, Lagos; The Government Printer, 1960, p. 64 ff.; and United Nations, Economic Commission for Africa — UNESCO, *Conference of African States on the Development of Education in Africa*, Paris; UNESCO, 1961, *passim*.

large plants will be confronted, if economic development and industrialization in Africa are successful, with a much larger number of men running
small and medium-scale businesses, who will unquestionably have to have
extensive managerial abilities, but who need not be university graduates
or even have gone through an extensive training in secondary schools.
Many of the most successful entrepreneurs in western economic development had little formal training and had never been near a university until,
in their more mature years, they received honorary degrees in recognition
of the benefactions they had made to university education.

But rather than argue from historical analogy, it suffices to discuss this
problem from the viewpoint of the social and economic needs of African
entrepreneurial developments. Entrepreneurship implies the exercise of
leadership. It is aided by maturity of character, by a sense of security, and
this is enhanced by information about relevant matters. This means that a
person in an entrepreneurial position must be able to read and write and
must have knowledge of accounting and related skills. It is helpful in some
lines, and imperative in others, that he know something about the
technical aspects of production. This is especially true of agricultural
entrepreneurs, but also of many traders and industrial business leaders.

But the entrepreneur must be principally a 'generalist', not a technical
or economic specialist. In this he is distinguished from the expert manager
of a large private or public enterprise. This latter is employed because of
his specialized knowledge. He is in charge of some technical aspect of a
productive enterprise, of purchasing, labour relations, or some other
strictly circumscribed sphere of action. Hence his special skill is of value.
But the entrepreneur of a small or medium plant must be not only a man
with some knowledge of the productive techniques employed in the
plant he owns and runs, but a person who makes the chief decisions
relating to supplies, to sales, and to relations with labourers and employees.
In the case of the manager his degree of skill is much more important than
the psychological aspects of his personality. In the case of the entrepreneur
it is safe to say that the reverse is true. Though the possession of knowledge
and skill are not unimportant, the small and medium-scale entrepreneur
must above all have the required characteristics of personality and leadership, the willingness to take risks, and the desire to innovate and experiment, in order to perform his role properly.

But if we assign first rank to personality characteristics and only second
rank to skill and information, it is not implied that the latter are of no or
little importance. For the tasks with which an African entrepreneur is
confronted — as compared to his western European counterpart — are
made complex by the unavailability or excessive scarcity of well-trained
fully committed industrial workers. If the African entrepreneur could hire

a western labour force his task would be much easier. For a western labour force is made up of persons who not only have a good deal of education themselves and who, therefore, can calculate, write, interpret instructions, read blueprints and circulars, and perform all kinds of tasks which may appear excessively complex to less well-educated persons, but are also deeply committed to the industrial way of life. These characteristics of a labour force which is firmly committed to industrial work as a way of life and which is saturated with the culture of industrial society are of great importance for the person who is to lead this labour force. A labour force which in culture, personal commitment, skills, educational background, and general outlook, is not committed to industrialism is a much more difficult body of persons to lead and is likely to present many more problems and make the entrepreneur's task substantially more difficult. This is so regardless of whether the entrepreneur is a European, an Asian, or an African.

The African entrepreneur is likely to have to recruit his labourers from a pool of manpower in which industrial culture is as yet only faintly known and appreciated. The men whom he can hire still have strongly traditional backgrounds, are as yet uncertain about their role in industrial society, and often accept industrial jobs or wage work of any kind only as a temporary expedient rather than as a regular way of life. The consequence is that this labour force is highly inefficient and hence that total labour costs, even though real wages paid to African workers are much lower than those paid to European workers, are often much higher than in the western countries.

The difficulties confronting the African entrepreneur owing to the lack of efficiency of his labour force have been well described by J. C. Champion. He shows that the lower wage cost incurred by entrepreneurs in Africa will be often more than offset by the following factors: (1) Low *per capita* productivity which leads to the need for large staffs, which in turn leads to poor utilization of labour and frequent absenteeism; (2) High costs of training the labour force, which is made worse because of a high labour turnover and the lack of familiarity of labourers with factory techniques and rational methods of modern production; (3) High rate of breakage of machinery and implements, owing to the poor skills of workers and their lack of interest in industrial work and discipline; (4) Poor quality of output, owing to often shoddy methods of work and lack of adequate inspection and quality control of the products turned out, and (5) High cost of supervision and management owing to the inadequate training and attention span of workers.[18]

In other words, the chance of successful performance of entrepreneur-

[18] See Champion, op. cit., pp. 26–27.

ship in Africa not only depends upon the skills and training of the potential entrepreneurs themselves, but also on the emergence of a more highly skilled and, in particular, more fully committed labour force than is available at this time.[19] We have discussed earlier the need for adjustment in the physical environment required for the more adequate development of indigenous entrepreneurship. To this should be added the requirement of providing a more adequate human environment, i.e., one which not only consists of persons accustomed to market transactions and monetary calculations, but also one characterized by the development of skills and attitudes among the potential wage earning population which will make it perform more efficiently in industrial, transport, commercial, and associated enterprises. It will also require a similar, though perhaps not quite as intensive training of the young men in the rural areas, since in these parts of African countries will be found some of the markets for the products of new industrial establishments, and the farmers, in turn, will have to relinquish their traditional forms of subsistence agriculture and turn to more modern methods of cash crop production. For it can be surmised without excessive imagination that among the most likely industrial developments will be first the growth of plants for processing agricultural commodities for export and secondly with the development of African urban centres the growth of processing plants for foods and other agricultural products which find a market in the urban population. In more concrete terms, the first types of industrial establishments will be plants processing tea, coffee, cocoa, palm oil, and other export products of African agriculture, and the second will be breweries, bakeries, packing plants, canneries, and other food processing industries which prepare indigenous agricultural products for the urban consumer. This will require that not only export crops, but also traditional subsistence crops be converted into cash crops. But this, in turn, requires education and the development of agricultural extension services, as well as the establishment of agricultural experiment stations whose findings will have to be transmitted to the new agricultural entrepreneurs.

As already implied throughout this section, the role of education is substantial, but its impact must be exerted not merely on the potential entrepreneurs themselves, but also on those who will form the labour force in the new establishments. Hence, it may be argued that because of the probable size and composition of African enterprises, what is needed is not special provision for the training of a large corps of high-level manpower. What is more urgently needed is an educational programme

[19] The problems of commitment of a labour force are discussed in Wilbert E. Moore and Arnold S. Feldman, eds., *Labor Commitment and Social Change in Developing Areas*, New York: Social Science Research Council, 1960.

which will provide the elements of a general education applicable to the exercise of industrial, commercial, and agricultural enterprise on a small and medium scale. This education should be supplemented for the entrepreneurial recruits by some technical education in some of the areas in which they will actually establish new enterprises, and this training can best be obtained by some on-the-job programme in countries in which such enterprises already exist. For example, an entrepreneur who wishes to start a foundry should be enabled to obtain access to such an enterprise in some African country where foundries already are in operation — or if this is not easy, to a foundry in some country in Asia or the Middle East — and should spend some time there in order to acquire enough technical expertise to run his own enterprise on his return. These programmes may be supported by governmental agreements and preferably by the expenditure of public funds for travel and maintenance of the trainees.

In addition to these semi-vocational and semi-general programmes of education, provision must be made for widespread elementary education which, at the same time, will produce gradually, if not immediately, the manpower for these new urban and rural (i.e., agricultural) enterprises. In some African nations the problems of school leavers are already acute and rapid growth of African enterprise is required to make possible their better and more fruitful employment.[20] In these cases the educational efforts already made and the sponsoring of entrepreneurial development supplement one another.

From the various points raised in this paper it will, we hope, become apparent that the fostering of entrepreneurship is not a special process which can be embarked upon without consideration of a whole set of associated changes. In fact, wherever we look we find that the development of more and better entrepreneurial talent in developing countries is closely integrated with the overall trend of economic development in these societies. In a certain sense the growth of entrepreneurship may be regarded as an almost 'natural' concomitant of economic development, in general, and if the latter is assured the former will eventually be forthcoming, provided some scope is left for private decision-making in such economic spheres as allocation of resources, investment of capital, and determination of output. What we have suggested in this paper, therefore, is not so much a series of policies which will guarantee that an entrepreneurial corps among Africans will actually emerge, but merely some steps which will facilitate its growth and enhance the likelihood of its rapid emergence.

[20] See Archibald C. Callaway, 'School Leavers in Nigeria,' *West Africa* (25th March, 1st, 8th and 15th April 1961), pp. 325, 353, 371–2 and 409.

8

SOME ASPECTS AND PROBLEMS OF TRADE IN AFRICA

BY P. T. BAUER

*Professor, London School of Economics and Political Science,
University of London, UK*

I

The invitation to this symposium asked me to examine from the African standpoint the principal aspects of trade in Africa, and to suggest improvements to enable it to serve better the African interest. In particular I was asked specifically to consider the defects of commerce in Africa; the possibilities of efficient modernization; and the merits of encouraging labour-intensive service industries.

Highly selective treatment is inevitable in the examination of these topics.[1] I shall review some aspects and implications of trade which I hope are of some general interest, which are prominent in public discussion and which have given rise to government action. I shall proceed largely, but not only, by setting out issues rather than by suggesting policies. The distinction between description and analysis on one hand, and suggestions for policy on the other, will be made clearly throughout.

I begin with two points which are partly introductory but which also bear on the substantive discussion.

First, I shall deal with specific issues (though I hope of some general interest) which bear on trade as an instrument for an effective deployment of resources and for the promotion of their growth. A discussion in terms of specific topics may understate the wide and pervasive influence and potentialities of trade in the underdeveloped world. Trade contributes to material progress in various ways, including among others by the husbanding of scarce resources, notably capital; by the extension of markets, with the resulting promotion of specialization and of production for sale, and thus the creation of an agricultural surplus (chiefly by

---

[1] I may mention here one general limitation. I shall deal only with trade outside the so-called subsistence sector. There is exchange and trade in locally produced goods and services within the subsistence economy, usually confined to the village, tribe and some other narrowly restricted community. The interest of this symposium is clearly with trade which is less restricted in its range and scope.

providing a market for agricultural produce and at the same time bringing new crops, methods and inducement goods to the notice of farmers and within their reach); by stimulating the accumulation of capital; by bringing to prominence and influence trader-entrepreneurs accustomed to an exchange economy; and by acquainting people with the processes of the exchange economy and promoting the habits and attitudes appropriate to it. Moreover, by linking local communities to the outside world and acquainting people with the habits of a money economy, trade promotes (for good or evil) the disintegration of the traditional local attitudes, customs and institutions.

These considerations are particularly relevant to the situation in Africa where subsistence production is still so extensive. Production for wider exchange and sale is indispensable for the achievement of even a reasonable standard of living. The inducement and even the possibility of production for wider markets depend greatly on the terms on which producers can buy or sell, which in turn are much affected by the effectiveness of the trading system which is therefore of great significance for the progress of the peoples of Africa, as of most underdeveloped countries.

My second point concerns the ambiguity and complexity of the concept of the African interest. The concept of a group interest is rarely simple. Even disregarding the important and complex philosophical or quasi-philosophical problems of the interest of a community, and of the time-horizon envisaged (involving the interests of different generations), there still remains the highly relevant problem of the discrepancy between the interests of particular groups or sections, and the interests of other groups or sections of the population. Whenever economic specialization has made some progress, members of each specialized group can improve their *relative* position (and up to a point also their real income) by restricting their numbers, and thus increasing the scarcity value of their services. Any benefits gained are at the expense of the rest of the community; and the economic cost of such measures from a less effective allocation of resources usually appreciably exceeds the benefits to the sectional interests.

II

In almost every African country foreigners are prominent or even pre-dominant in trade outside the subsistence sector.[2] In all major countries

---

[2] I use the term foreigner or expatriate as synonomous with non-African. Many of the European, Indian and Levantine traders have lived for decades or even generations in Africa, and it is therefore inaccurate to refer to them as foreigners or expatriates. But these terms are less cumbersome than non-African, and I shall use them to refer to people of non-African origin.

the import and export trade is largely handled by foreigners, who often also play a large role in subsequent stages of the distribution of imports and in the earlier stages of the assembly of exports. This situation is often regarded as anomalous; and the predominance of foreigners in external trade is often termed as a monopoly situation.

The use of the term monopoly here is unfortunate. It reflects and encourages confusion between two logically and practically quite distinct situations, the first in which an activity is largely in the hands of a geographically or ethnically distinct group, and the second is one in which those in a particular activity can exercise a degree of monopoly by deliberate restriction of supply or entry, which enables them to secure prices, trading margins, or returns on capital, higher than would prevail under more competitive conditions. The two types of situation are quite distinct, and one can, and often does, exist without the other. The frequent identification of these two types of situation is particularly unfortunate in African conditions because there the predominant position of foreigners sometimes is accompanied by a measure of monopoly, but often it is not, and this difference is obscured by the indiscriminate use of the term to cover both. And as I shall suggest shortly, the confusion is apt to issue in policies designed to limit the predominance of expatriates, which in fact strengthen whatever element of monopoly they may possess.

The prominence of foreigners in African commerce reflects the advantages of the possession of capital and of access to it, as well as of skills and attitudes such as technical and administrative skills, thrift, the ability to perceive and take advantage of economic opportunity, and various other aptitudes and attitudes, derived in part from the background of societies long accustomed to the ways of a money economy. Foreigners, including foreign traders, have been prime agents of economic change in Africa, and have been largely responsible for linking these economies to the outside world, and for the provision of human and material resources which have made these links possible.

The prominence of non-Africans in trade does not in itself imply the presence of monopoly in the usual meaning of the word. There is, nevertheless, a substantial degree of concentration in external trade in several African territories, notably West Africa. The principal reason for this is to be found in the large capital requirements in some branches of tropical trade, which in turn derives from the long distances and poorly developed communications, and also from the necessity of financing local intermediaries and often even local producers, because of the low level of liquid capital in the indigenous economies. The wide and rapid swings of prosperity and depression also tend to benefit those with large capital by enabling them to weather the slump, and even to buy up firms in difficulties. In one or two instances historical accident, such as the administration of certain territories by chartered trading companies, has promoted concentration. A high degree of concentration is in itself likely to result in a situation in which trading margins are wider than if the number of competitors were larger. This likelihood is enhanced if there are market-sharing agreements among the firms, agreements which are facilitated when there are few firms. A substantial measure of concentration and periodic market-sharing agreements have been prominent in the external trade of British West Africa, an area in the economic life and development of which external trade has been of the greatest importance.

Both the width of the trading margins and the stability of market-sharing agreements are much affected by actual and potential competition, notably by the presence of outsiders (that is, both firms other than those which account for the high degree of concentration, and firms not participating in or observing the market-sharing agreements), by the number of participants in the market-sharing agreements (which tend to be less effective when numbers are large), and by the possibility of the entry of effective new competitors. In practically all branches of trade outside small-scale retailing, the most effective competitors of foreign trading firms are other foreigners and foreign trading firms. Such actual or potential competition may come from three sources: foreign firms with experience of some other branches or stages of trade in the local country; foreign firms with trading experience elsewhere, notably some other poor country; and foreign firms engaged in economic activity other than trade in the same country. Empirically, the first two categories have been much the more important. The technical and administrative skills and experience, the knowledge of market conditions, and at times the local connections of such enterprises, are of obvious value in challenging the position of established firms.

It would seem that neither the high degree of concentration, nor the market-sharing agreements have generally secured substantial monopoly profits, or exceptionally wide gross margins to the firms for any prolonged period, except when government controls have restricted entry or stifled competition.[3] Without such controls the advantage of the possession of large capital is generally not sufficient to sustain monopolistic margins or profits for long.

However, the combination of the prominence of foreigners in trade,

---

[3] There are a few exceptions where special circumstances, notably control of important transport or port facilities, have placed certain firms in a particularly strong position. This was of some significance in the past, for instance in the trade in oil palm products in Eastern Nigeria. It is of no general interest or importance at present.

and of a high degree of concentration in external trade, present difficult political and administrative problems, even without monopolistic practices, organized barriers to entry, or abnormally wide profit margins. Indeed the absence of these aspects and practices enhances the dilemmas of policy which are often ignored in a politically highly charged atmosphere. In many African countries (and indeed throughout the underdeveloped world) there are controls to ensure larger local participation in trade by prohibition or severe restrictions of the immigration of foreign traders and trading employees, restrictive licensing of trading enterprises, and rationing or licensing of supplies. They are almost invariably said to be introduced to increase the volume of trade in African hands. This formulation ignores the essential problems and their attendant dilemmas.

Such restrictions diminish the aggregate volume of trade and of economic activity in the territories concerned, and they thus affect adversely the economic interest of African producers, consumers and workers. They do this because the activities of more efficient firms and individuals are reduced to provide opportunities for less efficient firms and individuals. Moreover, and this is perhaps particularly noteworthy in this context, it is virtually certain that the volume of trade handled by African traders is reduced by these restrictions. It is of course true that African traders whose activities depend on these restrictions would be displaced or find their scope curtailed. But the expansion of the total trade which would come about in the absence of these restrictions would benefit the African traders in those stages of trade, or in those distributive activities which would still remain in African hands. On all but extreme assumptions, the total volume of trade handled by African traders would increase even though some would be displaced in certain branches of trade. This conclusion is reinforced if the effects of the activities of foreigners on the growth of the economy as a whole are considered.

In practice, however, those who benefit from the restrictions and would lose by their removal are aware of these losses (or even overestimate them), whereas those who would benefit from their removal do not realize this. The losses from the removal of restrictions are direct, localized and are readily perceived, whereas the benefits would be widely diffused, would be indirect (in the sense of reaching the beneficiaries at one or more removes only), and would permeate the economy only gradually. The losses suffered by African trading interests would also suggest that the subservience of Africans to foreign merchants had increased. This type of asymmetry in the perception of benefits and losses from the imposition or removal of restrictions is usual.

Let me now consider some further economic effects and implications of these restrictions. In the trading activities in which they are imposed, competition is reduced and the trading margins of both Africans and foreigners are widened. Where the controls are effected by restrictive licensing and allocation of supplies, they result in windfall profits to the favoured traders, secured at the expense of their customers, and at the expense of those excluded from the protected activity. The wider distributive margins affect adversely the customers of the traders, including farmers who have to pay more for their supplies, and to receive less for their products, and they therefore generally tend to reduce the growth of production for the market. Moreover, such regulations necessarily exclude numbers of people from trading, many of whom may for various reasons be substantially disadvantaged by this enforced restriction on their occupational mobility. And whatever the basis of allocation of licenses and supplies, it necessarily implies an element of privilege and favouritism. This sets up obvious political, social and administrative strains, particularly in multi-racial societies.

Such regulations and controls are also apt to convey misleading ideas about commercial activity and of its difficulties and rewards. They ensure easy profits. As a result both the favoured traders and other members of the community tend to underestimate the difficulties and risks of commerce, and indeed to regard it as involving no more than the mere collection of riskless and effortless profits, which indeed it largely is in these conditions. So far from promoting commercial and economic education, and serving to train members of the local population for a more effective participation in economic life, such controls have the effect of misleading people about the tasks of commercial life, which leaves them less rather than better prepared to face subsequent vicissitudes.[4]

There are thus substantial disadvantages in attempts to promote the interests of African traders by restriction on competition in trade, especially by restrictive licensing and by the control and allocation of supplies. These disadvantages are particularly important when a large part of the economy is still in the subsistence stage, because, as already noted, the ability and readiness of subsistence producers to produce for the market is much affected by the volume, variety and terms of the available trading services.

It does not, however, follow from the foregoing that deliberate government action may not be required in this sphere. For instance, without it the local population may feel that it is separated from the outside world by an impenetrable layer of alien traders. This in itself may induce a sense of dependence, which is sharpened when these traders are

---

[4] These arguments apply whether the favoured traders are private firms or co-operative societies. The position of co-operative societies is considered in section V, below.

2 P. T. BAUER

members of economically and socially more advanced communities. And when the degree of concentration is high, both the feeling and the reality of dependence on particular firms are naturally further increased. This can lead to a politically explosive situation, particularly when some or many of the expatriate traders have over a period of years achieved considerable prosperity, even though their profits may not represent either abnormal returns on capital, or monopolistic margins.

There are no simple solutions to the problems and dilemmas of such a situation. The drastic suggestion sometimes heard for the elimination of expatriates from all or most branches of trade would severely retard economic progress in areas where continued growth cannot be taken for granted.

The most appropriate course must depend on local circumstances, particularly on social, political, economic and administrative conditions and possibilities. It would be affected by the extent, depth and intensity of the feelings of masses of producers and consumers, which often may differ considerably from those ascribed to them by vocal groups of local traders. Although generalized policy recommendations are of very limited use, I must follow the injunctions of the invitation to this symposium, and put forward some suggestions which I hope will serve as starting points for discussion.

For social, political and economic reasons it may be thought desirable to subsidize Africans in various branches of trade. The costs of such a policy should be brought out into the open and borne by the community as a whole in accordance with some recognized canons of equity, which are presumably reflected in the tax structure as far as it is politically and administratively possible. This suggests that wherever possible assistance should take the form of a government subsidy. This ensures that the cost is appreciated, and is borne by the community at large, and not by an arbitrarily selected group, namely by the customers of traders, and by those who are excluded from trade by the restrictive measures designed to protect African traders. Such a subsidy is also less likely to impede economic development than a rise in the cost of trading services.[5]

A subsidy could be given to African traders, co-operative societies or government-owned corporations or government departments engaged in trade. It could also be given to expatriate firms to encourage the employment of Africans in responsible posts. For instance, a subsidy could be related to the proportion which payments to Africans bear to total salary payments in certain senior grades. This would in effect be a subsidy designed to promote the training of Africans in trade. Service with

[5] Whether a subsidy is less of an impediment depends largely on the system of the subsidy and the structure of taxation.

unsubsidized trading firms (i.e. firms unassisted except for this particular subsidy) is suitable training for independent commercial activity, and possibly for subsequent industrial activity as well. It is likely to be more fruitful training than independent commercial activity in an officially-created non-competitive environment, that is in conditions in which profits are virtually assured. An increase in the number of Africans in senior positions with foreign firms would also help to serve to dispel some of the popular misconceptions about the activities of these firms and about their profits.

Thus direct government subsidy for securing African participation in trade offers a wider range of possibilities than protection of African traders by the restriction on their competitors, a policy which is inflexible and circumscribed, besides having the other special disadvantages already described.

I may refer to another specific suggestion. Given the admission of a certain number of expatriates to an African country, it would promote economic development if they were allowed to move freely between different occupations and activities without being prohibited from entering any particular activity or range of activity, especially trade.[6] If they are allowed to move between different commercial activities, they are likely to deploy their capital and skills in directions yielding the highest return, and they will thereby usually contribute most to economic development. They will normally engage in those activities in which the Africans are least likely to compete effectively in the near future, since it would be uneconomic for foreigners to enter these. This suggestion runs counter both to current practice, and to widely-held notions. It may indeed prove politically impracticable if opposition to foreigners is especially vocal and effective in particular activities.[7]

III

In many poor countries in Africa (and elsewhere) a large number of intermediaries is a conspicuous feature of the local scene. This multiplicity of intermediaries is often held responsible for the high costs of distribution and is widely regarded as a major defect of African commerce. This complaint is not so highly charged politically as those about the prominence of expatriates, but it is a frequent and influential theme of the official

[6] On political and social grounds this may not apply to mining, or to the acquisition of real property. This, however, has no bearing on the argument of the text.

[7] The case for this suggestion may be strengthened if such immigrants are given permission to reside for a given number of years, but without expectation of political rights, or assurance of an extension of this period.

literature, and it has had important effects on the course of events.[8] It was largely responsible for the introduction of restrictive licensing of ginneries and traders in the cotton industry of Uganda, a series of measures which has not only raised the cost of these activities, and reduced the marketing facilities serving Africans, but has also secured large monopoly profits to favoured licencees. This type of complaint was also partly responsible for the establishment of export monopolies over all major West African agricultural produce, which has had very far-reaching results.

The argument is that unnecessary intermediaries place themselves within the distributive chain thereby raising its costs. As a corollary the compulsory elimination of these redundant intermediaries is proposed. However, neither these suggestions, nor the consequent policy proposals stand up to examination.

The complaint invites the question why the allegedly redundant inter-mediaries are not by-passed by those with whom they deal. An intermediary will normally be used only if the price he charges for his service (that is, his margin) is less than the value his customers place on his service. He will be by-passed without official intervention if he provides no services (that is if he is redundant), or if his services exceed the costs incurred by his customers if they performed these services for themselves. This will happen unless neither of the parties served by them realises that it would be cheaper to by-pass them, or unless institutional arrangements preventing the adoption of more economical direction methods of dealing. Let me consider these possibilities.

The allegedly redundant intermediary necessarily must stand between another middleman and the producer, or between a middleman and the final consumer, or between two middlemen. Thus at least one of the parties served by the supposedly redundant intermediary is himself an intermediary. Even if it were true that the average farmer does not know his marketing alternatives, or could not perform simple commercial calculations, a redundant intermediary would still be eliminated if his middleman customer could effect a saving by dealing direct. It is most unlikely that those who live by trading, and whose profits and livelihood thus depend on their margins, would ignore economic opportunities in their own field of business, or fail to take advantage of them. Moreover, there is ample evidence of the awareness of African farmers of their marketing alternatives, and of their eagerness to sell at the best price; and

[8] For instance the following characteristic passages in the official *Report of the Nigeria Live-stock Mission* (London: H.M. Stationery Office, 1951) well illustrate these complaints . . . 'the handling of almost the entire trade by a host of redundant dealers and middlemen, the frequent handlings of stock' are among the factors that 'represent for Nigeria economic wastage on a prodigious scale and in large measure accounts for the unjustifiably wide gap between the prices received by the producer and those paid by the consumer', p. 95.

this is not surprising in view of their low cash incomes and of the often low opportunity costs in the disposal of their time.[9] Thus, an intermediary whose margin exceeds the value of his services to the parties served by him will be by-passed.[10]

Thus the compulsory elimination of classes of intermediaries (say, itinerant buyers or commission agents) implies that their services must be performed at greater cost (in terms of real resources) by one or other of the parties between whom they stand. This implies an uneconomic measure of vertical integration, together with a reduction in the marketing alternatives open to the parties. These adverse effects are serious in under-developed countries which are least able to afford the resulting waste.

Institutional arrangements sometimes deny customers the right to use certain methods of marketing. For instance, restrictive practices may prevent customers from by-passing middlemen even if they preferred to do without their services. This is against their interests. Such practices are much more significant in developed than in underdeveloped countries, though they are not unknown in the latter. For instance, in some West African ports market women are said to have prevented fishermen and their wives from retailing their catches. But clearly the interests of the fishermen will not be served by a compulsory restriction in the numbers of intermediaries whose monopolistic position would thereby be strengthened.

African producers are often said to be prevented from selling their crops on the best terms because they are indebted to particular inter-mediaries and have to sell to them. But a compulsory reduction in the number of trader lenders aggravates the situation of the producers instead of improving it. Such a measure reduces the volume of credit available to producers, and thereby weakens his position. The combined terms of the loan and the price would be worse; and it is this combination which concerns him. The weakness of the buyer derives from his need for a loan; reduction in the number of potential lenders aggravates this weak-ness. This is a specific example of the general point that the position of the customers of traders is usually not improved by a compulsory reduction in the number of traders, since this merely reduces the alternatives open to customers.

It is also often suggested that there are too many intermediaries or processors *at any particular stage* in the distributive chain, and that this results in unnecessary multiplication of facilities which raises overheads

[9] But even if they did not know the alternatives open to them, or more generally their own commercial interests, their position is unlikely to be improved by a compulsory reduction of the services available to them.

[10] This is so unless the customers are not free agents for institutional or other reasons, a matter which I shall consider later in this section.

which in turn forces the intermediaries to pay producers unnecessarily low prices. However, such a situation could be expected to induce the intermediaries to bid up producers' prices to get larger supplies, which would then lead to the elimination of the redundant intermediaries. There is indeed ample specific evidence in Africa that the so-called excessive competition tends to raise producer prices rather than depress them. If there really were significant economies in the operation of fewer and larger trading and processing establishments, the interest of intermediaries and processors and of the responsiveness of producers to the higher prices offered by them, could be expected to establish such a market structure with a relatively small number of local units, without compulsion. A situation would result in which the possibilities of the economies of scale are balanced with producers' valuations of the convenience of marketing (especially the proximity of traders or processors), and of the availability of a range of independent alternatives. This again is amply confirmed by empirical evidence in many African territories. For instance, it is borne out by the contrast in a number of countries between the few large timber processing enterprises compared to the multiplicity of cotton ginneries, which reflects the economies of scale in the former activity and their absence in the latter, which prevents larger ginneries from offering significantly more favourable terms to the producers than do the smaller dispersed units.

The multiplicity of intermediaries in a large measure reflects certain essential aspects of the economies of many African territories. The principal factor behind this multiplicity of intermediaries is that production for sale is undertaken by large numbers of farmers who individually produce on a small scale, and as they have little storage capacity and small cash resources they have to sell in small lots at frequent intervals. Moreover, many or most farmers operate far from the points of assembly, the principal markets or the ports of shipment. There is a heavy cost of assembling and conveying to the distant market large numbers of small parcels of produce.

Even the simple economics of this matter are so imperfectly understood that a numerical example may be useful. If each of five farmers situated twenty miles from the nearest village or town himself marketed his own very small weekly output, this would require five return journeys of forty miles each. If, however, one middleman (who may in fact be one of the farmers acting for the others) intervenes and carries the produce to the market, the number of journeys is reduced by four-fifths, saving scarce and valuable capital (in the form of animal or lorry transport), as well as labour. This last economy may also be important, since, even if there is a general surplus of labour, the harvesting of produce has to be accomplished within a given short period so that at times the farmer cannot afford to leave his holding. The same principle applies at the next stage; if each small middleman carried his purchases direct to the large markets the number of journeys would be greater than if another intermediary stepped in and carried the purchases of several traders; and so on all along the line.

The task of bulking cannot be avoided. So long as there is competitive entry into trade the producer is not affected whether the performer of the service of bulking and transport is remunerated by salary or by the profits of trade. If the farmers formed themselves into a co-operative society, these services would be undertaken by the servants of the co-operative society, whose time and effort would still have to be paid for.

Thus the distributive task in these economies absorbs a large volume of resources. The type of resource used depends on the relative supplies and prices of different resources, especially of capital and labour, on technical conditions, and also on institutional factors. Compared to conditions elsewhere, capital in African economies is generally scarce relative to unskilled labour. The lack of telephones and the low level and poor quality of the roads increase the capital required for a given flow of production and consumption. Most intermediaries are themselves poor so that they operate on a small scale; and small-scale distribution requires comparatively little capital and training. For these reasons, distribution tends to be labour-intensive.

There are some institutional factors originating outside commodity distribution which enhance the labour-intensive nature of trading activity in Africa. These are the restrictions on the access to land, and, more important, the establishment of minimum wages for hired labour in organized industry and commerce. These regulated wages do not apply to small-scale trade, nor of course to self-employment which is prominent in small-scale trade, which thus becomes an overflow activity into which are forced those who cannot secure wage employment.

In short, although the marketing arrangements in commodity distribution, especially small-scale trade, in Africa, are technically primitive compared to those in economically more advanced societies, they are not wasteful in African conditions. Arrangements which are economically efficient in one society will not be efficient in another where the availability of resources is different. Thus attempts to force marketing arrangements more closely into line with those prevailing elsewhere lead to waste. This applies notably to measures designed to bring about a larger measure of vertical integration by enforcing direct dealing between consumers and producers through the compulsory eliminating of intermediaries. Such measures increase unnecessarily the capital and administrative skills required in distribution (that is, they enforce increased employment of a scarce resource which can be used elsewhere), while setting free manpower with little or no alternative opportunities. They thus raise the real cost of marketing. They also deny marketing facilities to many producers, which may prevent them from entering the exchange economy or remaining within it.

IV

Complaints about the prominence of expatriates and those about the alleged wastefulness of the multiplicity of middlemen, usually stem from different sources and move on a different plane. But they often issue in similar policies, which reinforce an important and undesirable feature of African trade, which has received little publicity. This is the prevalence of restrictive tendencies.

There is in many African economies a pronounced tendency towards restrictionism, which draws strength from two distinct sources: the pressure of sectional economic interests and tribalism or xenophobia. As already noted, the tendency towards restrictionism is a feature of economies in which there is some measure of specialization. In such societies people often try to increase the scarcity value of their services by restricting entry into their own or related activities, because by such means they can improve their relative position and up to a point their real income.

Distrust or dislike of strangers is another familiar feature of many societies. In tribal or near tribal societies it is often pronounced. There are also prominent individuals and groups in such societies who think that their position would be jeopardized by extensive contact with other societies, and they therefore try to obstruct such contacts. Tribal sentiment and xenophobia therefore tend to reinforce the more narrowly economic motives of restrictionism.

Restrictive measures have become much more significant and effective with the extension of government intervention in economic life because government support is often necessary for their maintenance and effectiveness. Public opinion, especially vocal and influential opinion, is often ready to support restrictionism, with the result that its acceptance may give governments less trouble than attempts to resist it. Politicians and administrators often welcome restrictive measures for these reasons, as well as for others such as the resulting closer control over economic life and the apparently tidier economic system which results.

Although for obvious political and administrative reasons such measures are particularly effective and popular when directed against foreigners or members of ethnically or linguistically distinct groups, they are often directed also against other members of the local population (other than the beneficiaries).

For instance, it is well known that in West Africa there has for many years been a vocal and politically influential opposition to the activities of expatriate traders. Less familiar is the frequently equally vehement opposition to the entry or activities of Africans from other tribes, regions or districts. Such opposition is often directed against people who are ethnically and linguistically indistinguishable from, or even identical with, those who oppose their entry and activities, so that the essentially economic basis of the opposition is clear.

In recent years and decades there has been much officially supported restrictionism in many important branches of African commerce (including transport) effected by such measures as the restrictive licensing, the establishment of zonal monopolies, the confinement of trade to certain markets, and various other devices.

Restrictionism in trade raises the cost of the indispensible service of commodity assembly and distribution and reduces the alternatives of the population. By narrowing markets it retards the expansion of production for the market as well as the growth of specialization, and thus the development of the economy; for these reasons it not only retards the growth of agricultural production for sale but also increases the frequency and severity of local shortages, especially of food. It increases the unemployment stemming from the lack of co-operant resources (including the uneven local incidence of the scarcity of these resources) by preventing the most effective deployment of the available capital and skill. It also retards the spread of ideas and of new techniques and thus confines economic horizons. It enhances people's sense of dependence on the privileged traders which exasercbates political tension especially, but not only, when these are foreigners. It often strengthens the position of local monopolies. It leads to the growth of pressure groups and to political and economic strife. Further, in many African territories the local population itself is heterogeneous, so that restrictionism is particularly likely to result in extensive fragmentation of the economy.

Such restrictive measures, which are now so effective, have been introduced in many underdeveloped countries at a comparatively early stage of their development. Many of the African economies have hardly emerged from tribal restrictionism before being overtaken by more narrowly economic restrictionism. Thus they have not experienced a comparatively long spell of unrestricted activity of the earlier history of the developed countries. Moreoever, in European countries certain forms of restrictionism, notably the local monopolistic restrictions, disintegrated in the course of the accelerated economic advance of the eighteenth and nineteenth centuries. The early emergence of economic restrictionism (superimposed on or even juxtaposed with tribal restrictionism) affects adversely their economic position and prospects. Very poor economies, in which advance from a subsistence to an exchange economy is necessary for material progress, are particularly harmed by such restrictionism.

A specific example is served to illustrate some implications of the foregoing discussion. It has been known for many years that there is a large internal trade in local produce in Nigeria, much of it over long distances. There are wide seasonal fluctuations in the prices of these products and also large inter-district and inter-regional price differences. These fluctuations and differences reflect the narrowness of markets, the poor communications, and the low level of physical and money capital. In such a situation there are considerable possibilities of profits for enterprises with the requisite capital and organization. This was recognized by the United Africa Company in the early 1930s when it entered this trade. Its activities aroused such fierce opposition from local trading interests that the government asked the company to refrain from trading in local produce, and since about 1932 the company has not in fact participated in this trade. This episode incidentally illustrates the divergence between the sectional interests of certain African groups (the traders in local produce) and the interests of the African population as a whole, since the population generally would undoubtedly benefit from the smoother flow of internal trade.

For political reasons the European firms are still barred from participation in internal trade. Indeed they are more effectively barred than in the past, as local trading interests are more vocal and politically influential than in the 1930s. Newspaper and political opinion reflects their interests and views to a far greater extent than it does those of the rural population at large.

A general suggestion arises from the subject of this section.[11]

Governments and administrators could make greater efforts to resist restrictionism. A fairly close study of West African trade and some work on Uganda, suggest that in Africa the political pressures for restrictionism are not overwhelming, especially when they are directed primarily against other Africans. In Uganda the demands for restrictive licensing of ginneries have come entirely from expatriates; and as already noted in West Africa, much of the restrictionism is directed primarily against Africans. Governments and administrators have supported or accepted restrictionism for a variety of reasons, including over-estimate of the strength behind it; failure to recognize the heterogeneity of the African

[11] A more specific suggestion is discussed in section 6 below in the context of the modernization of distribution.

economic interest, especially the discrepancy between sectional interest and that of the rest of the community; the official preference for apparently tidy structures; the failure to see through the hollowness of the arguments for restrictionism; and a failure to appreciate its adverse results. In African conditions official support is very generally necessary for the effectiveness and maintenance of restrictionism. Thus official support should generally be withheld from restrictionism; and it might even be replaced by effective discouragement.

V

The co-operative movement is supported by governments in many, possibly most, African countries. The development of co-operative trading societies is widely regarded as the best way to remedy many of the real or alleged defects of African commerce, notably the predominance of expatriates, the high costs of distribution, the liability of producers to exploitation, and so forth.

Government support to co-operative societies takes varying forms, usually representing a mixture in varying degrees and combinations of such ingredients as special legislative facilities for the formation and registration of societies; provision of advisory and supervisory services by a government department; official participation in, or control of, decision-making and management; financial assistance ranging from the guaranteeing of loans to the payment of subsidies and grants in aid; and restrictions on, or the prohibition of, activities of competing private undertakings; preferential treatment in allocation of licences or supplies; and so forth. Quite often government departments have in fact become partners in co-operative enterprises in which they have become deeply involved. In these circumstances, co-operative societies are really extensions of government departments rather than independent organizations.

The case for government support of the co-operatives is often regarded as axiomatic. Yet the case for it is not obvious. A co-operative society is simply a form of business enterprise whose capital is provided, and whose activities are organized, by its suppliers or customers. A co-operator is both a part owner and a customer of the society.

Generally the economic or commercial services of co-operative societies such as credit, marketing or consumer societies are essentially similar to those supplied by private firms. When a co-operative society does not receive substantial privileges, preferential treatment or financial support from the government, its economic success can be measured by its ability to survive, and to satisfy the commercial needs of its members, who can

9

always turn to private firms if they are not satisfied. If, in such conditions, the society survives or expands, it means that its members prefer it to privately owned firms. Its advantages may stem from various sources, such as efficiency, or perception of commercial opportunities ignored by private firms. Or it may operate in a field where there is little competition among private firms, so that there is room for an independent supplier. Or the society may benefit from the loyalty of its members, or from the knowledge of their credit worthiness, or simply from their preference to deal with their own organization. But whatever the reasons for its success, this provides its economic justification, if it is gained without special privileges and support denied to private competitors.

There are certain other economic activities which cannot be easily undertaken by private organizations but which can possibly be undertaken by co-operatives. These include such important agricultural activities as pest control and soil conservation. These yield indiscriminate benefits, which means that firms undertaking them could not collect charges from the beneficiaries, since the benefits accrue whether or not the beneficiaries pay. Thus they will not be undertaken by private firms. The individual producer may also be reluctant to spend money on these activities as part of his expenditure will accrue to the neighbours without cost to them, and his own efforts may be frustrated by their neglect. These difficulties may be overcome by a co-operative embracing all the producers in its area of operation. This could obviously overcome the obstacles which are pro-hibitive to private enterprise in this field. At the same time it may be preferable to performance of these tasks by a government department, which is unlikely to know conditions in the particular area, or the circumstances of the producers, so well as a local co-operative society. There are great difficulties in the way of establishing such societies in underdeveloped countries, notably Africa. But it is noteworthy that there is a wide area, important for agricultural improvement, in which the co-operative effort would be complementary and not competitive with private effort, and may also be preferable to direct government inter-vention.

When co-operative societies enjoy sustained and substantial government support, then of course the simple test of survival and progress no longer indicate that economic usefulness, because they enjoy advantages which arise from privileges created for them by the government, and not from their commercial efficiency of their ability to satisfy the demands of their members. Thus the basis of rational economic assessment is removed. This is particularly so whenever the support and assistance is general rather than specific, and involves not only, or mainly, financial grants, but such matters as restriction on the activities of competitors, or preferential treatment in the allocation of licences or trading sites. Moreover, there is also the practically very important advantage that once the government has begun to subsidize co-operatives, further help can always be expected in the case of difficulties which the government cannot refuse. The government faces a contingent liability to assist societies which have run into financial difficulties, a liability which may be particularly onerous when these societies have acquired many members with the help of this support.

It is often argued that co-operatives, especially co-operative trading and credit societies, should not be judged in the basis of commercial success, because co-operation is desirable on wider grounds, for instance, by encouraging the virtues of self-reliance and thrift, or acquainting producers with problems of organization and marketing. This may justify government assistance in the form of advisory service or technical assistance. But this can hardly serve as an argument for large-scale government assistance, which becomes practically government participation. Such assistance, and the expectation of its continuation, undermine the self-reliance of the co-operators. Membership is valued not for its own sake but because of the privilege and support enjoyed by the society. Moreover, there is little or no educational advantage in co-operation in such conditions, rather the reverse, since any apparent commercial success is in a large measure the result of the special privileges granted to society by government rather than of the ability to serve the needs of customers.

Certain special arguments are often urged in Africa in support of the co-operative principle and of government support to co-operatives: that co-operatives to some extent resemble the communal shared economic activity of tribal life and is thus particularly suitable to African conditions; that co-operation helps African farmers to secure loans on tolerable terms, chiefly because the management has personal knowledge of the debtor; and that co-operation redresses the inequality of economic strength between the farmer and the middleman. But in themselves these arguments do not justify government support to co-operatives. If co-operatives are so suitable to African conditions, it would not be necessary to subsidize them. Again, the individual producer is known also to the small trader and money-lender. The high rate of interest on loans to farmers reflects largely the scarcity of money capital, the high cost of administering small loans and the high risks. High rates of interest may also involve an element of monopoly profits, though I believe this to be comparatively unimportant because of the ease of entry into small-scale trade and money-lending. But if competition is weak, this is precisely a condition in which there are opportunities for *unsubsidized* co-operative enterprise.

Essentially the same applies to the alleged inequality in bargaining strength between producers and money-lenders. If this were a substantial factor adversely affecting the terms of trade of producers[12] to be redressed by co-operation, the resulting improvement in these terms would secure the adherence of producers without government support.

It may be argued that such support is still required to overcome initial difficulties even if ultimately the society becomes viable, a suggestion along the familiar infant-industry argument for protection. But this argument is weak, and it would not justify subsidization or support of co-operative societies compared to private undertakings in which the same reasoning could be applied. In any case this has nothing to do with substantial and continued large-scale assistance to the co-operative movement.

Counsel has been darkened in this sphere by misleading comparisons with the success of the British consumer co-operatives over the last hundred years. This analogy is wholly irrelevant for the following reasons, among others. First, the British co-operatives were not subsidized by government. This in itself should suffice to dispose of the comparison. Second, the co-operative movement benefited greatly from the availability of latent managerial and administrative talent among the British working and lower middle classes for which in the nineteenth century and early twentieth century there was very little outlet in commercial or public life, and which was therefore available relatively cheaply to the co-operative movement. In Africa, however, the exact reverse applies. There is a great dearth of administrative and managerial talent locally, and there is ample opportunity in government service or private commerce for this talent which is therefore not available to the co-operatives. Third, in the nineteenth century competition in retailing in Britain was often weak, which helped the rapid progress both of the co-operative societies and, towards the end of the century, also of various other new types of retail organizations.

I may now turn to some policy implications of the foregoing. In those activities in which co-operatives compete with private firms, there is no general case for subsidizing co-operative societies rather than private African undertakings. If, however, co-operatives are supported, this is best done by the provision for a limited period of advisory and supervisory services. If it is decided to assist them beyond this limited extent,

---

[12] This is unlikely whenever there are a number of competing traders, or whenever entry into small-scale trade is easy (which it generally is, especially because farmers themselves often also act as traders) since actual or potential competition in trade forces the traders to bid for supplies. This compels them to offer prices which secure only competitive returns to the traders, regardless of differences in commercial skill or sophistication between themselves and the producers.

there is a case for doing so by direct cash subsidies, rather than by restrictions on the activities of the competitors.[13]

If it is thought desirable that the government should participate in a particular trading activity, it would seem preferable that it should do so directly through a government department or a government-owned corporation, rather than indirectly or covertly through government-subsidized co-operative societies, which are co-operatives in name only. It is often thought that government-supported co-operatives represent the best of both worlds in that they serve the public interest without the political and administrative difficulties presented by government operation. The truth seems to be rather the reverse. Such organizations are not subject either to the commercial or competitive test of the market, nor to the public scrutiny to which government agents or corporations are often exposed.

Lastly, it may be better to concentrate or even confine support for co-operatives to activities yielding principally indiscriminate benefits, such as pest control and irrigation (as distinct from ordinary commercial activities), which for reasons indicated earlier in this section cannot be undertaken by private enterprise, while at the same time are not particularly suitable for government departments.

VI

The two specific topics of modernization, and the encouragement of labour-intensive service industries, which I have been asked to examine, may be conveniently discussed together as they are related in the field of policy.

It is not quite clear what is meant by modernization of distribution which is an ambiguous concept. For instance, it could refer either to an increase or to a decrease in the volume of services rendered to the ultimate consumer. Home deliveries to consumers were at times regarded as essential in many branches of retailing in advanced economies, while now they are exceptional in the advanced economies of North America. Again, specialization is generally regarded as a feature of advanced economies, but the department stores and supermarkets of western countries, as well as of the more sophisticated commercial centres of Africa, are in some ways the opposite of specialization. Capital-intensive or technically-advanced methods are often regarded as characteristic of modern types of economic activity. But the economic desirability of the adoption of such methods is essentially a matter of costs and returns, and

[13] For the same reason as in the analogous instance noted in section II above.

it depends on factor supplies, technical conditions, the pattern of consumer wants and institutional arrangements. There is no special merit in adopting capital-intensive or technologically-advanced methods if these absorb a larger quantity of valuable resources in satisfying consumer wants than would simpler methods.[14] The foregoing is simply an example of the familiar confusion of technical and economic efficiency, that is of the assessment of the results and merits of economic activity regardless of cost.

It is, of course, economically desirable that commerce should be modernized in the sense that it uses resources most productively, and at the same time in a fashion most likely to conduce to their growth. I shall now put forward first some general suggestions, and then one more specific proposal for the promotion of this aim.

First, whenever possible resources should be used to satisfy consumer requirements at lowest cost, that is on the basis of economic and not merely technical efficiency. Second, trading enterprises should be allowed to operate unfettered by restrictions which raise their costs and which reduce the alternatives open to their customers. In particular, as far as possible trading enterprises should have unfettered access to new markets and methods, even if this affects existing vested interests. Third, the *economic* modernization of commerce, in the sense of closer approximation to its conduct in more advanced societies without waste of resources, is likely to be promoted by measures which advance the progress of the exchange economy. These include the suitable modification of the land tenure system, introduction of appropriate taxation, improvement in communications, resistance to restrictionism, and the provision of agricultural extension work.

The trade in agricultural produce for local consumption is an activity which seems to offer considerable scope for economic modernization and which is of great significance for economic progress in Africa. The specific suggestion I would like to make (and to which I referred earlier) concerns this broad area of commerce. It is provoked by the incident mentioned in section IV, the enforced withdrawal of the United Africa company from internal trade in West Africa in the face of pressure by African trading interests, a pressure which at present would be even more effective and powerful than in the 1930s.

---

[14] It is sometimes thought that the adoption of capital-intensive methods or of technically-advanced methods in some activities would help to promote technical progress and thereby raise the economy on to a higher plane. This view, which essentially ignores costs, is facile. Among other factors it disregards the fact that as a result of the adoption of these more capital-intensive methods in particular activities, methods elsewhere become less capital-intensive as less capital is available there. Consideration of the allocation of the resources may not suffice to provide criteria for policies designed to accelerate growth. But it does not follow that the adoption of unnecessarily costly methods in certain activities in some mysterious way promotes growth to offset the wasteful allocation of resources which it implies.

It is fairly obvious and well recognized that the expatriate merchant organizations could contribute substantially to the improvement of the efficiency of internal trade, which in turn would benefit the economy greatly, especially but not only by improving the marketing of crops and thus stimulating the output of local agriculture. African governments might therefore consider the promotion of a company for trading (including warehousing) in local produce, to be owned jointly by a government department or corporation, and by one or more expatriate merchant firms and possibly African commercial interests. Such a company could appoint expatriate merchants as agents either for a fee or for a participation in profits. These firms often have branches in many trading centres, and they would be well qualified to act as buying or selling agents. The experiment might at first be limited in scale and scope to minimize the risk and capital involved and to test its suitability in local conditions. Its extension would depend on results, which would be affected by such matters as the local political situation, the resources of the participating trading firms, and the efficiency of its competitors. It is clear that the experiment would be significant only if competitors were in no way hampered by official restrictions on their activities. Nor must the organization be in receipt of favours, privileges and concessions denied to its competitors. Of course, if successful, the experiment could be extended to other branches of trade and transport, as it already has for manufacturing industry (but not for trading) in some African countries.

The experiment might be politically practicable if the organization were known to be semi-official and to include influential African elements. The improvement in the methods and productivity of local food production is now widely and rightly recognized as a major factor in African progress, and one on which viable industrialization is likely to depend. Progress in this field is much affected by the efficiency of marketing. Moreover, acute local food shortages still occur in many parts of Africa and their removal or reduction could alleviate human misery; and in this sphere again such an organization could make a contribution. It would also serve to reduce the wide intra-seasonal price fluctuations. It would also provide valuable training to Africans in long-distance commerce. Lastly, it might help in unifying the local economies and counteracting the tendencies towards fragmentation. Altogether, if successful, it might contribute appreciably both to current economic welfare and to the promotion of economic progress. These wider advantages would be additional to any direct profits secured by the organisation.

Let me now turn to the question of the encouragement of service industries on the ground of their labour-intensive nature and their significance, therefore, as a source of employment. Service activity, especially distribution, is not necessarily more labour-intensive than other forms of activity. For instance, the large-scale substitution of capital for labour is a characteristic feature of distribution in the more recent development of the advanced economies of North America. But it is true that in emerging economies distribution, especially small-scale trade, is more labour-intensive than many, or even most, other activities outside the subsistence sector. This is so partly because unskilled labour can be substituted more readily for capital in small-scale distribution than elsewhere, and also because small-scale trading represents one of the overflow activities into which are forced those who cannot secure employment at the institutionally fixed minimum wage.[15] There is a general case for not discouraging trade in emerging activities, since this is a potent instrument in economic advance. Further, there is no reason for disparaging labour-intensive activities in these societies. But at the same time there is no general case either for encouraging or subsidizing an activity simply because it is labour-intensive; there is no merit in encouraging such an activity unless there is a market for the output at a price higher than its real cost in terms of the alternative uses of the resources employed in its production.

[15] In large-scale distribution, especially in establishments owned by expatriates, wages are raised above the opportunity costs by labour by this wage regulation. This somewhat hampers the progress, and restricts the activities of these enterprises.

TAXATION AND TAXABLE CAPACITY IN UNDERDEVELOPED COUNTRIES

BY DAVID WALKER

Professor, Dept. of Economics, University of Exeter, UK

I have been asked to answer the following questions:

> In general terms what is the taxable capacity of an underdeveloped country?
>
> What are the most appropriate taxes in an underdeveloped country?

From the way the questions are put it is clear that I am supposed to try and deal with them in general terms and not consider particularly the problems of Nyasaland. This I will do — though I add a few comments relevant to the Nyasaland situation towards the end of the paper.

I. EXPENDITURE

It is difficult to discuss taxation problems completely independently of other aspects of the public finance situation. I am not asked to consider the appropriate level of government expenditure. (Nor am I asked to comment on any of the alternatives to taxation, i.e. borrowing or credit creation.) This implies, I think, that the view is taken that the ability to raise taxation is the main factor determining the level of government expenditure; with the implication that there are always excellent ways in which governments could spend additional money and that what prevents the expansion of government spending is the rigidity of the tax system and the general difficulty of raising revenue. On the whole this is not an unreasonable attitude. In poor countries (and indeed in rich countries as well) one is always conscious of opportunities that exist for state help and action. There always seems to be a need for more police, or schools, or public housing, or higher civil service salaries — and there is the tendency to think that if only the tax system was more efficient or more highly developed then these gaps could be filled.

On the whole I believe there is an extreme need for revenue in underdeveloped countries. In addition to the reasons often given for this state

of affairs — the need for governments to do more in such countries
because of the weakness of private enterprise and the need to catch up
with the past — there is the important fact that poor countries, particularly
in Africa, are often faced with a price and salary structure with respect to
public expenditure which is out of line with the general level of incomes.

Very often discussion of tax requirements runs in terms of the need to
raise a certain percentage of the Gross National Product. With this
approach there is often the implication that after making allowance for
certain services which may not be needed on the scale needed in developed
countries — such as defence — and making adjustments for additional
services which may be needed — such as expenditure on industrial
promotion schemes — there is some sense in saying that governments of
underdeveloped countries need to raise roughly the same percentage of
the Gross National Product as in countries such as the UK or the USA.
For some purposes this may be a useful way of putting things but in my
view it often gives a too favourable and less challenging indication of the
public finance problem facing underdeveloped countries. For in this as in
so many other instances percentages do not tell the whole story. If a
government of a poor country raises the same percentage of its GNP as
a government of a rich country clearly — after adjustment to a *per capita*
basis — the amount of money available in the hands of the poor country's
government is much less than that in the hands of the rich country's
government. Now if the level of salaries which the poor government has
to pay and the level of prices which it faces with respect to the goods
which it buys are also considerably lower than the level of salaries and
prices relevant to the rich country's government this would not matter
too much for a similar percentage of total real output would be obtained.
But in most cases this is not the position. Governments of underdeveloped
countries very often have to pay salaries to expatriate officers which are
higher than salaries such officers would earn if they were employed in
their own (much richer) home countries. Perhaps more important has
been the effect the employment of expatriates has had on the salaries paid
to indigenous people having similar qualifications; such salaries have
tended to approximate to that of the expatriates and thus constitute a very
much higher proportion of the average national income of the country
than the salaries of expatriates constitute with respect to the average
national income of the countries from which they come. Similarly with
respect to goods. A substantial proportion of government expenditure in
a poor country goes on goods purchased from overseas at prices which
are in line with incomes in these countries. It follows that the same
percentage of a poor country's national income raised in taxation tends
to purchase a smaller proportion of available real output than the same

percentage of a rich country's national income. This factor is a very powerful influence in producing a great search for revenue in under-developed countries.

To a very substantial extent the level of public services which can be made available to a people depends on the wealth and productivity of the economy. If a country has only half the *per capita* income of another and that country is raising 15 per cent of GNP in taxation it would be necessary (ignoring the factors discussed in the previous paragraph) for the poor country to raise around 30 per cent of GNP in taxation if it is to approach the standard of public services available in the richer country. Similarly, if *per capita* incomes were one quarter of those of the richer country something like 60 per cent of GNP would be required. In the case of Nyasaland her level of *per capita* income is about one twentieth of that of the UK which makes it, of course, quite unrealistic for her to contemplate a UK level of public services — even though the UK may devote a high proportion of her public spending to defence.

There is, however, little doubt that the standard of service which is available in the richer parts of the world does tend to have an effect on the demand and desire for services in a poor country and thus the pressure builds up for more and more government expenditure. In considering this it has to be appreciated that in normal circumstances an increase in the level of government expenditure is only possible at the expense of private consumption or investment expenditure. It is necessary always to get behind the money veil and realise what the taxation and government expenditure transfers mean in terms of the use of real resources. It is necessary to compare the distribution and utilization of real resources at different levels of taxation and government expenditure. When one approaches the question in this way it often becomes obvious that an increase in government expenditure matched by a corresponding increase in taxation would *not* be beneficial from the point of view of the country concerned.

Now these considerations are outside my terms of reference but before beginning to answer the questions put to me I felt it necessary to express the view that it is not self evidently true that more and more government expenditure matched by more and more taxation is *necessarily* the best way to utilise the resources of a country.

II. SOME GENERAL CONSIDERATIONS

It is useful to begin by noting some of the general principles which are important when considering the application of taxes in underdeveloped countries; five sets of factors may be distinguished:

a. It is most important to keep the *costs of collection* as low as possible.
    Every penny spent in collecting revenue reduces the contribution
    that the revenue makes to financing useful expenditure. Three
    rather separate points may be made in this context. First, as the
    salaries of tax collecting and assessing officials are likely to be
    higher in an underdeveloped country than in a developed country
    in relation to average incomes the cost of collection point is
    particularly important. The second point is that it is desirable to
    make use of an existing administrative structure to obtain revenue
    or to increase the revenue rather than establish an entirely new
    organization. It is, therefore, usually more economic to increase
    an existing tax than to establish a new one and to impose taxes at
    points where the citizen is in contact with the administration
    anyway for non-tax reasons. Finally, it is always difficult and
    expensive to collect taxation if the people of the country
    fundamentally disagree with the system and level of taxation
    which is being imposed and this implies the need for a dynamic
    and informed leadership as well as a fair and enlightened public
    finance system.

b. The second consideration is the question of *Equity*. There are two
    issues here. In the first place there is the need to ensure that
    people in similar circumstances are treated alike, i.e. that some
    account is taken of the taxpayer's family responsibilities; that net
    and not gross income is taxed; and that income no matter how
    derived is taxed in a broadly similar way. The second point
    concerns the rate of progression. On the whole it is now generally
    accepted that the higher a person's income the higher the
    proportion of that income which should go to the State. There
    is, however, little agreement as to what is the appropriate rate of
    progression and economists have little special advice to offer on
    the question. At any moment of time it tends to be a matter for
    political decision in the light of some of the other considerations
    in this section and the general climate of opinion. One of the
    main taxation problems in underdeveloped countries is in fact
    the designing of a set of taxes which will satisfy these equity
    criteria and yet also be acceptable in the light of the other con-
    siderations — particularly from the cost of collection point of
    view.

c. The third group of factors to be taken into account may be put
    under the heading *Incentives*. The tax system must not be such as
    to impair the will to work either of people in salaried occupations
    or in business or in farming. Secondly, it must not be of a type

to inhibit the growth of productive investment either by domestic enterprises or by foreigners. Thirdly, the tax system must not be one that actively discourages saving. In other words in designing a tax system it is necessary to have in mind not only the need to raise revenue and so develop the public sector of the economy but also the need for economic growth in the private sector.

d. The fourth set of factors may be discussed under the heading *Democratic Association*. A number of issues are involved here. It is probably most desirable to make clear in people's minds the association between the taxation that they pay and the benefits they receive from government expenditure. The closer there is this link the more it is likely that people will be willing both to pay taxes (thus helping to keep down the cost of collection) and, perhaps more importantly, to work harder in order to earn to pay them. It has to be recognized, however, that it could work the other way and that people may not wish to have the products of government expenditure *and* the associated level of taxation. Faced with this possibility some economists have suggested that there is a case for a tax system which hides the burden of taxation (i.e. that indirect taxes are for this reason always to be preferred to direct taxes) in order to limit as much as possible opposition to the level of expenditure. This is, of course, essentially an un-democratic argument but in a period when great changes are required it is not necessarily to be rejected. It is believed, however, that if people can be shown the close association between items of government expenditure (and told of the effects such expenditures are likely to have on the development of the country) and the consequent need for taxation they will respond.

e. The final set of considerations are related to the need for the revenue to be *elastic* in an upward direction. There is considerable evidence to suggest that as the national income expands there is a tendency for the government sector to expand at a greater rate. This in turn implies the need for government revenue to expand. It is desirable that this should occur naturally and without the need for increases in tax rates and this can be achieved if the tax system is designed so that the marginal rate of tax is in excess of the average rate, i.e. that as incomes go up a higher proportion of the increase in income tends to flow into the hands of the government. It is, of course, equally desirable that the tax system should *not* be too elastic in a downward direction, for if the level of national income falls due to falling export prices or some natural catastrophe it is most unlikely that the level of government expenditures will tend to fall. Though in such circumstances modern fiscal theory would suggest the need for a large budget deficit the finance of such deficits often pose serious problems for underdeveloped countries.

It is clear that in some cases particular taxes will be judged favourable from one criterion and unfavourable from another. It may be, for example, that a particular sort of income tax may be thought desirable on equity grounds but expected to have bad incentive effects. Or, on the other hand, it may be that an export tax is judged desirable on cost of administration grounds but rejected for equity or incentive reasons. There is no such thing as an ideal tax or an ideal tax system. There are objectionable features with respect to all taxes. What is important is to choose the tax system which is least objectionable and what this implies is being fairly certain which of the criteria are of first importance at a given moment of time and which are only of second or third importance. If, for example, it is agreed that *equity* or *elasticity* considerations are not of first or even secondary importance the problem of choosing an appropriate set of taxes is much simplified.

III. TYPES OF TAXES

When considering how to classify taxes economists commonly make two sorts of division: first as between Direct and Indirect taxes and secondly as between Income and Outlay taxes. By Direct taxes is meant those taxes in which the tax payer is in direct contact (or in contact through corre-spondence) with the tax assessor or tax collector whereas Indirect taxes are those in which the taxpayer is not in direct contact. The second dis-tinction relates to taxes that fall on income independently of how that income is spent or indeed whether it is spent or not—Income Taxes—and those taxes liability for which only arises when one comes to spend money — Outlay taxes. To some extent the two sets of classification overlap; the taxes that are direct tend to be taxes on income and *vice versa*. The overlap is not, however, complete. In the case of export taxes, for example, the taxpayer is not in any sense in direct contact with the tax collector and under the first classification such taxes would rank as indirect taxes. The burden is, however, with respect to income and is in no sense associated with the expenditure pattern of the taxpayer. It would, there-fore, rank with the second classification as an income rather than an outlay tax. A similar division arises with respect to real property taxes such as rates. In this case the taxpayer is often in direct contact with the tax collecting authority and yet the liability depends in part at any rate, on the fact that the taxpayer has chosen to spend his money in a particular way, i.e. has chosen to live in a house of a particular character. For our purposes these two classifications are a little narrow and it will be convenient to divide taxes into the following six main categories and then look at them one by one:

A. Income Taxes
    1. On personal income
    2. On company income
B. Taxes on Foreign Trade
    1. On imports
    2. On exports
C. Taxes on Domestic Trade
    1. Excise taxes
    2. Sales taxes
    3. Cesses
D. Personal Taxes
E. Property Taxes
F. Fees, Licences, Charges.

IV. INCOME TAXES

By income taxes I mean taxes similar to the taxes of that name that are in existence in the UK and USA and, indeed, in the Federation of Rhodesia and Nyasaland. The characteristics of such taxes are:

a. With respect to Personal Income

   (i)   they do not weigh very heavily on taxpayers earning much below about £500 a year;

  (ii)   they are progressive with respect to incomes above the level at which they become effective;

 (iii)   there are very complicated legal provisions with respect to the definition of income, expenses, allowances, etc., an important object of which is to ensure that taxpayers in similar circumstances are treated alike;

 (iv)   for the effective administration of the tax considerable reliance is placed upon the honesty and competence of the taxpayer himself in providing details of his income, expenses, dependants, etc., to the tax collecting authority.

b. *Company Income.*— In this case the tax rate is usually proportional at a fairly high rate with respect to the undistributed income of the company. Again, there are very complicated legal provisions relating to the tax and the company itself has heavy responsibilities with respect to the preparation of the accounts upon which tax liability is based.

In connection with both personal and company taxes of this type there is need for a highly skilled and sophisticated tax administration and — as we have seen — considerable responsibility is imposed on the taxpayer with respect to assisting in the determination of his own tax liability which in turn means that he must be able to read and write — or employ those who can — and have some understanding of financial matters. I believe that an income tax of this type has a part to play in an under-developed economy. Such a tax, however, is only really suitable for literate taxpayers with fairly high incomes. The reason for this lies essentially in the cost of collection criterion that we noted above. It is not an economic proposition to carry the full apparatus of the income tax down to individuals earning relatively small incomes, nor to individuals who are unable to read or write. It follows that in most underdeveloped countries one cannot rely upon the income tax producing a large share of the country's revenue. It could only do this if one had the rather exceptional conditions of a country such as Northern Rhodesia in which large mining or plantation companies dominate the economic scene and make very large profits which can be taxed.

There is a case for having a (western type) income tax in order to deal fairly and effectively with the people in the country that do earn large incomes and the (mainly foreign owned or controlled) companies which make large profits. It would be wrong not to tax such individuals and companies up to the limit — the limit being set by considerations of incentives, equity, etc., but in a country with the economic characteristics of Nyasaland such taxes are unlikely to produce more than about 3 per cent of GNP in revenue.

It is, of course, possible up to a point to simplify the income tax: to reduce the rates of progression, to limit the allowances that can be claimed, have very simple, definite and inflexible rules as to what is and what is not a cost of production and to make very considerable use of taxation at the source devices and thus reduce the extent to which reliance has to be placed on self assessment procedures. Such devices should be used as much as possible but it has to be recognized that there are fairly drastic limits to the extent to which such simplifications can go without reducing some of the equity advantages of the tax which are one of its main features, and one of the reasons why it can be pressed so hard in favourable circumstances.

V. Taxes on Foreign Trade

From the point of view of raising revenue a country which has a high ratio of imports and exports to the Gross National Product is in a fortunate position. The reason for this is that the cost of collecting taxes levied on foreign trade is usually very low and — which amounts to the same thing — can be carried out fairly easily and without the need of large numbers of highly skilled and expensive staff. Taxes on commodities are most easily levied when there are a small number of channels through which the goods to be taxed have to pass. Imports and exports satisfy this criterion very well for they have to flow through ports or along main railway lines and roads. At these points they can be checked and taxed. Moreover imports and exports are usually handled by a small number of merchants and this in turn simplifies the administrative task as compared with taxing many domestically produced and purchased products.

If a country imports and exports 10 per cent of Gross National Product, i.e. the total of imports and exports represents 20 per cent of GNP, and a tax rate of 20 per cent is imposed on both imports and exports then this means that something like 4 per cent of the GNP flows to the government in the form of taxes on foreign trade. If a 50 per cent tax rate was imposed then some 10 per cent of the GNP would flow to the government. If on the other hand we are considering a country in which foreign trade is more important, i.e. in which imports and exports both amount to 25 per cent of the GNP, i.e. foreign trade in all represents 50 per cent of GNP then a 20 per cent tax rate on foreign trade would bring in 10 per cent of the GNP in tax revenue and a 50 per cent rate no less than 25 per cent of the GNP. In 1953, i.e. before federation, Nyasaland's exports amounted to about £7m, her imports to about £7m and her Gross Domestic Product to about £24m, i.e. value of foreign trade was about 60 per cent of domestic money incomes. With such a ratio of foreign trade to national output, Nyasaland was in a fairly strong position to raise revenues.

There are, of course, limitations to the rates of tax that can safely be imposed on foreign trade. Let us first consider *imports*.

The first consideration is the extent to which demand for the products concerned changes with respect to price. If a high rate of tax is imposed on a particular good consumption may fall and the flow of revenue be smaller than it might have been with a lower rate of tax. This possibility is likely when there are reasonable substitutes to the taxed commodity. It is quite often suggested in underdeveloped countries that rates of tax on very expensive motor cars should be very high. A less expensive motor car is, however, a fairly good substitute for a more expensive one and an

10

effect of discriminating heavily against the expensive type may be a reduction in the revenue. A second important consideration is the effect that high prices of imports may have on the overall cost of living and, in due course, upon the economic price of exports. This is perhaps not a very important point with respect to an economy like Nyasaland but there have been underdeveloped countries which, trying to establish their economies by building up exports, have to some extent priced themselves out of markets by taxing imports which have in turn produced a high cost export sector. On the other hand it should be remembered that the taxation of imports does tend to have a favourable effect on the local development of import substitute industries. The third consideration relates to the equity argument. Since an import duty enters into the price of goods it increases the cost of living and this affects the standard of living of everyone in the country. Now it is true that in most under-developed countries there is a high income elasticity with respect to imports, thus the lower one's income the lower the proportion of it that is spent on imports. This means that a standard rate import duty tends to be progressive, to some extent, with respect to income. It is also possible to tax commodities which are consumed by the better off sections of the community at very much higher rates of tax than the commodities which are consumed by less well off people. Nevertheless the inability to discriminate in favour of poor people or people with particularly large families suggests the need not to push import duties quite as far as might be considered desirable on cost of collection grounds. There is, too, always the danger of substantial smuggling occurring.

Even though there are objections to very high rates of customs duties it is believed that in many underdeveloped countries such duties are often too low. It is often forgotten that an import duty levied at 100 per cent on the import value may represent only an effective rate of 30 to 40 per cent at the retail level; and this is the effective point when considering the burden of such taxes with respect to the average level of incomes or marginal increases in them. Some governments are reluctant to levy rates of tax approaching or even exceeding 100 per cent on imports yet rates of this order on luxury articles are probably essential if governments are to raise the sums of money they need.

Export taxes.—On the whole, in African conditions export taxes fall upon the producers of the commodity concerned as in very few cases do the crops or commodities which are produced constitute a high propor-tion of total world output. In these conditions it is not possible to pass the tax forward to the consumer.

There are two main arguments against imposing heavy rates of export taxation. On the one hand such taxation tends to inhibit the production of export crops by reducing the yield to the producer and in most African countries an expansion of exports is a prerequisite for sound economic development. It is true that our knowledge of the response of producers — particularly African peasant producers — to the effects of changes in the net rate of return is pretty rudimentary but I believe it would be wrong to base policy on the belief that the *long run effect* of a decline would be favourable to output. The second argument is connected with the first. Taxes upon exports discriminate against export earnings as compared with income from other forms of production and are, therefore, inequitable. During the period of boom in Uganda producers earning their incomes from cotton and coffee growing were being taxed at a rate of about 40 per cent whereas individuals with similar pre-tax incomes making their living through producing food crops for the towns or engaged in cattle trading were not being taxed at all.

It is believed that there are two rather different arguments in favour of export taxes. First, relatively low rates of export taxation, say 5 per cent, may well be justified on cost of collection grounds, and such a rate is not likely to have a serious disincentive effect. Second, and in addition, there is a strong case for the existence of sliding scale export duties so that if there is a substantial rise in export prices a good part of these increased earnings are transmitted to the government. This can be justified on the ground that the gain is to some extent in the nature of a windfall; moreover, such taxes also have advantages from a stabilization point of view. On both counts care has to be taken not to press the tax so hard as to reduce the will to work and produce.

VI. Taxes on Domestic Production

Three rather different sorts of tax may be distinguished. First there are taxes — commonly called excise taxes — levied at fairly high rates (different rates) on a few commodities which are consumed in large quantity, e.g. taxes on beer and spirits, on tobacco and cigarettes, on sugar and, perhaps, on tea and coffee. In most underdeveloped countries such taxes are imposed; and they have the great advantage of being fairly easy and cheap to collect as production of such commodities is usually fairly localized. Again there are factors which set a limit to the amount which can be collected. In the case of taxes on drink if they become too high consumption is affected both by people reducing their alcoholic intake or by shifting to home-made brews. Similarly with tobacco. If 'factory' cigarettes are taxed too heavily there will be attempts in those areas in which tobacco can be grown for substitute 'home-made'

products to be manufactured. Such taxes may also tend to inhibit production particularly of the 'back-yard' type of enterprise. There is also a
degree of inequity about them which though probably acceptable in the
case of drink and tobacco is not so acceptable in the case of sugar and tea.
Nevertheless, there is a case for taxing home produced commodities that
have got a fairly inelastic demand and which can be caught at relatively
low costs, fairly heavily.

In many developed countries there are general sales or purchase taxes,
i.e. taxes levied at fairly low rates over all or most forms of production or
consumption. There are many varieties of this broad type of tax. Some are
levied at the retail stage; others at the wholesale or production end. Some
are 'single stage' taxes, i.e. if once levied on a portion of value added that
portion is then exempt from tax no matter how many further productive
processes the commodity may undergo; others are 'multi stage' or turnover taxes such that at every stage of production the gross value of sales
and not the value added is taxed. Some are confined to goods and exclude
services; some are all-embracing.

It seems very doubtful if these forms of taxation are desirable or
practicable in African conditions at the present time for they demand a
considerable degree of sophistication in the wholesaling or retailing sector
and a great deal of paper work. In a country with a very low ratio of
foreign trade to national product the need for revenue might force a
country to introduce such a tax, administrative costs and injustices not-
withstanding, but in a country with a good deal of foreign trade this
should not be necessary. Moreover, such a tax might well tend to encourage subsistence or barter transfers and generally inhibit the growth
of money transactions and the money economy.

Finally, we have to consider Produce Cesses. One of the great problems
in underdeveloped countries is to obtain tax revenue from poor farmers.
A high proportion of the national output comes from this sector of the
economy and unless it makes its contribution to the national exchequer
very small sums of tax revenue will be collected, and yet there are clearly
great difficulties in raising money from this sort of taxpayer. In the next
section we will look at what is perhaps the best way of doing this but it is
worth referring here to the method of having produce cesses which was
tried in East Africa, especially in Tanganyika and Kenya, during the post-
war period; though it should perhaps be stated that in perspective it cannot
be judged to have been particularly successful.

These cesses began by being concerned with 'controlled' produce, i.e.
produce that was necessarily sold through official markets at fixed prices.
As the produce came to market it was classified and weighed, on the basis
of which the price and tax to be received and paid was calculated. The

seller received the price net of tax and the actual tax was collected from the buyer later who was generally speaking a wholesaler or other intermediary. Later the system was adapted to deal with produce not subject to controlled prices. This was much more difficult and never worked really well.

One of the drawbacks with this sort of tax is that it can make no allowance for family responsibilities nor can it very easily be levied at other than proportional rates, or take notice of costs of production. There are also many opportunities for evasion and downright fraud and only in a very tightly controlled marketing system could it effectively operate. It is, however, important to bear this type of tax in mind as it does provide a way of getting at commodities which are important in domestic trade such as cattle and basic foodstuffs and this may well be necessary and desirable particularly if it is planned to impose export taxes at fairly high rates. It is perhaps worth mentioning here that very often the extent of domestic trade is underestimated — often because statistics are available for foreign trade and not for domestic trade or because (especially in colonial societies) the government is particularly interested in exports. May I illustrate this point with reference to some Uganda figures. Cotton and coffee sales completely dominate the export scene constituting some 85 per cent of total export earnings. It would, however, be wrong to think of cotton and coffee *completely* dominating the agricultural (and related) cash sectors. In 1959 the value of cotton and coffee sales amounted to about £27·5m. Other important sales were: food crops to urban Africans £0·6m; to non-Africans £1·6m; of cattle £5·6m; of milk £1·7m; of locally made beer £5·9m; and of fish £1·6m. In all, these sales amounted to a considerable sum of money and all of it a legitimate target for the tax collector. Clearly it would be wrong to tax the income accruing from exports because it is easy to tax and not that from domestic sales; and in the absence of a better and more comprehensive system of dealing with income arising from agricultural and related activities a case can be made out for produce cesses — even though they present formidable administrative problems.

VII. Personal Taxes

I referred above to the need to tax income arising in agriculture. In various parts of the world attempts have been made to do this by forms of land taxation. On the whole these have not been very successful — except, perhaps in Japan. The main reason for this is fairly obvious. Either land valuations must be revised frequently, which is expensive and uses personnel which are in very short supply, or else it must be accepted that only rough justice can be done as between taxpayers which tends to limit the amounts which can be collected. If a simple land tax with, say, only five possible values for each acre was generally acceptable to the public a considerable revenue might be collected from such a tax with little cost. But such simple taxes on the whole are not generally welcomed — and, of course, there are objections to them. It is not easy, for example, to take account of the differing family responsibilities of the taxpayer nor to deal with a man with income from a number of sources. On the other hand a tax which is related to the potential productivity of the land might well have an encouraging effect on production. However, in African conditions it is doubtful if a tax based on land valuations is really a practical proposition in view of the absence in many parts of the continent of any real system of individual tenure. I am fairly convinced myself that what is needed is a form of personal tax and would like to illustrate what I have in mind with reference to the type of tax which is in operation in Uganda.

By a personal tax I mean a 'simple' income tax, i.e. a tax the burden of which depends on the size of a person's income and which takes some cognizance of the differing obligations and family circumstances of the taxpayer — as with a 'proper' income tax — but which is relatively cheap and easy to collect and administer. A main object of the tax being to tax people (the great majority of the population) with incomes below the exemption level for the 'proper' income tax.

In most parts of Africa one of the first taxes to be imposed by the colonial rulers was a simple poll tax, with the objective both of raising revenue and stimulating work. Such taxes are very unsatisfactory. They cease to be at all equitable as soon, as with economic development, incomes become different. Secondly, as the rate cannot be raised above the ability to pay of the poorest a severe limit is put on the total revenue that can be raised. In a number of different parts of Africa, however — notably Tanganyika, Uganda and Nigeria — such poll taxes have evolved into simple income taxes, very often at the local authority level. In Uganda such a tax, known as the Graduated Tax, has been introduced as a local authority tax to such good effect that in 1958/9 it brought in over £3m which was nearly as much as the revenue in that year from the income tax; more than was collected through excise taxes; about half what was collected through duties in imports; and in all amounted to about 10/- per head of the total population.

The Uganda tax is administered as follows. A list is drawn up in each of the local authorities of the *main sources of income and wealth* in the area. These would include income from farming (by type of crop both for export, home sale and subsistence), from fishing, from cattle, goats and chickens, from milk and beer sales, from trading, transport, and manufacturing activities and income in the form of wages, salaries and pensions.

The next step is the crucial one of deciding on the method of aggregating the various types of income or income yielding assets. The basis of the calculation is the taxable capacity of wage or salary income and an attempt is made to apply reasonable and consistent conversion rates for other types of 'income'. In the case of a crop such as coffee each tree is assumed — on the basis of realistic calculations — to yield, say, 3/– a year in income. Similar calculations determine appropriate conversion rates for other crops — both those grown for sale and those used for subsistence. There is a tendency to pitch the conversion rates somewhat below the level that could be achieved by an average farmer on average land so as to encourage output and it is always possible, at the time of individual assessment, for a taxpayer to plead that his land or his trees are below average quality. A similar procedure is followed with respect to livestock. The possession of a cow, for example, is assumed to yield, say, 15/– a year (even though in Uganda cattle are not for the most part owned for their income producing value) and corresponding values are established for goats, etc. In the case of income derived from trading or transport activities a consistent and reasonable method is used. The stock of shops, for example, may be valued and a ratio between income and stock of, say, 2 : 1 assumed in order to arrive at estimates of income arising. The broad object of all these calculations being to provide a basis so that the various sources of income or potential income of individual taxpayers can be aggregated.

Having ascertained in this way the incomes of the various taxpayers rates of tax can be declared and imposed. These may be progressive. A given percentage may be levied on taxpayers having £50 a year and higher percentages on those with incomes between £50 and £100 and those with incomes between £100 and £150 — and so on. It is also possible to take note of the number of persons dependent on a particular income and even of special claims upon it, e.g. school fees and medical charges.

There are two main distinguishing features of this type of tax. In the first place there is the attempt to bring into the tax net most of the items that affect taxable capacity even though they do not directly lead to a flow of money income. This is not only more equitable than a system which relies only on taxing money income but also permits a higher revenue to be collected. The way this is done has advantages from an administration point of view as well. It is often easier to take account of the fact that a man has so many coffee trees or acres of a particular crop under cultivation than to find out the money income which he has derived from sales in a given year. This applies particularly to crops which are grown for the domestic economy and to cattle and livestock. The second important characteristic of this type of tax is that assessments are made not on the basis of declarations or returns — as with an ordinary income tax — but by local assessment committees who judge following a consistent and recognized procedure a man's taxable capacity and finally determine his assessed income and thus his tax liability. This has the advantage that a man's assessment does not depend on his honesty or his ability to complete forms; the taxpayer need not be literate and no expensive administration is required. On the other hand there is clearly the possibility of abuse and a proper system for appeals is required.

Though such a tax could be operated by the Central Government, I believe there are strong reasons for linking such a tax to local authority needs. If the local assessment committees are concerned with raising money for local purposes and know the area well it seems more likely that the system will be operated with justice and efficiency. On the one hand the members of the committees will have personal knowledge of the general standard of living of an area and, therefore, be in a better position to determine relative taxable capacity — they may also be able to use the evidence of a person's standard of living and consumption as a means of determining his taxable income and capacity. On the other hand the taxpayer will feel that his affairs are being examined by people familiar with his problems and difficulties and may feel a more direct or positive willingness to be assessed and taxed if the proceeds are to go to meet local needs.

A possible disadvantage of making this sort of tax a local authority tax is that it may be too successful with the effect of providing local authorities with too much money in relation to the services they are expected to provide — and leaving the central government with too little. In Uganda until recently a maximum of £20 was laid down. Clearly there are many fiscal devices, e.g. laying down that a share — perhaps an increasing or declining share — of all collections should go to the central government, for keeping the yield to the local authorities under control and for ensuring that the central government is not penalized unduly.

Our discussion so far in this section has been directed to the special problems of rural areas, important distinguishing features of which being the need to take note of features which increase a person's taxable capacity though not necessarily his flow of money income and the fact that a taxpayer's assessed income has to be arrived at by adding up the income he has received from a number of different sources. The extent to which a tax similar to the Uganda graduated tax is needed for urban areas varies from country to country. In some underdeveloped countries urban areas are so big that it is doubtful if such a tax could operate — or is needed. A high proportion of the income that needs to be taxed is wage/salary income and it is probably better to deal with it by a straight wage tax at source rather than through direct assessment. A simple percentage tax on a weekly or monthly basis (depending on which is the normal pay period) is probably the best way of taxing the poor workers in the towns: no attempt needs to be made to organize it on an annual basis. If desired the tax can be progressive — a wage of 100/- a month being taxed at, say, 1 per cent and a wage of 200/- at 2 per cent and, though with much greater administrative difficulty, an attempt can be made to have different rates for taxpayers with similar monthly incomes but differing family responsibilities. The taxpayer would receive a card showing his tax payments and this would be evidence against 'rural' tax obligations if he were to return to the country. Urban income other than that arising in the form of wages and salaries would mainly be profits from trade or manufacturers or from running a transport business. At the income levels we are considering (i.e. levels below that at which the 'proper' income tax becomes effective) such incomes might be taxed by a payroll tax, i.e. so much tax per person employed, or through a property tax. Alternatively, he could be compelled — as with a proper income tax — to declare his profits and be taxed at the current tax for wages. Clearly there are administrative snags with this but these would not be so serious if such a tax was confined to urban areas.

In some underdeveloped countries — and Nyasaland may be one — the size and population of the urban areas may be so small as not to necessitate any special action; the type of tax applicable to rural areas can be applied without much amendment in the urban areas.

With both the graduated tax in the rural districts and the wage tax in the towns a problem arises when the incomes of taxpayers approach the level at which they become liable for 'proper' income tax. Though in many ways it is an irrational emotive response many taxpayers react very strongly to anything which smacks of 'double taxation'. To have one's income taxed under both a personal tax and a 'proper' income tax often produces strong adverse public criticism. There are many ways in which this can be dealt with equitably: a useful one is to allow payments of personal tax as an offset to income tax liability; in this way no real injustice will arise and public antagonism will be avoided.

I have no desire to be dogmatic concerning types of personal tax. What it is desired to stress is the need to obtain a large total revenue from general (i.e. excluding taxes such as export taxes) direct taxation from individuals who are too poor and illiterate to be taxed through an orthodox income tax. In a poor country such individuals — say with below £500 a year — must surrender a substantial portion of their incomes to the State. The need for a large contribution from general *direct* taxation, i.e. from taxes related to income and taxable capacity rather than to expenditure or outlay, arises for two main reasons. First, that through such a tax, unlike an indirect or outlay tax, it is possible to take account of many of the factors that influence taxable capacity including family responsibilities and — which is so important in African conditions — the possession of assets and the consumption of unmarketed produce. Second, it is possible to do much more with a direct tax than with even a complicated system of indirect taxes to make the tax structure somewhat progressive. Not only is this desirable on equity grounds but it is also necessary if really large sums of money are to be raised. My conclusion here is that I do not see how an underdeveloped country can do without a simple direct tax. To discuss the details of the form of such a tax most appropriate for particular countries would go outside the scope of the present paper.

VII. Property Taxes

There are a number of different sorts of property tax. Almost certainly there is a limited role for such taxes in African underdeveloped countries but on the whole it is doubtful if they are going to be particularly important as revenue raisers.

In the previous section I referred to two types of property tax. I suggested that a tax based on land valuations was not likely to be very successful in African conditions as a means of taxing income arising from agricultural activities. On the other hand I suggested that a property tax might well be a suitable tax in urban conditions. There is, of course, a long tradition in the African towns and cities that have had a link with the UK of financing a good part of their expenditure out of a local property tax. Such taxes have taken a number of different forms. Some have been taxes based on the annual value (rent) of the properties; others have been based on the capital value of the properties. And in turn there were variants on each of these. Some were linked to current use values of the land and buildings combined: some to a hypothetical unimproved site value basis. This is not the occasion for a full discussion of the problems of urban property taxation and I propose just to make two brief points. First that there is a good case for levying such taxes. Not only do citizens and businesses in the towns usually enjoy many services not available to citizens elsewhere, but citizens occupying property in the urban areas tend to have and might be expected to have a very considerable taxable capacity. Moreover such taxes are common throughout the world and are expected by such occupiers. The second point is to state my opinion that on balance a capital value basis is better in an underdeveloped country and that there is a good case for a divided rate structure — one rate falling on the value of the building and the other (higher) rate falling on the unimproved site value. This dual system provides both an encouragement to the development of sites and yet, by including the existing use value, both ensures a greater stability in the yield and takes into account specifically taxable capacity.

Other types of property tax are death duties, annual capital taxes, capital gains taxes and capital levies. It is considered that there is little to be said concerning such taxes with reference to an African underdeveloped country. A striking characteristic of the African economic scene in the areas without major concentrations of expatriates is the small amount of capital. A major task is to develop the stock of real capital and, also, establish some modest holdings of private wealth. There are few great fortunes and concentrations of wealth and no real problem of waste through large scale conspicuous spending. It is believed there may be a case for death duties but on the whole scarce administrative skills can probably be much better utilized than in thinking about or designing capital taxes; and it is not proposed to discuss them further here.

Clearly, the above paragraph reflects in part an implicit belief that private or capitalist enterprise is expected to play a considerable part in the development process. If this is not the case and state enterprise is expected to be the dominant element then, of course, the need for private holdings of wealth is that much reduced.

IX. FEES, LICENCES, CHARGES

We now come to fees, licences and charges. It is believed that it is necessary and desirable in underdeveloped countries to raise considerable sums of money from these sources. In the case of licences, e.g. driving licences, motor vehicle licences, trading licences, etc., it seems important given that such licences have to be issued for administrative reasons to raise something more than purely nominal sums of money from them. In this way cost of collection and administrative expenses generally will be reduced to a minimum. As regards charges the position is a little more complicated. First of all there is a strong case for charging the full economic cost for the services provided by the government which are not of a directly social character. I am thinking here of postal services, and the provision of public services such as electric power, water, transport and rented housing. If an economic charge is not levied for these services it follows that they constitute a burden upon the overall budget which in turn means that the cost is spread generally throughout the economy through taxation. In exceptional circumstances there may be a case for not charging the full price but given the great shortage of revenue the balance is normally in favour of charging the full economic price — and perhaps even a little more. When it comes to the main social services such as education and health the position is a little more complicated but here again it is thought that if society is not sufficiently rich to make such services readily available to everybody then there is a good case for using the price mechanism; both as part of the machinery of deciding who shall enjoy them, and in order to help finance them. In the case of higher education — including within this term education leading to the higher school certificate — a good case can be made out for charging and making available loans which can be repaid after the students have taken up their jobs.

Certain advantages may follow an emphasis on licences and charges. In each case the so-called 'voluntary principle' is involved. The citizen is not forced or compelled to take out a licence or pay the charge. If he therefore does so it is because in part at any rate he feels it is worth it. Such 'taxes' tend to have a favourable effect on incentives as the goods and services for which charges and licences are made and issued tend to be in strong demand. Another advantage of using charges as part of the rationing process for services in short supply is that if people are prepared to pay for something this is evidence that the something is prized and this may ensure that services are not misused or over expanded. I am well aware of the considerable number of arguments that can be deployed against using charges and licences to raise considerable sums of money but am not entirely convinced of their validity in very poor countries.

A discussion of licences and charges takes us very near the question of 'assigned taxes'. Though on the whole most unpopular with fiscal experts there is a good deal of evidence that taxes imposed with the explicit intention of helping to finance a particular service — usually a social service — and named accordingly (e.g. Social Insurance Contribution, Education Tax, Health Service Levy, etc.) are regarded with less disfavour by the public than most ordinary taxes and probably have less disincentive effects. Whilst appreciating the orthodox fiscal arguments against it — it is uneconomic, misleading and confusing to tie or appear to tie a given piece of expenditure to a particular tax — it is believed that up to a point these considerations are offset by the other factors we have mentioned and that there may well be a case for special 'assigned' taxes and levies.

X. ANSWERS

My answer to the second question put to me will be clear from the fore-going paragraphs and there is little more to be said at this stage:

a. Orthodox personal and company taxes should be used up to the limit compatible with cost of collection and incentive considerations. It is believed, however, that these considerations make it unlikely that large sums of money will be raised by such taxes in underdeveloped countries that do not have large expatriate mining, plantation or settler sectors.

b. The cost of collection criterion justifies the fairly severe taxation of foreign trade. We noted, however, some factors which put effective limits on the amounts of revenue which should be raised — particularly through export taxes — in this way.

c. In considering taxes on domestic trade it was considered that there was a good case for fairly heavy excise duties on such commodities as drink and tobacco and, perhaps, on tea and sugar. On the whole it was not thought that general sales taxes or produce cesses were likely to be particularly useful revenue raisers in African conditions — though it was noted that in those countries in which foreign trade was not very important they might have to be imposed.

d. Great emphasis was put on the need for a personal tax. It was argued that it was important to have suitably designed direct taxes to bring in substantial sums of money from individuals with incomes well below the level at which an orthodox income tax can be operated economically. The great need in African conditions to raise considerable sums of money from poor farmers was emphasized and it was suggested that a tax similar to the graduated tax in Uganda seemed to be valuable in this connection. In large urban areas a simple wages tax might be useful.

e. Except for raising revenue from the occupiers of urban land and buildings there does not seem a great deal of scope for property taxes.

f. It was argued that a good case existed in African conditions for:
   (i) raising revenue from licences;
   (ii) charging at least the full cost for public utility type services;
   (iii) making some charges for medical and education services;
   (iv) making at least a limited use of 'assigned' taxes.

g. In connection with a number of ways of gathering revenue — notably personal taxes — it was pointed out that there were advantages in having them operated as local authority measures.

It is not easy to give a clear answer to the first question. Some relevant qualitative observations have been made with respect to the problem of raising a given percentage of the national product:

a. The existence of a substantial group of persons and companies who can be reached through an orthodox income tax simplifies the problem.

b. As does a high ratio of foreign trade to national product.

c. Good political leadership and an understanding of and sympathy throughout the country for what the government is trying to do enables more income to be raised at less cost. This is particularly important as regards personal taxes, charges, and special 'assigned' taxes.

There are a number of other relevant considerations.

a. Taxable capacity depends in part on the use that is made of the tax proceeds:

(i) the higher the proportion of government expenditure that is spent overseas the more difficult it tends to be to raise a given percentage of the Gross Domestic Product in taxation for the circular flow of income and expenditure and taxation is then broken.

(ii) the higher the proportion of government expenditure that goes in the form of transfer payments and does not directly employ or utilize real resources the easier it is on the whole to raise a given percentage of the GDP in taxation for in this case 'taxable' income tends to exceed the GDP thus making a given set of taxation measures more effective.

b. Whatever may be the long run taxable capacity of a country at a given moment of time it does not follow that such a level of taxation could quickly be reached from an existing much lower level. There are always serious obstacles — political, administrative, and economic (I am thinking under this heading mainly of incentive considerations) — to a rapid increase in the burden of taxation. What may be possible in the long run — over a five to ten year period — may be impossible all at once. Some things, of course, help to increase the rate at which the current level of taxation can be brought nearer the capacity limit (and, perhaps, help to increase the capacity level itself). If the level of *per capita* incomes is rising either through increases in domestic productivity or through an improvement in the terms of trade it becomes easier to increase the average rate of taxation; for in taking a larger share of a bigger total the government is still able to leave the taxpayer in a better position than he was before the 'improvement' and the tax change.

It is not easy to move from the general considerations of the two previous paragraphs to a conclusion as regards the percentage of its GNP that an underdeveloped country might raise in revenue. To approach appropriate orders of magnitude it is perhaps useful to note the experiences of two African countries — Uganda and Tanganyika — whose basic economic characteristics are not dissimilar to those of Nyasaland — though, of course, they are both much larger countries. (The figures quoted in the next four paragraphs are designed merely to indicate the broad orders of magnitude; no attempt has been made to put them on an exactly comparable basis.)

In 1959 Uganda had a Gross Domestic Product of about £150m and a Gross Money Product of about £108m. Having a population of about 6·5m there was, therefore, a *per capita* GDP of about £23 and a money product of about £17. Imports and exports amounted to about £80·5m, giving a foreign trade/GDP ratio of about 54 per cent and a foreign trade/money product ratio of about 74 per cent. During the financial year 1958/9 the total revenue collected by the central government on current account amounted to about £21·4m, i.e. about 14 per cent of GDP and 20 per cent of money product. It included the following:

Item	Amount £m	Percentage of GDP	Percentage of Money Product
Income tax	3·5	2·3	3·2
Export tax	5·9	3·9	5·5
Customs duties	5·1	3·4	4·7
Excise taxes	2·2	1·5	2·0
Licences	0·6	0·4	0·6
Court fees	1·2	0·8	1·1
Rents and charges	1·0	0·7	0·9

A further £4·0m was collected by the local authorities, i.e. 2·7 per cent of GDP and 3·7 per cent of money product. Of this total £3·3m was collected through the graduated tax and most of the rest through licences, fees and charges.

Thus in 1959 the central and local governments in Uganda collected on current account about £25·4m which constituted some 17 per cent of

GDP and some 23·5 per cent of money product, amounting in all to about £3·9 per capita.

In 1958 Tanganyika had a GDP of about £174m and a gross money product of about £104m. With a population of about 8·8m this implies a per capita GDP of about £20 and a per capita money product of about £12. Imports and exports amounted to about £89m, giving a ratio foreign trade to GDP of 51 per cent and a ratio foreign trade to money product of 85 per cent. During the financial year 1957/8 central government revenue amounted to about £19·4m, i.e. some 11·2 per cent of GDP and 18·6 per cent of money product. The revenue included:

Item	Amount £m	Percentage of GDP	Percentage of Money Product
Income tax	3·5	2·0	3·4
Personal tax	1·3	0·7	1·2
Other direct taxes	0·6	0·3	0·6
Customs duties	6·7	3·8	6·4
Excise duties	2·1	1·2	2·0
Licences	1·1	0·6	1·1
Charges for goods and services	1·3	0·7	1·2
Property income	1·8	1·0	1·7

A further £2·5m was collected by the local authorities (of which about £0·6m was in the form of produce cesses) constituting 1·4 per cent of GDP and 24 per cent of money product.

Thus in 1957/8 some £22m was collected in current revenue constituting some 13 per cent of GDP and 21 per cent of money product; in all amounting to some £2·5 per capita.

It would be wrong to try and build too much on these examples from Uganda and Tanganyika. I would like to make two points:

a. The figures suggest that a taxation/GDP ratio of around 15 per cent and a taxation/money product ratio — which in many ways is the better figure to take for comparative purposes as there are such differences in the way subsistence output is calculated — of around 20 per cent can be achieved in African countries which are poor and which do not have a dominant expatriate sector. It will be noted, however, that both countries have a substantial foreign trade ratio.

b. I am convinced from my knowledge of the economic and fiscal situation of the two countries in 1959 and 1958 that the revenue limit had *not* been reached. In Tanganyika, for example, I believe that £1·5m to £2·5m could have been raised in export taxation. I believe that in both countries more revenue could have been squeezed from income tax — particularly from companies — and from import duties and excise duties without causing any economic damage. I also believe that the graduated tax in Uganda and the personal tax in Tanganyika could have been pressed harder without adverse economic consequences.

It is doubtful if it is possible to be at all precise as regards what constitutes taxable capacity. The most useful meaning that can be given to the concept is probably something like this. That it is: the maximum percentage of the GNP that can be collected in taxation without certain undesirable phenomena such as revolution (or serious political unrest), inflation, reduced rates of growth, etc., occurring as a result or consequence. This is rather vague but does, I think, convey the gist of what is usually in mind when economists and others speak of taxable capacity.

Earlier in the paper I have indicated a large number of factors that are relevant in determining or influencing taxable capacity. In conclusion I would hesitate to offer more than a negative view. I believe that the government of even a poor African country with, say, a *per capita* income of around £20 would not find it impossible over the long run to raise 20 to 25 per cent of GDP (and perhaps as much as 30 per cent of money product) without producing serious adverse economic effects so long as the government commands the support of the people *and* there is a fairly high ratio of foreign trade to domestic product.

XI. NYASALAND FOOTNOTE

There are three features of the contemporary Nyasaland economic and fiscal scene which require emphasis when considering questions of taxable capacity, and related matters. They will be no more than noted here; almost certainly they will be discussed at length during the symposium.

It would seem that the subsistence sector is a very high proportion of the GDP. In 1959 out of a GDP of about £53·0m some £27·0m was from the subsistence sector. (Subsistence income as defined by the official statisticians does not entirely exclude monetary transactions: it includes those within the African rural economy.) This poses serious problems for a government wishing to raise a high percentage of the GDP in taxation and suggests the need for a special concentration on taxes which can take some account of non-monetary income — such as a Uganda type graduated tax — and on measures which may stimulate the demand for money income such as charging for social services. (With a population of about 2·8m GDP *per capita* in 1959 was about £19 and *per capita* money product about £9.)

A striking characteristic of the Nyasaland economy is, of course, the high proportion, the working population that is employed outside the country. In 1956 some 309,000 Nyasas were employed in the Federation: only 155,000, however, were employed in Nyasaland; the rest having jobs in Southern Rhodesia and Northern Rhodesia. These employees outside the country remit money to Nyasaland which though not part of the GDP is, of course, part of the total of Personal Income and represents income which can be taxed. In 1957 (the last year for which I have figures) these migrants' remittances were estimated at £1·7m and amounted to about 12 per cent of total African personal incomes in the country — the remainder consisting of wages and salaries at £7·2m and profits of unincorporated businesses at £5·2m. Given the general poverty of the country these remittances should bear their share not only of the indirect taxes which are levied but also of the direct taxes — even though the factor incomes from which they have been derived may already have suffered direct taxation in the country in which they have been earned.

We referred earlier (part V, 2nd para.) to the fact that in 1953, before federation, foreign trade at £14m constituted some 127 per cent of gross money income and, probably, about 60 per cent of GDP. In the absence of federation it seems reasonable to suppose that these ratios would have continued to exist and this emphasis on foreign trade would have provided a good basis for the imposition of import and export taxes. With federation, however, Nyasaland ceased to have any direct responsibility as regards the fixing of customs duties: these became a federal responsibility. Another effect of federation was to alter the effective tariff structure with respect to imports into Nyasaland which has probably had the effect of increasing the share of 'imports' coming from her partners in the Federation.

With federation, too, the income tax became a federal responsibility (though individual territories may themselves levy a limited surcharge on the income tax payable to the federal government). Excise duties also became a federal tax.

There are, of course, offsetting fiscal benefits from federation. The Nyasaland Government receives through the federal public finance machine 6 per cent of the total federal proceeds of the income tax and customs and excise duties. Nyasaland also gains from the various services provided by the Federal Government in and on behalf of Nyasaland. Indeed it has been suggested by two informed and sympathetic observers (A. Hazlewood and P. D. Henderson, *Nyasaland: The Economics of Federation*) that Nyasaland benefits fairly substantially from these fiscal transfers. What it is desired to emphasize here, however, are the following two points:

a. An effect of federation has been to deprive Nyasaland of considerable fiscal autonomy and freedom: the range of choices open to the Nyasaland Government and Parliament has been narrowed very considerably.

b. The second point, of course, is to emphasize how the present position of Nyasaland with respect to the Federation makes it difficult to appraise fully her future fiscal position. Though it seems almost certain that Nyasaland will leave the Federation it is not impossible that after succession Nyasaland will be able to negotiate agreements with some of the other countries of East or Central Africa which might enable her — in return perhaps for certain trade concessions — to receive some financial help. Such an agreement might also have the effect of putting certain limits on her fiscal freedom. Without knowing in some detail the content of such developments it is too hazardous to offer a view on the proportion of domestic product that might be raised in taxation.

THE CHOICE OF TAXES IN DEVELOPING COUNTRIES

BY NICHOLAS KALDOR

Fellow of Kings College, University of Cambridge, UK

I. GENERAL INTRODUCTION

The question posed above does not admit of any general answer. The only feature that is common to 'underdeveloped' countries is that they all suffer from a shortage of revenue, and that their 'taxation potential' is rarely *fully* exploited — though the extent to which the amounts raised in taxation could be augmented through a reform of the tax system varies greatly as between different countries.

The 'taxation potential' of a country — defined as the maximum proportion of its national income that could be diverted for public purposes by means of taxation — is obviously greatly dependent on (i) real income per head; (ii) the degree of inequality in the distribution of income; (iii) the sectoral distribution of the national income, and the social and institutional setting in which the output of particular sectors is procured; (iv) the administrative competence, etc., of the tax-gathering organs of the Government.

It is a commonplace to say that taxes can only be paid out of the 'economic surplus' — the excess of production over the minimum subsistence needs of the population. Moreover, in so far as such surplus is not consumed by the people to whom it accrues, but is saved and invested, it can only be made available for the purposes of public expenditure at the cost of reducing the rate of capital accumulation of the community, which in turn is bound to react adversely on the country's economic development — unless the capital investment which is reduced thereby itself served the purposes of inessential or 'luxury' consumption (such as luxury housing). It would be more correct to say therefore that the taxation potential of a country depends on the *excess of its actual consumption over the minimum essential consumption of the population.*

In practice, however, the 'minimum essential consumption' of a community cannot be defined or measured; it is not just a matter of the strict biological requirements of subsistence (which themselves vary greatly with climate and location) but of social conventions and habits, and the actual standard of living to which the *bulk of the population* of any particular community has become accustomed. Since governments ultimately depend on the consent of the people whom they govern, it is impossible as a matter of policy to compress, by means of taxation, the actual standard of living of the mass of the population outside fairly narrow limits. If this were not so, the taxation potential would vary enormously with the actual level of real income per head. Supposing this potential were 10 per cent in a country with an income per head of £20 a year, it would be no less than 82 per cent in a country whose income per head is £100 a year. Yet even in the richest countries with the highest incomes per head find it very difficult to raise more than 30–35 per cent of their GNP in taxation.

It is for this reason that the taxation potential of any country is strongly dependent on the prevailing inequality in the distribution of the national income, which in turn is closely linked to the relative importance of incomes derived from property, as against income derived from work, and to the degree of concentration in the ownership of property. As between two countries with the same real income per head, the accustomed standard of living of the bulk of the population will evidently be the lower in the country in which a larger share of total incomes accrues to a minority of wealthy individuals.

From this point of view the underdeveloped countries of different regions of the globe (or even individual countries within the same region) show the widest differences. At one end of the scale a country such as India, with a very low income per head of population, has a high ratio of property income in total income (a ratio that is comparable to that of the country with the highest income per head, the United States) and in consequence has a relatively high taxation potential in relation to real income per head.[1] (In many of the countries of Latin America the share of the national income accruing to property owners is higher than in any European or North American country, and the proportion of the GNP that is taken up by their consumption may be three to four times that of the corresponding ratio in highly developed countries such as the US or the UK.) At the other end of the scale there are some underdeveloped countries (particularly in Africa) in which incomes derived from property ownership are relatively insignificant and in which a wealthy property-owning class can hardly be said to exist. From the point of view of 'taxation potential' the African countries thus appear to be less favourably placed, in relation to real income per head, than the countries of Asia or Latin America.

[1] Although the 'coefficient of utilization' of that potential appears to be rather low.

It is possible on the other hand that the amount of food produced in a country could be limited, not by the availability of natural resources (land) or by knowledge or ability, but by the immediate needs of the agricultural population, who prefer to have maximum leisure and a minimum of material income, and therefore work just hard enough to cover their immediate and essential needs. In such circumstances additional taxes levied on them would tend to make them work harder and produce more — i.e., to reduce their leisure, rather than their standards of material consumption. Taxation would then act as an incentive to produce more (rather than force the people to consume less) and this may not encounter the same kind of resistance, particularly if the increase on taxation is a gradual one. From this point of view, the countries of Africa — where, in general, shortage of land is not a critical factor in agricultural production — are more favourably placed than the underdeveloped countries of Asia.

There are some underdeveloped countries which, while they lack a domestic property-owning class, have important foreign enterprises in their territory (for the exploitation of valuable minerals or the product of plantations), so that a considerable share of their gross *domestic* product accrues to non-residents. Since the right of a country to tax all income arising within its jurisdiction is now firmly established, this provides a source of taxation that is essentially similar to that of a wealthy domestic property owning class. There is a danger, however, that owing to the comparative ease with which this source can be tapped (by means of export duties, or taxes on income and profits) such taxation may be carried to the point where it inhibits the development of export industries which may be vital to the development of the economy.[2] On the other hand many underdeveloped countries have recently been competing with one another in according all kinds of tax privileges and immunities to newly established foreign enterprises in an attempt to attract foreign capital to their own territory, with adverse consequences on their ability to collect revenue. Whilst it can plausibly be argued that an underdeveloped country gains from the inflow of foreign capital even if the income accruing from the investments is left untaxed — owing to the wage and salary incomes generated as a result, and the increased export earnings — it is an uncertain matter how far the total flow of capital investment from the developed to the underdeveloped areas is enhanced in consequence of such policies, and if it is not, such 'beggar-my-neighbour' policies of

---

[2] It is said, for example, that the excessive taxation of the foreign owned copper mines in Chile was largely responsible for the decline in the share of Chile in the world copper market.

stimulating development deprive the underdeveloped countries of revenue without any compensating benefit.[3]

Underdeveloped countries differ also as regards the relative magnitude of the 'non-monetized' or subsistence sector, and the 'monetized' or market-exchange sector, as well as the nature of the prevailing type of enterprise in each. The most appropriate forms of taxation will be different in an economy where commercial and manufacturing activities are carried on by small traders than in one where they are concentrated in the hands of large-scale business enterprises. Similarly, the prevailing forms of land tenure, the nature of social and family relationships, the extent of economic inequality, etc., call for differing methods of taxation of the subsistence sector. The general tendency in most underdeveloped countries is to throw a disproportionate share of the burden of taxation on the 'monetized' or market sector, and an insufficient amount on subsistence agriculture. The reasons for this are partly administrative and partly political — taxes levied on the agricultural community are far more difficult to assess and collect, and are socially and politically unpopular because they appear unjust — the people in the 'subsistence sector' are, individually, always so much poorer than the people in the market sector. Yet for reasons set out below, it is the taxation of the agricultural sector that has a vital role to play in accelerating economic development; the disproportionate taxation of the 'monetized' or market sector tends to retard economic progress by reducing both the sources and the incentives to accumulation.

Our general conclusion then is that the question 'which taxes are the most appropriate for maximum revenue of an underdeveloped country?' can only be answered in concrete terms in the light of the particular circumstances of each individual country. The main considerations that are relevant in this connexion are: (i) the forms of land tenure, and the distribution of land ownership; (ii) the nature of enterprises in the so-called 'secondary' and 'tertiary' sectors of the economy; (iii) the role of foreign enterprise; (iv) the nature of exports and of imports; (v) the competence of the administrative organs of the Government.

In the remainder of this paper I shall examine the implications of the above considerations under four separate heads: (1) the taxation of the

[3] Any *particular* country with unexploited natural resources will normally stand to gain by the offer of such tax concessions, since this will tend to attract capital and enterprise that would otherwise have been attracted to some other country. Its gain, however, may be at the expense of some other under-developed country which is deprived of foreign investment as a result. This necessarily leads to an unhealthy competition between different under-developed countries in the offer of such tax concessions which will thus collectively impair their revenue without benefiting any of them, since the competing concessions offered largely cancel out each other. The remedy to this lies in international agreements among the under-developed countries themselves limiting the nature and scope of such concessions.

agricultural sector; (2) taxes on commodities (customs and excise, export duties, a general sales tax); (3) direct taxes on income and capital; (4) compulsory savings; (5) problems of tax administration.

II. The Taxation of the Agricultural Sector

The most important common feature of underdeveloped countries is that a high proportion of the total population is occupied in the so-called 'primary' or subsistence agricultural sector; indeed the proportion of the population engaged in the provision of food supplies for domestic use is the best available index of the stage of economic development of a country. In the poorest and most backward economies it reaches 80–90 per cent; in the relatively poor but semi-developed economies it is around 40–60 per cent; in the highly developed areas it is 10 per cent or less. This means that as development proceeds, the proportion of the working population engaged in producing food is steadily reduced, and the proportion engaged in manufacturing, commerce and services is steadily increased. In order to make this possible the proportion of food produced on the land which is *not* consumed by the food producers must steadily increase; this in turn inevitably involves that each family engaged in food production should sell a steadily larger part of its output for consumption outside the agricultural sector. Unless this happens it is impossible for the non-agricultural sector to expand so as to occupy an increasing proportion of the community's man-power. Such an expansion of the 'agricultural surplus' cannot be relied upon to arise automatically as part of the overall process of growth in the economy. Economic incentives do not operate in the same way in the 'subsistence sector' as in the case of industry and commerce. A shortage of food is not likely to call forth increased production; a rise in the price of locally produced food may even lead to a *decrease* of the amounts which are offered for sale since it may cause the agricultural families to reduce their amount of work (or increase their own consumption) if their own needs for things which can only be procured with money can now be satisfied in exchange for a smaller quantity of foodstuffs. But since, on account of the nature of food as a primary necessity, a very large part (and if necessary an increasing part) of the urban worker's income is spent on food, it is the supply of foodstuffs to the non-agricultural sectors which limits the effective demand for the products of those sectors. Hence it is the growth of the demand for labour outside agriculture which is limited by the proportion of food production which goes to the market (as against the food consumed by the food producers themselves) and not the other way round.

It follows that the taxation of agriculture, by one means or another, has a critical role to play in the acceleration of economic development since it is only *the imposition of compulsory levies on the agricultural sector itself* which enlarges the supply of 'savings' for economic development in the required sense. Countries as different in their social institutions or economic circumstances as Japan and Soviet Russia have been similar in their dependence on heavy agricultural taxation (in the case of Japan, through a land tax, in the case of Soviet Russia, through a system of compulsory deliveries at low prices) for financing their economic development.

An annual tax on land, expressed as a percentage of the value of the produce per acre, is the most ancient form of taxation both in Europe and in Asia. Up to the beginning of this century the land tax still provided the principal source of revenue in the countries of the Middle East, in India and many other areas (in Europe its relative importance had been declining for a century or so as a result of the diminished relative importance of agriculture in the total national income). Since that time, however, political pressures, combined with monetary changes, have succeeded almost everywhere in 'eroding' the weight of this tax almost completely, and its rehabilitation now faces heavy political and administrative obstacles. Yet there can be little doubt that with heavier agricultural taxation the rate of development of all these countries could be much accelerated.

The main political objection to this tax is that it is socially unjust in its incidence since (taking into account needs) it hits the poor family far more heavily than the rich farmer. However, it would be possible to avoid the anti-social features of the tax by making it a progressive tax varying with the total size of family holdings. Since in most countries that are relatively overpopulated, and in which land is scarce, the distribution of the owner-ship of land is very uneven (with something like one-half of the available land being owned by 10 per cent or less of the agricultural families in typical cases) it is quite possible to exempt the very small farmer from this tax altogether and yet collect adequate revenue by making its incidence progressive on the owners of the larger holdings. A progressive land tax naturally raises the most fierce resentment in all countries where a land-owning class exists, and, to my knowledge, it has not yet been put into practice anywhere.

Another objection frequently made against a land tax is that it requires relatively frequent periodic reassessment of each individual holding — a task which is extremely costly and difficult to perform. It would be possible however to assess the potential fertility of varying pieces of land *in relation to the national or regional average* on the basis of more or less permanent

162 NICHOLAS KALDOR

criteria (such as average annual rainfall, irrigation, slope and inclination of the land, porousness or other qualities of the soil, etc.), and once this work of evaluation of 'potential relative fertility' is accomplished, it need not be repeated at frequent intervals. On the other hand the actual assessment to tax of each holding could be changed year by year by estimating the average value of output per acre for the country or region as a whole,[4] and multiplying this by the coefficient which relates the fertility of any particular acre to the national average.

In most areas of Africa the traditional social customs and the prevailing system of land tenure, etc., have made the establishment of a system of an annual land tax hitherto impossible. Instead resort was generally had to an inferior substitute — the poll tax — which is levied simply on the basis of the numbers of adult males in each region. The great advantage of the poll tax is the ease of assessment; and in countries where there is not much economic inequality in the rural areas this tax is not so obnoxious as it would be in older over-populated countries where a high degree of economic inequality prevails. Nevertheless a poll tax can never fulfil the same functions as a land tax based on the *potential* fertility of land. A poll tax, unlike a land tax, does not give the same incentives to improve cultivation; it does not make for greater fluidity in the ownership and/or occupation of the land which can alone secure that the land is cultivated by the most capable farmers. And because it can take into account economic inequality, a land tax is capable of yielding a much larger revenue than a poll tax.

The importance for economic development of an efficient system of taxation of the agricultural or subsistence sector of the community cannot be overestimated. Sooner or later the countries of Africa must develop a system whereby they can tax the *produce* of the land, and not just the inhabitants of the land. Indeed I would regard it as one of the most urgent tasks of the newly emerging independent countries of Africa to make a thorough investigation as to what is the most appropriate form of agricultural taxation suitable to their particular conditions.

In the absence of a direct tax on the subsistence sector — either in the form of a land tax or a poll tax — this sector can only be taxed indirectly through taxes on commodities which are bought by the agricultural sector. Such methods of indirect taxation can never, however, fulfil the same function: they do not provide the same incentives for increased

[4] One way of doing this is by making an estimate of the total output of foodstuffs for the country or region and then dividing it by the estimate of the number of cultivable acres in that region. Once statistical estimates had been made for a sufficient number of years, the average value of the produce per acre could be calculated as a moving average of, say, the past five years. In years of drought the tax could be remitted altogether either on a local or a national scale, as the case may be.

production or an increase in marketable supplies, and may even tend to retard the development of the rural regions. Since, moreover, it is impossible to differentiate in indirect taxation between various classes of consumers, and since only a small part of the real income of the subsistence sector is absorbed by the consumption of products bought for money, the scope for such indirect methods of taxing the subsistence sector are severely limited.

III. Taxes on Commodities

While commodity taxes are not an adequate method for taxing the agricultural sector, they are bound to be one of the principal methods of taxing the economy at large. As a method of taxing the 'monetized' or exchange sector they are superior to direct taxes in all cases where the economy largely consists of small enterprises, with few employees in each; in these cases the income tax is not an efficient instrument for taxing either the profits of the employer, or (through the PAYE, or deduction-at-source method) the wages and salaries of employees. Such taxes are relatively easy to assess and collect on commodities which pass through the frontier, particularly in the case of countries with access to the sea, and where imports and exports pass through some port. And to an extent which is not always realized, they can be used as an indirect method of taxing the profits of the *producers* or *suppliers* (domestic or foreign), and not only the *consumers* of the taxed commodities.

Thus in the case of commodities imported for domestic consumption, where particular imports are under the control of a single company, or a limited number of companies (this may be the case either because the bulk of the local markets is controlled by a single great merchanting house, or because — as with oil and petrol — the imports are controlled by world-wide concerns) the price to the domestic consumers tends to be fixed at the optimal 'monopoly' price, so that it does not pay the importer to pass on the full incidence of the tax to the local buyer. In this case the import duty is partly a method of taxing the profits of the importer (generally a non-resident company) and only in part a method of taxing the domestic consumer.

Similarly in the case of the exports of minerals or plantation products, an export duty is a method of taxing the profits of the producing companies which may be more effective than an income tax, particularly in those cases where the local operating company is a subsidiary of a foreign company who is also its trading partner, and where therefore the profits shown by the local company may be arbitrary. The danger is, however, that once export duties are imposed, the exigencies of revenue cause them to be fixed at excessive levels with the result that the development of export industries is inhibited.[5]

Though it is possible to differentiate in the weight of commodity taxes according to the degree of luxuriousness of the commodity, and thereby introduce a certain progression into the tax system, the revenue potentialities of taxes on luxurious goods are limited, since the import of such commodities is relatively small, and their consumption may be substantially reduced by heavy taxation. To get 'maximum revenue' it is necessary to tax articles of mass consumption — cotton cloth, sugar, flour, beer, tobacco, kerosene, etc. — and this raises all the political difficulties associated with a reduction in accustomed standards of living of the mass of the population. But this is not a peculiar feature of such taxes, but of taxation in general. It is impossible to increase the amounts raised in taxation suddenly or substantially without public resistance — whatever form the taxation takes.

There is finally the possibility of a *general sales tax*, collected from retailers on a very wide range of articles. Such taxes are a common feature of many developed countries; the experience of India shows that they can be successfully imposed also in underdeveloped areas, though it is a matter for investigation how far they represent a promising form of taxation under African conditions.

IV. DIRECT TAXES ON INCOME AND CAPITAL

The relative importance of progressive direct taxes necessarily varies with the stage of economic and social development. The experience of a wide variety of countries shows that taxes on income or profits can only be successfully imposed on large scale enterprises or on the employees of such enterprises. In underdeveloped areas the bulk of income tax revenue comes from a few large business firms and from government employees. The extension of the tax to small traders, artisans or professional persons meets with serious administrative difficulties — as there is no way of ascertaining income where no proper books are kept, no regular accounts are prepared or audited. It has often been suggested that a more promising form of bringing small and medium traders within the scope of direct taxation would be by means of a tax assessed on the value of their property — by means of a net wealth tax — since property (whether in the form of land and buildings, plant and equipment or stock-in-trade) is more difficult to conceal than income. However, in the few underdeveloped

---

[5] The expansion of the Ceylon tea industry is said to have been severely hampered on account of excessive taxation by means of export duties.

countries where graduated taxes on net wealth have been introduced (such as India and Ceylon) they operate with a huge exemption limit, and they are intended as an additional form of taxation on wealthy individuals and not as a tax on small and medium business, so that there is no actual experience to show how successful such a tax would be in practice.

V. COMPULSORY SAVINGS

A relatively new form of raising internal resources for development purposes is compulsory savings: this has recently been introduced in a number of countries, i.e. Turkey, Ghana, British Guiana, Brazil, etc. The most common form of these schemes is one where the contributors are given interest bearing but not negotiable bonds in exchange for their contributions which are repayable, together with accrued interest, after five, seven or ten years. The fact that the contributors will get their money back together with accrued interest makes it possible to levy a contribution on the *whole* of their income at a flat rate (which is normally 5 per cent) instead of at a graduated rate above a certain exemption limit, as is the case with income tax, though normally only people whose income exceeds some minimum level are brought within the scope of the scheme. The scheme is usually administered in connection with income tax or (in the case of Ghana) in connection with the purchase of cash crops by a marketing board. A similar obligation is imposed also on the profits of business and professional persons, generally with a contribution at a higher rate (which in Ghana is 10 per cent).

It is possible to combine such a scheme with a lottery scheme which might make it more attractive to the majority of contributors who are given a chance to win large cash prizes even before the bonds are due for redemption. The lottery element however makes the administration of this scheme far more complicated; also, it was found in Ghana that both the churches and the farmers' organization objected to a compulsory lottery.

It is possible also (though this requires far more administrative preparation) to make the scheme into a universal contributory pensions scheme, drawn up on an actuarial basis whereby the repayment takes the form of a pension upon retirement, the size of the pension depending on the amount of the annual contributions made. A compulsory savings scheme which results in a universal old age pensions scheme is found to be far more popular than a scheme where the contributors get non-negotiable bonds in exchange for bonds repayable after a fixed number of years.

A scheme of this kind is only appropriate, however, to those underdeveloped countries which are already sufficiently developed to bring a considerable section of the population within the scope of direct taxation; or where there is a major cash crop (such as cocoa in Ghana) which is purchased by a central marketing board at fixed prices. (In Ghana, 10 per cent of the price of cocoa is now paid in the form of such bonds.) The possibility of its application to countries which have more primitive forms of direct taxation (such as a poll tax) remains to be investigated.

VI. Problems of Tax Administration

It cannot be emphasized too strongly that the efficacy of the tax system is not just a matter of appropriate tax laws but depends on the efficiency and integrity of tax administration. In many underdeveloped countries the low revenue yield of taxation can only be attributed to the fact that the tax provisions are not properly enforced, either on account of the inability of the administration to cope with them, or on account of straightforward corruption in the administration. No system of tax laws, however carefully conceived, is proof against collusion between the tax administrators and the taxpayers; an efficient administration consisting of persons of high integrity is usually the most important requirement for obtaining 'maximum revenue'.

One important condition for this is that the government departments concerned with the administration of taxes should not be overburdened and this in turn requires that complicated taxes should be avoided until the administration is sufficiently developed to be able to cope with them. Many underdeveloped countries suffer both from an insufficiency of staff and from the relatively low grading of the staff of the tax administration departments. Persons of ability and integrity can only be found for these jobs if sufficient recognition is given to the importance of the tasks which they are asked to perform, and this should be fully reflected in their status, pay, prospects of promotion, etc. Any additional outlay incurred in improving the status and pay of the officials of the revenue department is likely to yield a very high return in terms of increased revenue.

THE OUTLOOK FOR AFRICAN EXPORTS

BY WALTER A. CHUDSON*

*Assistant Director, Technological Division,
Centre of Industrial Development, United Nations*

In view of the heavy dependence of African countries on exports an appraisal of export prospects is fundamental to an attempt to estimate the capacity to provide from their own efforts the savings and the foreign exchange resources required for their economic development. By the same token, such an appraisal is basic to an estimate of their requirements for external financial assistance and, indeed, of the capacity to obtain capital from abroad on commercial terms.

For many years to come, trends in the national product of most countries of the region will continue to be dominated or strongly influenced by the evolution of export proceeds; in some cases the transition from subsistence to commercial production may increase the dependence on exports. There is certainly no immutable relationship between export income and domestic savings, but it can safely be predicted that the level of total investment and public expenditure will depend heavily on exports. All of which goes to say that development programmes and projections of economic growth, if they are to be realistic, must take into account the probable trend of the volume and price of the leading export commodities and the likely range of fluctuation in export proceeds.

THE 1950S

As a point of departure, it is useful to recall that from 1950 to 1960 the value of exports from tropical Africa (excluding countries on the Mediterranean fringe and the Republic of South Africa) rose by about 70 per cent, which was not far below the growth of world trade as a whole. This was an impressive performance, particularly in comparison with sluggish growth of exports from Asia (excluding Japan) and with the virtual stagnation of Latin America's exports. In consequence, Africa's share of several major commodities (for example, coffee, cocoa, groundnuts and palm products) increased appreciably.

* The views expressed by the author do not necessarily represent those of the United Nations Secretariat, with which he is associated.

The greater part of the expansion took place in the early part of the decade when an increase in quantity was reinforced by rising prices. The shape of things to come was foreshadowed in the second half of the 1950s when an increase in the *quantum* of exports of over 25 per cent was offset by a decline in export prices, with the result that the value of exports rose by only 15 per cent.

Almost all countries shared in the expansion and in the slow-down. It is worth noting, however, that the expansion of exports from the former French territories took place within a sheltered market, in most cases at prices above world market levels and in several instances with a guaranteed volume of sales. Africa benefited also from internal conditions restraining the growth of exports in competing countries elsewhere. There was little progress towards the diversification of exports or towards a higher degree of processing, with such exceptions as the up-grading of palm oil products in Nigeria.

The facility with which the output of tropical products was expanded during the 1950s was impressive and surprised not a few qualified observers, who tended to think in terms of diminishing returns in agriculture. For many agricultural commodities, including tropical food-stuffs and agricultural raw materials, large increases in output were obtained by increasing productivity as well as by extending the area of cultivation. Rising prices and the attraction and availability of consumers' goods proved a powerful incentive to small-scale producers, and these forces were supported by the expansion of transport and marketing facilities and by agricultural extension measures. Whatever disincentive effect may be attributed to the relatively low prices paid to producers by Marketing Boards in countries such as Ghana, Nigeria and Uganda, it was apparently outweighed by technical aids to production often financed by the Boards.

Although the income-elasticity of demand for tropical foodstuffs and beverage crops is generally greater than that for temperate-zone food-stuffs (which are more subject to the limitation of one stomach per person), the rapid growth of output in Africa and elsewhere led inevitably to the sharp decline in prices already mentioned, and this decline has in some measure persisted or, as in the case of coffee, been arrested or slowed down only by restriction of the volume of exports. What, is the out-look for the years immediately ahead?

OUTLOOK FOR THE 1960s

The making of economic projections in the commodity field is beset with many traps for the unwary. Projections are, in any case, not forecasts. It is of interest, nevertheless, to consider the implications for Africa of certain projections of world demand for and supply of agricultural commodities that have recently been made by the Food and Agriculture Organization of the United Nations.[1]

The projections of demand were based on an assumed growth of population and on upper and lower estimates of gross national product of 'high-income' and 'low-income' countries. As a first approximation, agricultural output was projected on a country-by-country basis assuming no change in relevant national policies and prices remaining at the 1957–9 level. Coefficients representing the assumed increase in *per capita* consumption associated with increased *per capita* income were derived on a commodity-by-commodity basis.

The projections of the agricultural exports of 'low-income' countries (assuming unchanged export prices) are shown in Table 1. It will be noted

TABLE 1

Projected demand for agricultural commodity exports of 'low-income' countries in 1970[a]

A. Commodity	To 'High-income'[a] Countries	To Sino-Soviet Bloc	Total
	(at constant prices, 1957–9 = 100)		
Sugar	106–107	+ 3 million tons	142–143
Vegetable oils	96	222	100
Beverage crops	129–135	409–574	136–146
Coffee	132–138	428–643	138–149
Cocoa	134–136	320–400	150–158
Tea	106–115	118–127[b]	106–115
Agricultural raw materials	112–138	86–125	106–134
Fibres (cotton wool, jute)	107–128	82–125	100–127
Rubber	117–146	90–125	111–141
Total (including citrus fruit)	117–127	183–237	123–137

B. Importing country	1957–9	1970
		(Billions of dollars)
Western Europe	5·1	5·8– 6·2
United States — Canada	1·4	1·5– 1·6
Japan	0·7	1·1– 1·2
Sino-Soviet Bloc	0·6	1·2– 1·5
Total — including net exports by Australia — New Zealand	6·9	8·5– 9·4
excluding net exports by Australia — New Zealand	7·8	9·6–10·5

Source: FAO, *Agricultural Commodities — Projections for 1970*, Special Supplement to *FAO Commodity Review*, 1962 (Rome, 1962), pages 1–35.

[a] 'Low income' countries are those in Central and Latin America, Africa and the Near East, and Asia and the Far East (excluding Japan). 'High income' countries are those in Western Europe and North America together with Japan, Australia and New Zealand.
[b] Net exports.

[1] See FAO, *Agricultural Commodities — Projections for 1970*, Special Supplement to *FAO Commodity Review 1962* (Rome, 1962).

12

that they take into account the much-pondered question of the potential expansion of exports to the Sino-Soviet bloc. The projections do not indicate Africa's share in the indicated expansion, but they give a rough idea of the possible growth of effective demand for products on which the exports of tropical African countries heavily depend.

In order to draw conclusions from this table it is necessary to ask whether, in the light of the projected growth of supply, the assumptions that national policies will not change and that world prices will remain at their 1957–59 levels are reasonable. The answer given by the FAO to this question varies:

1. For coffee and soft oils (including groundnuts and other liquid edible oils), the present large world surpluses of production over effective demand are expected to increase if current production trends and national policies continue.
2. For cocoa, jute, tea, sugar, rice, and citrus fruit, world surpluses could well occur if current trends persisted.
3. For certain agricultural raw materials, notably cotton and rubber, the main problem is expected to arise from competition from synthetic products, tending to exert a downward pressure on prices.

For several commodities of major importance to African countries the projections thus imply no improvement in the terms of trade but rather a further deterioration unless specific measures are taken to affect supply, although some measures tending to increase demand, such as reducing internal taxes on tropical beverage crops in western Europe, may also be effective. On the rather improbable assumption of no further decline of export prices during the current decade, the projected expansion of total exports of 'low-income' countries from $7·8 billion to $9·6 to $10·5 billion (including exports to the Sino-Soviet bloc) represents between 2 and somewhat more than 3 per cent per annum. This excludes, of course, the potential expansion of mineral exports which, in several countries such as Liberia, the Congo (Leopoldville), Nigeria and several other countries may be important. It also excludes any expansion in exports of manufactures that may occur, but it is not likely such exports will play a significant part in African trade during this period.

To carry the analysis further in terms of its implications for African economic development it would be necessary to make some assumption regarding the imports required to attain assumed rates of growth. I do not propose to attempt this here, except to point out that in rough calculations made in connexion with proposals put forward recently by the Secretariat of the United Nations for promoting what has come to be called the

United Nations Development Decade it is suggested that for the less-developed countries as a group an average increase in imports of something like 5 per cent per annum might be required in order to meet an annual growth target of 5 per cent in national income.

If, as assumed in the United Nations proposals, foreign aid were to rise to 1 per cent of the gross national product of donor countries and then increase in step with it, the exports of less-developed countries would have to grow by about 25 per cent over the decade to provide the additional foreign resources needed. This is not far out of line with the FAO's minimum projection for the growth of agricultural exports of 'low-income' countries as shown in Table 1, *provided* (as is, however, unlikely) that their terms of trade do not deteriorate in the course of the decade. It also assumes a substantial expansion of exports to the Sino-Soviet bloc as indicated in Table 1.

SOME IMPLICATIONS

It seems beyond much doubt that, even assuming no further decline in export prices, the high rate of growth of African export income during the 1950s will not be repeated during the 1960s and that, indeed, some further decline in export prices in many countries cannot be ruled out. These hard facts must (or should) be taken into account in formulating African development programmes, as has been done, for example, in the Nigerian development plan for 1962–8. Given the prospect, what are the lines of policy that should be pursued and what are the limits of the feasible?

One avenue of 'escape' to which much attention has been given is exports overseas of manufactures and semi-manufactures. For tropical African countries generally (which excludes Egypt and South Africa) this is, however, the least promising solution at their present stage of development. Nevertheless, attention should be given to the possibilities of a higher degree of processing and of upgrading traditional export commodities (for example, the export of cocoa butter and cocoa paste instead of cocoa beans).

Another avenue of escape is intra-regional trade. This should not be underestimated, but it carries two important qualifications: it will not quickly assure much of the needed supply of capital equipment and industrial raw materials; more important, the creation of common markets and other forms of economic union by the stroke of a pen will not suffice. Until transport and communication facilities are expanded, and, indeed, the size of the market increases through rising incomes within existing boundaries, the mere abolition of customs and fiscal barriers will not have an appreciable effect. (This observation should not be interpreted, however, as implying that a disintegration of existing common markets and common services would not be costly, at least to certain of the participants.)

It is also well to bear in mind that a country's dependence on imports is not unalterable. The outlook for African export trade adds further grounds — if these were really necessary — for the most careful scrutiny of development expenditure in order to see that the structure of production is adjusted to impost capacity.

It remains to consider what measures can be taken to deal specifically with problems of African commodity trade. For this purpose it is convenient to distinguish between national and international action.

NATIONAL ACTION

The main lines of internal adjustment to changing long-term conditions have, I think, already been indicated above. Measures to increase productivity in regard to major export crops should also be encouraged. I have already referred to the importance of adjusting the composition of exports as much as possible to long-term market prospects.

Superimposed on longer-term trends in commodity markets we can expect the continuation of more or less disruptive fluctuations of a short-term nature, which, unless counteracted, may lead to the curtailment of imports in a way that can jeopardize development programmes and cause undesirable secondary repercussions. The use of price-stabilization funds by marketing boards or the corresponding *caisses de stabilisation* in French speaking territories or similar measures such as sliding-scale export taxation to deal with this problem is a subject unto itself, and I shall make just a few brief remarks on these devices.

It is important, and I think generally agreed by now, that marketing boards and *caisses de stabilisation* should be regarded as multi-purpose institutions, not merely as stabilization devices. On the usefulness of their technical and commercial functions, particularly when production is in the hands of many small-scale cultivators, there is now widespread agreement, though there are naturally those who favour solutions through increasing the degree of competition rather than through direct intervention by government agencies. Some of the technical functions can, of course, also be performed by co-operatives and agricultural extension services, but there seems little doubt that the marketing boards in African countries have usually performed these functions with reasonable efficiency.

The more difficult issues arise in relation to the internal price policies adopted by the marketing boards. I think there is general agreement that marketing boards can, if properly administered, avoid perverse responses of supply to fluctuations in export prices and also assist in mitigating harmful secondary repercussions of export fluctuations. Since the export sector is usually relatively large, the Boards (or the *caisses*) cannot, even if they would, continue to maintain producers' prices or incomes above levels warranted by world market conditions for a protracted period. The opposite is, of course, possible, namely to maintain producers' prices below export prices. In most African countries having such institutions the average price received by the producers during the 1950s has been below the average of export prices for these years, the funds withheld having been allocated to collective expenditure in the export sector itself or drawn upon for general development financing. An assessment of the merits of a 'trickle-down' policy (high pay-out to producers) as against a collective-saving or forced-saving or taxation policy (low pay-out) calls for examination on a case by case basis. It is worth noting that in several countries, the policy of low pay-out had been replaced, even before the persistent decline in export prices on the marketing boards' reserves, by reliance on sliding-scale export taxation.

The stabilization of producers' prices (or incomes) in the face of an upward trend in world prices seems to be feasible but, of course, poses the threat of misallocation of resources through loss of contact with the trend of prices, a danger which I think can be effectively guarded against. Stabilization in face of a persistent downward trend, however, seems to pose extreme difficulty because of the problem of accumulating reserves in the face of pressure to use reserves for development if not for current expenditure. If there is no pronounced trend, however, it seems feasible to achieve a fair amount of year-to-year stabilization of producers' prices and/or incomes, on the basis of competent forecasting or by using some kind of moving-average formula.

These remarks refer, of course, to the stabilization of the export sector itself. If such stabilization is to help in stabilizing development expenditure, the funds siphoned off or the proceeds of sliding-scale export taxation must be spent in an offsetting fashion. This in turn means that the average level of government expenditure must be geared to this policy — which seems a rather platonic ideal, given the very real pressures to which governments of less-developed countries are subject. Some adjustment may also be possible on the expenditure side, if a portion of a country's development expenditures is used as a buffer, by varying expenditure on road construction (the number of miles built per year can be varied), sewerage, soil erosion work and the like.

International Action

It is at least easy to state the objectives in regard to international action that the less-developed countries have or should have in common: (1) it is important to them that the industrial countries should offer increasing outlets for their commodities by pursuing policies of economic expansion and by adopting measures designed to reduce tariffs and other barriers to export; (2) they wish their foreign exchange earnings to be protected from excessive short-term fluctuations; and (3) they hope that the industrial countries will be prepared to import some of their present or prospective manufactured products, although, as already indicated, this possibility will remain of limited significance to African countries for some time.

Where does the international community stand in regard to forging an international commodity policy to meet these objectives?

There is no space here to give a full answer to this question, but I think it can be reasonably said that as a consequence of action taken under the auspices of the United Nations and other international agencies a certain consensus on the broad outlines of an international commodity policy is slowly emerging.

It may be said with confidence that such a policy will involve concerted action along several lines. One is through further efforts to stabilize commodity prices by direct intervention in world markets through international agreements. Examples are the negotiations for a five-year international coffee agreement now proceeding under United Nations auspices in New York and the recent action of the International Cocoa Study Group in preparing a draft international agreement.[2] The list of commodities for which such agreements exist or are under active consideration now embraces a fairly important segment of commodity trade (tin, wheat, sugar, coffee, cocoa, and, to some extent, lead and zinc). The mere extension of the list of commodities subject to such agreements is not, of course, an end in itself, and much remains to be done in formulating effective policies to govern the operation of these agreements and their co-ordination with other policies relating particularly to the less developed countries. If an international commodity agreement is designed primarily to prevent a collapse of prices that would otherwise result from a structural imbalance (as in the case of coffee, for example) it is obviously important that parallel action be taken during the 'breathing space' afforded by the agreement to encourage a shift of resources from the surplus sector. This implies not only appropriate action to reduce supply, if it is truly excessive, but positive measures to assist the transfer of resources to other lines of activity.

[2] The factual references in this section refer to the situation in mid-1962.

Another development has been the recent action under United Nations auspices to consider the establishment of new machinery or the enlargement of existing machinery to provide compensatory financing to countries suffering from adverse fluctuations or trends in their export income. There is a wide range of possible applications of this concept with a wide range of costs and alternative policies, and there are many practical problems that arise. Nevertheless, serious consideration is being given to this approach as a complement to other international commodity policies.

Much attention has also been given recently to the importance of reducing import barriers in industrial countries in order to assist the exports of the developing countries. I do not propose here to go into the vexing problems arising in connexion with the association of certain African territories with the European Economic Community. It must be recognized, however, that the withdrawal of preferential treatment from underdeveloped and highly vulnerable countries presents problems comparable to those faced by countries that may be harmed by discrimination.

To supplement measures of the above type it is desirable that other concrete steps be taken, for example intensified research aimed at developing new uses for African raw materials. Another is the seeking of new or expanded markets for primary commodities in the underdeveloped areas themselves and elsewhere, for example, in Eastern Europe and the Soviet Union.

SHOULD AFRICAN COUNTRIES FORM ECONOMIC UNIONS?

BY A. J. BROWN

Head of Dept. of Economics and Commerce, University of Leeds, UK

THE MEANINGS OF ECONOMIC UNION

The answer to the question which has been assigned to me clearly depends, like the answers to most questions, on interpretation. Economic union can mean a number of things. Perhaps the simplest thing it can imply is free trade between the constituent countries in goods. The next meaning that comes to mind is a true customs union — not only free trade in goods between the countries concerned, but the adoption by them of common tariffs (or other trade barriers) against goods coming from the outside world as well. Next, one may think of union as implying free movement between the territories of some or all of the factors of production. In so far as capital is one of the factors thus free to move, this leads on to the question whether the countries are to have, in some sense, a common monetary system, or at least a firm arrangement whereby their currencies shall be mutually convertible without restriction, or mutually convertible at a fixed rate, or both. Next, there is the question whether the development policies of the member countries should be worked out in common, or accommodated to each other in some way. And finally, the terms of an economic union may include some degree of pooling of part of the public revenues, or the joint development and ownership of public utilities such as transport systems, or of educational and research establishments, and possibly of some tax collecting machinery.

I need hardly remind you that union in most of these senses normally exists in a political federation; internal trade, migration, and payments are normally free, there is a common external tariff, a common money, and pooling of revenue at least to the extent needed to provide federal armed forces, central administration, and other services of the federal government. In some federations at some times — in the United States sixty years ago, for example — these central services have been at a minimum, and there has been neither much inter-state redistribution of revenue, much federal ownership of public utilities, nor much central direction or co-ordination of economic development. But as governments in general have moved away from a *laissez-faire* position, federal governments have taken up these functions, and, indeed, have often taken them up more vigorously than the governments of the member states.

On the other hand, many of the forms of union that I have mentioned exist to some extent in the absence of political federation. Tanganyika, Kenya and Uganda constitute a common market with an almost (though not quite) common external tariff, have a common monetary system, and operate a wide range of fiscal, research, educational, and transport services through their Common Services Organization. They even, to a small extent, redistribute public revenues through a pool in order to provide some degree of automatic compensation for inequities in the operation of the common market. In a different context and on a bigger scale, the Rome Treaty provides for the gradual creation of a common market with a common external tariff, freedom of internal migration and capital movements, common policies with regard to agriculture and transport, and, in very general terms, for the co-ordination of the economic policies of the member countries in the interests of internal and external equilibrium. The United Nations Organization itself, along with its specialized agencies, provides common services of information and research, machinery for the limitation and reduction of international trade barriers, the essentials of an international monetary system, and some distribution of development funds in the light of a central appraisal of competing claims. 'Economic union' covers a lot of possibilities.

FREE-TRADE AREAS — THE CONVENTIONAL TREATMENT

The possibility that receives most attention at present is that of a free trade area. How important is this for African countries? I do not think that most of the theoretical discussion of this subject helps us much. The treatment of Viner, Meade, Makower and Morton, Gehrels, and Lipsey (admirably surveyed by Lipsey in the *Economic Journal* for September, 1960), are concerned almost entirely with the effect of customs unions on economic welfare on the assumption that there are no productive economies of large scale. Whether this assumption renders the analysis unrealistic when applied to (for instance) the European Economic Community is open to discussion; I shall argue presently that it renders it wholly unrealistic when applied to African conditions. But first let us look at some of the results of the analysis as they might apply to Africa. For each member country, the introduction of free trade within the area eliminates any distortion by tariffs of the price-relations between goods from its own producers and those of other member countries, but introduces a distortion of the price relation between goods from its union partners and goods from the outside world. Lipsey points out that the former change — which may be assumed to improve the use of resources — is important in so far as there is much scope for trade between member countries. The second change — the introduction of a distortion, which presumably makes use of resources less efficient — is important in so far as the external trade (union and non-union) of the members is big. The case for a free-trade union is strong, in fact, when the member countries have little external trade in proportion to their internal production, but do a high proportion of that external trade with their union partners. The strength of the case depends also, of course, on the sensitiveness of the trade-pattern to tariff changes and on the relative efficiencies, in different countries, of the industries which the tariffs protect. If consumers do not regard goods from a union partner and goods from the rest of the world as being close substitutes for each other, then the free-trade union will not make much difference to the way in which resources are used, though it may make a considerable difference to the terms of trade between the countries. If protected and non-protected kinds of production are of about the same relative efficiency in different countries of the union, then, again, the union will not make much difference to the use of resources. In this case there will, in any event, not be much scope for trade between the union partners. The case for union is strong where the constituent countries are all trying to protect the same kinds of industry, but show markedly different values for the ratios of factor-efficiency in these industries to factor-efficiency in non-protected branches of production.

According to these criteria, the immediate gain from free-trade unions in Africa would be small. It is true that African countries apply import duties to broadly similar ranges of goods — in general, they all tax imports of most manufactured consumers' goods, partly for revenue and partly for protective purposes. It is probably true, also, that their comparative advantages in producing these manufactured goods and in producing other things vary a great deal from country to country. For one thing, different African countries (though they are all at an early stage of development as compared with the advanced countries) show very different degrees of immediate industrial promise. Some have the substantial beginnings of an industrial labour-force, an internal supply of industrial capital, and technical and commercial skills; others have not. Moreover, in some, the immediate possibilities of extending commercial agriculture or mining are good; in others poor. The relative possibilities of manufacture and primary production thus probably vary over a wide range. But, on the other hand, the actual volume of trade between African countries is still small in relation to their trade with the rest of the world, and their total external trade is large (as these things go) in comparison with their total domestic production. The total merchandise exports of African countries are probably more than a fifth of their total production of goods and services; nearly as high a proportion as one finds in the countries of the European Economic Community. In both of the notable common markets of Africa — the Central African Federation and East Africa — the trade between the constituent territories is only a fifth or a sixth of trade with the outside world; for all African countries together, it is less than one tenth, even if we include an estimate of the trade between the member countries in the two common markets that I have just mentioned. For the European Economic Community countries, the corresponding proportion is nearly three-fifths. In trade, Africa is an outward-looking continent — though perhaps not quite so outward-looking as South America.

The conclusion from these facts, taken with the theory of free-trade unions as it has so far developed, is that African countries ought to form such unions (if at all) with some of the advanced industrial countries. It is with these that they do most of their trade; both the African and the advanced industrial countries mostly protect their manufacturing industries, and in the present phase of development the industrial countries have a big comparative advantage in most kinds of manufacture. This is an argument against fostering manufacturing industry in Africa by any form of protection, and for making African trade even more outward-directed than it is at present. It is invalid for two reasons, one of which has already been mentioned.

The Longer View

First, it is based upon a short view; it takes comparative advantages and trade patterns as they are now instead of considering what they are likely to be, say, a generation hence. By that time, African comparative advantages in different kinds of production are likely to, or at any rate could, be greatly altered by the spread of education and technical knowledge, and by the increase of population. In some parts even today the prospect of extending primary production radically is poor; in such areas the comparative advantage shifts towards secondary industry as soon as skill, capital, communications, and the forms of organization and habits of life appropriate to manufacturing industry can be provided. This is beginning to happen already. As it goes on happening, the trade pattern will change. Experience of countries already semi-industrialized suggests that external trade at a somewhat later stage grows less fast than internal purchasing power. At this stage, too, trade between African countries — both between those already semi-industrialized, and between semi-industrialized countries and those with comparative advantages in primary production — would probably grow faster, proportionately, than trade with the outside world. The area of the economy over which free-trade unions between African states might be expected to improve the use of resources would thus increase with development, and the areas over which such unions would cause high-cost goods from within the union to be substituted for lower-cost goods from outside it would, relatively, diminish. Development would strengthen the case for unions between African countries, even according to the theoretical criteria at which we have looked.

ECONOMIES OF SCALE IN SECONDARY INDUSTRY

But the other weakness of these criteria, as they stand — the weakness already referred to — is probably more serious. It is that they take no account of economies of scale, and I shall argue that, in African conditions, these are crucially important. Admittedly, we know all too little about these matters. In spite of the importance of the subject, the only recent and substantial study known to me is that of twenty American industries by Professor Bain[1] — though I understand that relevant work is now in progress in Cambridge. What, therefore, are my grounds for believing that scale is important for our present question? The chief one is the fact that, in relation to any scales of production that either are declared to be optimal for engineering reasons, or are actually prevalent in advanced countries, the markets offered for most kinds of manufactures by most African countries are very small indeed. Let us first look at this small-ness.

Taking such estimates of national income as exist for African countries (independent or not), and making very rough estimates for the rest with the help of population figures, I arrive at the conclusion that the median income is about £50 million — roughly that of Nyasaland. The upper quartile seems to be about £180 million, the lower quartile about £15 million. These estimates are intended to include subsistence production; if one takes only money income these figures are reduced by anything from, say, 15 per cent in some cases to over 50 per cent in others. The money income of the 'median' African country is probably less than that of an English town of 100,000 inhabitants. This does not, of course, mean

[1] *American Economic Review*, March 1954.

that demand for each kind of manufactured good would be the same in our median African country as in our English town. Judging from East African data,[2] it seems that the African demand is several times as great for cotton textiles, about twice as great for cement, about the same for footwear, and much less for most other kinds of manufacture — for non-food manufactures in aggregate probably somewhat less than the English town's demand.

How do these markets compare in size with the optimum scales of production? Professor Bain's evidence is, admittedly, confined to industries where the technical unit of production is large — he was looking into the validity of the technical argument for monopoly or oligopoly in the United States. He reckons that, for nineteen out of his twenty industries, the capacity of the technical optimal productive establishment is more than one-tenth of 1 per cent of the United States market, and for ten of them (gypsum products, tyres and tubes, rayon, soap, farm machinery, cigarettes, automobiles, copper refining, tractors and typewriters) it is more than $2\frac{1}{2}$ per cent of the United States market. His figures relate to the year 1951; converted to the prices of 1958 (to which year most of our African income data relate) one-tenth of 1 per cent of the United States national income of 1951 would be about £116 million. Only one-third of African countries have as large a money income as that. $2\frac{1}{2}$ per cent of United States income, in the same terms, is some £2,900 million — considerably more than the money incomes of the two largest African economies (Egypt and the Republic of South Africa) added together. Moreover, because expenditure in Africa is distributed differently from expenditure in the United States, the optimum establishment of most of these industries would need a market area with a money income several times larger in African conditions than in American conditions. Few African countries provide a market large enough for the optimum establishment in any of the twenty industries in question. For the ten industries for which the optimum establishment demands $2\frac{1}{2}$ per cent or more of the United States market, no existing African country would come near to providing an adequate outlet for one such establishment.

Of course, these are the extreme cases; we are looking at the industries of largest optimal plant-size in the largest economy in the world. It is possible to go further only by looking at the sizes of plant that are *prevalent* (without being able to ascertain that they are technically *optimal*), in other advanced countries. The sizes of plant prevalent in the United Kingdom in 1951 have recently been analysed by Professor Sargent

[2] A. J. Brown, *Yorkshire Bulletin of Economic and Social Research*, May 1961.

Florence.[3] He finds that, out of 129 industries, twenty-six show so wide
a dispersion of plant sizes that no typical size emerges, but that the
remaining 103 can at least be classified as to the broad size groups (in terms
of employment) into which their plants predominantly fall. The pre-
dominant size of plant in these industries can be fairly well indicated by
employment in the 'median' plant — using this term to mean the plant of
which it is true that as many people are employed in the industry in
larger ones as in smaller ones.

For the present purpose, we are interested not in size of plant as such,
but in the size of the market that one plant supplies. The convenient first
step to this is the ratio of total employment in the industry to that in the
'median' plant — the number of plants of median size that would be
required to supply the whole market that the British industry in question
does, in fact, supply, This number varies, naturally, over a wide range,
from something like 20,000 in the building industry to a mere half-dozen
in mineral oil refining. It is, however, less than 200 in about three-quarters
of the 103 industries, less than 140 in about half of them, and less than
fifty in about a quarter. Bearing in mind that the United Kingdom is a
net exporter of manufactures, supplying a total market that is bigger by
perhaps a fifth or a quarter than the home market, one may conclude that
in three-fifths of all British industries (including in the total those with no
predominant plant size), the 'median' plant requires the equivalent of a
British market with an income of £110 million or more to absorb its
products. Three-quarters of the separate countries and territories of Africa
do not possess a money income of this size. Because of the difference
between British and African expenditure patterns, a still higher proportion
of them would fail to provide an adequate market for the outputs of most
of the 'median' plants in question.

Moreover, I do not think it can be maintained that size of plant is
relatively large in the United Kingdom because the market is large —
rather than for any technical reason. In the article cited, I have shown that
plant size is apparently much the same in East Africa as in most of the
corresponding industries in the United Kingdom, just as Florence has
shown that plant sizes are much the same in corresponding industries in
the United Kingdom as in the United States.

How much does all this matter? As I have said, we lack much information about the optimum scales of production, still more we lack
information about the degree in which working at less than the optimum
scale reduces output per man. All that can be said is that there is a pre-
sumption that working within the limits of single African countries, even
with a single plant, would in the majority of industries reduce the attain-
able level of productivity substantially. The reduction would be all the

[3] *Post-War Investment, Location and size of Plant;* Cambridge, 1962.

more substantial in that the rough calculations just described do not take account of the fact that different plants classified as belonging to one 'industry' in Britain or the United States are often not competing plants, turning out similar products, but complimentary plants turning out different components of a product, or performing different processes, so that several plants may go together to form a productive system which could not be broken up without loss of efficiency. At all events, it seems that, so far as manufacturing industry is concerned, a large part of it is likely to work to substantially greater advantage within market areas bigger than most African countries than it would work within most of those countries singly. This means that, in so far as reliance is placed upon enterprise from outside, this will be attracted preferentially to the larger African economies, or to free-trade unions. Even if development is largely independent of enterprise from outside, the larger countries, or unions, will tend to obtain a substantial competitive advantage from their size as development proceeds.

The Problems of the Free-Trade Unions

I have dwelt at length on this matter of the advantages of free-trade unions. What is to be said against them? Perhaps the most obvious thing is that they present administrative difficulties, or limitations on freedom of fiscal policy, or both. If the union is of the simplest kind, with the constituent countries retaining different tariffs against the outside world, it will not generally be possible to dismantle the internal tariff barriers lest foreign goods should flood into the lowest-tariff member of the union and from there supply the other members without paying further duty. It will be necessary, also, to be able to distinguish adequately at the frontiers of the higher-tariff members between these goods and the products of other members — for which their importers may try to pass them off. On the other hand, if these problems are avoided by organizing a full customs union, with a common external tariff and no internal tariff frontiers, the governments of the member countries have to agree what that tariff shall be, and, what is more serious, have to give up the use of variations in the tariff as a means of adjusting their individual national revenues to requirements. They thus find themselves in what has been described, with some feeling, as 'a fiscal strait-jacket'. This is a main reason why, in a federation, customs revenue is usually federal, or, if it goes in part or in whole to the state governments, is distributed to them according to a predetermined formula.

These are problems to be aware of, but they should not be insuperable.

They are probably much less important in the long run than the economic strains which arise from disparities of development between the members of a free-trade union — or, for that matter, between states of a federation or even different parts of a unitary state.

I have emphasized that, in African conditions, at least, a good deal of the case for free-trade union rests upon the large output of the efficient modern manufacturing plant. It follows from this that, especially while purchasing power is still low, production of any one type of manufactured good must be very highly localized. Indeed, experience shows that there is a strong tendency for many kinds of manufacturing activity to congregate together, and for a fairly high degree of aggregation of manufacturing industry to remain even when the economy has grown and made room for many plants in each of the main industries. I need not go into the reasons for this, except to say that they may well be especially strong in the early stages of development, when poor transport facilities limit the choice of locations, and anything like a body of experienced factory-labour is much smaller and more localized than in later stages of growth.

In these circumstances, there is a strong tendency for the benefits of the union to be localized in the member-territory that happens to become the main focus of manufacturing industry and commerce. The other member-territories then tend to complain, on two grounds. First, they are apt to covet the development of secondary industry which has passed them by, and to believe that, with tariff protection against their partners, they would have attracted some of it for themselves. I think it follows from my previous argument that this belief is largely invalid when the territories in question offer markets as small as most African territories can provide today. Without the union, the growth of secondary industry would simply have been smaller, and would still have been preferentially attracted to certain territories — probably the largest and richest of the economies concerned.

The second ground of complaint, however, is more substantial. If we assume that the non-industrial territories pay prices for manufactures of their partners which are equal to the prices of competing imports, including import duty, then by being in the union they lose revenue equal to the duty on the manufactures which they buy from their union partners instead of from the outside world. Probably this loss of revenue brings about a reduction of public expenditure, leading to a reduction of total income. Correspondingly, of course, the industrialized territory gains in total income, because of the existence of its secondary industry. The taxation on this income will compensate its government (indeed, probably more than compensate it) for what it loses in import duty by producing manufactures at home instead of importing them. This is not the whole story; there are mitigating considerations. In so far as the increased income of the industrializing territory leads it to buy more from its union partners, the benefits of its industrialization are diffused. But there are cases where this diffusion is slight; where, for instance, the non-industrializing territories sell little to the industrializing one, or where what they sell to it is simply diverted from export to the outside world, and is sold at a price no higher than its export price.[4]

There are a number of things to be said about this problem of uneven development within a free-trade area, and its consequences. The first is that it may be possible to avoid it to some extent by interterritorial, or international, planning of development, which might make the rates of advance in the different territories or countries more nearly equal than they would otherwise be. It must be faced that the most effective use of the resources available for development within the territories, taken together, is likely to demand more rapid advance in some of them than in others. It is nevertheless true that, in the interests of preserving the free-trade area, on which the whole development depends to such a large extent, it may be worth departing from optimal distribution of effort in order to produce greater interterritorial equality of growth.

Secondly, more rapid, and more uneven, development can be reconciled with interterritorial equity to some extent by financial transfers. Within a unitary state or a federation a certain amount of this may happen automatically through the ordinary channels of public finance; for instance, if some part of the central (or federal) revenue is divided between districts or states in a predetermined proportion, then all will get some share of the extra revenue from new secondary industries, and all will share the loss of customs revenue as home production displaces imports. Transfers of this kind can operate to some extent even between separate countries; the method of financing the non-self-contained services of the East African Common Services Organization and the operation of the associated distributable pool, are designed to produce exactly this effect between Kenya, Tanganyika, and Uganda — offsetting certain inequities in the operation of the East African Common Market. Another method of effecting some such compensation is for the government of a territory which admits free of duty from a neighbour goods of kinds that are dutiable if imported from elsewhere to receive some specific payment from that neighbour for each unit of such goods admitted. I believe that an arrangement of this kind existed between the Union of South Africa and Southern Rhodesia some years ago.

[4] I have discussed this and related matters at greater length in the *Yorkshire Bulletin of Economic and Social Research*, November 1961.

The Role of Free Factor Movements

Thirdly, the problem of unequal growth within a free-trade area is mitigated from one point of view, though not from another, if there is free movement of factors of production between the member territories. So far as labour is concerned freedom of movement makes it possible for people to move to those areas where advance is fastest thus partially correcting the maldistribution of population in relation to resources on which the inequality of development is likely to be at least partially based. This is, indeed, the way to secure the highest possible rate of growth in total income, and at the same time to promote greater equality of incomes between the people of the free-trade area. But this very process may accentuate the divergence between the aggregate incomes, and government revenues, of the member territories; the poorer lose population to the richer, receiving some compensation in the form of emigrants' remittances, some useful skills brought by returning emigrants, and a reduction of the pressure on their natural resources. In terms of economic welfare, these are substantial compensations, though to the patriotic eye they may appear insufficient.

A similar consideration may arise with capital. In general, freedom of capital transfer, as of payments generally, within an area wider than most single African territories is of great help in promoting the most profitable distribution of scarce capital resources, and in making investment in the area attractive to external capital. Investment of capital from a less rapidly developing territory in a more rapidly developing one provides one of the ways in which the prosperity of the latter can be both assisted and diffused. It is true that in such a case the less rapidly developing territory would often be more benefited if its own savings were invested in it and not outside — the returns on the capital might be lower, but labour which is otherwise virtually unproductive might be drawn into employment. Nevertheless, to obstruct the outflow of capital from the less rapidly developing territories would probably not be sufficient to secure a corresponding increase in their internal investment, and would almost certainly do more harm than good to them. Freedom of capital-transfer is, of course, most complete within a common monetary system.

Common Services

From the advantages and difficulties of free trade in goods and the associated question of free movement of factors of production, I should like to turn now to the advantages and difficulties of sharing the overhead costs of public services. This is another neglected subject, though a good deal that is relevant to it, as to the rest of my topic, was presented to the

1957 meeting of the International Economic Association, and is published in *The Economic Consequences of the Size of Nations*. There are some services which can be pooled between territories, for the spreading of their overhead costs and the increase of efficiency, only if the territories in question are in effect federated; most of the services grouped together as general administration are clearly among these, though East Africa has the remarkable feature of a common tax-collecting service. Some part of defence and some part of education are in the same case, though it is not excluded nowadays that other parts of these should be shared between sovereign states, as in NATO in the one case and the University of East Africa in the other. The operation of transport systems and research organizations of international scope is a matter on which there is a larger body of experience. Without for the moment going further into the political conditions for these various types of pooling, can one estimate their economic importance?

To a large extent, one has to rely here upon general presumptions. Economies in the large-scale operation of public services, like those in large-scale manufacturing, come from the indivisibility of certain units in the organization. In all services, some of these units are simply individuals of unusual ability and training, capable of extending their beneficial activities over a wide geographical area. Sometimes they are teams; sometimes they are pieces of plant or equipment — laboratory facilities, repair shops and the like. The larger the costs of these specially qualified individuals, or these special facilities, bulk in the total cost of the service in question, the greater the probability that there are economies of scale. Research services provide perhaps the clearest example; the optimal geographical scope of an establishment is limited only by the prevalence of the physical and economic conditions to which its findings apply. The same is true of a central banking organization, or, to a considerable extent, of any advisory service. In the educational field, it is mainly the institutions of higher education and vocational training that show large economies of aggregation, and, among them, pre-eminently the faculties or schools that deal with small proportions of the total populations at high cost per student — above all, the medical schools, with their need of teaching hospitals. In elementary and secondary education, however, there are also economies of scale up to a point — it is widely held that the larger county authorities in the United Kingdom, for instance, have considerable advantage over the smaller ones, especially in the range of specialized services they can provide.

In all these cases, the principle of aggregation applies — it is necessary to operate on a relatively large scale to provide an adequate field for specialists.

The case for seeking these economies of scale, moreover, is stronger where specialists are scarce and expensive than where they are relatively plentiful, and therefore command salaries not so much above the general level. Africa in particular needs to economize its specialists for this reason.

The only firm quantitative evidence known to me on the size of economies of scale in public services is that provided by Professor Prest,[5] from the statistics of the Australian Commonwealth Grants Commission, this being a case where the qualities of service provided by the different states concerned have been subject to careful inspection and comparison. The Commission estimates the extra cost per head of providing the services of education, health, and law and order in Tasmania (population 319,000) as compared with the corresponding cost for services of similar 'standard' quality in New South Wales (population $3\frac{1}{2}$ million) to be about 12 per cent. The difference appears to be largely due to scale; other relevant factors, such as average population density and proportion of children of school age in the total population, show little difference between the two states. Because of the relatively high cost of specialist services under African conditions, I should expect margins of this kind to be larger in Africa — a 20 per cent difference between large and small territories would hardly be surprising.

In some services, there are further technical sources of economy from common operation over large areas. Transport (both rail and air), for instance, not only provides a strong case for a sufficient scale to secure the full use of specialized services and machines of large capacity; there are often interterritorial differences in the seasonal pattern of traffic, so that it is specially advantageous to be able to shift vehicles between the internal services of different territories. Another consideration of importance here is the interrelated nature of local and interterritorial services — the former partly feed the latter, but the latter often cover their direct costs better. There are clearly gains to be made from operating on a geographical scale that may well be more than national. Where a common defence organization is politically possible, that also presents great possibilities of economy, especially for contiguous territories. Not only does an arrangement of this kind remove the need for even token garrisoning of the common frontiers but there is a gain from the pooling of reserves to meet contingencies, quite apart, of course, from the possibility of sharing the more obvious overhead costs of staff and training establishments. If one is considering not merely a functional co-operation between states but their actual political federation, there are, of course, other possible economies in governmental costs, of which that in the cost of diplomatic representation abroad is perhaps the most obvious, and by no means a negligible

[5] *The Economic Consequences of the Size of Nations*, Chapter 15.

one — especially where the supply of personnel of the required high ability is small.

Finally, there are what we may call the economies of planning on a large scale. These do not arise only from the fact — though it is an important fact — that planning staffs and other organs of economic policy require scarce and expensive kinds of personnel, and need to grow only less than proportionally to the size of the economy with which they have to deal. They arise largely from the fact that planned development is co-ordinated development of complementary resources. It may not be worth carrying out a power project or building a railway unless production of some kind is developed to use the power and the railway; the production, similarly, cannot be profitably started without these facilities. Private enterprise alone may not be moved to undertake any of these three things because of the risk that the other two will not be undertaken, or not for a long time, and because private capital may not be available under single control on a sufficient scale to undertake all three projects at once. By government initiative, with or without the participation of private enterprise, all three projects can profitably be undertaken because it is known that they are all being proceeded with at once. If the power-source, the agricultural, mining, or industrial area to be developed, and part of the railway lie in three separate territories, the government initiative will not be forthcoming without a joint planning organization of some kind. Needless to say, the probability of desirable development failing to materialize through lack of a planning organization of sufficient geographical scope is very considerable when the planning areas are small, and decreases sharply (though no doubt at a diminishing rate) as they become bigger. Needless to say, also, the technical inter-relations between branches of economic activity, and between localities, that development involves are vastly more complicated and widespread than a simple example of this kind suggests, and are more likely to be critical in an undeveloped economy than they are in a developed one, which has nearly every kind of industry, skill, and service already in existence, most of them with some excess capacity at any given time.

SUMMARY AND CONCLUSIONS

I have now said something of a rather general kind about the scope for economies from union (in various senses) between countries in Africa. Let me first summarize it and then try to draw some conclusions:

1. African countries, in general, present rather poor cases on the (not very realistic) grounds of conventional theory for mutual

free trade in goods, in as much as the amount of their mutual trade is small.

2. Nevertheless, not only will this situation probably change as development proceeds, but the extreme smallness of the demand for most manufactures within most African countries means that they will be severely handicapped in developing manufacturing industries unless they can in some degree pool their markets.

3. The smallness of African national or territorial economies also means that the advantages of scale to be got from pooling many of their public services are substantial, especially since some of the expertise required for these services in present African conditions is so scarce. Among the 'services' to which these considerations apply strongly is the planning of economic development.

4. The smallness of territorial economies, and the diversity of their present development and scope for future development mean that, for the people of the continent as a whole, there are enormous advantages in freedom of interterritorial movement and payments.

5. Interterritorial differences of both actual and potential income levels give great scope for raising welfare by public finance transfers between territories. Some transfers of this kind may also be necessary, or at least helpful, for reconciling the less fortunate territories to an arrangement that raises the rate of growth of an interterritorial union as a whole at the cost of continued, or increasing, differences in the social products of its geographical parts.

My conclusion from all this is that Africa split into fifty economically separate states makes no sense at all. The four biggest economies — the Republic of South Africa, Egypt, Nigeria, Algeria — which together account for nearly half of the continent's income, have big advantages in the race for development by virtue of the sheer sizes of their markets, even though these are, on the average, only about as big as the internal markets of Norway or New Zealand. The rest of the African countries or territories carry an enormous handicap to their separate development in consequence of their smallness — a handicap outweighed only for a small minority of them by some such advantage as their richness in exportable minerals. Union, combination, close co-operation of some kind seems to be absolutely necessary to give reasonable prospects of growth. But what kind of union, and between which territories?

Obviously, I can adduce only very general principles in reply to these questions. To go into specific detail would be impossible without an enormous amount of study, and in any case specific proposals for inter-territorial union, like proposals for marriage, have to take account of many factors other than economic ones. But here are a few general pre-sumptions that may be of some use in considering specific cases.

First, in so far as considerations of scale are of primary importance in African conditions, any union that involves pooling of markets and/or services is advantageous, but the more so the smaller are the territorial economies within it.

Second, since considerations of scale are most important in manufactur-ing industry and in some of the services usually publicly provided, it follows that unions are most advantageous:

1. where they are of a political and geographical form that facil-itates common public services (whether by a central political authority or a Common Services Organization), and/or
2. where one or more of the constituent territories has compar-ative advantages that mark it out, at least in the long run, as more suitable for manufacturing industry than for production of export-able primary products (e.g. a high population density in relation to natural resources).

Third, in so far as union tends to facilitate movement of factors of production (especially labour) between the constituent territories, it will be most advantageous to their populations as a whole where it links territories with markedly different levels of living, or territories with poor development prospects on the one hand with territories with good development prospects on the other. The benefits are greatly reinforced in such cases if the union is of such a nature that its public finance system transfers income from richer to poorer territories.

Fourth, the benefits of a union may be very unevenly distributed; some territories may in extreme cases lose by it though such losses are out-weighed by the gains elsewhere. The territories least likely to gain, or most likely to lose, even though the union increases total income, welfare, and rate of growth are:

1. territories with strong comparative advantages in primary pro-duction selling their union partners only goods that they could equally well sell to the outside world. They receive benefits only through the improved quality and/or reduced cost of public services, possibly improved access by their inhabitants to centres of development in the rest of the union, and (if the union is close enough, and they are poor enough) through public finance;
2. territories which, basically, have comparative advantages for

some secondary industry (notably a high ratio of population to primary resources), but fail to attract such industry in a union because one or more of their partners is ahead of them in supply of skill and enterprise, provision of basic services, or convenience of location in relation to the internal market as a whole. Without special measures of policy these areas will, for a long time, get from the union only the same advantages as the primary producing areas described in sub-paragraph (1), though with greater importance attaching to facilities for emigration of labour. If, however, the form of union permits planning of development, it is possible in a case like this, often at only a relatively small cost in aggregate growth, to spread the secondary industry between the territories. In the first instance, at any rate, this will tend to mean that each territory specializes mainly upon agreed branches of manufacture for the whole union market.

Fifth, the chance of forming a union, and its stability when formed (so far as these depend upon economic factors) are presumably greatest where the advantages are not only substantial, but also well spread between the participants. From this, and the foregoing considerations, it seems to follow:

1. that the most beneficial and stable economic unions are those involving small territorial economies, all of which are suitable for some development of secondary industry, but that a necessary condition of stability may well be an effective plan allocating industrial projects between the territories;

2. that unions in which the prospects of secondary industry are much brighter in some territories than in others are likely to commend themselves most strongly to these potentially manufacturing territories, and to bring comparable advantages to the other territories only if these find in the union improved outlets for their labour, naturally or artificially protected markets for their produce (e.g., for perishable foodstuffs), or substantial financial transfers in their favour;

3. that unions between areas whose strength and prospects, within the practical horizons of policy, lie in exporting primary products to the outside world and not in secondary industry may bring substantial economies in common services, but present neither so strong an economic case as those between potentially manufacturing territories, nor such a powerful mixture of advantages and probable tensions as those between territories that will industrialize and others that will not.

I am aware that these are only very crude generalizations, and that, in any case, the political and psychological aspects of an association between territories can have stronger effects on their development, or lack of it, than the more purely economic factors to which I have confined myself. There is one other general consideration that I should like to mention in conclusion. I have been speaking, for the sake of simplicity, about various forms of economic association between groups of territories, which were tacitly assumed to be the same for each of those forms; the free trade area co-terminous with the monetary area, the common services area, and so forth. The practical (as opposed to the expository) advantage of this is that a single interterritorial organization can then take account most fully and easily of the mutual repercussions of decisions taken in regard to the different fields of co-operation. But this may be too simple. There may be a case for a free trade area, or a monetary area, much wider than the areas over which it would be easy or useful to operate interterritorial services; these services may themselves be operated over wider interterritorial areas in some cases than in others.

This would clearly make for complication in the political organization of co-operation. But if one starts with fifty economies as small (in general) as the economies of the African countries and territories today, it seems to me that there are only two organizational roads to progress. One is political coalescence into 'all purpose' unitary states, or into federations or confederations with various divisions of powers between central and state authorities — the aggregations being much bigger than most African territories now. The second possibility is of a complex but effective pattern of *ad hoc* functional co-operative organizations, linking the existing political units in various groupings.

The possibility seems worthy of serious contemplation, at least as an alternative to the only remaining one, which, I fear, is that of economic stagnation; but time does not permit a discussion of its problems here.

THE ROLE OF AN EXPERT ADVISORY GROUP IN A YOUNG GOVERNMENT

BY GERALD M. MEIER

Stanford University, Stanford, Calif., USA

Development programmes, National Planning Boards, and Industrial Development Corporations now abound throughout the less-developed parts of the world. These reflect a widespread conviction that government must be the primary agent in accelerating the development of a poor country. In attempting to meet the urgency of this challenge, governments have sought advice from outside 'experts', and there is now scarcely an underdeveloped country without its advisory group, foreign consultants, or visiting mission. Economic advisers in particular have had substantial influence in shaping the development programmes of many countries. But if the retention of expert advisers was originally based upon optimistic expectations, subsequent experience has too often been sobering. It has become increasingly clear that there is a need to reconsider what should be the appropriate roles of a development economist as adviser and of a young government as client. It is essential that the government recognize the uses — and abuses — of advice from outside experts. This paper attempts to provide some perspective on this problem. It does not intend to catalogue the varied duties of an adviser, or to discuss in any detail the many substantive issues on which advice may be given, but rather to explore more broadly the problems and prospects of advising a government on its development programme.

It is readily understandable why national economic planning should now be more attractive to the governments of poor countries than was ever true in the historical experience of the presently advanced western countries. Part of this appeal stems from a distrust of the dictates of the price system for attaining the objectives of development. It is believed that the market mechanism is either ineffective, unreliable, or irrelevant. The price system may exist in only rudimentary form: the inflexibilities and rigidities of the economy may give no play to market forces, or they may be too weak. Even a fairly well-defined price system may be considered unreliable when market prices of goods and factors are not a true reflection of the opportunity costs of these goods and factors to society.

And it may be thought that the price system must be superseded when the amount and composition of investment are too important to be left to a multitude of individual investment decisions, and when the tasks of the economy entail large structural changes over a long period ahead instead of simply marginal adjustments in the present period. For these reasons, it may be contended that the variety of interdependent activities involved in the process of development cannot be co-ordinated effectively from without by a market system but must be co-ordinated from within a programme.

The desire to avoid the errors and wastes of the price system is, however, only part of the appeal of planning, and it is not a different kind of argument from that which would also be relevant in rich countries. To a more significant extent, planning has been adopted in poor countries because of a belief that since the obstacles to development are now more pervasive and more intense than they were for western countries in their pre-industrial period, the scope for private calculation and individual action is accordingly less than it ever was in western development.

The very level of *per capita* income from which development must now proceed is much lower than it was in the currently rich countries before they entered their phase of active industrialization. Another basic contrast between the problems of development a century ago and now is the failure of many poor countries to have yet experienced a sufficient increase in agricultural productivity to provide a favourable base for industrialization. Population pressures are also now more severe, in so far as population growth is associated mainly with a declining death rate due to medical advances and is therefore independent of the rate of economic development, unlike the situation in western countries during the nineteenth century when it could be maintained that the population growth was induced by development. Nor is there the nineteenth century outlet of international migration. Even though the overall density of population may be rather low in some poor countries, the concentration of the population in certain areas or the primitive methods of cultivation may still put considerable pressure on the land. Furthermore, a most important difference is that the institutional structure and value system of these societies are much less conducive to development. Social and cultural traditions place less value on the individual, and the core institutions of the family, religion, and education tend to be inimical to development. Political independence may also have been only recently attained, and national disunity and political instability are still common. In short, there has not been a suitable underpinning of sociological and political development for the process of economic modernization.

Yet, at the same time, the popular demand for higher levels of living is unprecedented, and any young government must be committed to quickening the pace of development. Given the insistence on modernization, but confronted by pervasive obstacles that have for so long limited economic change, the governments of recently emergent countries have turned to the practice of some form of planning for development. And with this has come a reliance on the advice of outside experts. But the difficulties involved in utilizing such advice should not be underestimated, and the results to be derived should not be overestimated. The lessons of recent experience are that the client government should temper its expectations of what may be gained from the use of an expert advisory group, and that the adviser should exercise restraint and know the limitations of his advice.

The real difficulty is not that of deciding whether an expert advisory group is a necessity or not, but to determine as clearly as possible the conditions under which such a group can make a maximum contribution to the client government. There need be no hesitancy in seeking economic advice from outside. Every government official cannot fancy himself an economist, and the proper technical knowledge for development may have to be derived from abroad. In this respect the problems of a young government are similar to that of new domestic enterprise. The remarks of W. Arthur Lewis are as appropriate for a young African government as for African enterprise: 'African entrepreneurship is deficient in technical knowledge, managerial capacity, and in capital. Of these three, the easiest to remedy is the deficiency of technical knowledge. For this can be learnt ... Besides, technique can usually be hired. African businessmen should not hesitate to employ expatriates who have special knowledge: some already do so, and more should follow their example. For an African to hire a European (or Indian or Japanese or whomsoever has the skill) should be regarded neither as treachery to the racial cause nor as a source of added prestige; it is often simply the quickest way to establish an African business on a sound foundation.'[1]

Similarly, the most expeditious way to meet the need of framing a development plan may be by drawing upon the technical knowledge of outside experts. No developing country is immune from the fact that knowledge is the scarcest of resources, and it should be no reflection on the capability of a young government that it retains advisers. Indeed, it is a mark of maturity of government leaders to seek guidance from specialized consultants, if the alternative is simply to be dependent either

[1] W. Arthur Lewis, *Report on Industrialization and the Gold Coast*, Government Printing Department, Accra, 1953, p. 12.

upon abstract ideological theories for public policy, or upon the advice of personal associations and friends.[2] Whether the use of outside advisers might be a reflection on the capacity of the government and weaken popular support will ultimately depend on whether the advice is productive of results. For if it helps the government to succeed with a wisely formulated development programme, then popular support of the government will be strengthened.

A client government is understandably chary of having the outside expert become involved with political, social or personal factors. Even short of this degree of involvement, however, an economic adviser can make significant contributions in aiding the formulation of a development programme. His principal role is that of an elucidator. He may indicate what will happen in the economy if no changes are made, and he may reveal what can be made to happen by policy measures that control certain strategic variables. In his role of elucidator, the economist may present a set of calculations designed to clarify decision-taking by making the policy-maker aware of the consequences to be expected from alternative courses of policy action. His major contribution thus consists in pointing out and illuminating the choices of governments, so that those responsible for policy decisions can assess the benefits and costs of alternative measures before the decisions are made instead of afterwards.[3]

What is distilled from his advice may finally be embodied in a development programme. The development programme then serves several functions: as a register of decisions, a method of communicating decisions, a focus of decision-making, a method of delegating decisions, and a measure of the success of the plans which it embodies.[4] An expert advisory

[2] Cf. Max F. Millikan and Donald L. M. Blackner (eds.), *The Emerging Nations*, Little, Brown & Co., Boston, 1961, p. 73.

[3] It is instructive to compare the position of economic advisers in advanced governments. A number of British economists have written about the role and status of economists in government. See R. L. Marris, 'The Position of Economics and Economists in the Government Machine,' *Economic Journal*, December 1954; Sir Robert Hall, 'The Place of the Economist in Government,' *Oxford Economic Papers*, June 1955; H. Tyszynski, 'Economic Theory as a Guide to Policy: Some Suggestions for Re-appraisal,' *Economic Journal*, June 1955; A. K. Cairncross, 'On Being an Economic Adviser,' *Scottish Journal of Political Economy*, October 1955; I. M. D. Little, 'The Economist in Whitehall,' *Lloyds Bank Review*, April 1957; Ely Devons, 'The Role of the Economist in Public Affairs,' *Lloyds Bank Review*, July 1959; Sir Robert Hall, 'Reflections on the Practical Application of Economics,' *Economic Journal*, December 1959; P. D. Henderson, 'The Use of Economists in British Administration,' *Oxford Economic Papers*, February 1961.

[4] Cf. A. K. Cairncross, 'Programmes as Instruments of Co-ordination,' *Scottish Journal of Political Economy*, June 1961, pp. 88–89. For other general discussions of the scope and techniques of development programming, see Jan Tinbergen, *The Design of Development*, Johns Hopkins Press, 1958; Hollis B. Chenery, 'Development Policies and Programmes,' *Economic Bulletin for Latin America*, March 1958; Gustav F. Papanek, *Framing a Development Program*, *International Conciliation*, March 1960; United Nations, ECAFE, *Programming Techniques for Economic Development*, Bangkok, 1960; United Nations, ECAFE, 'Economic Development and Planning in Asia and the Far East,' *Economic Bulletin for Asia and the Far East*, December 1961.

group will have performed a most useful role if it has helped to ensure that the decisions taken are feasible, consistent, and co-ordinated. This it can do by stressing the analytical basis for decision-taking, and by giving shape and logic to empirical investigations.

Indeed, for a young government the *process* of development programming may be of even more benefit than the actual programme itself. In the process of programming, the adviser has three important functions beyond the actual formulation of the programme: (1) to indicate the deficiencies in empirical information and to point out how the data may be acquired, (2) to indicate the necessary administrative organization needed to implement the programme, and (3) to stimulate as much local training and 'counterpart' personnel as is possible, so that ultimately the outside adviser may be replaced.

On the other side, however, it is just as important that the government realize what economic advisers cannot advise on as it is to recognize their potential use. There has been a tendency for governments to overestimate the contribution that advisers can make, and in many instances advisers have not exercised the restraint which should come from a realistic awareness of their own limitations.

These limitations are bound up with the fallibility of the economist's judgement on even the purely economic elements of the development process and from his disregard or relative neglect of non-economic aspects. The fact that a development programme is finally promulgated should not conceal the very real likelihood of biases in judgement and errors committed in the process of formulating the programme. The value of economics lies in its power as a technique of thinking, but as we are constantly reminded it is not a body of settled conclusions immediately applicable to policy, and a government cannot expect to receive from an economic adviser a ready-made set of categorical answers to its development problems.

Indeed, in no other area of economic policy does the distance between theory and policy tend to be as great as it does for developmental problems. There is no analytical model of development that can be readily translated into policy. All models of development are simply ways of looking systematically at the general development process. They relate to the 'economics *about* development' — the way one looks at development in the abstract and from the outside, but they do not immediately constitute the 'economics *for* development' — the pragmatic way one must use economics in the daily administration of a development programme. The approach of the outside analyst is not the approach that is needed by the local practitioner of development programming. Unlike the Keynesian model of income determination which may form a basis for establishing routes to full employment or the model of pure competition which may serve as a basis for deriving rules for resource allocation in a socialist economy, the principles of development are not as immediately suggestive of policy measures. A model of development can never be interpreted as if it were a simple recipe for development; unfortunately, however, governments have sometimes retained expert advisers in the expectation that the adviser can reveal the recipe, or that access to the teachings of modern economics might have some new magical quality.

The scope for professional economic advice is also restricted when statistics of the economy are highly imperfect or the requisite data are unavailable. Economic policy measures necessarily assume quantitative estimation for their formulation and for the evaluation of the effects of decisions taken. The illumination of policy choices is therefore handicapped when the existence of historical statistics is negligible and the measurement of key variables is deficient. Errors may be large when the data are inadequate to calculate such variables as total savings, capital coefficients, the extent of disguised unemployment, or the value of an investment project. The first task of an adviser may, therefore, be to indicate the need for specific data and to make recommendations to fulfil the needs.

The contribution of the outside expert is also limited if he has difficulty in overcoming a parochial outlook. There is a natural temptation for the foreign adviser to place special emphasis on the factors that he believes have been strategic in the history of his own country's development. But the emerging countries are unwilling to follow simply the sequence of their predecessors. An adviser should be free of ethnocentrism and should realize that development cannot be achieved through any simple attempt at duplication: each country needs its own solution to its own development problems. Necessary actions will not be taken by government leaders if they feel that the 'advisers do not understand our local problems.'

The specialist's approach to the very subject-matter of development is also likely to be parochial in so far as one is tempted to attach major significance to his own particular field of interest. The international trade specialist tends to emphasize the role of foreign trade, the money and banking specialist the role of monetary institutions and monetary phenomena, the agricultural economist the position of agriculture, etc. A part of the problem may then be mistaken for the whole. The myopia of a parochial outlook must be guarded against — by taking care in the initial selection of individual advisers, by providing a suitable balance within the group of advisers, and by subjecting the advisers to searching questions of realism in terms of the local economy.

An even stronger and more unfortunate temptation is for the adviser to give the client government what he believes the government wants —

rather than what it more appropriately should have. A young government may believe that its status is enhanced when it draws advice based upon the most advanced economics. Whether it be due to the operation of an international 'demonstration effect' among governments or the dominant influence of intellectuals in the government, there is often a desire by the young government to be advised of the most refined model, the newest technique, the latest element of expertise. If an advisory group succumbs to this desire, it may cause policy-makers to borrow and imitate at too high a level. The attraction to the ornamental in economics and the appeal of the ultra-sophisticated technique are then likely to carry over into the development plan and make it too refined for practical implementation.

At their present levels of political, social, and economic development, most poor countries would derive more benefit from advice that conveys a sound understanding of the fundamental elementary principles of economics than from advice predicated on the highest-style theory. From this standpoint, much of the effort devoted to the use of econometric models and the technique of linear programming in framing a development programme has been premature and inappropriate. These models and techniques have not only focused too exclusively on the magnitude and composition of investment, but they have also at the same time made the economic analysis too over-refined for most poor countries,[5] and they have made more difficult the problem of communication between economics and other social sciences which is especially regrettable for development issues. In dissenting from the use of the methods of operations research in the practice of national planning, Charles Hitch warned that 'High level jobs have allure, but the level does not measure the importance, and is inversely correlated with tractability.'[6] Advisers on development should always be mindful of this warning.

The temptation to operate at too advanced a level of analysis also reinforces the tendency to neglect the non-economic components of the development process. The more rigorous is the economic analysis, the less is it capable of incorporating non-economic elements. Yet it is a misconception to think that development programming is solely or even overwhelmingly a matter of economic analysis. More compelling than the question of how much economic change can be induced is the problem of how much political change and cultural change the society can absorb

---

[5] Even at the level of technical analysis, linear programming has shortcomings: the introduction of diminishing returns or increasing returns raises difficult computational problems, relationships that cannot be expressed in quantitative form must be omitted, and the 'criterion function' must also be quantifiable.

[6] C. J. Hitch, 'Operations Research and National Planning — A Dissent,' *Operations Research*, October 1957, p. 722.

and how quickly. For a country that is in only an early phase of development it is especially important that attention first be given to whether the total environment is favourable for development, before concentrating on the purely economic factors. Unless this is done, the concern with the economic barriers to development will come to nought. As Professor Galbraith observes, 'on even the most preliminary view of the problem, effective government, education, and social justice emerge as critically important. In many countries, in diagnosing the barriers to advance, it is lack of these that is of critical importance. And it follows that until these barriers are removed little will come from capital investment and technical assistance. While plans may be big on paper they will be small in result.'[7] Regardless of the economic logic of a development plan, its success in gaining popular support and participation will depend on cultural elements, values, attitudes. It must be recognized that the social and political environment is an important determinant of the appropriateness and probable success of particular economic policy measures.[8]

In sum, if the shortcomings in the advice of an expert advisory group are to be guarded against, it is most appropriate for an adviser to concentrate on a lower-level analysis, and to strive for an analysis that is comprehensive in giving due weight to strategic non-economic factors, even if this analysis must be less precise than the purely economic. And in retaining advisers to formulate a development programme, the government cannot think that the hard choices of development policy will be solved by the act of programming in itself. A programme, as Professor Cairncross remarks, 'is a focus, not a substitute for decision-making . . . it is nonsense to think that a programme settles everything and that no sensible decisions can be taken without one. It furnishes no more than a systematic way of trying to co-ordinate decisions and improve on unco-ordinated decisions. Although unco-ordinated decisions may be bad or costly so also may co-ordinated decisions: there is no magic about a programme that transforms the quality of decisions beyond the virtue that co-ordination lends.'[9] It is essential to realize that the mere act of co-ordination does not guarantee in any way the merit of the particular decisions that are being co-ordinated.

In addition to being aware of the possible limitations of the advice it receives, the government must also realize that no amount of advice can remove the responsibility that the government must have for the choice of policy objectives and for the selection of the policy instruments that are

---

[7] J. K. Galbraith, *Economic Development In Perspective*, Harvard University Press, 1962, pp. 9–10.
[8] Cf. W. H. Nicholls, 'Accommodating Economic Change in Underdeveloped Countries,' *American Economic Review, Papers and Proceedings*, May 1959, pp. 156–68.
[9] Cairncross, op. cit., p. 90.

actually to be used. Although a government may properly look to an adviser for an indication of what may be done, in the sense of being made aware of different objectives and the range of choice of policy instruments, it should not be under the illusion that there is anything in the professional knowledge of the adviser which qualifies him to *prescribe* what should be done. It is sometimes thought that linear programming models of development provide a set of 'decision rules' that can serve as specific guides to action for the policy-maker. Although linear programming may serve this function for some types of business and military operations, it cannot do so for a process which is as complex and qualitative in character as is the development of an entire economy and a society. Such a basically humane undertaking should not be viewed as a mechanical process, and its diagnosis should not be reduced to a matter of pure technics.[10]

At many points in formulating a development programme, the policy-maker cannot escape from value judgements, and political decisions must finally be made — no matter how extensive is the economic analysis and how abundant the statistical information. This is true for both the setting of objectives and the choice among policy instruments to achieve any one objective. A conflict among multiple objectives is frequently encountered in development programming. Commonly accepted objectives in a development programme are the following: (i) a rapid increase in *per capita* income, (ii) a high level of employment, (iii) a relatively stable price level, (iv) equilibrium in the balance of payments, (v) a reduction of inequalities in income distribution, (vi) the avoidance of marked disparities in the prosperity and growth of different regions within a country, and (vii) a diversified economy.[11] Although each of these objectives may be desirable by itself, in combination they may be unattainable. When conflicts among them arise, it is necessary to decide which objective should receive precedence in planning. Actually, an adviser should be concerned with formulating not a single programme but alternative programmes according to the different weighting of the diverse objectives.

If only economic criteria were relevant for the choice of policy instruments, an economic adviser would be on surer ground. But for each

---

[10] Although he was not directly concerned with techniques of programming for development, the conclusion of Sir John Hicks in his survey of the techniques of linear programming is noteworthy: 'The "logic of choice" now that it has been fully mathematised, appears as nothing else but pure technics — the distilled essence of a general technology.

'Economics, surely, is a social science. It is concerned with the operations of human beings, who are not omniscient, and not wholly rational; who (perhaps because they are not wholly rational) have diverse, and not wholly consistent, ends. As such, it cannot be reduced to a pure technics, and may benefit by being distinguished from pure technics; for we can then say that its concern is with the use that can be made of pure technics by man in society. And that looks like being a distinctly different matter.' J. R. Hicks, 'Linear Theory,' *Economic Journal*, December 1960, pp. 707–8.

[11] Cf. United Nations, ECAFE, *Programming Techniques for Economic Development*, op. cit., p. 6.

economic criterion of a policy action there is also likely to be a non-economic criterion, and the economist alone cannot resolve a possible conflict between these criteria. On the matter of investment criteria, for example, a social psychologist may suggest investment in complex machines requiring maintenance rather than simple machines because servicing the former develops more of desired character traits — impulse control, initiative, general know-how, etc.[12]

This recommendation, however, will call for the choice of capital-intensive techniques in contradiction to the economic criterion of economizing on the scarce factor of production. An adviser may point out the various economic and non-economic consequences of different investment decisions, but once investment decisions are not to be left to the operation of the price mechanism, the ultimate choice of the amount and composition of investment will have to be a political decision. Similarly, for numerous other questions in development programming, the policy-maker cannot expect an adviser to furnish him with unambiguous answers that absolve him from the ultimate responsibility of choice. The more modest, but extremely important, function of the adviser is to enable the policy-maker's decision to be an informed decision, by having it reached in the light of as much information as possible with respect to various policy alternatives and their ramifications, and to ensure that the various policies taken are consistent.

Although an adviser's major contribution is made at the stage of formulating a development programme, the next stage of implementation will determine if practical results are to follow from his advice. The record of development policies in many countries makes it clear that problems of implementation now need to receive even more attention than problems of formulation. The major difference between an advanced government and a young government is not at the level of understanding economic policy, but at the level of execution of policies. Many governments have attained fairly rapidly an understanding of what development measures might be taken, but the capacity to implement these policies has remained limited.

The contrast between the consistency and balance of a development plan on paper and the inefficiency and inconsistency of actual planning has commonly been due to deficiencies in political and administrative requirements. Without sufficient political leadership and authority, a government is unwilling and unable to act upon the plan. No matter how inspired and dedicated the government may be, it should be careful not

[12] For an excellent discussion of the sociological and psychological dimensions of development problems, see David C. McClelland, *The Achieving Society*, D. Van Nostrand Co., Princeton, 1961, chapts. 5, 10. Also, Everett E. Hagen, *On the Theory of Social Change*, Dorsey Press, Homewood, 1962.

to overestimate its political power and its administrative ability. Political interests may also run counter to the economic rationale of the development plan if the political party in power is concerned with only the immediate or very short period of time, is willing to settle for 'showcase' projects and public symbols, succumbs to sectional interests, or wishes to prevent a loss in social status or political power for certain groups in the society. Deficiencies in executive and administrative machinery are especially severe impediments to effective implementation of a development programme. The organization of public administration in many poor countries still tends to be limited to the 'law and order' kind of administration. But this is not suited for the administration of developmental policies. The administration of economic controls is a sensitive art that cannot be practised in a mechanical or routine fashion, or subjected to indecision and delay. Nor can economic enterprises be operated as if they were administrative departments. An economic civil service and full-time economists within the administrative machinery itself are needed. Most importantly, it has to be realized that the very essence of economic policy decisions is their interdependence, whereas the independence of administrative departments may thwart central co-ordination and operation of economic policy. The body that formulates an overall development programme cannot be fully effective if it is merely in an advisory position without executive functions and without influence on the planning activities of individual government departments. Within the administrative hierarchy there must be a clear delineation of the responsibility for framing and carrying out economic policy, and the relative bureaucratic strengths of the respective agencies administering the development programme should not be allowed to determine the outcome of the programme. In addition, there must be provision for necessary revisions of the original plan and guidance on when the several departments and agencies ought to deviate from the originally conceived policies.

An adviser must, therefore, give particular attention to the workability of his policy recommendations. His task consists in more than discovering an 'obstacle', such as uneconomic land-use or inflation, and merely advising its removal. He ought to go beyond this and recommend how, by causing specific changes elsewhere in the economy, additional pressure could be brought on the obstacle to give way. This involves a detailed analysis of sequences in economic policy-making, so that an effective combination of pressures can be initiated.[13] It is desirable to set forth a

[13] Cf. A. O. Hirschman, 'Comments on "A Framework for Analyzing Economic and Political Change",' in *Development of Emerging Countries: An Agenda for Research*, The Brookings Institution, Washington, D.C., 1962, pp. 41–42.

definite chronological order of decision-taking. This may be an adviser's most difficult task since the workability of a set of policies can only be determined from experience and cannot be evaluated except in qualitative terms and by the use of judgement rather than formal analysis.[14]

From the foregoing considerations, I would conclude that it is generally more desirable and practicable to have an expert advisory group concentrate on a partial or light-type of development planning than on a comprehensive heavy-type of planning.

A comprehensive development plan aims at a forced take-off and high speed development, makes a large amount of public investment and deliberate industrialization the core of the plan, and supplants the market mechanism with physical planning that involves the government in decisions that are many in number and of a direct specific character.

Regardless of how much advice is received, this type of planning is likely to be premature for most poor countries at their present level of development. Although a few countries may have already laid the administrative, social, and educational groundwork that is necessary for an elaborate or complex development plan, most of the poor countries are not yet prepared for this type of planning.[15]

Comprehensive planning is also likely to have several undesirable results. It may easily exaggerate the significance of capital accumulation as a cause of development; lead to inflationary pressures; neglect the problems of allocation and distribution; react on the supply of private entrepreneurship and hinder the full realization of investment potentials in the private sector; lead to inefficient industrialization with projects that are handicapped by technical difficulties and excess capacity; and neglect the strategic importance of agricultural growth and foreign trade. It also becomes difficult to correct or revise a comprehensive plan when it is subject to cumulative errors, and it is impossible to do so when it involves decisions that are irreversible. Moreover, the distinction between *initiating* development and *sustaining* development is vital: while a plan may succeed in initiating development, the development process may not advance on to become self-sustaining unless there is a diffusion of individual activities, individual opportunities, and multiple centres of initiative.

More appropriate is the partial or light-type of planning in which greater reliance is placed on decentralized regulation through the market mechanism. Although priorities may be determined as among sectors, a dispersal of decisions may still be allowed for in the selection of single projects within a sector. Government policies would concentrate on creating the general conditions for development by providing social

[14] Cf. Chenery, op. cit., p. 61.
[15] Cf. Galbraith, op. cit., pp. 15–16, 36–38.

overhead capital (education, housing, health, etc.), economic overhead capital (transportation, communication, power, irrigation, soil conservation, etc.), and strengthening markets by institutional arrangements. In this approach to development the initial emphases would be placed on achieving the maximum utilization of existing resources, increasing investment in the areas of social overhead and economic overhead, and raising agricultural productivity. While light industry may be promoted, especially as a complement to agriculture, the development of larger-scale industry would only be induced more gradually from the progress in agriculture. As development proceeded, the economy would be able to use capital more effectively, and capital formation would result from the increase in income.

This type of planning conforms better to the present needs and capabilities of most poor countries. It is also likely to call forth expert advice that is more relevant and that has policy implications which should prove possible to implement. And it should avoid the too easy notion that problems of development are solved — and the costs of development are avoided — merely by engaging in national development planning.

NATIONAL BUDGETS AND THEIR USES

BY K. N. RAJ

Professor, Delhi School of Economics, University of Delhi

The questions that have been put to me relate to a technique of economic programming which ordinarily interests only the specialist. I presume that your main interest in raising them is to form a view on the worthwhileness of adopting national budgeting in African countries, and that you have no wish at this stage to go into the more technical issues. I shall, therefore, concentrate on what appear to me the basic problems involved in the adoption and use of national budgeting in the less developed countries.

In India, we have had to give some thought to this problem in recent years. In fact, one of the first questions to which attention was given soon after India attained independence was the feasibility of adopting national budgeting as an aid to planning and to the formulation of economic policies. In the course of the last decade we have also got to know some of the problems it throws up. I shall, therefore, answer the questions posed to me against the background of our experience in India and, since there are many features common to our countries, I hope it will be of some use to you, at least as a starting point for further consideration of the whole problem in the light of conditions in Africa.

A national budget is simply a statement of the income that is likely to be available to a country over a year, the sources from it is expected to accrue, the likely magnitude and composition of the total expenditure, and the means of covering any excess of expenditure over income. It is thus, in essentials, like any other budget. The main difference from the other budgets to which we are accustomed is that it relates to the entire country, and not just to a constituent part of it. Unlike a government budget, which is concerned with only the income and expenditure of the government, a national budget covers the income and expenditure of all the income-receiving and spending units in a country, whether they are households, business enterprises, or departments of government.

It will be obvious from this that what a national budget helps to do in the main is to take an overall view of the economic activity of a country; and, more particularly, to determine whether there is a balance between the resources available for its use in a given year and the demand for them. If the total demand for resources falls short of the available supply there may be a tendency for unemployment to grow and prices to fall. On the other hand, when demand is in excess of supply, inflationary pressures are created in the economy which may have other adverse consequences. A national budget is, therefore, intended to help in detecting the possibility of such imbalances developing in the economy and in working out ways of correcting them.

One of the first implications of adopting national budgeting is naturally that it should be possible to estimate quantitatively the main constituents of demand and supply of resources in the economy concerned. In other words, it has to have a certain statistical foundation. Data should be available on the national income of the country, on how it is distributed, how much of it is devoted to consumption requirements, on the volume and pattern of investment, and so on. In the less developed countries, such data are usually not available in the required detail, and even when they are (as in India) their reliability is often open to question.

A more difficult problem arises from the fact that the different con-stituents of the demand and supply of resources in an economy are inter-related in a variety of ways. Since the purpose of national budgeting is to detect the possibility of imbalances developing in the economy, and since the sources of such imbalance must be located *in advance* if they are to be corrected, it is, obviously, not enough to have quantitative estimates of national income, or of consumption and investment, for periods which have gone by. It is necessary to forecast the future. This requires some kind of an analytical frame about the nature of the inter-relationships between different factors over time; the dependability of the forecast will depend not only on the data available but on the correctness of the relationships so postulated. In other words, national budgeting has to have also a theoretical basis.

There is nothing very new about the broad notion underlying national budgeting, that, in making economic policy, one should be guided by the balance of demand and supply in the economy as a whole, and not just by the need to balance demand and supply in any constituent part of it. Attempts to measure statistically magnitudes such as of national income, consumption, investment, etc., have also a fairly long history. What is of relatively recent origin is the attempt to *forecast* these magnitudes under *alternative* assumptions of *governmental policy*, so as to choose that alternative which appears to be the best taking all the relevant considera-tions into account.

Historically, the development of national budgeting can be traced to two different kinds of stimuli. The first came, in the nineteen-thirties, from the new ideas associated with the Keynesian theory of income and employment. Keynesian theory postulated certain relationships between the demand and supply of resources, as also between some of their constituent elements, and thus provided, so to say, the theoretical basis of national budgeting. The second stimulus came from the outbreak of World War II, which made it necessary for countries to make the fullest use of the available resources for the prosecution of the war without creating inflation. It was in fact under the pressure of these war-time exigencies that economists and statisticians got together and developed the actual technique of national budgeting.

The preparation of a national budget goes, broadly speaking through three stages. At the first stage, an estimate is made of the gross national product that would be realized if all the available manpower were fully employed; then of the consumption expenditure that would be incurred (on private and government account) from the incomes so created; and finally, of the total investment outlay that might be expected to take place if the existing investment plans in the public and private sectors were pushed through. If the total demand for resources (as represented by the estimate of consumption and investment expenditure) exceeds the value of the gross national product at market prices, and if the excess is larger than the deficit in balance of payments which the country concerned can afford to have, it indicates the need for adopting corrective measures for narrowing the gap. This preliminary exercise helps to determine the magnitude of the imbalance that would develop if existing policies and programmes were to continue unchanged.

At the next stage, the alternative measures that can be taken by the government to correct the imbalance are taken into account. Theoretically, many alternatives are open to the government. If the aggregate demand seems likely to exceed available supply, and there is, what is often described as, an inflationary gap, the government may take special measures for increasing the volume of output; or reduce disposable incomes through direct taxation with a view to reducing total consumption expenditure; or raise the market value of the gross national product by increasing indirect taxation at carefully selected points; or simply enforce a cut in the investment. Which one or combination of these measures is in fact adopted will depend on various considerations, some of them economic and others political; in either case, what they involve are basic policy decisions which cannot be taken by economists or statisticians. At this stage, therefore, the framers of the national budget consult the political leaders who have to take these decisions, indicate to them the implications of alternative policies, and thus try and get a solution that is economically satisfactory as well as politically acceptable.

Once this process is completed, and the likely effect of the proposed governmental measures is taken into account in the estimates, the national budget becomes something more than a mere forecast. It reflects a programme of action. And it is only when this stage has been reached that national budgets generally appear in print; the earlier processes are gone through, so to say, behind the scenes.

Since the national budget in its final form is in the nature of a politically-accepted prognosis, in which the magnitude of the constituent items are the end-results of an economic policy that has already been charted out in some detail, it should be possible to check at the end of the period the actual performance with what was anticipated and proposed at the beginning of it. In other words, some kind of an annual verification of the national budget with the final accounts can be done in much the same way as in the case of government budgets.

A national budget can also be prepared in considerable degrees of detail. Instead of confining oneself to estimating merely the aggregates like the gross national product, consumption and investment, one could break them down further into their various components and estimate each independently before attempting any kind of aggregation. The Norwegian national budget used to be broken down, for instance, into a series of 'global' budgets like production, consumption, and manpower budgets, and then into a multitude of sub-budgets, including commodity budgets, worked out in great detail. Their purpose, in theory, is to bring out sectional imbalances, and indicate bottlenecks, that would not otherwise be evident.

A technique such as this, which offers so much scope for elaboration, refinement, and technical virtuosity, and which appears, at least on the surface, to be so useful for policy formulation, is naturally fascinating to the expert in the line, and often even to the administrator and the politician whom it is intended to help. Without denying the value of the approach underlying national budgeting, it is important, however, to maintain a certain amount of scepticism as to what it can really do in practice. This is not only because of the vast amount of statistical information that would be necessary to estimate the relevant magnitudes with any degree of confidence but on account of the complicated relationships which govern economic activity. Economic theory presents some of these relationships in a simple form, and this is useful for many purposes, but to attribute to them a degree of completeness and precision that they do not have can be extremely misleading when dealing with the problems of the real world.

For this reason, even in the developed countries of the west where the technique of national budgeting came to be developed first, and where vast improvements have since been made in the statistical basis and methods of forecasting, there has grown considerable doubt about the dependability of detailed estimates relating to the future. Some countries like Sweden were always sceptical about the worthwhileness of working out national budgets in very great detail, and confined themselves therefore to broad notional estimates of the more important aggregates. In other words, they regarded national budgets as providing only a kind of frame, indicating in a rough and ready way the kind of problems that might have to be faced by the economy concerned, rather than as the counterpart of a detailed programme of action based on comprehensive forecasting of the future. Other countries, which had originally more extravagant hopes in national budgeting, have generally tended to accept this position.

It may be relevant to mention in this connexion that the usefulness of national budgeting depends to a large extent on the degree of control that is exercised by the government over economic activity. The closer the degree of control, the more a national budget approximates to a programme of action; the estimates begin to have the status of targets. For this reason, I think it would be broadly correct to say that it was found more useful in western countries during war-time than after the dismantling of controls following the end of the war.

In the less developed countries, there is the additional problem that the available statistical data are also extremely deficient. India has a vast statistical organization — perhaps the largest to be found among the less developed countries — and large sums of money are spent annually on sample surveys for collecting various kinds of data. Yet, even today, if one were to ask a simple question such as 'how much additional food grain is likely to be consumed if there is a given increase in national income?', no satisfactory answer can be found. Still less do we know how much consumption expenditure in the aggregate is likely to increase when there is a given increase in income, and how high, therefore, is the value of the marginal propensity to save. With such lack of knowledge regarding some of the basic relationships governing economic activity, it would be rash and misleading to pretend that one is in a position to use national budgeting as a technique of programming and policy formulation.

The fault is not wholly that of the statistician. The less developed countries, once they start developing, undergo important structural changes, and under these conditions even statistical relationships which might otherwise be presumed to hold true cannot be taken for granted. Moreover, so little is still known of some of the relationships which govern the growth of income in these economies that, even if one had accurate data regarding the present, it would be extremely difficult to venture a forecast of the future. For instance, we know extremely little yet of the kind of relationship that obtains between increase in commodity production in these economies and increase in income from services. And without some idea of this relationship, it is difficult to estimate the likely increase in national income even if one has a precise estimate of the likely increase in commodity production. The statistician's task in any kind of year-to-year budgeting is also complicated by the extreme dependence of these economies on agriculture and the variability of crop output in response to weather conditions.

This is not to suggest that we should dismiss national budgeting as something irrelevant to the less developed countries, or make no attempt to study quantitatively the kind of relationships, to which I have referred above, pertaining to their economies. An understanding of the basic notions underlying national budgeting is extremely important, at least as a safeguard against the formulation of governmental policy on narrow and irrational considerations, such as dogmas about balancing the government's own budget. There is also no greater stimulus to the collection of data relevant to rational policy-making than a commitment to produce national budgets, initially as a broad frame of reference and gradually as the basis for more sophisticated programming.

This is broadly our approach to the problem in India. We do not have year-to-year national budgets, but we have end-point estimates for each Five-Year Plan period (i.e. relating to the last year of each plan) covering the more important aggregates like national income, consumption and investment. These estimates will not bear very close scrutiny, as their statistical foundation is still weak; still they serve a useful purpose in that they provide a broad frame of reference. Hunches are better than no hunches in practical matters, and quantified hunches are better than non-quantified hunches because they can usually be verified, if not immediately, some time in the future. But what I want to say is that more than this should not be expected of national budgets in the less developed countries for some time to come, and that the somewhat colourless and difficult job of collecting the basic statistical data required in these countries (and I presume that Mr Jackson will be indicating in his paper what these basic data are) should not be allowed to suffer from the dispersal of effort that might ensue from exaggerated ideas about the importance and urgency of national budgeting.

NOTES ON GOVERNMENTAL MEASURES TO PROMOTE INDUSTRIALISATION

BY BEN W. LEWIS

Oberlin College, Oberlin, Ohio, USA

In discussing this subject, my purpose is to offer, not formulas or specific prescriptions or a rounded survey, but rather a few general propositions intended to stimulate discussion. I claim no originality for these propositions. I shall confine my remarks almost exclusively to industrialization through private investment, and in the main I shall talk about *foreign private investment*. This is not to decry industrialization through government investment or through domestic private capital. Indeed, on my own scale of values, both of these channels rank high. Limits on time, however, necessarily impose limits upon scope. Also, much of what I shall say about private investment from abroad applies equally to domestic investment, and is also relevant to government investment.

I shall phrase my remarks as though I were offering advice to concerned responsible authorities of a developing country.

First, make up your mind whether or not you want to industrialize, and precisely why. Do not seek to industrialize just because others have done it or are doing it. You may do it on either economic or essentially political grounds (or on a combination of these), but in any case be sure of your grounds, and count carefully the prospective disadvantages against the prospective advantages. In this connection, be aware of the requirements for successful industrialization, both generally and for specific industries, and be realistic about your own limitations. For instance, at the moment you do not have a large supply of skilled industrial labour; you do not have unlimited funds in your Government Treasury; you do not have a large and flourishing internal market for all industrial products. Don't put a false front on your assets. Above all, don't fool yourself.

Be prepared for a long, long pull. Industrialization does not materialize overnight. If you seek industrialization because of its value as a symbol of progress, remember that unsuccessful (uneconomic) industrialization may prove to be a symbol of progress–in–reverse.

Second, make up your mind whether or not you want foreign private capital. I do not urge you to seek it, or to seek it indiscriminately, although

my own conviction is that, in today's world, the alleged dangers of
'domination by foreign capital' and 'capital colonialism' are considerably
overemphasized. You have the power, if you have the will, to confine
these dangers. Let me elaborate this proposition. It is politically fashionable to rake up old charges against colonial governments and to inveigh
against 'economic colonialism by foreign capitalists'. My best advice to
you, if you really want economic development, is not to live morbidly in
the past. You are — or are about to become — politically independent
sovereign states. You have the power to protect your people from
economic oppression whether by Africans or by foreigners. Use this
power intelligently and realistically, with an eye to the present and future,
not to the past. Do not be so protective that you repel foreign investment
which you greatly need, and which is willing to come to you on reasonable, businesslike terms.

Investment from abroad need not be pre-emptive, or in any sense
destructive of domestic investment. Indeed, to anticipate a later point, it
is hoped that some of the qualities of entrepreneurship embodied in
foreign investment will 'rub off' and will contribute to the development
of domestic entrepreneurship.

My present point, however, is simply that you should decide whether
or not you want foreign private capital, and if your decision is affirmative
it should be both firm and confident. If you really want foreign private
capital go after it, get it, hold it and keep it coming. Above all else, do not
invite and attempt to attract it, and at the same time behave toward it as
though it were suspect and unwelcome. If you really want it, make it
really welcome. In this area you cannot afford ambivalence.

The attraction of foreign private ownership capital is itself a *business*: it
calls for clear purpose, organization, skill and hard work. Foreign private
capital for investment in developing countries is not unlimited — in fact
it is very scarce — and competition to attract it is intense. The market for
such capital is, today, a sellers' market. It will not flow to your country
automatically. It must be sought by methods and in terms — profit and
risk — which it understands.

The capital we are talking about is ownership, 'risk' capital. It is the
embodiment of a factor which, in the developing countries, is perhaps the
rarest of all factors necessary for industrialization — *entrepreneurship*. It is
my observation that, more than sheer capital, these countries stand in
need of entrepreneurship, the special quality associated with ownership
investment that *senses* when and where and how to undertake a business
or industrial venture, and how to get it off the ground. It involves a
willingness to weigh the chances of gain against the risk of loss, and to
say 'yes'.

It is your job, if you want such investment, to tip the scales in favour of investment in your country enough (probably just a little more than enough, but not too much more) to induce it to say 'yes' to your invitation. Let me be more specific: private risk capital is attracted by one thing — the possibility of profit in relation to the risk of loss. It is irrelevant to talk about the 'duty' of such capital and what it 'ought' to do. This may or may not be the way to talk to the UN or AID or the Foundations, but this is not the language of private capital, and if you want to communicate you must talk the language it understands. You must show it a prospect of profit sufficiently great to overcome any voluntarily accepted risk of loss, and the margin must be more attractive than any margins shown by competing opportunities elsewhere. You have heard a good deal about the 'human' aspects of development; I invite you to consider that the investor is very, very human. In simple, down-to-earth terms, this means that your programme must be built of greater profit and lesser risk. It's a bargaining situation and if both parties are satisfied, it's a deal!

One footnote: you must be realistic, but you need not be reckless. You need not (and, of course, should not) offer too much, and most certainly you never need to offer more than you are willing to offer — the 'market' is entirely voluntary on both sides. An investment incentive programme is a matter of business, and being businesslike involves restraint as well as daring.

Governments sometimes behave as though they believe that profits paid to foreign companies on their investments in developing countries represent a complete loss to the countries. It is said: 'We want investment from abroad as long as the profits are spent here — otherwise the foreign investment is nothing but a drain on our economy.' You know better than this: don't be misled. Profits (when they are earned and received) are the *price* you pay for the capital and entrepreneurship you want. If you buy machinery and supplies from abroad, you expect to pay for them; if you buy the services of experts from abroad, you expect to pay for them; and in both cases you are not worried if your payment is received and enjoyed abroad. In precisely the same way, you should expect that some of the payments (profits) made for the services of capital and entrepreneurship furnished by foreigners will be received and enjoyed abroad. If foreigners *care* to reinvest their profits within your country, this is fine, but they are under no moral or economic obligation to spend their profits in the countries where they are made, and the value of the capital and entrepreneurial service they render is in no degree lessened by the fact that the profit which they earn (if any) leaves the country. For the foreign investor, any reinvestment in the country of earned profit should be made for exactly the same profit-and-risk considerations that prompted his original basic investment.

The distinction that some authorities seek to draw between foreign capital used to exploit natural resource concessions (which is said to benefit the foreign country primarily, and to be conditioned by its needs rather than yours) and foreign capital employed in conventional industries in your country (which is said to serve your needs more explicitly and to be patterned in the light of your needs) is not particularly useful. Mineral resources are, of course, exhaustible and, once gone, cannot be replaced, and in bargaining for their development by foreign capital this fact should be kept in mind. But it also should be kept in mind that mineral resources without capital equipment to develop them are useless. Your bargain consists in trading some of the undeveloped resources for capital — a trade of assets for assets — for mutual benefit. There is certainly nothing questionable in trading assets. The demands for your minerals are no more determined by outside 'interests' than the demand for any of your other products — and your grip on the situation is not inherently weaker in the former than in the latter case. In both cases, if the terms of trade are against you, the advantage to you of the trade will be less than you might have hoped, but the converse is equally true. If in either case you are met by monopoly buyers you are unfortunate, and you must plot your course carefully. But this is a problem of *monopoly*, not a problem of foreign oppression. Treat it as such. Don't be afraid to act. You now have ample power to make the most of your resources and to protect your people. Don't use it to dry up your resources and to deny their value to your people. But, equally, don't be in too great a hurry to realize on your exhaustible natural resources. *Bargain carefully — they won't spoil!*

If you decide actively to seek foreign private capital, prepare your programme with great care. It must be carefully thought out, well organized and effectively publicized. It should not be over-glamourized, but it does require a professional touch, and you probably would do well to seek professional advice.

As a general condition, political and monetary stability are absolutely essential. This goes without saying, and, of course, such stability is not something to be undertaken solely in order to attract foreign private capital, nor is it properly to be considered as part of an investment incentive programme. Nonetheless, it is just as well to realise that the most alluring incentive measures and devices will be useless in an atmosphere of political unrest and instability. I shall not labour the obvious point that investment will flow more readily, too, if the government shows an active interest in, and has embraced a positive programme of education, roads, power, communications, etc. In this regard, however, the potential investor will form some impressions from this programme that will affect his willingness to invest — impressions about whether or not the government is chasing rainbows, and whether or not it can operate without undue waste.

Potential foreign investors are fearful of the future of their investment. They are concerned about (a) nationalization without adequate compensation, (b) required Africanization of ownership, and (c) compulsory Africanization of staff. They need to be assured by practice as well as by words that nationalization will occur, if at all, only on terms and by procedures carefully spelled out at the time capital is sought and committed. They may well desire immediate or scheduled association of local governmental or private capital, but, they are not likely to look with favour upon the prospect of compulsory loss of their ownership control. You may not like this attitude, but it is one of the facts of life which you must face if you want foreign private capital. As a simple measure of economy, foreign owners are quite likely to be eager for Africanization of staff as rapidly as is consistent with efficient operation, and it is in their financial interest to speed up the process and to train African workers. Expatriate staffs are costly. But, if *you* want Africanization at a more rapid pace than is dictated by considerations of cost and profit, you must be prepared to accept a slowing down of the inflow of foreign private capital.

A wide array of special devices to attract the foreign investor is available for use by any government (including governments other than your own) which desires foreign private ownership capital. They are designed to reduce risks, lower costs and increase revenues, and they are not to be thought of as measures to increase the profits of 'foreigners' above reasonable levels necessary to attract the investment you want. They are in no sense *guarantees* of profit. You would be wise to consider all of them in the context of your particular situation: your needs, resources, administrative machinery, political atmosphere and competition from other capital-seeking countries. Tailor your selection and adaptation of these devices to your own situation — do not employ all of them indiscriminately. No one but you and your experienced advisers, familiar with your situation and problems, are in a position to draft an incentive programme suited to your needs. The devices include: protective tariffs, customs relief on imported capital goods and materials, a variety of tax advantages (temporary or permanent, general or selective), and the provision of land, facilities, amenities and finance.

There is little new to be said about protective tariffs. They are deceptively attractive. I can offer no special advice other than to repeat the cautions which economists have been advancing for decades, and to point out that

15

even the most economically advanced countries today find it difficult to rid themselves of the burden of protective tariffs too eagerly employed in the earlier stages of their development.

Along the same line, think long and hard before granting monopoly rights to any new industry, and, particularly, on alleged grounds that, otherwise, the market will be oversaturated and destructive competition will ensue. We are talking about private investment, and the essence of private enterprise is competition. Monopoly may help the favoured firm to get started, but monopoly is inherently *restrictive*, and it can rarely have a proper place in a programme for *development*. If monopoly is indicated, it should be government-regulated or government-owned. And, categorically, *no guarantee of profit*.

Customs relief on imported capital goods and materials is frequently a logical and relatively inexpensive incentive device.

You should give consideration to the general level of your personal and corporate income taxes in relation to incentive, and to the possibility of using some form of the 'pioneer certificate' device to provide calculated temporary tax relief during the early years of industrial enterprises. Generically, this is an excellent device, but its administration is difficult and sometimes has produced more in the way of annoyance than incentive. If it is to be administered selectively, the qualifications for selection should be in terms of defined categories and should be made clear to everyone, in order to avoid delays, unexpected rejections and frustration. Make clear just whom and what you want; don't play games with applicants, or you will end up with applicants who like to play games.

Land, housing, roads, docks, rail sidings, power, etc. (industrial estates) have proved to be useful in attracting industrial investment. These are necessary and costly items in the calculations of potential investors. The incidence of the cost of these items is a matter for bargaining — no general rule can be stated except that, at the outset, you should decide firmly whether your objective is to make a profit on the items, or to use them to induce investment. If the latter, decide firmly whether, if necessary to induce investment, you are willing to bear part (and how much) of the cost. There should be the closest co-operation between the government agency administering these items and the agency responsible for economic development. In negotiating with potential investors, state your terms — all of them — and stick by them. Be clear, make firm decisions, avoid uncertainties and delays, be helpful. If this is part of an incentive programme, don't let it degenerate into a programme of frustrating annoyances.

Some foreign private investors may be attracted by an arrangement under which the government puts up some of the risk capital. This lessens the burden on (and, of course, lessens the profit going to) the private investor, and gives him some assurance of government goodwill and co-operation. This will cost you something, but it may prove profitable. Before going into such a joint venture you should be well satisfied of its economic soundness, and you must provide (both with your private partners and within your own organization) for the effective representation of your ownership interests. The extent of control which you may exercise, either immediately or in time, is, again, a matter of bargaining and, again, whether and how much you want foreign private capital. In any event, all arrangements should be clearly stated and clearly understood.

Do not confuse your power to compel priorities in public investment with your power only to suggest and to induce priorities in private industrial investment. You can, of course, prevent private investment in industries which are harmful to the economy, but you cannot compel private investment in the precise order and pattern which you may consider to be ideal. Welcome all industry that is not harmful: seek out and make special inducements to industries and firms which are particularly suited to your needs. But don't offer too much for too long.

If you decide that, in the existing market, foreign investors are placing too high a price (in the way of special concessions) for their contribution of capital and entrepreneurship, consider the alternatives, and weigh them very carefully. You may be able to get some industrial investment funds from the international agencies, but the amount at best will be small. You can threaten to adopt government investment and ownership — but with what? Your government resources are very, very limited, and there are many more ordinary and development claims upon them (that only the government can appropriately try to satisfy) than your government can possibly meet. This does not mean that you are at the mercy of foreign private investors; there is still room for a negotiated bargain. But it does serve to remind you that capital is a scarce good, and that the road to development through industrialization is a long, rough road. Before using scarce government funds for industry, always ask — and insist on a convincing answer — 'why isn't private industry willing to undertake this venture on our terms?'

FISCAL MEASURES TO PROMOTE
FOREIGN INVESTMENT

BY DAVID WALKER

Professor, Dept. of Economics, University of Exeter, UK

It is not easy to give a sensible answer to the question without straying outside narrow fiscal matters. There is a temptation to consider at length the extent to which an underdeveloped country should be encouraging foreign investment and the particular fields in which promotional activities should be directed. There is also a temptation to consider (and, perhaps, contrast with fiscal measures) other types of government action that can be taken to encourage foreign investment. I suspect that there will be other papers at the Symposium which deal with these aspects. However, it will be necessary for me to make a few brief references to such considerations in order to make my position clear on the fiscal aspects of the problem.

I propose to begin by indicating some of the fiscal measures that can be taken. Then to touch on some of the other measures that are possible. Finally, in the light of a brief discussion as to the extent to which foreign investment ought to be encouraged to suggest how governments might act.

Throughout these discussions I shall for the most part be confining my attention to *private* foreign *direct* investment. This implies two limitations. First, the term *private* implies that investment by governments and international organizations is excluded from consideration. It is most important to be able to mobilize as effectively as possible assistance from these sources but I am sure a consideration of how this may be done lies outside the scope of an answer to the present question. Second, the term *direct* implies that we are concerned with the actual establishment (or extension) and operation by foreign firms or individuals of business enterprises of one sort or another. I am not concerned in the paper with what is usually called portfolio investment, i.e., the purchase by foreigners of stocks or bonds issued by the government of an underdeveloped country or by a public utility or by a locally based private enterprise. In the past this type of investment has been important: in the great hey-day of British foreign investment in the years before 1914 a high proportion of it was in this form. At the present time, however, such investment is running at a low level and it seems doubtful if it is likely to expand very much in the foreseeable future. For this reason and because it is doubtful if fiscal changes in the underdeveloped country can influence it very much this form of investment is not discussed.

We are, therefore, concerned in the paper with the following sorts of foreign investment:

1. An overseas company, partnership or individual establishing a branch enterprise;

2. An overseas enterprise establishing a wholly owned subsidiary company;

3. An overseas enterprise establishing with a local enterprise a new subsidiary company;

4. An overseas enterprise taking a definite interest in an existing local enterprise.

I. Fiscal Measures

Four types of fiscal measures may usefully be distinguished: those involving government spending; those relating to indirect taxes; those relating to the definition of taxable income; and those relating to rates of direct taxation.

A. Government Expenditure.—There are a large number of ways in which government expenditure can encourage foreign investment.

1. Financial help may be given towards the cost of sites, buildings and equipment. In Ireland at the present time, for example, grants of up to 100 per cent of the cost of sites and buildings and up to 50 per cent of the cost of plant and equipment can be made to encourage investment in manufacturing industry in the more underdeveloped parts of the country and — on rather more restrictive conditions — grants of up to $66\frac{2}{3}$ per cent of the cost of sites and buildings and up to $33\frac{1}{3}$ per cent of the cost of plant and equipment can be made with respect to investment in the other parts of the country. Grants are also available towards the cost of training workers.

2. Steps can be taken — through direct government subsidy or in some other way — to enable foreign firms to purchase power, water, transport services and other inputs at prices below the full economic cost. Loans can be made at terms more favourable than the current market rate.

3. The government can establish trading estates and permit foreign firms to rent prepared sites and, indeed, whole factories, at subsidized rates.

Foreign enterprises are not likely to be attracted to a country unless it has a fairly well developed infrastructure, a set of public utilities, and a supply of reasonably well educated and trained labour. The provision of all this is the responsibility of the government and implies a substantial level of government spending.

There are advantages in measures which involve government expenditure. Foreign firms can recognize and measure the degree of help, and for them this is evidence of the goodwill and good intentions of the government. There is also an advantage from a narrow public finance point of view. By helping foreign investors through measures which involve a direct burden on the budget the real cost of the encouragement is revealed. This is good from the point of view of encouraging a full discussion of priorities; of the advantages and disadvantages of alternative expenditure patterns. It may, of course, by providing ammunition for vocal extremists hinder or prevent rational or coherent decisions being taken. Another disadvantage is that government funds are usually in short supply and there is great pressure on revenue resources. This often makes it easier to assist foreign entrepreneurs by measures which involve losing or giving up revenue in the future rather than by expenditure in the present. Not only is it easier to push things away into the future but there is always the belief or hope that the income generating effects of the foreign investment will permit a higher total revenue in the future even though various concessions on tax rates are made.

B. Indirect Taxes.—There are two rather different ways in which such taxes can be used. First, there is the use of a protective customs duty to keep out imports and thus 'guarantee' the home market to a foreign industrialist. This is a measure likely to be used when a foreign firm is being 'persuaded' to establish a factory to cater for the demand for a good which is being imported. The normal argument used to justify this sort of measure is that new industries need protection for a time till they reach a level of efficiency similar to established industries elsewhere. Clearly, one would expect new industries in non-industrial countries to be high cost industries during their first years of life and tariff protection can be a useful way of improving the profitability of basically sound projects during the running in stage. The great danger of this sort of measure is that the pressure to become efficient and competitive is reduced and there is the chance that the country concerned will be saddled with high cost, inefficient businesses which become a drain on her resources. This is a particularly important point if we are considering a small country in which there is only likely to be scope for one or two plants for a number of years.

In connexion with the use of protective duties it is important to bear in mind what may often be an unintended effect of a particular set of tariff rates. Very often customs duties are fixed in such a way as to tax 'luxury' imports at much higher rates than other imports — particularly those in common use. This may be entirely satisfactory from a narrow fiscal point of view but it may make it more profitable to invest in a 'luxury' industry than in an industry producing other (more necessary) goods with the effect that scarce resources may get involved in projects of rather low priority.

The second way in which changes in indirect taxes can be used to help foreign enterprises is the negative one of ensuring that the inputs of such enterprises — raw materials, power, the purchase of capital goods, etc. — pay no customs or excise taxes. This enables the firm to meet foreign competition more easily.

It will be noted that the measures discussed in the last three paragraphs would normally be applicable to all locally established enterprises. It *might* be possible to confine the benefits to foreign enterprises and even to foreign enterprises in particular spheres of activity but to do this would almost certainly cause unrest amongst other enterprises and would lead to administrative difficulties.

C.   *Taxable Income.*—Foreign investment may be encouraged by reducing the burden of taxes falling on business profits. This can be influenced in two main ways. Either by reducing the rates of taxation — this we consider in the next section — or by adjustment to the legal provisions which define what is and what is not taxable income — aspects of this we consider in the following paragraphs.

Since the income tax is a tax on income, i.e., gross revenue minus the expenses of production the effective burden of the tax depends in part on the extent to which costs of production are recognized for taxation purposes. What we have in mind here is really the removal of a disincentive rather than the giving of a positive incentive — though in practice this amounts to the same thing. Foreign investment is encouraged in a country if the tax system ensures that expenditure which the firm regards as a cost of production is recognized as such under the tax legislation. In some cases countries are reluctant to allow certain sorts of capital expenditure to qualify for tax free depreciation allowances. Though buildings and plant which are designed for directly productive activities usually qualify for such treatment it is not uncommon for the capital which goes in providing housing accommodation for workers not to be so allowed, and yet in many underdeveloped countries the provision of such accommodation is absolutely necessary. Similarly, expenditure on the construction of roads connecting the factory to the main highway system of a country is also not always allowed as a cost of production. Often, too, there is a reluctance to recognize expenditure on the education and training of staff, on the provision of recreational and amenity facilities, on scientific research, on passages for expatriate staff, and on advertising and selling expenses, etc. This is not the occasion to go into detail but an important incentive is to ensure that a liberal view is taken of what constitutes a deductible expenditure for income tax purposes.

So far we have been considering fiscal measures in very general terms. What we have written for the most part has been equally applicable to foreign investment in agriculture, mining and manufacturing. It is believed that in this context fiscal incentives are particularly important with respect to mining and agriculture, as special problems exist in these sectors.

There is a good case for generous fiscal incentives for mining companies. There is need for such companies to be able to charge as an expense for tax purposes their exploration and pre-production expenses; need, too, for recognition that mining companies are concerned with wasting assets and need depletion allowances and fairly short writing-off periods for capital expenditures; and it also needs to be recognized that in under-developed countries mining enterprises often have heavy expenses with respect to the housing of staff, construction of roads, etc. — all of which are often legitimate charges against gross revenue. On the other hand if valuable minerals are discovered and exploited the taxable capacity of the enterprise will be substantial in the long run and great care has to be taken not to give over-generous very long run concessions which might prevent the country concerned receiving a proper benefit from the exploitation of its resources.

Similar considerations apply to agriculture. If it is desired to encourage foreign investment in agriculture, either in plantation type enterprises or in mixed farming or ranching type enterprises, a good deal of attention needs to be given to the legal details as to what does and does not con-stitute an expense. In the case of many agricultural enterprises a consider-able amount of investment needs to be made over a period of years before much is seen by way of return. Moreover, in African conditions there is often need for extensive expenditure of a quasi public works type — such as construction of roads, dams, pipe lines, etc. — before even the work of clearing the land and getting it ready for its first commercial crop can be got under way. It is important to ensure that all these various pre-produc-tion costs are allowed as costs for tax purposes and that losses can be carried forward.

A common method for encouraging foreign investment — and indeed investment generally — in underdeveloped countries has been to allow firms to write off their capital expenditures for taxation purposes over a shorter period of time than the capital assets would normally be expected to last. This incentive of 'accelerated depreciation' can take a number of forms. It is possible to legislate that capital assets can be written off in a short fixed period such as five years, even though their average life is expected to be much longer. Or, alternatively, the device of initial allowances can be used so that a substantial proportion of the cost of an asset — say 50 per cent — can be written off in the year of purchase thus leaving a much smaller quantity to be written off over the rest of the life of the asset.

The incentive effect of accelerated depreciation arises for two main reasons. In the first place it makes available to the firm — on the assumption that sufficient gross profits are earned — a substantial tax free loan which may be useful for financing additional investment or repaying short period borrowings previously made. Secondly, and probably more importantly, it tends to reduce risks as the firm can expect to recover the cost of its capital expenditures in a shorter period of time than would otherwise be the case. This is of particular importance if firms in planning their investment expenditures insist on earning a rate of profit sufficient to cover the cost of capital assets over a shorter period than the normal economic life of such assets.

There are certain disadvantages with this sort of measure. In the first place it is only really effective as an incentive device if the firm expects to make gross profits in the years immediately following the investment spending for otherwise the benefits cannot be obtained; though this point can in part be met by allowing accumulated depreciation allowances to be carried forward against future profits. A second disadvantage is that it reduces government revenue in the period when the capital expenditure takes place and this may necessitate higher rates of taxation on other sectors. A third possible objection is that if it is expected that rates of taxation will be higher in the future an effect of accelerated depreciation is to increase the average burden of taxation on the company over the years.

A number of other measures should be mentioned though they are of general relevance and could probably not be confined to incomes arising from foreign investment:

1. There is need for the law to permit the carrying forward of losses and at least a limited freedom to carry them back and set them against profits made elsewhere.

2. There is need, particularly where individuals are concerned and in agriculture, to permit some flexibility as regards the averaging of incomes for tax purposes.

3. It is also important not to confine attention to effective tax rates on the *investments* of business enterprises. Businesses are owned and controlled by men — and men have wives and children! Tax measures designed to encourage foreign businessmen and foreign executives and technicians may have a good effect on the level of investment.

D. *Direct Taxes.*—A common device in underdeveloped countries is to give exemption from company income tax in whole or in part for a number of years with respect to profits arising from new investments.

In Ireland at the present time there is a great desire to encourage investment (foreign and domestic) in industries which will be able to export a substantial proportion of their output, and there are a number of tax concessions linked to this objective. There is relief on taxation of company profits ranging from 25 per cent to 100 per cent with respect to profits obtained from new exports. The full relief is available for ten years with a tapering off period of a further five years. In addition there are measures to provide for remission of local property taxes. Two-thirds of the local rates payable on new industrial buildings are remitted for the first seven years after their construction and in the case of the underdeveloped parts of the State there is remission for ten years.

A number of objections arise with respect to such special provisions. Perhaps the most important is that on first examination the provision of tax holidays and reduced rates seem to be of doubtful value as incentive devices. Such measures do not become effective unless the investment yields a profit; whereas what mainly worries the investor is whether or not costs will be covered and a profit earned at all. Much more important would seem to be help from the government to ensure that costs *are* covered. It is usually more important to do things which enable a company to make a profit than to grant exemptions when a profit is made. Moreover, if a profit is earned it seems not unreasonable that taxes should be paid for then special help is hardly needed. It has, however, to be recognized that business psychology may be somewhat irrational: tax free periods do seem to have good incentive effects and they must, therefore, be included amongst the useful weapons at the disposal of a government. There is also the difference between expectations and the eventual reality. A firm may attach great importance to avoiding a loss, and measures to prevent or hinder this are a vital incentive, but if it did not expect to do more than break even it would not decide to make the investment. A firm expects and requires profits and the promise of a reduction in the rate of tax on profits, implying an increase in the net rate of return, can be an effective incentive.

A second objection is that there is a definite limit as to how far government should go in giving special concessions with respect to foreign investments. Each concession tends to mean a heavier average burden of taxation for the rest of the community. A crucial general issue for governments to face is the extent to which they wish to offer a series of special concessions as against the general incentive of low rates of taxation. If it were judged administratively feasible and politically possible to confine special concessions to foreign investments then, because of the orders of magnitude involved, there would be little impact on the overall level of taxation. But if concessions were extended to all investment then the effect on the general level of tax rates would probably be significant and might have some disincentive effects.

One final point here: due to the operation of double taxation agreements and the income tax law in the countries from which the foreign investment is likely to come it is possible that a reduction in income tax liability in the underdeveloped country will be offset by an increased tax liability in the investor's home country. The main impact of the incentive reductions — assuming that the underdeveloped country's tax rates are below those of the investing country — will be to encourage the investor to:

1. change his residence so as to get full advantage from the concessions;
2. keep the profits within the underdeveloped country, i.e., not to repatriate them and thus keep the advantage of the concessions;
3. operate through local companies and specially formed subsidiary companies rather than through branches.

Clearly in planning tax concessions it is important that the government concerned should be very well aware of the tax legislation of the countries from which it hopes to obtain a flow of investment.

II. Other Measures

I have little doubt myself that in African conditions fiscal action is not likely to be a particularly powerful inducement to a foreign investor. Other conditions and measures are likely to be much more important and effective. I should like to refer briefly to some of these.

The foreign investor attaches importance to the existence and maintenance of what he calls 'political and industrial stability'. A number of factors are covered by this phrase.

1. The need to be convinced that the government of the under-developed country has the intention and ability to maintain law and order and prevent the destruction of property and the disruption of ordinary economic and commercial life.
2. The need to be persuaded: that there will be no arbitrary government interference by the government in business affairs; that commercial contracts will be enforced in the courts; and that no undue pressure will be exerted in connection with wage negotiations or industrial relations generally. In particular the foreign investor needs persuading that foreign enterprises will not be adversely discriminated against — in relation to domestic enterprises — or have to face competition from a state owned or controlled enterprise.
3. The foreign investor needs a definite assurance that if for any reason the government should nationalize his enterprise he will receive full compensation— assessed, perhaps, with the assistance of independent experts.

It is important that the laws of the underdeveloped country should be conducive and acceptable to foreign investors. I am thinking here of laws relating to economic and commercial matters: company law, contract law, bankruptcy law, town planning law, and the statutes under which banks, insurance companies, etc. operate.

It is also important that a country's administrative procedures should be geared to the end of encouraging foreign investment and that unnecessary delays, paper work and red tape be eliminated. It is not unknown in developing countries for the excellent efforts of a Department of Trade or a Development Corporation to be rendered more or less useless by some other agency of the same government — perhaps the department concerned with import licences, or immigration or urban building standards.

Of vital importance to the foreign investor is the ability to convert into his home currency the earnings on the capital that has been invested. Equally important is the ability to sell his investment to local entrepreneurs and convert the proceeds into foreign exchange. Also important is the need for expatriate employees to be able to obtain foreign exchange and transfer 'home' at least a good proportion of their earnings.

Foreign investment in these days has to be wooed. Investment resources are in short supply and are being sought by many countries. If a country wishes to succeed in the struggle to obtain foreign investment representatives of the government concerned must travel the world seeking it, making contacts and — in the contemporary jargon — projecting a favourable image of their country in the minds of investors in the financial and economic centres of the world. A number of other things need to be done:

1. Suitable advertisements need to be placed in carefully selected publications. This is important so as to make known the tax and other advantages that the country is offering and the opportunities that are available.

2. It is of great value if the government concerned knows what it wants and has a fairly clear picture of how it wishes the country to develop and the role of foreign investment in the development process. In this context it is often useful to have a development plan — particularly if it has been drawn up with the help of an international agency.

3. It is important that the country's political leaders (both government members and those who oppose the government) should avoid not only 'wild' actions, i.e. actions disliked by foreign investors — but also 'wild' words in domestic and international gatherings.

A main barrier to the development of manufacturing industry in underdeveloped countries — and, therefore, to foreign investment — is the size of the market. An important way in which governments can encourage foreign investment is by working for customs unions or free trade areas in the orthodox general sense or with respect to particular commodities.

There are a number of other measures which can be used:

1. In support of or in addition to a protective customs tariff a government can by an import licensing system forbid the importation of a particular commodity.

2. By introducing an industrial licensing scheme a foreign firm can be given monopoly rights as regards the production of a particular commodity.

3. Government influence and legislative powers can be used to encourage a responsible trade union movement.

4. Foreign investors are often favourably impressed if the government of a country or some special agency such as a development corporation or development bank is prepared to put capital into a project or subsidiary company in some fairly equal ratio with them. They are also impressed if the government will make some statement about its intention to ensure that the new enterprise makes a profit with the implicit guarantee that if it does not then

some action to produce a profit — by tariffs or licences, etc. — will follow.

III. Development Policy

In the previous paragraphs we have listed a considerable number of measures which can be taken to encourage foreign investment and — particularly in connection with those discussed in the last section — we have implied that a good number of them would probably *have* to be taken. Some of the measures are costly in terms of revenue and may be unpalatable from a general political point of view. It is, therefore, not unimportant to consider briefly what resources or degree of effort *should* be expended in encouraging foreign investment.

A. Types of Investment.—Within our chosen field of private direct investment it is useful to distinguish three rather different activities to which such investment might flow.

1. First, it might go into mining or agricultural enterprises concerned, for the most part, with the production and limited processing of a commodity for export.
2. Second, it might go into manufacturing industry and into enterprises primarily concerned with supplying domestic demand for a commodity previously imported.
3. Third, it might go into manufacturing industry with a main object of producing for an export market.

These categories are clearly not exhaustive or all-embracing. It may be desired to encourage private direct foreign investment in transport, especially in air and road transport; in the provision of banking, insurance, and financial services; in the import/export trade and the distribution sector; in the tourist industry; and in the construction industry. On the whole these are not the sectors in which government effort is usually directed either because local capital and enterprise is more active in these fields or because foreign investment seems to occur in them without the need for much special effort, and it is considered that little will be lost by not specifically considering such investment outlets.

The last of the three categories mentioned above was included for the sake of completeness. (It also happens that in Ireland, where I am working, development effort at the present time is being concentrated in this direction). It is not considered that it is of any great relevance for most African countries. Such countries are unlikely for a number of years to provide a good base for the establishment of industries capable of exporting manufactured exports at competitive prices. On the whole those countries that are making a success of exporting manufactures (or are likely to make a success of it) fall into two categories. On the one hand there are the relatively rich countries of the world which are fairly well endowed with cheap fuel and raw materials, and have good supplies of capital, skilled labour, and inventive and adventurous entrepreneurs and exporters. On the other hand there are countries like Hong Kong and Puerto Rico which have become substantial exporters of manufactured goods even though they lack a good number of these advantages by making effective use of their assets of extremely cheap labour (in relation to productivity) and easy access to cheap sea transport. African countries do not tend to fall into either of these categories. Almost by definition they do not possess the first set of characteristics and, as regards the second those that have low labour costs (in relation to productivity) tend to be away from the coast and sea transport which makes it difficult to build up industries based on importing raw materials and exporting the finished product. The countries on the other hand which do have good access to sea transport tend to be countries with labour shortages and rather high wage costs (in relation to productivity).

In due course the exports of manufactures may become an economic proposition and African countries may be able to compete on the world markets with India, Japan, Hong Kong, etc. At the present time, however, when for the most part the home market cannot yet be supplied economically, it is hardly realistic to concentrate much attention on development through the export of manufactures. Emphasis needs first to be placed on production for the domestic market and on the extension of that market through customs unions, etc.

Our problem then is to consider the first and second categories.

A. Plantation Agriculture and Mining.—Investments in this field are often attractive to foreign investors.

1. As the earnings are in foreign (world) currencies no economic difficulties arise with respect to the foreign investor and the expatriate employee transferring funds to their home countries.

2. Unlike manufacturing industry there may be a real desire in the developed country that is providing the investment for the products that the overseas enterprise is going to produce. From the developed country's point of view overseas investment in primary production may be complementary with domestic production. In the case of manufacturing investment the product of the enterprise may through displacing imports compete with the output of the developed country and reduce domestic profits.

From the underdeveloped country's point of view there is a danger with these types of enterprise that an 'export enclave' will be built up and little real benefit accrue to it. If most of the inputs other than unskilled labour come from overseas and if the wages of such labour are kept low by the pressure of population in subsistence agriculture, and if the profits accrue to foreign shareholders there is a likelihood that the contribution of such enterprises to the economic development of the country will be slight — confined almost to the payment of wages to local labour and the amount of local expenditure (as distinct from remittances home and expenditure on imported goods) of the expatriate employees. There may, of course, be substantial local payments for power, transport, water and other materials—and the government may obtain revenue from taxes and royalties. There is also the possibility that the establishment of mines and plantations will disturb fairly considerably — and perhaps adversely—the living pattern and way of life of the people, and thus produce social strains.

It is important that governments should not be influenced too much by such considerations. The possession of mineral ores and of land suitable for operation by plantation enterprises are economic assets, the economic exploitation of which is a desirable end and often an essential pre-requisite for developments elsewhere in the economy. Often, too, there is much more linkage between mining and plantation enterprises and the rest of the economy in the longer run — and, therefore, more indirect benefits to the economy — than occurs in the early years of operation.

In very few cases would an underdeveloped country have the capital, technical skill or managerial resources to exploit these natural assets, or the marketing contacts through which to dispose of the output. Foreign help is, therefore, required.

On the other hand, great care has to be taken to ensure that too much is not offered by way of inducement in these primary producing fields. It must be borne in mind that foreign enterprises often have an intense interest in the possibility of such investments.

B. *Manufacturing Industry for domestic market.*—Governments of under-developed countries are usually keen to get manufacturing industries established and often seem prepared to take fiscal and other measures to encourage them out of keeping with even the long run advantages of such developments to the economy. Three beliefs seem to be important here:

  1. that by broadening the basis of the economy and reducing the extent of dependence on primary production a country will be less susceptible to the considerable fluctuations that take place from time to time with respect to the demand, supply and prices of such commodities;

2. that such broadening also provides a better foundation for future development both because of the existence of external economies in manufacturing industry and also because of linkage effects;

3. there is, too, the belief that industrialization is the key to economic development and that without industrialization standards of living cannot be increased at all substantially.

Given the desire to get manufacturing industries established it becomes important to attract foreign investment not only because capital is in short supply but — and perhaps more important — because managerial ability and technical competence is in short supply at all levels from the point of view of industrial development.

C. The Development Problem.—This leads on straightaway to a crucial issue. In a poor country the scope for profitable investment in manufacturing activity geared to domestic sales is limited. Demand is small; for with low *per capita* money incomes little is left over after food purchases and rent payments have been made and tax obligations met. In addition low levels of output are associated in many industries with high unit costs, with consequential pressures on profit margins if competition from overseas has to be faced.

To embark on a policy of encouraging manufacturing industry — using the measures discussed in Parts I and II — without paying great attention to the size of the market and the long run viability of the ventures in the absence of special measures of government help, is likely to lead to a misallocation of resources and to check rather than encourage economic development.

A point needs to be made here which should, perhaps, have been explicitly made earlier in the paper. The question asks about 'measures to encourage foreign investment'. My response must not be taken as implying that foreign investors *always* require and need special incentives. In a good number of instances foreigners may be willing to invest without being specially persuaded. This is probably more likely to be the case with mining and agricultural enterprises than with manufacturing — though it can happen in this sector too. Such investment is almost always beneficial from an economic point of view. The stock of capital is increased, workers are employed and earn wages, profits are made which can be taxed, foreign exchange is earned or saved — and the whole operation involves no hidden burdens or costs to the community in the form of higher prices or higher levels of government expenditure.

I am not really concerned here with those forms of investment which need no special encouragement but with those that do. Nor am I concerned with the arguments which economists have used for many years to

16

show that there are a large number of occasions when things should be done — investments made or encouraged, for example — which would not be profitable in a narrow commercial sense and which, therefore, need government help and intervention if they are to be brought to fruition. The paper is mainly concerned with the much narrower question of what measures might be used to operate a given line of policy, i.e. the encouragement of foreign investment. In this section, which is really a digression from the main theme, what is stressed is the need to consider the costs as well as the benefits before deciding to embark on the policy. There is a lot to be said for encouraging those investments which least need encouragement!

In conjunction with measures designed to stimulate manufacturing investment for the home market it is important not to lose sight of the need for measures to stimulate other sectors of the economy. The development of an (import-saving) industrial sector will have a favourable indirect multiplier effect on the level of incomes by reducing the import leakage. Excepting in a very large poor country, however, a bootstrap operation is not likely to be successful and in the absence of growing incomes elsewhere — from exports or other activities — out of which the demand for manufactures arises the development of an industrial sector based on import substitution is likely to peter out as the economic and not too uneconomic industrial possibilities — given the level of incomes and demand — are exhausted.

To attempt to meet this problem by giving more and more concessions to potential investors in manufacturing industry instead of using the available scarce resources to increase incomes elsewhere would almost certainly be unwise.

In the case of foreign investment in mining and plantation agriculture there is, as we noticed above, the danger that most of the economic advantage will go to foreigners. On the whole this danger is well recognized. What does not seem to be so well appreciated is the corresponding danger with import substitute manufacturing industry. If pressed too far the policy of 'encouraging' foreign enterprises may involve the country concerned in paying out substantial sums by way of subsidy; and with prices for the relevant goods considerably in excess of imported goods, and these burdens may hinder the development process.

It will be clear from what has been written that there is no easy, obvious answer to the question. In conclusion I would like to make two observations.

1. The most important question for a government in this general field is to decide, in the light of a general appraisal of the country's economic, natural and human resources and needs, and in the

light of world trends with respect to the demand and prices of the raw materials which it produces what its development strategy is to be. This in turn should throw up the opportunities for foreign investment, and the contribution it might make to the development process. In some cases such an analysis may show little scope for foreign investment (of a private direct type): in others it may reveal scope in the mining and agricultural spheres or in manufacturing for the home market — or both. The analysis should also indicate the extent to which subsidies and other assistance will be needed and this knowledge is clearly a key factor to be taken into account when deciding the 'planned role' for foreign investment; the advantage of using government resources as a 'bait' for foreign investors having to be compared with the advantages that might flow from their deployment elsewhere.

2. Once it has been decided that there is a real place and need for foreign investment (and that it won't flow to the interested country of its own volition) then decisions have to be taken as to how it is to be attracted. Various measures and devices have been mentioned earlier in the paper. I would myself attach considerable importance to those discussed in Part II. Of the fiscal measures the pattern is to some extent set by what other (competing) underdeveloped countries are doing, by the various double taxation agreements into which the country may have entered, and by the tax legislation of the countries from which it hopes to attract investment but I would place emphasis on the points I made relating to taxable income in Section C of Part I and the points made in Section A of Part I concerning government expenditure.

INVESTMENT POLICY IN UNDERDEVELOPED COUNTRIES

BY ROBERT E. BALDWIN

University of Wisconsin, Madison, Wisconsin, USA

I

On a general level there is little disagreement among economists concerning the key requirements for raising *per capita* income levels in underdeveloped countries. The crucial requirement is quite simply an increase in the rate of capital accumulation. Greater investment — not merely in physical resources but also in human resources — is necessary to accelerate the rate of growth. Not only is there a consensus regarding what is needed, there is also general agreement concerning why this requirement is so difficult to satisfy in the underdeveloped areas of the world. Low *per capita* income levels make it extremely difficult for the people in these areas to reduce production directed at satisfying current consumption needs in order to devote a larger part of their economy's production potential toward investment activities. In addition, the lack of detailed knowledge by foreigners of investment opportunities within underdeveloped countries and the high risks associated with many of these projects make extensive foreign borrowing very expensive.

One line of investigation that quite naturally stems from these obvious generalities is to consider various financial policies that might be adopted to raise the internal volume of saving in underdeveloped countries despite low levels of *per capita* income and to increase the flow of capital funds from foreign countries despite the difficulties associated with these endeavours. However, another line of thought suggested by the preceding statement of the development dilemma is to examine the matter of achieving the best utilization of the investment funds that can be raised. This is the topic that will be discussed here. It is a subject too often overlooked in development discussions and yet one that actually occupies a large part of any development planner's time. Moreover, because of the high expectations of the people and the hardships that involuntary saving programmes impose upon the people, the leaders of those nations suffering from mass poverty can ill-afford to use inefficiently the hard-earned investment funds that they can secure. They must know exactly what their nation's various goals of economic and social policy are and ensure that the available resources for investment are utilized in such a manner as to achieve these goals in the best possible manner. Otherwise, they cannot be regarded as successful leaders.

Unfortunately any policy-maker desirous of fulfilling this role receives little comfort concerning the proper way to proceed when he examines the economic literature on the subject of investment criteria. He is confronted with an amazingly large number of seemingly contradictory investment rules, and for each rule there seems to be an expert who considers it the 'best' rule.[1] In large part much of this diversity is simply due to differences in objectives, although too frequently the particular set of goals on which a selection criteria is based is not explicitly stated. Clearly, the particular importance assigned to such objectives as increasing employment or redistributing income in addition to increasing the rate of growth will affect a country's 'proper' investment policy. But the matter is more serious than this. Among writers who claim they are seeking the same objective there is considerable disagreement on the proper investment rule to follow. It is little wonder, therefore, that policy-makers in underdeveloped countries are inclined to employ such divergent investment criteria in their development programmes.

The purpose of this paper is to help clarify the apparent contradictions among writers concerning the appropriate investment criteria that planning authorities in underdeveloped economies should utilize. Specifically, we shall examine the implications for investment policy of various economic and social goals that frequently are mentioned in underdeveloped economies. By doing this it is hoped that, given a particular set of goals, those responsible for influencing investment policy will be better able to implement their goals.

II

It is useful to begin the analysis of investment criteria on a fairly abstract

---

[1] Two interesting works illustrating the wide divergence in views on the subject are: United Nations, Economic and Social Council, Economic Commission for Latin America, *Manual of Economic Development Projects* (58,11.G.5) (New York, 1958), and Center for International Studies, Massachusetts Institute of Technology, *Investment Criteria and Economic Growth* (New York: Asia Publishing House, 1961). A few of the better known articles in the field are: Hollis B. Chenery, 'The Application of Investment Criteria,' *Quarterly Journal of Economics*, LXVII (February 1953), pp. 76–96; W. Galensen and Harvey Leibenstein, 'Investment Criteria, Productivity, and Economic Development,' *Quarterly Journal of Economics*, LXIX (August 1955), pp. 345–70 Otto Eckstein, 'Investment Criteria for Economic Development and the Theory of Intertemporal Welfare Economics,' *Quarterly Journal of Economics*, LXXI (February 1957), pp. 56–85.

but, nevertheless, fundamental level. Suppose we are concerned with achieving the Pareto optimum welfare conditions for the contemporary households who make up an economic community. The satisfaction of these conditions — it will be recalled — means that it is impossible to increase anyone's welfare without thereby decreasing the welfare of some other member of the community. Since we are interested in optimizing over the entire time horizons of contemporary households, the optimum conditions must cover not only the allocation of resources for consumption purposes but also for investment activities. Given this framework, the subject we wish to analyse first is what conditions may exist in the real world that prevent the achievement of the optimum production and exchange conditions under a free market mechanism. In other words, tentatively accepting the goal of maximizing real income for the contemporary members of the economy, what grounds are there for the possible intervention by the government in the economic scene? Until one understands the issues involved in this question, there is little use in discussing particular investment criteria.

As is well known, on the production side — to which we shall limit our attention here — there are four main reasons why a free market mechanism may fail in the attainment of the Pareto optimum conditions.[2] These are: (A) the existence of increasing returns to scale; (B) the existence of collective goods; (C) the existence of technological externalities; and, finally, (D) the existence of imperfect markets due to the lack of perfect knowledge or institutional factors. Let us consider each of these in turn.

A.   Increasing returns to scale mean that a certain percentage increase in inputs results in a percentage increase in output that is greater than the given percentage increase in inputs. With constant input prices, it follows that the average cost curve of a firm producing this output will be downward sloping. Since monopoly behaviour will emerge in such an industry under a free market system, the optimum condition that price equal marginal cost will be violated. However, the difficulty is not just the existence of monopoly behaviour. Since marginal cost will be below average cost, setting price equal to the level at which the demand curve intersects the marginal cost curve results in losses being incurred by the firm. Consequently, even should a private firm be induced to set price equal to marginal cost, it still could not remain in business with a single price policy unless subsidized by the government.

Closely related to the case of increasing returns to scale in the output range relevant for existing demand conditions is the case where returns to

---

[2] For a comprehensive analysis of the factors that may prevent the attainment of the optimum conditions under free markets see: J. de V. Graaff, *Theoretical Welfare Economics* (Cambridge: Cambridge University Press, 1957), chaps. 2–4.

scale are decreasing but a monopoly problem nevertheless arises under free market conditions. This situation occurs when average costs for a producer fall over such a wide range of output in relation to total market demand that one or a few firms with non-decreasing unit costs exhaust the market. Under these circumstances competition in the market cannot be relied upon to ensure marginal cost pricing. However, unlike the previous case, marginal cost pricing in this situation does not mean that a firm would incur losses.

To what extent might one expect increasing returns to scale in under-developed countries to cause the above sort of difficulties? Probably most would agree that in the so-called public utility field — covering such industries as electric power, railway transportation, telephones, and telegraph — increasing returns to scale are significant in relation to the demand for these services. Consequently some form of government intervention to ensure optimum pricing is justified. In other sectors of the economy little can be said on a general level. The number of domestic firms in most industries usually are sufficiently large to ensure competitive behaviour or the opportunities for importing identical or similar commodities are favourable enough to prevent monopolistic behaviour in cases where there are only a few domestic producers. However, in any area where local or foreign competition is weak a case does exist for some form of government intervention or regulation to ensure the optimum pricing results that pure competition would bring.

B. Collective or public goods are those commodities that are consumed collectively by members of the community. The usual example given is national defence. Another illustration is the services from a flood control project above a town. The essential aspect of these types of commodities is that they are not — usually for institutional reasons — subject to the exclusion principle. When one individual consumes the service other individuals also consume it, e.g. your flood control protection is my flood control protection. A free market pricing system will result in the underproduction of these goods from a social point of view. The difficulty is that individual consumers will equate the money exchange ratio for the public commodity to their individual marginal rates of substitution between the commodity and all other commodities, whereas a social optimum requires an equality between the exchange (and marginal cost) ratio and a weighted sum of the above marginal rates of substitution for all the individuals in the community. Another problem with a free pricing system is that each consumer in an attempt to induce others to pay for the collective commodity is not likely to reveal his true preferences.

Because of these characteristics of collective commodities the appropriateness of government intervention in determining the output of these goods has long been recognized. However, there is no automatic guarantee that by government action we will come any closer to the social optimum position than without intervention. It would seem that we usually produce more than would be called forth under a free price system, but there is the possibility that government intervention results in overproduction of these commodities.

One method of handling the problem is to set up arrangements which exclude the collective consumption of the commodity. It is almost never impossible to devise some sort of exclusion method. For example, a wall can be put around a park and admission keys given to those who wish to pay for enjoying the park. Similarly, roads could be privately owned and tolls charged for using the roads. However, the cost of the resources involved in preventing collective consumption may be greater than the efficiency benefits that would result from the exclusion. Consequently, most economists would agree that, despite the difficulties of ascertaining the optimum output for public goods through political processes, government intervention is appropriate in order to improve upon the obviously nonoptimum result under a free pricing system.

C. Technological spillover effects arise because of physical interdependences among different production functions.[3] A change in the input or output rate by one producer influences the physical output other producers can obtain from their physical inputs. The most frequently cited example is the interaction between apple producers and honey producers. A farmer who produces honey benefits from the expansion of a nearby apple farm, since his bees are able to gather a greater quantity of nectar in a given period of time. Similarly, an increase in the number of bees increases apple output by increasing the degree of pollination. Because these physical interactions exist and yet each producer is not able to capture the benefits his expansionary actions have on other producers, a social optimum will not be achieved. Government intervention in the form of subsidies and taxes is one method of handling technological external economies and diseconomies. Another method is to make changes in ownership arrangements, since it is the divorce of scarcity from effective ownership that causes the misallocation of resources when technological spillover effects exist. In the honey-apple case combining the two activities into one firm will eliminate the divergence between private and social costs and benefits.

The opinion of most writers on the subject seems to be that in a static economy technological externalities — not offset by ownership arrangements that eliminate the divergence between social and private costs and

[3] For an especially clear analysis of technological externalities see: Francis H. Bator, 'The Anatomy of Market Failure,' *Quarterly Journal of Economics*, LXXII (August 1958), pp. 351–79.

benefits — are not very significant.[4] Under static conditions the types of external effects most unlikely to be offset by voluntary ownership arrangements are ones involving many producers. Therefore, the collective commodity problem already discussed arises. An example of this is the discharge of pollutants into irrigation water by a user of such water. This action reduces the output of other farmers who subsequently use this water. Yet it is likely to be difficult to get the other producers to voluntarily get together to bribe the initial farmer to refrain from discharging the pollutants. Some new type of legal device or outright government control probably is required in this case.

Although there is general agreement that uncompensated technological spillover effects are not especially important in a stationary economy, there is general agreement that they are very significant in a dynamic, growing economy.[5] The training of labour by employers is usually presented as perhaps the most important type of technological externality that operates over time. The problem associated with on-the-job training is often stated as follows. In ascertaining the extent to which training is profitable an employer compares the costs of training with the additional profits that accrue to him during the period that the trained workers remain with him. However, the social benefits from trained workers last over their entire working lifetime and not merely while employed by the employer who trained them. But, since slavery is not permitted, an employer will not be able to capture the extra income the workers gain after they leave him. Consequently, in underdeveloped countries where turnover rates are especially high, training programmes will fall short of what is required to achieve the social optimum.

The above analysis seems at first sight to be reasonable but in fact it is not complete. It neglects the equilibrating tendencies in the market for trainees. Although an employer considers the returns he will secure from a trained worker only during his expected period of employment, a prospective trainee in offering himself for training considers the extra income he earns during and after his employment with the firm which trains him. The prospect of obtaining extra income after leaving the initial employer will act to depress the wage at which trainees will work during their training period. Indeed as long as they can gain by such training they will be willing to pay the employer for the training. In a free, competitive market the fact that employees move from one employer to another during their lifetime will not bring about a different result in

[4] For example see Tibor Scitovsky, 'Two Concepts of External Economies,' *Journal of Political Economy*, LXII (April 1954), p. 145, and Francis M. Bator, 'The Simple Analytics of Welfare Maximization,' *American Economic Review*, XLVII (March 1957), p. 42.

[5] Scitovsky, op. cit., pp. 145–51; Bator, 'The Anatomy of Market Failure,' op. cit., p. 365; de V. Graaff, op. cit., p. 14.

terms of training than if they remained in one employment during their lifetime. One does not need the institution of slavery to get this result. The same point holds with respect to the other types of dynamic externalities mentioned in the literature. Of course, imperfections in the market such as minimum wage rates or imperfect capital markets can prevent the dynamic externalities from being fully exploited. But one should understand that these are the factors and not some other institutional arrangements that give rise to uncompensated externalities.

There is, however, one other type of external effect that does not fit the preceding description of externalities very well, and yet may have very important growth repercussions in an underdeveloped economy. Expansion of one industry may encourage the utilization of improved technology in other industries whose demand or supply conditions are affected by the initial industry. This type of externality is not a technological one in the sense that the production functions of these industries are interdependent. On the other hand, the use of better techniques does involve a real increase in production possibilities.

One important factor operating to hold down the rate at which new techniques are introduced is the high risk aversion that low income producers possess. A subsistence producer prefers a lower expected income to a higher expected income if the range of possible outcomes is smaller in the lower expected income case. The risk element may be considerable even when existing techniques are employed, but it is still greater when new methods first are employed. Although aversion to risk influences all producers no matter what their income levels, a rise in income seems to reduce the degree of risk aversion. Consequently, as a subsistence producer's income rises under existing productive methods because of a change in market conditions, he becomes more willing to assume innovational risks. Therefore, a purely pecuniary externalty such as an expansion of demand in a particular market may lead to repercussions that raise the economy's national product.

Another reason why an expansion of one industry that increases the demand for the output of another industry may lead to the introduction of better techniques in this other industry is because market imperfections and indivisibilities exist. For example, the introduction of a particular improved technique by a rural producer may require the purchase of some 'lumpy' capital good, but the existence of an imperfect capital market prevents the producer from borrowing the needed funds. However, when the demand for the firm's output rises because of the expansion in another sector, the increased profits accruing to the producer may enable him now to purchase the capital goods and introduce the new method of production.

To the Hon. Secretary, of the Chisiza/Makata Memorial Appeal, Fircroft College, Birmingham, 29.

I enclose a contribution of £   s.   d. to the above Appeal.

Signed :   NAME ....

ADDRESS ....

....

....

Cheques and Postal Orders should be crossed and made payable to the Chisiza/Makata Memorial Appeal.

Chizisa/Makata Memorial Appeal

DEED OF COVENANT

I, ...

of ....

hereby Covenant with FIRCROFT COLLEGE (hereinafter called 'Fircroft') of Birmingham that for a period of seven years from the date hereof (or during my lifetime whichever period shall be the shorter) I will pay annually on the

.... day of .... in each year to Fircroft such a sum as will after deduction of the Income Tax thereon leave in the

hands of Fircroft a net sum of £ ....

(...) the said sum to be paid from my general fund of taxed income so that I or my estate shall receive no personal or private benefit in any of the said periods from the said sum or any part thereof.

IN WITNESS whereof I have here set my hand and seal this ....

day of...19...............

Signed, Sealed and Delivered by the said :

....   SEAL

in the presence of :

Witness
- (Signature)...
- (Address) ....
- ....
- (Occupation) ....

(NOTE.—The date chosen for the annual payments must be later than the date on which you sign the deed.)

NYASALAND

CHISIZA/MAKATA MEMORIAL APPEAL

Those who read the papers of the Nyasaland Economic Symposium in this volume will be aware of the effort and skill needed to organise such a gathering. This brilliant organisational work was done by Dunduzu Chisiza, who himself read one of the most striking papers at the conference and who was also responsible for drafting the Nyasaland Development Plan before self-government was granted.

Chisiza's only formal education was a one-year course in economic and social studies at Fircroft College, England, in 1957-8 but he avidly followed up these studies during his period of detention in 1959-60. It was a tragic blow to Malawi, and indeed to Africa as a whole, when Chisiza was killed in a car accident soon after the end of the Symposium.

In the same year, Lawrence Makata, Executive Member and Deputy Chairman of the Malawi Congress Party, also died in a car accident. Makata, an astute businessman, used his money to help the cause of the Malawi Congress Party but, during his period of detention, his business collapsed and he lost everything. Had he lived, he would probably have been the first African Mayor of Blantyre.

In memory of these two men the Chisiza/Makata Memorial Appeal was set up in the United Kingdom under the Secretaryship of Philip Hopkins, Warden of Fircroft, where Chisiza had studied. Members of the Sponsoring Committee are Hon. David Astor, Ernest Bader, Mary Benson, Charles Brooke-Smith, Christopher Cadbury, Sir Jock Campbell, Lord Hemingford, Edward F. Jackson, Edward Mwasi and Alderman St. John Reade, and George Thomson, M.P. acted as the Chairman before his ministerial appointment.

Money collected in this country (at present totalling £2,730) is to be used to send a Malawi student to Fircroft (Chisiza's old College) each year for seven years. It is intended that the student will return immediately after the end of his year to contribute to the economic and social development of his country. Rising costs make it necessary to find more money and all donations will be gratefully received.

[P.T.O.

D. The most obvious requirement for the achievement of an optimum allocation of resources over time is the existence of perfect markets. One aspect of this is the requirement of perfect knowledge. For example, both investors and savers must know future prices and what new techniques will be introduced in the future in order to make optimal investment and saving decisions. Only if perfect futures markets, extending indefinitely into the future, existed for all goods would firms and households possess the information for making rational saving and investment decisions concerning the future.

Since such futures markets do not in fact exist, the requirements for the attainment of an optimum over time are clearly not fulfilled. However, the interesting question at this point is not whether they are or are not fulfilled but whether government intervention in the investment process can be justified on the grounds of imperfect knowledge. For some writers the answer is emphatically yes. These authors stress two points — the interdependence among investment projects and the indivisibilities associated with many investments.[6] The first point refers to the fact that an investment in, say, industry A affects the profitability of an investment in industry B. If an investor in industry B is unaware that investment is taking place in industry A and if this investment does affect profits in industry B, then he lacks the necessary knowledge for an optimal investment decision. On the other hand, if all investment decisions are co-ordinated and taken simultaneously, these pecuniary interdependencies can be exploited immediately.

There seems to be general agreement that if capital accumulation takes place by small increments this type of interdependence does not cause much difficulty.[7] Successive mutual adjustments within the various industries involved will tend to bring about an economically efficient level. Furthermore on the basis of past experience businessmen may also be highly successful in anticipating pecuniary externalities and thus come close to making optimum investment decisions.[8] However, there is no doubt that better information would be available if investment decisions were centrally made. Therefore, the real economic question is — setting aside the relative merits of private versus government decision makers in terms of mechanical efficiency and the possible political consequences of

[6] Scitovsky, op. cit., pp. 148–50, and Scitovsky, 'External Economies, Investment, and Foresight: A Reply,' *Journal of Political Economy*, LXIII (October 1955), pp. 450–1; P. N. Rosenstein-Rodan, 'Programming in Theory and Italian Practice,' in Center for International Studies, op. cit., pp. 19–32. For an excellent summary and critical analysis of this subject see Marcus Fleming, 'External Economies and the Doctrine of Balanced Growth,' *Economic Journal*, LXV (June 1955), pp. 241–56.

[7] Scitovsky, 'A Reply,' op. cit., pp. 450–1; R. N. McKean, *Efficiency in Government Through Systems Analysis* (New York: John Wiley and Sons, 1958), pp. 142–3.

[8] J. A. Stockfisch, 'External Economies, Investment, and Foresight,' *Journal of Political Economy*, LXIII (October 1955), pp. 446–9.

government intervention (both of which are irrelevant for the theoretical problem) — whether the additional costs associated with collecting and evaluating investment information from all industries and then centrally co-ordinating this data are greater or less than the additional social benefits that could be derived by utilizing this information. Apparently, where investment proceeds by small increments there is general agreement that the costs are greater than the gains.

When investments can take place only in large 'lumps', the existence of strong interdependencies could — all would agree — lead to more serious errors than in the previous case. For example, there may be two inter-dependent investment projects each of which is not profitable without the other and each of which must be undertaken in large 'lumps'. Under these conditions neither investment may be undertaken by private interests for fear the other will not be undertaken. Therefore, government interven-tion into the investment process may be required to exploit the inter-dependencies fully.

The allocation problem arises — it should be noted — because of the indivisibility of certain types of investment projects. However, it is in these investment areas where monopolistic or oligopolistic market behaviour will emerge in a free market and therefore where a recognition of the interdependence of investment decisions both within an industry and among closely related industries will exist. Since the number of firms is comparatively small, the costs involved in making co-ordinated business decisions through some private arrangement among the firms involved is also relatively small. In other words, in the 'lumpy' investment case the misallocation error can be large if interdependences are ignored, but this is precisely the kind of situation where private firms are most likely to make arrangements for taking them into account if they are significant. More generally, if co-ordinated decision-making among complementary industries increases national product when the economic costs of making these decisions are taken into account, private producers in a free market system will try to make private arrangements to undertake a co-ordinated investment policy.

The other main aspect of the requirement for perfect markets that should be mentioned is the actual existence of rigidities and frictions, of irrational behaviour, and of monopoly and oligopoly behaviour — all of which prevent the achievement of an efficient allocation of resources. The most important of these conditions from the point of view of corrective policies is the existence of monopoly actions. We have already touched on the consequence of these actions in connection with the increasing returns to scale problem. But it should be recognized that monopoly behaviour does not just stem from this phenomenon. Many forms of monopoly can undoubtedly be broken up into competitive units without sacrificing any real benefits to the economy. Where this applies, vigorous anti-trust action by the government is needed to prevent self-oriented groups from benefiting at the expense of the community as a whole. Unfortunately, in efforts to redistribute income the government itself often needlessly acts to misallocate resources. Such actions as exchange control, price control and subsidization of certain agricultural commodities, and the enforcement of minimum wage laws clearly contribute to a misallocation of economic resources.

III

The preceding analysis has led to the conclusion that there are grounds for government intervention in the economic process, given the goal of achieving an optimum resource allocation over time for contemporary households. Most economists agree that in such areas as electric power, roads and railways, education, defence and police protection, etc., there is no question about the need for government intervention of some type in the economic allocation process. However, there are some writers who argue that on the basis of the four factors previously discussed, government intervention in underdeveloped countries should be much more extensive. In particular they argue that unless comprehensive investment programming is undertaken by the government an optimum allocation of resources in a dynamic sense does not have a chance of even approximate achievement. The market mechanism is, in other words, a poor method of allocating resources over time.

We would like to suggest here that the analytical arguments presented to support this position seem superficially convincing but lose most of their force under more careful examination. The rather casual side remark made by some theorists that underdeveloped countries illustrate the best cases where a free price mechanism will not work well does not seem to be based on careful reasoning.[9] One of the two main points these writers usually have in mind is that dynamic technological externalities are especially important in underdeveloped countries and are not likely to be handled properly in a free market system. The second point is that lumpy investments are more important in underdeveloped than developed areas and therefore the investment interdependence problem is more serious in the former areas.

It is not possible to decide on the basis of casual empiricism if technological spillovers are in some sense more significant in underdeveloped

[9] See, for example, Scitovsky, 'Two Concepts of External Economies,' op. cit., p. 150.

than developed countries. However, the point to make is that the analytical reasons usually given to support the significance of uncompensated dynamic technological externalities are not conclusive. Of course, if restraints hinder the operation of a flexible, free price system, then the externalities may not be made internal through private property arrangements. But the cure here would seem to be to try to remove the restraints through government intervention rather than to accept the restraints and use government intervention to get around them.

The matter of the significance of lumpy investments in underdeveloped countries is also impossible to evaluate on general grounds. It is argued here that this does not constitute a serious problem in terms of achieving optimal investment decisions except to the extent that monopoly behaviour will tend to develop under these conditions with free market arrangements. The monopoly problem may be more serious in underdeveloped countries although one is hesitant to make this statement. But, even if it is, this problem is hardly likely to lead one to the conclusion that centralized planning is essential. Certainly, the misallocation caused by monopoly has not been used as the main argument by those who do advocate this policy.

Even if the view that extensive central planning is necessary to maximize income over time is rejected, there still are — as has been previously mentioned — wide areas where government intervention is desirable in order to maximize over time. One form of this intervention that is sometimes appropriate is government investment activity. Granting this, what investment rule should the government follow to achieve the Pareto optimum conditions?

The answer is quite straightforward. If the present value of the benefit stream resulting from a particular investment project is greater than the present value of the cost stream connected with the project, the investment should be undertaken. In other words, the standard present value rule is the correct one to follow. It is sometimes useful to express benefit and cost streams in terms of level annual flows. Under this equivalent rule, any investment that yields annual net benefits greater than zero should be adopted.

In determining benefits and costs the government must, of course, be concerned with social rather than private benefits and costs. As previously noted, this involves taking technological externalities into account in estimating the net benefits associated with a particular project. In addition the existence of all sorts of market imperfections due to institutional arrangements means that prices do not adequately reflect real costs. In general, the government should take measures that eliminate these imperfections, since they distort the allocative process. However, if for some reason this is not done, the government in its investment decision-making should correct market prices to reflect actual opportunity costs. It should, in other words, use so-called shadow prices.

The discount rate that the government should use in determining present values for any particular project, given the optimizing goal under discussion, is one that reflects the rate at which the government could borrow funds for the particular project in a competitive capital market and if the repayment power of the government bond is limited to the expected benefits derived from the project, i.e. a revenue bond rather than a general credit bond is used. To make public investment calculations comparable to private ones the government project also must be treated as if it pays the same level of taxes as private firms do.

IV

It is apparent that the actual investment activities undertaken by most underdeveloped countries differ significantly from what would seem to follow from the preceding analysis. In numerous countries there are, we suggest, many projects undertaken by the government that the people would reject if the government was obliged to use the market place to secure its investment funds. Obviously, this leads to the question as to why governments do in fact run counter to the preferences expressed by the people in the market place.

The main justification usually given by planners is that the present generation does not give sufficient weight in its saving and investment decisions to future generations. Contemporary households are too short-sighted and consequently devote too large a share of their income to consumption purposes rather than to saving.[10] It is the duty of the government — so the argument goes — to represent the welfare interests of future generations as well as contemporary households. Therefore, the government must act to increase the current rate of investment.

Whether the people of underdeveloped countries actually do want their governments to adopt this attitude might be debated, but it is a widely accepted goal by those who influence governmental development planning. Accepting it as a goal, we wish to ask how it modifies the conclusions previously reached when only contemporary households were considered. In general all that can be said is that saving and investment rates should be greater than under the previous goal. Once the goal of achieving a Pareto optimum for contemporary households is abandoned the optimum rate of investment becomes largely a political matter.[11] In

[10] Advocates of this position do not claim that contemporary households completely ignore future generations in allocating their income over time. The point is simply that they do not give sufficient weight to future generations in their decisions.

[11] See de V. Graaff, op. cit., pp. 99–105, for an excellent discussion of the implications of this point

particular those making investment decisions must themselves determine the time horizon over which national income is to be maximized as well as determining the terminal capital equipment when the horizon is reached. They must also, of course, decide in some way the particular nature of the preference functions of future generations that are to be used in the social welfare function. All these decisions will influence what the optimum investment rate is and they must be specified in order to determine the optimum rate.

Different value judgements as expressed through the political process concerning the most desirable distribution of income is another major factor accounting for differences with regard to what is an appropriate investment programme. Satisfaction of the Pareto optimum conditions does not imply any specific income distribution. There are, in other words, many income distributions possible with the Pareto conditions still being fulfilled. Under a free price system the particular distribution that emerges depends upon the initial ownership arrangement regarding the factors of production. If a government does not wish to accept this distribution, it theoretically can still achieve a Pareto optimum with the income distribution it does prefer.

One important expression of value judgements by governments on this matter concerns the distribution of income over time. It seems that many governments are prepared to give relatively high weights to the preferences of future generations in the social welfare function being maximized. The present generation is being asked to make heavy sacrifices to benefit future generations. This takes the form of restricting present consumption in order to increase the rate of present investment.

Although rejecting the preferences of contemporary households regarding their valuation of present versus future income enables the government to influence the shape of the income paths possible with investment, it does not provide a direct method for discriminating among different types of current outputs. Yet those in political power in under-developed countries also wish sometimes to reject the sovereignty of consumer preferences among commodities. Planners may not, for example, be willing to accept the fact that an increase in the number of movie theatres may increase the value of national income more than a steel mill no matter what discount rate is employed. The justification for this viewpoint is an extension of the kind of argument given in connection with the control over the production of such items as narcotics. Obviously, the more extensive this sort of interference with consumer choice, the more necessary a completely planned economic system becomes in order to achieve the goals set forth by the government.

Governments also take measures to influence not only the distribution of income over time but also among members of the community at any particular time. One method is to select investment projects that mainly benefit a particular group, e.g. an irrigation project in a particular rural area. The great danger with this procedure is that projects are not selected that bring about the largest possible net increase in the economy's national income. Growth is needlessly sacrificed in order to achieve the desired distribution of income. Sometimes this may be necessary, given the actual institutional constraints within which the government operates. Too often, however, poor planning is the cause. There may, in other words, be ways other than investing in the area where income is regarded as too low by which the desired income distribution can be obtained without holding back the economy's overall growth rate. Since the capital resources of the typical poor country are already so low it is essential that particular groups be subsidized only when their case on grounds of social justice is unusually strong.

The goals of maintaining full employment, a stable price level, and equilibrium in the balance of payments also often conflict with the growth goal in underdeveloped countries. Governments, for example, select investment projects that are more appropriate for the employment goal than the development objective. We would argue — as in the income distribution case — that many of these conflicts arise because of the lack of determination and imagination on the part of the planners. They do not fully consider the politically feasible alternative ways of achieving these other goals without sacrificing growth.

Similar considerations apply regarding such non-economic goals as maintaining political stability or trying to create certain changes in social attitudes among the people. Clearly the optimum investment rate and the distribution of investment funds among projects can differ depending upon the weights assigned to these goals. But planners must be careful to consider all the possible measures that can be taken to achieve these goals. They should not merely consider projects that yield mainly economic benefits and have certain secondary effects on these other goals. Measures designed primarily to achieve these other goals must also be included in the overall project array from which selections are made.

V

On the basis of what has been said it should not be surprising to find governments differing significantly concerning investment policy. Different value judgements on such matters as the time horizon over which

17

income is to be maximized, the desired distribution of income over time and among households within a particular period, and the weight to be attached to non-economic goals will result quite properly in differences in the volume of investment and its distribution among alternative projects. Likewise differences among governments concerning the feasibility and effects of various policy measures cause differences in investment policies.[12]

There is more, however, to the disagreements over investment criteria than a difference in goals. Writers agreeing on the same goal suggest different criteria. Most authors approach the investment criteria problem by assuming a fixed investment budget. The objective is to allocate these investment funds in such a way as to maximize the increase in output. Framing the problem in this manner immediately introduces an important element of inefficient planning.[13] Obviously it is possible with a fixed budget for a divergence to arise in the marginal rate of return on investment between the private and government sectors or, even if the government undertakes all investment, between the marginal productive rate of return on investment and the marginal time preference rate implied in the social welfare function. The decision concerning how much to invest, i.e. the size of the investment budget, should be made in conjunction with an analysis of investment possibilities and time preference. Otherwise only by accident will economic inefficiency be avoided. If the volume of investment funds were in fact fixed for an underdeveloped country, this formulation of the problem would be appropriate. But except for short periods it is difficult to conceive of situations where the government could not increase (or decrease) from internal or external sources the size of its investment budget. Of course, it probably will be required to pay a higher interest rate but that does not affect the general argument. Consequently, one sets up an artificial problem in framing the investment issue in underdeveloped countries in terms of absolute capital rationing.

When the problem is not framed in this manner the formal rule for determining the optimum investment rate is similar to that expressed in the third section. Benefit and cost streams should be discounted at the interest rate (subject to corrections concerning risk) that is consistent with the various political judgements concerning investment that have been discussed previously.[14] One should hasten to add that this interest rate will

---

[12] See H. Leibenstein, 'Why Do We Disagree on Investment Policies for Development,?' *Indian Economic Journal*, V (April 1958), pp. 369–86 for a comprehensive discussion along these lines.

[13] It is interesting to note that the 'practical' planning literature does not frame the investment problem in this narrow way. See, for example, United Nations, Economic Commission for Asia and the Far East, *Formulating Industrial Development Programmes* (61.II.F.7) (Bangkok, 1961), chap. 2.

[14] A constant interest rate over the relevant time horizon is usually assumed in discussing capital accumulation but this is not necessary.

be quite different from that which would prevail if government restricted its goal to maximizing income for contemporary households. On a general level all one can say is that this interest rate (corrected for risk differences) should be used to discount benefit and cost streams in all sectors and that all investment projects producing a net stream of benefits with a positive present value should be undertaken. Unless these conditions prevail, it simply means that the government is not achieving its own goals in the best possible manner.

Although viewing the investment allocation problems in terms of capital rationing is generally misleading and improper, there may be cases where short-term capital rationing is relevant. For example, one can imagine a situation where it can be regarded that the investment budget is fixed for the current planning period, e.g. the next three months. Ranking alternative investments under these conditions is a fairly straightforward process. The net receipts resulting from a project at the end of the first time period and every period thereafter can be reinvested at the market rate of interest since capital rationing will no longer prevail. Similarly, borrowing can take place at this rate. Therefore, beginning with the net receipts of period one, the net recipts resulting from each project should be compounded to some common terminal date. Ranking the ratios of the compounded values for each project divided by the outlay on the project in the current period enables planners to make the correct project selection.[15] The planner goes down the list until the fixed current budget is exhausted. If capital rationing actually does prevail over a number of periods the method of selecting projects is somewhat more complicated and will not be discussed here.[16]

Perhaps the most striking differences among investment rules under capital rationing concerns the nature of the denominators and numerators in the ranking ratios.[17] Most economists use a present value measure of the net receipt (benefit) stream in the numerator and investment costs (usually assumed to occur entirely in the current period) in the denominator. This is essentially the same as has just been suggested. Actual planners, however, often reject this ratio in favour of one that includes a measure of all costs in the denominator and either all benefits or net benefits in the numerator. The justification for including all costs is that it is the productivity of all resources that matters and not just capital.[18] The latter part of this state-

[15] See J. Hirschleifer, J. De Haven, and J. Milliman, *Water Supply* (Chicago: University of Chicago Press, 1960), chap. 7, for an excellent analysis of this rule and others that are equivalent to it.
[16] See J. Lorie and L. J. Savage, 'Three Problems in Capital Rationing,' *Journal of Business*, XXVIII (October 1955), pp. 229–39, for an analysis of this situation.
[17] See United Nations, *Manual of Economic Development Projects*, op. cit., Pt. II.
[18] J. Tinbergen, 'The Relevance of Theoretical Criteria in the Selection of Investment Plans,' in Center for International Studies, op. cit., p. 4, is one who gives this reason.

ment is obviously true, but this does not mean that all costs should be included in the denominator. When in obtaining the numerator such costs as wages (corrected, if necessary to reflect real opportunity costs) are subtracted from benefits to obtain the stream of net benefits, the productivity of other resources are taken into account. The denominator should consist of the net outlays on the project during the time that the capital rationing constraint applies. Since usually it is assumed that funds are limited for the current period, the current outlays on a particular project (i.e. the investment expenditure on the project) are the appropriate denominator. As has been repeatedly stressed by certain writers on resource problems in advanced countries, it is incorrect to include under these circumstances all costs over the life of the project. Similarly net benefits rather than total benefits should constitute the numerator.[19] Yet there are repeated statements in practical guides to planners in underdeveloped countries that the benefit-cost method (or one of its many variations) is a superior or equivalent criterion for allocating investment funds to one based upon the social marginal productivity of capital.[20] But ranking projects on a benefits-cost basis will not rank the projects properly in terms of the increase in national product associated with the investment in each project.

VI.

Extensive participation by governments in the investment process is now a widespread and well-established practice in underdeveloped countries. The objective of this paper has been to consider the various reasons that have been given as to why government intervention is justified, in order to understand better why investment policies differ so much among underdeveloped countries. We concluded that a strong case can be made for some government interference with the operations of a free price system even under the assumption that the preferences of the people currently constituting the economy are what matters in allocating resources. Activities usually covered by the term 'social overhead capital' are ones where some form of government intervention is most likely to be needed. We rejected as inconclusive, on the basis of the usual arguments given, the view that extensive centralized planning also can be justified under the consumer sovereignty goal when a developing economy is considered. Instead, it was suggested that an unwillingness of govern-

---

[19] McKean, op. cit., chap. 7, presents one of the clearest explanations of why these various ratios are incorrect except under limited circumstances.

[20] United Nations, *Manual of Economic Development Projects*, op. cit., Pt. II, chap. IV, and United Nations, *Formulating Industrial Development Programmes*, op. cit., p. 21.

ments to be guided by the economic preferences of contemporary households with respect to the relative importance of present versus future income is the main reason for extensive government intervention in the investment process. There are a number of other economic and non-economic goals whose attainment also requires government participation in the allocation process.

It is not the primary role of economists to comment upon the 'correctness' of these various goals. This is a matter to be decided on the basis of the value judgements of the people in the underdeveloped countries. However, economists can point out the various possible conflicts among the different social and economic goals with which a government is concerned. In particular, we have emphasized that under immediate political pressures governments are apt to adopt non-optimal policies in terms of their comprehensive goal system. Furthermore, the objective that most frequently seems to be sacrificed needlessly for some other goal is economic growth. Governments of underdeveloped countries are not unique in facing this problem, but, since the growth goal is stressed more strongly in underdeveloped than developed countries, it may constitute a more politically serious problem.

In addition to urging that investment policy be considered within a comprehensive framework of goals, we pointed out that the practice of analyzing investment decisions under the assumption of a fixed budget almost invariably leads to inefficient and non-optimal decisions. Planners in general should simultaneously consider the productivity of investment funds and the wishes of the community regarding the importance of current consumption. Moreover, when capital rationing is an appropriate assumption, planners must be careful to rank investment projects by using a ratio that maximizes the increase in income in terms of the funds actually rationed.

MONEY, INCOME, AND THE FOREIGN BALANCE

BY RUDOLF R. RHOMBERG*

Chief of the Special Studies Division, International Monetary Fund, Washington

In comparison with other problems of development the question of the proper management of the economy's money may at first glance appear to be of secondary importance. Yet the history of money is full of examples of monetary disorders which have nullified the economic efforts of a whole nation for months and years. Even in less extreme cases inappropriate monetary policies may deprive an economy of part of the fruits of its development effort, no matter how excellent the development program is in other respects. For this reason it is important to incorporate considerations of monetary management into the general economic development plans. This in turn requires a quantitative assessment of the relations between money and other economic magnitudes.

I. Money, National Income, and the Balance of Payments

The last decade has seen a revival of interest in monetary theory and policy. Modern monetary economics is leaving behind not only the simplifications of the original quantity theory ('a change in money affects only the price level'), but also the confining special case which Keynes' early followers had pulled out of the *General Theory* ('a change in money affects, in the first place, only the interest rate'). The new approach is more general. Money is one of a number of real and financial assets which households and businesses hold. Starting from an analysis of the factors on which the public's demand for money and for alternative assets depends, one can describe the probable reaction of the private sector of the economy to changes in the supply of money.

A. The demand for money.—The public holds money balances (currency and demand deposits at commercial banks) for two principal reasons. First, cash balances must be held by households and business firms in

* The views expressed in this paper are those of the author and not necessarily those of the International Monetary Fund.

order to bridge the temporal gap between receipts and payments, the size of the cash requirements for this 'transactions' purpose depending on the customary payments arrangements in the economy — the frequency of wage payments, and of payments for rent, food, and so on. Changes in the demand for transactions balances may be presumed to be more or less proportional to the value of the national income at current prices, or better, to that portion of it which is bought and sold in the market.[1]

Second, individuals and businesses may hold a part of their assets in the form of money balances. Such idle balances, in contrast to other assets, do not earn interest, dividends, or profits, but compensate the holder for this loss of potential income by their perfect liquidity.[2] The importance which the individual holder attaches to the liquidity of the marginal dollar diminishes as the proportion of his assets held in the form of money increases. Consequently, given their income and the total value of their assets, economic units will be willing to increase their holdings of cash balances if the importance they attach to liquidity as such rises, say, because of increased uncertainty about asset prices in the future, or if the expected yields on alternative real and financial assets (including expected changes in their capital values) decline.

The demand for money as an asset depends thus on the aggregate value of all assets and on the yields of assets other than money. Given the payments customs of the society, the total demand for money, both for transactions purposes and for purposes of asset holdings,[3] rises with an increase in income and in the aggregate value of assets, and declines with a rise in the yields or the expected appreciation of other assets. It is, however, not possible, in practice, and perhaps not even in principle, to distinguish the effect of the income level on the demand for money from the effect of the total value of assets, for — given the yields of the assets — income and the value of assets are closely related. The level of assets is thus best left out of consideration; its influence will then be reflected in the two remaining factors, income and asset yields.

---

[1] In developing economies part of the upward trend in the demand for money is due to the fact that, as development progresses, an increasing portion of output is channelled through the market and exchanged for money.

[2] Perfect liquidity is the property of an asset that allows it to be used instantly for the purchase of any other asset without loss. The liquidity of assets other than money diminishes with the market loss that must be expected if they are to be sold instantly for the purpose of acquiring another asset. Thus government bonds are less liquid than money, but (ordinarily) more liquid than inventories of goods, which are in turn more liquid than the machinery in a factory.

[3] In a very elegant derivation Milton Friedman subsumes the transactions demand under the demand for money as an asset since the former depends on the same factors as the latter. For example, higher yields on alternative assets will induce changes in payments habits designed to economize transactions balances. [*Studies in the Quantity Theory of Money* (M. Friedman, editor), University of Chicago Press, 1956. Chapter I.] From the long-run viewpoint Friedman is no doubt right, but since the payments customs normally change only slowly, the concept of a transactions demand may still have a place in short-run analysis.

B. The supply of money.—We must now turn to the question of how the money supply is determined. Since a later section reviews the instruments of central bank policy, the discussion can be held brief at this stage. Provided that there is sufficient demand for credit at the going interest rate at which the commercial banks make loans to their customers, the volume of loans and thus of bank deposits will be a certain multiple of the reserve assets of the banks. This multiple depends on the statutory or customary reserve ratio to which the banks adhere. The reserve assets of the commercial banks usually comprise mainly their deposits at the central bank and their foreign exchange assets. Where the banks are required to surrender most or all of their foreign exchange holdings to the central bank or to a separate exchange control authority, they obtain additional central bank deposits in return. In either case commercial bank reserves will vary with changes in the country's foreign exchange reserves.

The other set of influences on the reserve assets of commercial banks, and therefore on the money supply, can be subsumed under the heading of central bank credit. By making loans to, or buying assets from, the commercial banks, the public, or the government, the central bank can bring about an increase in the money supply either directly or via an increase in commercial bank reserves, and by reversing these operations it can accomplish a reduction in the money supply.[4]

It is important not to exaggerate the precision with which the central bank can control the money supply. Apart from the effect of the balance of payments, the reaction of the commercial banks to central bank credit changes must be taken into consideration.[5] If the commercial banks always extended credit to the full extent permitted by their reserve assets, we could link the money supply by a simple formula to the combined amount of the nation's foreign exchange reserves and central bank credit. In practice, however, banks will expand the volume of their loans in the short run only if there is sufficient demand at the going bank loan interest rates, and will reduce these rates in order to stimulate demand only gradually if excess reserves persist for some time. For now we may content ourselves with the statement that the money supply will in the long run depend on the commercial bank reserve ratio and on the sum of the central bank credit and of the country's gold and foreign exchange reserves; and while it can never exceed the level so determined, it may in the short run occasionally remain below it.

---

[4] Textbooks on money and banking give a precise formula for the 'money multiplier', in which the ratio of currency to demand deposits and other details are taken into account. The exact formula can be given only with reference to the banking legislation and the institutional features of the country in question.

[5] See J. Ahrensdorf and S. Kanesathasan, 'Variations in the Money Multiplier and Their Implications for Central Banking,' IMF, *Staff Papers*, November 1960.

C. Money and spending.—In tracing the effects of changes in the money supply on the economy it is convenient to take as point of departure a hypothetical equilibrium situation in which the money supply is equal to the 'long-run normal' demand for money. In such a situation the real national income will, by hypothesis, be at its long-run normal level, given the country's resources, its stage of development, and the average levels of its exports and of its capital imports, if any. The price level and the foreign exchange rate will be constant, and all asset yields and interest rates will equal the marginal productivity of capital goods minus the appropriate liquidity premium for each type of asset.

Such a long-run equilibrium situation is unlikely ever to exist in reality, since the monetary equilibrium is constantly disturbed by changes in the money supply or by short-run changes in the factors which determine the demand for money. But these disturbances will produce reactions in the economy which will tend to re-establish monetary equilibrium either by changing the demand for money or its supply, or both. It is, therefore, possible to describe the course of economic events in a country as a path along which the sectors of the economy react to disturbances of the monetary equilibrium.

The mechanism by which this readjustment takes place is simple: whenever the quantity of money actually held exceeds (or falls short of) the long-run normal demand for money, individuals and businesses will attempt to reduce (or increase) their cash balances by purchasing (or selling) other assets.

The adjustment process is as follows:

1. To the extent that the additional money is spent directly on foreign securities or foreign goods, foreign exchange reserves and the money supply will be reduced. (In the unlikely event that the entire addition to money would be spent on imported goods and securities, the original money supply would be restored and this would be the end of the story.)

2. To the extent that the additional money is spent on domestically produced goods (producers' or consumers' durables or inventories of non-durables to be held in business or household stocks), money national income will rise, either as a result of a rise in output or of price increases, with three consequences: first, a leakage into imports as under (1); second, an increased demand for cash balances;[6] third, higher prices for real capital assets implying

---

[6] The nominal cash balances demanded change in proportion to the price level so that the real cash balances (i.e., cash balances deflated by the price index) remain constant. If real income also rises, the demand for real cash balances will itself increase.

reduced yields and thus a larger demand for cash balances, provided that expected future prices of these capital goods and of the goods they help to produce are not revised upward in proportion to the rise in present asset prices.

3. Finally, to the extent that cash holders attempt to spend the additional money on domestic securities, they will bid up their prices and reduce their yields without, of course, being able to reduce the cash balances which they, as a group, hold.[7] At the lower interest yields of securities the demand for money will be increased. This is the pure Keynesian short-run case, where interest rates fall until the demand for money has increased sufficiently to absorb the rise in the money supply. But even in this case one should expect two further reactions in the longer run: first, the lower domestic interest rates may tend to induce a capital outflow or a reduction in the capital inflow with consequences as under (1) above. Second, the lower yields on securities will lead to additional spending on real assets (say, capital goods and inventories), as long as the marginal productivity of real capital is unchanged. In other words, there will be a tendency to return to an equilibrium between the yields on financial and real assets through sales of securities and purchases of capital goods, including inventories, with further consequences as under (2).

A similar analysis would show how monetary equilibrium tends to be re-established following different types of disturbances, such as a loss of export income, an increase in capital inflows, a budgetary deficit, or an autonomous wage increase. The only difference in the analysis would be that one would have to allow for the initial impact of these disturbances on national income and on asset yields, and thus on the demand for money, before tracing the further monetary consequences in the manner exemplified above.

D.   Summary.—The scheme of monetary analysis sketched in this section is not, by itself, sufficient for a full appraisal or a forecast of short-term economic processes. As we have seen, there are several ways in which the public may react to, say, an increase in domestic credit creation or to a decline in the capital inflow. In order to go beyond a listing of possible outcomes, or an explanation from hindsight of events in the past, it is necessary to obtain some quantitative knowledge of the likely reactions of households and businesses to changes in the magnitudes which the discussion has singled out for special consideration.

---

[7] The attempt on the part of the cash holders to acquire additional real estate or (domestic) art treasures would have similar consequences as the attempt to buy additional securities.

Some of the quantitative knowledge may be quite easily accessible in the case of a particular economy at a given time. For instance, if capital movements are tightly controlled, the probable capital outflow as a result of an increase in the money supply may be put down as zero. Again, in many of the less developed countries the market for securities is quite 'thin' or non-existent, and the main alternative assets are money, foreign exchange assets, and real assets (real estate and goods); in these cases a whole class of possible reactions to an increase in the money supply can probably be ignored.[8] By making use of known features of this sort it is usually possible to restrict the range of possible outcomes of a given situation. Beyond this it is necessary to base the analysis on experience as reflected in the available data and on one's judgement as to the acceptability of past experience as a guide to the future.

When it comes to an assessment of some of the longer-run consequences of changes in the factors on which a country's economic activity depends, we are on somewhat firmer ground. The reason for this is that the final outcome does not depend on the precise magnitude or timing of the short-run reactions of the economic units. We know, for instance, that (under fixed exchange rates) the money supply will tend to increase (decrease) as long as there is a balance of payments surplus (deficit), unless these externally caused changes in money are constantly offset by changes in central bank credit. We know further that it is impossible in the long run to offset the effect of a continual external deficit on the money supply through central bank credit, since in that case the country must soon run out of foreign exchange reserves. Nor can the monetary effect of a persistent external surplus be offset indefinitely, at least in practice, since the central bank would sooner or later run out of domestic assets to sell.[9] It follows that in the long run imports will equal exports plus capital inflows, money income will tend to a level such that imports conform to this equality, and the money supply will adjust itself to a level at which it satisfies the demand for money at that money income (and at the long-run level of the yield of capital).

Although this simple scheme leaves a number of important questions unanswered, there are others that it answers quite adequately: (a) What-

---

[8] See J. J. Polak, 'Monetary Analysis of Income Formation and Payments Problems,' IMF *Staff Papers*, November 1957, and J. J. Polak and L. Boissonneault, 'Monetary Analysis of Income and Imports and its Statistical Application,' IMF *Staff Papers*, April 1960. In Polak's approach use is made of the assumption that changes in the desire to hold securities (and physical assets not currently produced, such as real estate) can be ignored even in the short run. This makes it possible to postulate that money income will change in proportion to the money supply. See also Section IV below.

[9] In principle, a central bank could continue indefinitely to sell obligations of its own which are specially introduced for this purpose, or raise reserve requirements if necessary to 100 per cent or higher.

ever the influence of monetary policy may be in the short run, in the long run it cannot have a large role to play in the determination of income and imports, given the restraints imposed by the foreign balance. This is not to deny that inappropriate monetary policies during successive short-run periods may disturb the adjustment of the economy to its long-run equilibrium, i.e., to its growth path, and thus make matters worse than they would otherwise have been. (b) A permanent rise in exports will raise imports by an equal amount,[10] and it will raise money income by an amount which depends on the income and price elasticities of import demand, but does not depend on the conventional Keynesian multiplier. If output would have been at its full capacity level without the rise in exports, the increase in the money income will be mainly in the form of price increases. (c) A permanent rise in capital imports, say, in the form of foreign aid, will have the same effect on imports and money income as a permanent rise in exports. (d) A permanent rise in the propensity to import will bring about a decline in money income, which may manifest itself either as a reduction in (the growth path of) output or as a decline in the price level, or a combination of both.

As J. J. Polak has pointed out,[11] these are essentially the conclusions of the classical economists analyzing foreign trade and lending under gold standard conditions. This is not surprising since at the present level of abstraction the classical assumptions are indistinguishable from those underlying the long-run scheme set out above: fixed exchange rates, the money supply determined by the foreign balance, money income determined by the money supply, and imports determined by money income. But in the analysis of year-to-year changes in money, income and imports some of these assumptions must be modified. We return to this topic in Section IV.

II. EMPIRICAL EVIDENCE

A. The relation between imports and income.—The relation between imports and income has been extensively investigated,[12] both for the inter-war period and the post-war period. As a result of these studies there can be no reasonable doubt that, barring unusually incisive exchange control

[10] Note that the Keynesian model leads to the conclusion that imports will rise by less than exports provided that the marginal propensity to spend is less than unity. The difference is due to the fact that the Keynesian model does not allow for the effect of the foreign balance on the money supply.

[11] J. J. Polak, op. cit., p. 29.

[12] See the survey of statistical results by H. S. Cheng, 'Statistical Estimates of Elasticities and Propensities in International Trade: A Survey of Published Studies', IMF *Staff Papers*, April 1959.

measures, imports rise with income. Furthermore, the income elasticity of imports is typically greater than unity. Table 1 shows the marginal pro-

TABLE I

Marginal Propensity to Import and Income Elasticity of Import Demand, Twenty-One Countries, Generally 1949–60[a]

		Marginal Propensity to Import[b]	Income Elasticity of Imports[c]
1.	Austria	0·43	1·7
2.	Belgium	0·63	2·0
3.	Canada	0·18	1·1
4.	Costa Rica	0·41	1·7
5.	Denmark	0·71	2·4
6.	El Salvador	0·36	1·7
7.	Finland	0·31	1·5
8.	France	0·12	1·2
9.	Germany	0·26	1·8
10.	Greece	0·34	1·8
11.	Guatemala	0·26	1·4
12.	Italy	0·26	1·8
13.	Japan	0·16	1·2
14.	Mexico	0·18	1·4
15.	Netherlands	0·69	1·6
16.	Norway	0·56	1·7
17.	Peru	0·27	1·4
18.	Sweden	0·54	2·4
19.	Switzerland	0·50	1·7
20.	United Kingdom	0·29	1·5
21.	United States	0·04	1·2

[a] Data: Commodity imports deflated by import prices; GNP deflated by cost of living index. Source: *International Financial Statistics.*

[b] Regression coefficient b of the function $M = a + bY$, where M is real imports and Y is real GNP.

[c] Regression coefficient b of the function $\log M = a + b \log Y$.

Note: In all cases R^2 exceeds 0·85 (for most countries it exceeds 0·90), and the regression coefficients are at least five times as large as their standard errors (in most cases they are ten to twenty times as large).

pensity to import and the income elasticity of imports in twenty-one countries for which these values could be reliably estimated[13] from post-war data.

National income data for longer periods of time are not available for most countries. Moreover, the structural changes which occur over a longer time period, especially during and after major wars, make it difficult to estimate the long-run relation between imports and income.[14]

[13] The criteria of reliability chosen were that income variations explain 85 per cent or more of the observed variations in imports, and that the standard error of the estimated coefficient be reasonably small relative to the value of the coefficient (one fifth or smaller).

[14] It should be remembered that Eugene Staley has argued that commodity imports will tend to rise less fast than GNP as an economy develops, since the latter will contain an increasing proportion of services which are not internationally traded. (See his *World Economic Development,* International Labour Office, Montreal, 1944.) But it is, of course, entirely possible that imports will tend to rise more than in proportion to the nonservice components of GNP.

B.   The long-run relation between money and income.—In this area, too, it is difficult to obtain consistent time series covering a longer period. From the data which they have been able to piece together, some students of this field have concluded that money tends to increase faster than income and that the income velocity of money declines with the secular rise in income. There is little doubt that this conclusion is justified in the case of the early development of the United States, where the ratio of income to money has declined considerably from 1800 to the present century. The evidence on the behaviour of the income velocity is less conclusive with respect to the last sixty or eighty years.[15] In accordance with the reasoning in Section I we should, however, not look for a stable ratio of money to income but for a stable relation of money to income and the long-term yield of capital.

For the United States reasonably consistent data on money (currency plus demand deposits) are available for several decades. A long-run demand function making the demand for real cash balances depend on real gross national product and the long-term corporate bond yield (as an admittedly imperfect substitute for the yield on capital assets in general) has been fitted to the annual data for 1900 to 1961:

$$\text{(II–1)} \qquad\qquad \frac{L}{P} = 0.72 \; \frac{\left(\dfrac{Y}{P}\right)^{10.1}}{i^{0.65}} \qquad (R^2 = 0.98)$$

where L = money, Y = gross national product, P = price level (GNP price deflator, 1929 = 1), and i = bond yield in per cent.[16] The equation shows that the income elasticity of the demand for money was almost precisely 1 (with a negligibly small standard error of $\pm$ 0.02), while the interest elasticity of the demand for money was — 0.65 (with a standard error of less than one-tenth of the size of the coefficient).[17] Over the last six decades the demand for real cash balances in the United States tended thus to vary in proportion to real income and was inversely

[15] See, e.g., Ernest M. Doblin, 'The Ratio of Income to Money Supply; An International Survey', *Review of Economics and Statistics*, August 1951, and Richard T. Selden, 'Monetary Velocity in the United States', in *Studies in the Quantity Theory of Money* (M. Friedman, editor), University of Chicago Press, 1956.

[16] The data for L/P and Y/P are taken from Edward S. Shaw, 'Money Supply and Stable Economic Growth,' Chapter 2 of *United States Monetary Policy*, The American Assembly, 1958, pp. 55–56 for 1900–28 and from the *Federal Reserve Bulletin* (L) and the *Survey of Current Business* (Y and P, which were then converted into 1929 prices) from 1929–61. The yield, i, on 20-year highest-grade corporate bonds is taken from William Fellner, *Trends and Cycles in Economic Activity*, Holt, New York: 1953, for 1900–45, and from the *Federal Reserve Bulletin* for 1946–60.

[17] For a different approach see Milton Friedman, *The Demand for Money: Some Theoretical and Empirical Results*, Occasional Paper 68, National Bureau of Economic Research, New York, 1959. Our results are in line with the findings of Henry A. Latané, 'Income Velocity and Interest Rates: A Pragmatic Approach', *Review of Economics and Statistics*, November 1960. Latané's article also contains a discussion of Friedman's approach.

related to the long-term interest rate. At an earlier stage of development, however, when the whole financial system develops more rapidly
than the rest of the economy, the demand for money is also likely to rise
faster than income.[18]

III. ECONOMIC GROWTH, MONEY, AND PRICES

In a closed economy the money supply should increase at a rate which is
sufficient to satisfy the growing demand for cash balances which the rise
in real income with stable prices brings about. But in an economy in which
foreign trade plays a large role an additional factor must be considered.
With a given domestic cost and price level, the rate of growth of a
country's exports is not necessarily equal to the rate of increase in its
imports which will result when output and employment are maintained
at satisfactory levels. In the construction of long-range plans it is, therefore, important to allow for this possibility, and to establish overall
guidelines for monetary policy which are compatible with the appraisal of
long-term domestic and foreign developments.

Given a long-run demand function for money of the type discussed in
the preceding section, there is a rate of growth of the money supply
which will tend to maintain domestic price stability. Suppose that real
income grows at a rate of y per cent and that the marginal productivity of
capital and the level of interest rates remain constant over time.[19] If the
income elasticity of demand for real cash balances is g, then the rate at
which the money supply must grow to maintain a constant domestic price
level is yg. As was argued in Section II, it is likely that in the early stages
of development g is greater than one, since the financial institutions will
develop more rapidly than the rest of the economy and since a growing
portion of the nation's output will be exchanged against money at some
stage of the process of production and distribution. In this case the money
supply should grow faster than output in order to prevent deflationary
tendencies. At a later stage of economic development the value of g is
likely to be closer to unity and the money supply should then grow at
approximately the same rate as output.

It has sometimes been argued that a rate of growth of the money supply

[18] See J. G. Gurley and Edward S. Shaw, *Money in a Theory of Finance*, Brooking's Institu-
tion, Washington D.C., 1960, especially Chapter IV, and Graeme S. Dorrance and Eckhard
Brehmer, 'The Growth in Liquidity in Selected Industrial Countries', IMF, DM 62/19,
May 1962.

[19] This assumption, merely made for simplicity of exposition, is warranted if there are
underemployed labour resources available which are drawn into the productive process as
development continues, or if technological improvements continue to counterbalance any
tendency towards diminishing returns to capital as they have done historically in the
industrially advanced countries.

which induces some price inflation may also raise the rate of growth of output. But while it may be possible for a relatively short period to increase the levels of saving and capital formation through the redistribution of income which price inflation brings about (i.e., through the so-called process of 'forced saving'), this cannot result in a permanent increase in the rate of economic growth. Inflation is a relatively inefficient form of taxation, since the speed of inflation would have to continue to accelerate merely to provide a constant amount of additional saving. An accelerating rate of inflation must soon result either in the application of restrictions or in the breakdown of the market system and what little may have been initially gained will then be lost as the economy is subjected to a painful readjustment process.

These considerations apply particularly strongly to economies in which foreign trade plays a large role. Table 1 (Section II) shows that many countries are highly dependent on imports, and a computation of the proportion of national income derived from exports would, of course, give a similar picture. Exports are often concentrated in a few specialized products. Only a small portion of the output of these industries can be utilized by the domestic economy. In these circumstances domestic cost and price inflation would rapidly lead not only to a loss of the country's foreign exchange reserves, but to a reduction in output and employment in many of the export industries as well.

As already shown, in an economy which is highly dependent on foreign trade, as most of the underdeveloped economies are, the money supply will in fact tend to grow at a rate which, over the long run, maintains the foreign balance roughly in equilibrium. The monetary authorities can intervene to smooth short-run fluctuations in the money supply, but they cannot indefinitely counteract the long-run trend unless they are also prepared to alter the foreign exchange rate from time to time. The alternation of 'stop' and 'go' signals which domestic producers receive under a policy of domestic price inflation with intermittent exchange depreciation favours neither development nor the inflow of foreign capital. In the long-run development effort monetary policy must remain a relatively passive factor, conducted with the aim of avoiding disruptive monetary disturbances both of the inflationary and of the deflationary varieties, rather than with the objective of making it an independent stimulant to economic growth.

IV. MONEY, INCOME, AND THE FOREIGN BALANCE IN THE SHORT RUN

Monetary policy is more effective in influencing the level of real income in the short run because of the absence of some of the restraints which are operative in the long run. First, in the short run imports need not equal the sum of exports and foreign receipts on capital account. Second, although the foreign balance does affect the money supply, this effect can be offset by central bank policy, at least for some time, provided (in the case of a foreign deficit) that the country has an adequate level of foreign exchange reserves. Third, in the short run the level of income and employment is subject to fluctuations, either due to variations in exports or to changes in domestic conditions, which monetary policy can attempt to counteract, whereas it cannot be nearly as effective in influencing the long-run growth path of economic activity.

A. Features of a simple short-run model.—To assess the influence of a change in the quantity of money on national income during a short period, one must estimate primarily two behavior relations. First, one must know how much of the additional money supplied will tend to be wiped out through an induced increase in imports and a concomitant decline in exchange reserves. Second, one must find out the extent to which the remaining addition to the money supply will increase the public's spending on additional domestic output (investment goods, inventories, consumer goods, etc.), and to what extent it will merely lead to higher prices, and thus reduced yields, of financial and real assets.

These estimates must then be combined in a fairly intricate manner: the drain on the money supply due to the induced rise in imports cannot be known until we determine the rise in income, which in turn is due only to the portion of the additional money supply not drained away through higher imports. In other words, imports, income, and the total money supply are simultaneously determined by a number of other variables which we may take as more or less independent, such as exports, domestic credit creation, and in some cases[20] perhaps also the net inflow of foreign capital.

In principle there is no limit to the number of refinements one can introduce into such a model. But if data are limited, as well as computing facilities, it should be kept as simple as possible. Moreover, there is virtue in starting with a simple model and expanding it only gradually as one gains experience in its application.

Guided by these considerations, J. J. Polak has constructed a model[21] in which the income velocity of circulation is assumed to be constant (at its

[20] For instance, when the net capital inflow consists chiefly of foreign aid and does not depend on domestic interest rates.

[21] J. J. Polak, op. cit., the model has been applied to thirty-six countries in J. J. Polak and L. Boissonneault, op. cit.; see also J. M. Fleming and L. Boissonneault, 'Money Supply and Imports', IMF *Staff Papers*, May 1961; S. J. Prais, 'Some Mathematical Notes on the Quantity Theory of Money in an Open Economy', ibid., May 1961; and S. Kanesathasan, 'Government Imports and Import Taxes in Monetary Analysis of Income and Imports', ibid., December 1961.

average level for the post-war period) and in which money imports are
determined by money income. The estimated annual values of income
and imports move in response to changes in the annual total of exports,
net capital inflows, and changes in domestic credit creation. The key
assumption of this model is the constancy of the income-money ratio.
With a given long-term yield of capital, the constant income velocity can
be interpreted as the long-run demand function for money. It is, therefore,
not surprising that the estimates for income and imports obtained from
the Polak model are found to correspond quite well to the average level of
the actually observed values of income and imports over several years, but
that they do not follow the year to year variations in the observed values
very closely. In other words, the estimated values give the appearance of
moving averages of the actual values. In order to get a closer explanation
of the year to year changes in income and imports we must try to estimate
more nearly the short-run relation between money and income. We can
do this only at the sacrifice of some of the simplicity of the Polak
model.[22]

B.   *Money and expenditure in the short run.*—In the familiar Keynesian
model private expenditure (i.e., consumption plus investment) is assumed
to depend on income and the rate of interest. An increase in the quantity
of money, other things being equal, is expected to affect private expenditure by first depressing the interest rate, which in turn will stimulate
(investment) expenditure. In other words, the public first bids up security
prices but not the prices of any other assets and it is only the concomitant
reduction in the cost of borrowing[23] which leads to an increase in private
expenditure. Since long-term borrowing rates are notoriously inflexible,
many economists have come to doubt that an increase in the money
supply will have an appreciable influence on spending and thus on
income.

   This reasoning ignores the change in demand for assets other than
securities which must have accompanied the rise in the demand schedule
for securities unless some kind of irrational aversion towards real assets is
assumed. Some of these other assets are, like securities, in temporarily or
permanently inelastic supply (real estate, art treasures, etc.). But others,
such as capital goods, including inventories of raw materials, and stocks of
consumer goods have supply schedules whose price elasticity is always
positive and increases with the length of the period considered. It is a
well-known principle of demand analysis that when spending in general
increases, more of the additional expenditure is devoted to a good in

---

[22] The Polak model is fully set out in the published sources given in the preceding footnote
[23] It is probably fair to say that the interpretation of the role of the interest variable in the
investment function as representing the 'cost of borrowing' was a red herring supplied by
some of Keynes' followers rather than by Keynes himself.

elastic supply than to one in inelastic supply, if the two goods are close substitutes for each other,[24] since the prices of the former will rise less than those of the latter for every additional dollar spent on each.

When interest rates decline and land values rise as a consequence of an increase in the money supply, an increase in spending on other assets must occur simultaneously, unless the demand for these assets has by chance declined for reasons unrelated to the increase in the quantity of money. The significance of the interest rate in the Keynesian expenditure function is not so much that it reflects changes in the cost of borrowing, but that it is an index of changes in expenditures on all types of assets, including securities and investment goods. The reciprocal of a real estate price index would, except for market imperfections, serve equally well as a variable in the investment function.

Rather than include in the expenditure function an interest variable which reflects the extent to which an increment of money was not spent on real assets (but instead on securities or not at all), it may be more straightforward to include instead the increment of money itself. The coefficient of this variable will then indicate the additional spending on goods which was necessary during a given period of time in order to lower the yields of these real assets (by raising their prices or by increasing their volume, or both) by a sufficient amount so as to induce the public to hold the larger quantity of money. This additional expenditure may be a fraction or a multiple of the original excess supply of money, depending on the length of the period considered, on the initial ratio of money to total assets, and on the elasticities of demand for and supply of the various asset classes, including money itself. While these individual elasticities will remain hidden behind the scenes, this approach should furnish a clue to the effect of an increase in the quantity of money on spending and thus on income, even in countries where security markets are thin and where published interest rates are not representative of the true yields of real and financial assets.

C. *The basic equations of the model.*—Assuming the long-run yield on capital to be constant, the long-run demand for money can be expressed as

$$(\text{IV--1}) \qquad\qquad L^{\star} = kY$$

where $L^{\star}$ are the desired cash balances which the public would wish to hold in the long run at an income level of Y, and where k is a constant. The deviation of the actual money supply from this desired level in any particular year t is $L_t - L^{\star}_t$. Private expenditure, E, is linearly dependent

---

[24] I.e., if their price elasticities of demand exceed unity. We are in this context not concerned with the case of different income elasticities of the demand, or complementarities among goods.

on current and last year's income and on the excess of actual over desired cash balances[25] some time ago.

Since L_t is the stock of money measured at a moment of time (at the end of year t) while Y_t is the flow of income during year t, we express the average desired cash balances during year t as $(L^*_t + L^*_{t-1})/2 = kY_t$, and the deviation of actual from desired cash balances during year t as $[(L_t + L_{t-1})/2 - kY_t]$. The private expenditure function is thus

(IV–2) $E_t = a_1Y_t + a_2Y_{t-1} + a_3[(L_t + L_{t-1})/2 - kY_t] + a_0$

if there is no lag of expenditure with respect to a change in the excess of desired over actual cash balances.[26] If there is a one year lag, the term in square brackets is replaced by $[(L_{t-1} + L_{t-2})/2 - kY_{t-1}]$, and if the lag is one half-year it becomes $[(L_{t-1} - k(Y_t + Y_{t-1})/2]$. The most promising form of the expenditure function would seem to be that incorporating a lag of one half-year or of one year, which gives adequate time for orders, price lists, production plans, and actual output to change.[27]

The model contains in addition an import function,

(IV–3) $M_t = mE_t + m_0$

which expresses imports as a function of expenditure (rather than income). Government expenditures on goods and services, G, may be taken as autonomously determined or they may be related to income, recognizing the fact that G must depend to a considerable extent on tax revenue which is itself a function of income:

(IV–4) $G_t = g_1Y_t + g_0$

The model is completed by two identities defining income and the money supply:

[25] For a discussion of such a model in terms of differential equations rather than difference equations see S. J. Prais, op. cit.

[26] That there is no substantive difference between the classical and Keynesian approaches, when both are formulated in appropriately general terms (i.e., without assigning specific causal significance to one particular variable or another), can be seen in this way: the Keynesian expenditure function (ignoring time lags) is $E = b_1Y - b_2i + b_0$ and a linear approximation of the liquidity preference function is $L^* = c_1Y - c_2i + c_0$. Substituting for i from the liquidity preference function into the expenditure function and combining terms in Y results in $E = (b_1 - c_1b_2/c_2)Y + (b_2/c_2)L^* + $ constant, which is the form of (IV–2) in the text with (b_2/c_2) equal to the coefficient a_3 in (IV–2). A Keynesian could thus interpret a_3 as the ratio of the effect of a change in interest on expenditure to the effect of a change in interest on the demand for money. For a fuller statement of the equivalence of the two systems, if properly stated, see J. M. Fleming, 'The Determination of the Rate of Interest', *Economica*, August 1938.

[27] The first reaction of an increase in spending will be a reduction in inventories accompanied perhaps by a rise in some prices. Since the model outlined here is in current prices (because of data limitations rather than by choice) the rise in prices will be reflected in private expenditure. But we should allow a long enough lag for inventories to be restored to their desired level, so as to express the effect of a change in money on both the price level and on the level of output.

$$(IV-5) \qquad\qquad Y_t = E_t + G_t + X_t - M_t$$
$$(IV-6) \qquad\qquad L_t = L_{t-1} + X_t + C_t - M_t + \varDelta D_t$$

where $X_t =$ exports, $C_t =$ net capital imports, and $\varDelta D_t =$ change in domestic credit creation (i.e., the change in money of domestic origin). These identities and the non–observable relation (IV–1) are the same for all countries. The behaviour equations (IV–2), (IV–3), and (IV–4) are given below for Norway, and in the Appendix (Tables A1 and A2) for four other countries (Costa Rica, Ecuador, Japan, and the Netherlands). The expenditure equation (IV–2) is estimated[28] in a form in which the coefficients of Y_t or of Y_{t-1} are combined into one coefficient, say, $(a_2 - ka_3)Y_{t-1}$.

D. *An example: Norway, 1949–60.*—The variables appearing below are measured in billions of kroner.

$$E_t = \frac{0.53}{(0\cdot10)} Y_t + \frac{0\cdot13}{(0\cdot11)} Y_{t-1} + \frac{0\cdot90}{(0\cdot47)} \frac{L_{t-1} + L_{t-2}}{2} - \frac{0\cdot12}{(1\cdot39)} \qquad \overline{R}^2 = \cdot995$$

$$M_t = \frac{0\cdot59}{(0\cdot02)} E_t - \frac{1\cdot41}{(0\cdot52)} \qquad\qquad \overline{R}^2 = \cdot98$$

$$G_t = \frac{0\cdot21}{(0\cdot01)} Y_t - \frac{1\cdot38}{(0\cdot34)} \qquad\qquad \overline{R}^2 = \cdot96$$

By combining these equations we can express each (current) dependent variable as a function of the independent and the lagged dependent variables. (The corresponding equations for the other four countries are given in Appendix Table A3.)

$$Y_t = 0\cdot09\, Y_{t-1} + 1\cdot76\, X_t + 0\cdot66 \frac{L_{t-1} + L_{t-2}}{2} - 0\cdot04$$

$$M_t = 0\cdot10\, Y_{t-1} + 0\cdot54\, X_t + 0\cdot73 \frac{L_{t-1} + L_{t-2}}{2} - 1\cdot49$$

This formulation shows that a rise (or fall) in Norway's current exports has tended to raise (or lower) current money income by about 1·8 times the export change, and current imports by about one–half of the current export change. A rise (or fall) in the money supply has tended to raise (or lower) money income the following year by two–thirds of the change in the money supply, and imports by almost three–fourths of the money change.[29] The change in money during a particular year depends, of

[28] The equations have been estimated by the two–stage least–squares method from annual data for 1949–60. The standard errors of the regression coefficients are given in parentheses below the estimated coefficients.

[29] This lag in the effect of a change in the money supply on income and imports is, of course, somewhat artificial. The adjustment of spending to the changes in the stock of money goes on all the time and some effect will already be present in the current year. We should really have an equation showing a distributed lag response of expenditure to changes in money. But the available data (short time series and annual values) make the fitting of more complicated functions impracticable for many countries.

course, itself on exports, capital inflows, imports, and the change in domestic credit creation in that year. The effect of a change in money in the preceding year on current money income and imports can be carried back to these other variables by substituting them for $(L_{t-1} - L_{t-2})$ in the two equations above. The import equation shows particularly clearly the extent to which it may be necessary to allow for the future effect of present monetary action on the foreign balance.

C. *Conclusion.*—In Norway as well as in the other four countries, a change in the money supply appears to affect expenditure appreciably with an average lag of one year (one-half year for Japan). The statistical significance of the coefficient of the money variable is, however, at a lower level than that of some of the other coefficients of the model. In Norway, a rise in the money supply tends to raise private expenditure (consumption plus investment) in the following year by an amount which is about 90 per cent of the increase in money. In the Netherlands, in Costa Rica, and in Ecuador, this proportion was higher, while in Japan it was much lower (and not significantly different from zero in the probability sense).

The statistical fit of the model as a whole is uniformly better for the five countries than that of the Polak model, as shown below:

Standard error of computed income*
(Per cent of average income)

	Polak model	Alternative model
Costa Rica	2·2	0·9
Ecuador	4·7	2·2
Japan	13·8	3·3
Netherlands	2·0	1·6
Norway	2·4	2·3

* Root-mean-square deviation of computed from actual income.

These figures give a rough idea of the average percentage error that one would be likely to make in forecasting income, if exports, capital imports, and the change in domestic credit creation were known in advance. Since these values must themselves be estimated for any future period, the actual forecasting error will probably tend to be higher.

The model is, however, not specifically designed for the purpose of forecasting, but rather to give a general understanding of the magnitudes and the timing of the short-run effects of autonomous changes in the money supply (domestic credit creation), as well as of changes in exports and in the capital account of the balance of payments. Having satisfied ourselves that changes in the money supply do have an effect on spending, income, and imports in the short run, we turn now to a brief discussion of the means by which the central bank can influence the money supply.

V. CENTRAL BANK CONTROL OF THE MONEY SUPPLY

A number of underdeveloped countries do not have a national currency of their own but employ instead a foreign currency as the circulating medium. In some other instances the so-called currency-board system is in effect, under which local currency is issued in exchange for foreign currency and other foreign exchange assets. In both of these cases the amount of circulating currency is always equal to the country's foreign exchange reserves. Moreover, the commercial banks tend to expand or contract their loans in accordance with variations in their reserves which consist of domestic currency and foreign exchange. In these circumstances, the money supply depends entirely on the foreign balance, not only in the long-run but all the time, and the direct effects of export fluctuations on national income tend to be magnified by the monetary effects of variations in the external balance.

As has already been indicated in Section I, a central bank can offset the influence of the foreign balance on the money supply by altering either its holdings of domestic assets or by changing the commercial banks' ratios of reserve assets to deposit liabilities. There are three widely used instruments by which central banks influence the money supply. First, the central bank can vary the interest rate ('discount rate' or 'bank rate') and other terms at which it buys ('discounts') private short-term debt instruments ('commercial paper') from the banks and at which it makes loans to the banks, thus influencing their loan policies.

Secondly, the central bank can raise commercial bank reserves by buying government securities (or other securities specified in the Central Bank Law) either directly from the commercial banks or from the general public, and it can achieve the opposite effect by selling such securities. If these 'open market operations' are carried out with the non-bank public rather than with the commercial banks, there will be a direct effect on the public's cash holdings in addition to the indirect effect via commercial bank reserves.

Thirdly, in many countries the central bank may prescribe a minimum ratio of bank reserves to deposit liabilities and may vary this ratio within certain limits set by law, thus limiting the potential maximum volume of outstanding commercial bank loans at a given level of bank reserves.

The extent to which these instruments can be applied depends on the degree of development of the financial structure of the economy. In many underdeveloped countries the volume of commercial paper and of government securities is small or non-existent. The commercial banks in some countries are branches of foreign banking institutions which can augment their reserves by borrowing from their head offices and need not rely on credit from the central bank. Moreover, in underdeveloped countries a large part — say, between one-half and four-fifths and in some countries probably more — of the money supply is held in the form of currency, so that measures which affect primarily the volume of bank deposits will have a proportionately smaller effect on the total money supply.

While the scope for monetary policy is reduced by these conditions, there would seem to be some compensation: although it is more difficult for the central bank to change the money supply, a given change may have a larger effect on spending and national income than it would have with more fully developed financial institutions and money markets, because of the absence of a number of the types of financial assets which residents of more developed economies can hold as alternatives to money. The asset holders' choice is thus restricted to holding either money or goods. There is, however, an important qualification to this statement. If the asset holders have unrestricted and convenient opportunities to buy or sell foreign securities, the range of their choice is at least as wide as it would be if there were a market for domestic securities. In fact, when businesses and the group of wealth-holding individuals are accustomed to holding a varying portion of their assets in foreign securities or foreign time deposits, the attempt to control the money supply may at times be frustrated by variations in capital movements which offset the effects of the central bank's policy measures.[30]

The problem of monetary policy in a developed economy has been described by saying that 'you can pull on a string but you cannot push on a string'. This means that it is possible to prevent the money supply from exceeding a desired level by restrictive central bank policies which force the commercial banks to restrain the volume of their loans, but that the central bank cannot force an expansion in the money supply in all circumstances, since it can neither force the banks to expand their loans nor make the businessmen borrow. When monetary and budgetary policies are considered jointly, one might say that the reverse difficulty exists in countries with underdeveloped financial markets. When monetary expansion is indicated, it can always be achieved by expanding government expenditures on one or several of the many pressing development projects and by financing the additional spending through an issue of government securities sold to the central bank. But when inflationary pressures make it desirable to restrict the money supply it may prove difficult for the

[30] This difficulty is, of course, not restricted to underdeveloped countries.

central bank to sell government securities to the commercial banks or to the public. For the reasons already given, the attempt to reduce the money supply through the use of the other instruments may also be unsuccessful. This asymmetry adds to the inflationary bias which is already present in developing economies.

In view of the limited applicability of the traditional instruments of central bank policy in the case of countries with undeveloped financial institutions, some countries have had recourse to measures designed to restrain the activity of particular sectors of the economy or to put maximal limits ('ceilings') on the amount of credit which banks may make available to the economy.[31] A particular technique which has been applied in a number of countries in recent years is that of advance deposits on imports.[32] In the frame of this paper it is not possible to comment in detail on these special techniques. Credit ceilings may be useful in times of strong inflationary stress, but are not very helpful as a means of continuous rational control of the money supply. The experience with advance deposits on imports is not entirely favourable. While it may bring quick results by sharply reducing excess liquidity, the continuous application of this instrument requires delicate timing and presents many pitfalls. The experience with advance deposits on imports is evaluated in the first of the two articles given in the last footnote.

CONCLUSION

It will be seen, then, that there are many special problems confronting the authorities in a newly emerging country, if they wish to use monetary policy for short-run stability and to permit maximum growth. What may be called for in these cases is an initial co-operative effort of the central authorities and the commercial banks to establish a set of suitable procedures for monetary control. In the western literature on monetary policy such co-operation is sometimes listed as a separate type of policy instrument under the infelicitous name of 'moral suasion'.[33] When the number of commercial banks is small it would not seem impossible to reach agreement on desirable changes in loan policies, on reserve ratios, or discount policy, on the holding of government securities by the commercial banks, and on similar matters. After some of the financial markets have developed, partly as a result of this co-operation, less reliance would have to be placed on the direct personal contact between the

[31] See G. S. Dorrance and W. H. White, 'Alternative Forms of Monetary Ceilings for Stabilization Purposes', IMF, *Staff Papers*, November 1962.

[32] See E. A. Birnbaum and M. A. Qureshi, 'Advance Deposit Requirements for Imports', IMF *Staff Papers*, November 1960; and I.O.W. Olakanpo, 'Monetary Management in Dependent Economies', *Economica*, November 1961.

[33] There is, of course, nothing moral about such a policy, and the persuasion has, in fact, often been of the '. . . or else' variety.

central bank and the commercial banks and increasing use may be made of the traditional instruments of central bank policy.

APPENDIX

Tables A1 and A2 give the estimates of equation (IV–2) to (IV–4) in Section IV for Costa Rica, Ecuador, Japan, and the Netherlands. Table A3 gives the reduced form equations for income and imports for the four countries.

TABLE A1

Expenditure Functions (IV–2)

	Regression Coefficient (Standard Error)			
	Y_t	Y_{t-1}	$\dfrac{L_{t-1} + L_{t-2}}{2}$	R^2
Costa Rica	—	0·42 (0·24)	2·8 (1·4)	0·99
Ecuador	0·07 (0·54)	0·20 (0·25)	5·0 (3·8)	0·99
Japan	0·96 (0·14)	− 0·20 (0·17)	0·12[a] (0·53)	0·99
Netherlands	0·54 (0·40)	− 0·22 (0·29)	2·7 (1·0)	0·99

[a] The money variable is L_{t-1} in the case of Japan (implying a lag of one-half year).

TABLE A2

Imports and Government Expenditures

	Import Function (IV–3)			Government Expenditure (IV–4)	
	Regression Coefficient (Standard Error)			Regression Coefficient (Standard Error)	
	E_t	$E_t + G_t$	R^2	Y_t	R^2
Costa Rica	—	0·23 (0·02)	0·93	0·20 (0·02)	0·89
Ecuador	0·25 (0·01)	—	0·97	0·18 (0·01)	0·96
Japan	0·16 (0·01)	—	0·93	0·19 (0·01)	0·95
Netherlands	0·69 (0·02)	—	0·99	0·20 (0·02)	0·92

TABLE A3

Reduced Form Equations for Income and Imports

	Coefficients of		
	Y_{t-1}	X_t	$\dfrac{L_{t-1} + L_{t-2}}{2}$
Income (Y)			
Costa Rica	0·38	1·18	2·47
Ecuador	0·23	2·03	2·42
Japan	0·02	3·86	1·50[a]
Netherlands	− 0·28	1·81	2·38
Imports (M)			
Costa Rica	0·12	0·06	0·76
Ecuador	0·07	0·13	1·43
Japan	− 0·03	0·58	0·24[a]
Netherlands	− 0·06	0·59	2·54

[a] Coefficient of L_{t-1}

THE DEVELOPMENT EXPERIENCE OF ISRAEL IN THE LAST DECADE

BY MICHAEL MICHAELY

Eliezer Kaplan School of Economic and Social Sciences, Jerusalem, Israel

In attempting to evaluate the experience of Israel I should be cautious and humble. Although I am fairly familiar with Israel's experience, I could not claim to have thoroughly analysed it; neither could I argue that the lessons I tend to draw from that experience are shared by all, or even most, observers of the Israeli scene. Moreover, and this is far more crucial, I am required to indicate conclusions which might be applicable to other emerging countries, about the circumstances and experiences of which I have at best some scant and vague knowledge. It may perhaps be best, therefore, to point out at the outset some of Israel's special attributes, so that the reader should be able to judge for himself whether the lessons of Israel's recent history are at all relevant to other specific countries, with each of which good many of the readers are certainly much better acquainted than I am. I shall then proceed to describe and analyse two aspects of Israel's development — the effect of capital imports to the country and the experiment in economic planning — where, I believe, some useful lessons might be gained.

1. A FEW CHARACTERISTICS OF THE ISRAELI ECONOMY

It should first be recognized that even at the dawn of its existence as an independent state, Israel was not strictly an 'underdeveloped' country — at least not in the sense that this term would probably be understood on the African continent. By the usual yard-sticks, Israel was from its inception beyond the Rostovian 'take-off point to a self-sustained growth'. This could be gathered from a few pivotal magnitudes:

    a.   *National income.*—In 1950, the first full year following Israel's war of independence, annual *per capita* GNP was roughly 450–500 dollars. Comparing it to other commonly-termed underdeveloped countries — bearing in mind the well-known reservations applying to geographical comparisons of national income — it is approximately the income level found today among the better-off countries in Latin America, such as Argentina, Chile, Cuba, Uruguay, or Venezuela. But it is twice the size of *per capita* income in Ghana, the richest of the newly independent countries in Africa; and it is some ten times the level of income among the least fortunate African nations — say, Niger, Somalia, Tanganyika, or Nyasaland — where annual *per capita* incomes range from 40 to 50 dollars.

b. *The level of education and proficiency.*—In a population of about one and a quarter millions in 1950, some one quarter of a million were enrolled in schools. Primary education was already by that time compulsory and universal. About one thousand students graduated that year from secondary schools, and approximately the same number graduated from technical and agricultural post-primary schools. Some 4,000 students were enrolled in institutes of higher learning. The rate of literacy at that period was about 90 per cent. Over three quarters of the population had at least full primary education, close to one-third had at least secondary education, and 6 per cent of the population were university graduates. This is a level of education about at par with that of the United States, and it is higher than educational levels in many present-day European countries. One important consequence of the widespread education was that the economy had at its disposal not only a large number of skilled personnel in many areas, but also an abundance of entrepreneural ability. This latter magnitude defies exact measurement; but the abundance could probably be indicated by the fact that in 1950 the country had, for instance, close to 5,000 engineers and 1,000 lawyers — groups from which 'entrepreneurs' very often spring. This position of Israel contrasts very sharply, of course, with that found today among African nations, in many of which — including Nyasaland — college graduates number not more than 10 to 20 per million, and sometimes even less than that.

c. *Occupational distribution.*—As is well recognized, underdeveloped countries are characterized by a very high proportion of employment in the primary sector.[1] In the poorest countries, this proportion may be as high as 80 to 90 per cent. And, as a rule, this proportion declines as the economy's development progresses, while the proportion of the labour force employed in secondary industries, and even more so in tertiary industries,

---

[1] See, for instance, Colin Clark, *The Conditions of Economic Progress* (3rd Edition) (New York: Macmillan & Co., 1957); or Simon Kuznets, 'Industrial Distribution of National Product and Labor Force,' *Economic Development and Cultural Change,* Supplement to Vol. V (July 1957).

tends to rise. Israel is certainly an exception to this rule. During the whole decade, the share of the labour force employed in the primary sector (agriculture, fishery, forestry, and mining) was less than 20 per cent; the proportion of employment in the secondary sector (manufacturing, power, and construction) was about one-third; and in the tertiary sector (services) about one-half. These proportions resemble those maintained today in the United States, the country with the highest *per capita* income. But they differ considerably not only from those prevailing in the least-developed nations, but also from those found among countries whose *per capita* income levels resemble that of Israel — say, Puerto Rico, Chile, or Cuba. There, the share of employment in the primary sector is about 40 per cent, in the secondary sector some 20 per cent, and in the tertiary around 40 per cent. The exceptional situation of Israel in this respect is explained probably to a large extent by the availability of capital imports and the existence of a large import surplus, which will be discussed later; since international trade is mainly an exchange of *goods*, not of services, a large import surplus leads to the provision of a large share of the country's need of goods from abroad, while the economy itself devotes a larger share of its resources to the provision of services than it would in the absence of capital imports. One result of its extraordinary situation was that Israel, probably alone among recently emerging nations, was engaged in the course of its development process, mainly in its early stages, in an effort of directing manpower *towards* agriculture, rather than away from it.

It may be worth noting a few other features of the Israeli economy, beside the fact that it was well ready for a process of economic development, which are certainly relevant in discussing this process and in which Israel differs from most other underdeveloped economies.

a.   *The rate of immigration.*—During the decade of the fifties, Israel's population increased twofold — from a little over a million at the end of 1949 to over two million by the end of 1959. Most of this spectacular increase in population took place through immigration: during these years, the number of immigrants to the country exceeded 600,000. Of these, over a half came in the two years 1950 and 1951 (the number of immigrants in 1949 was, indeed, even higher). But in the following years, too, the rate of immigration, and the rate of increase in population, was one not likely to be matched in other present-day underdeveloped economies.

b. *Capital imports.*—The amount of capital imports into Israel during the decade under consideration was roughly 3 billion dollars. This is obviously an extremely high magnitude. Capital imports amounted to about two-thirds of Israel's total imports of goods and services during the period, a rate approached in recent years only in very few other countries — Jordan, South Korea and Greece. The ratio of capital imports to the economy's gross national product during the period was close to 25 per cent, a ratio apparently far above that found in any other country save one — Southern Rhodesia — in the post-war years.

c. *The existence of a 'mixed' economy.*—Although other economies, including a few which are underdeveloped, could also be termed 'mixed', Israel's blend is probably strictly its own, and deserves, therefore, a brief description. The economy's public or semi-public sector consists of three major components.

First — the government. During the whole period, most of the investment in the economy was either undertaken directly by the government or financed from the government's resources. The government's share in financing investment was particularly heavy in the earlier years of the period; but even at the end of the period it amounted, by available estimates, to over one-half. This high share is explained by the fact, to which I shall return soon, that domestic investment was financed practically altogether by capital imports; and that over one-half of total capital imports to the country was received by the government — mainly from German reparation payments, from sales of development bonds abroad (primarily in the United States), from United States grants-in-aid, and from export-import bank loans. These governmental receipts were then channelled into investment through the government's development budget.

Another segment of the public sector is the Jewish Agency and a few related institutions. The Agency, established after World War I as part of the terms of the British mandate over Palestine, represents world Jewry, and in particular the Zionist movement. It receives large amounts of donations from Jews outside Israel — mainly in the United States — intended to finance immigration to the country and the settlement of immigrants. The Agency's transfers of money to the country constituted about a quarter of all capital imports, thus making the Agency an important source of financing the country's development. The Agency's investment tended to concentrate mainly, but not solely, in agriculture,

and was quite closely co-ordinated with the development
carried out by the government.

The third component of the public or quasi-public sector is the
'Histadrut' — Israel's general federation of labour. It is a federation with probably no parallel anywhere else. It comprehends about
half of the country's population, and besides functioning as a
labour union it is also the chief provider of health services in the
country and the largest single industrial employer. Enterprises
owned by the 'Histadrut' constituted, in size of employment and
of value added, some 15 per cent of Israel's total manufacturing
industries; their share in construction works amounted to over
one-third. The 'Histadrut' is also the mentor, and the roof
institute, of a very wide co-operative movement. Producers
co-operatives are significant mainly in agriculture, either in the
form of the 'Kibbutz' — a commune, or collective settlement;
or in the form of the 'Moshav', the more conventional co-operative
settlement. Together, these forms constitute the large majority
of Israel's agriculture. Another industry in which co-operatives
are important is transportation: most of the country's land
transportation system (excluding the governmentally-owned
railway network) is run by co-operatives.

I shall content myself with this brief description of some of the major
features of the Israeli economy — emphasizing once more that I have
deliberately chosen to consider mainly those in which Israel is likely to
differ from most other emerging nations. I shall now proceed to derive a
few lessons from the country's process of development.

2. The Role of Capital Imports

During the decade under consideration, the net national product in
Israel increased, in real terms, by close to 190 per cent; that is, the 1960
NNP was almost three times that of 1950. Part of this spectacular increase
is explained, of course, by the extremely high rate of growth of population and manpower. But even *per capita* NNP increased between 1950 and
1960 by some 70 per cent — an annual rate of increase of some 5·5 per cent,
which compares favourably even with the post-war record of most
developed economies.

Maintaining *per capita* income intact in the face of as high a rate of
increase in population as Israel has had — and *a fortiori* raising it by over
5 per cent p.a. — should obviously require a very substantial rate of
investment. Indeed, gross domestic investment in physical assets — con-

struction, equipment, husbandry and agricultural planting[2] — amounted during the decade to 28 per cent of the GNP. Although the rate of investment has been gradually falling, it was still quite high even at the end of the period: the proportion of gross investment to the GNP went down from some 40 per cent in 1950–51 to about 25 per cent in 1959–60.

As could be gathered from my earlier remarks, this rate of domestic investment could not have been maintained without the inflow of sizeable capital imports to the country. The only other alternative source of financing investment is domestic saving — and gross savings could hardly be expected to approach 30 per cent of the GNP. In fact, moreover, one finds that capital imports not only contributed to financing investment but were, in net terms for the economy as an aggregate, its only source of finance. Through the period under consideration as a whole net domestic investment amounted, in constant 1956 prices, to close to IL5·5 billion, while capital imports came to over IL6 billion. Capital imports thus exceeded net domestic capital formation; that is, not only were there no savings in the economy as a whole — net saving was even slightly negative. This situation is more typical of the earlier part of the period than of its later years, but even in the late 'fifties, when savings were no longer negative, they were practically nil. Since here lies one of the main lessons I chose to draw from Israel's experience, I should like to dwell on this point at some length.

Why are savings so low, or even negative, in the Israeli economy? It might be just that people do not care to save, for reasons connected with social or age structure, customs, and the like. But so far as households in the economy are concerned, this is apparently not true. Available consumer surveys show that individuals in Israel save, on the average, 5 to 6 per cent of their disposable income — about the same rate which is found in comparable consumer surveys in the United States or the United Kingdom, and presumably the same rate prevailing in most other countries.

Israel's low rate of saving is thus not the result of some unique tastes or time preferences of consumers in the economy. There must be some other explanation — and it seems that it lies mainly in the size of capital imports to the country. I see primarily three avenues through which the availability of capital imports tended to diminish domestic saving.

One is quantitatively very important in the case of Israel, but is probably not too relevant for most other emerging countries likely to receive capital from abroad, and shall therefore be dealt with only briefly. Of the total capital imports during the decade, some one quarter were transfer payments from abroad to private individuals in Israel, mainly in the form

[2] Data on investment in inventories are not available.

19

of gifts and pension payments and of personal restitution payments from Germany. These transfers, especially when they flow on a regular and continuous basis, are viewed by their recipients as part of their disposable income — the overwhelming share of which tends, naturally, to be consumed. Consumption thus increases without any parallel increase in the country's national income, as this term is usually defined; and this is reflected, in the economy's system of national accounts, in the decline of savings. Moreover, part of the transfers from abroad to the public and semi-public sector — mainly to the Jewish Agency — is destined in advance to increase, through various media of support, the disposable income of households, mainly that of new immigrants. This tends further to raise consumption and diminish the country's rate of saving out of its earned income.

Another avenue, which deserves particular attention, is that through which capital imports effect indirectly the amount of business savings. While there are no comprehensive studies of business savings in Israel, existing fragmentary information indicates clearly that business savings are meagre, and that the rate of business saving is much lower in Israel than it is in the average country. Indeed, in certain branches of the economy it is probably even negative, that is, business enterprises may not only refrain from reinvesting profits, but also fail to retain sufficient funds for depreciation allowances. This phenomenon, it seems, is closely associated with the existence of capital imports — in the following manner:

As has been stated earlier, the majority of capital imports to the country is received by the Israeli government and by the Jewish Agency which, in turn, channel most of these receipts (or, rather, of their counterpart in local currency) to domestic investment. However, the larger part of this investment is not undertaken directly by the government. The government's receipts serve, instead, to finance private investment (including that which is carried out by the 'Histadrut'). This is done sometimes — mainly in the agricultural sector — by outright grants; but most often it takes the form of long-term loans, on relatively easy terms (compared with those of the free money market), from the government (or the Agency) to the private enterprise. Due to the relative ease with which these loans could be secured, business saving was drastically diminished. This was the outcome both because the possibility of securing the required funds for expansion from the government relieved the private enterprise of the need to provide its own funds, through the accumulation of unallocated profits and depreciation allowances; and because the enterprise was free from the need of applying to the free money market where, most often, the ability to raise loans is conditioned by the soundness of the firm which, in turn, is partly determined by the ratio of the enterprise's own capital to its total indebtedness. The government, on the other hand, did not very often pay much attention to the solvency of the enterprise, as this is usually evaluated by business criteria. Thus, business firms did not feel the necessity, as in most other economies, to save and increase their own means in order to invest and expand.

The lesson I should like to draw from this outcome is that a government which is fortunate enough to have at its disposal foreign aid, or other forms of capital transfers from abroad, should beware lest its financing of domestic investment should reduce the motive of private enterprises to save. It should, on this count, invest itself (through government corporations) rather than be a source of finance to private business. And, when the government does transfer its receipts to private business, it should act as if it were a commercial bank. In particular, it should scrutinize carefully the enterprise's position with regard to the size of its own capital in relation to its total indebtedness, and examine the enterprise's performance in the past with regard to saving and increasing its own means.

The third main avenue through which capital imports acted on the amount of savings was through their effect on the government's current expenditures — although whatever could be said here is of a highly speculative nature. Throughout most of the period, deficits in the government's current budget contributed substantially to the reduction of the amount of savings in the Israeli economy. And it is likely that in creating the deficits, the government took into consideration the availability of capital imports — particularly the mitigating effect which capital imports, turned into an import surplus, are bound to exert on inflationary pressures created by budgetary deficits.

Again, my lesson here would be that governments enjoying capital transfers from abroad should conduct their current, regular operations — in distinction from their development undertakings — as if these capital imports did not exist at all. Moreover, if a government sees a possibility of creating savings and financing investment in the economy by retaining a surplus of income over expenditures in its regular, current budget, it should pursue this possibility when capital imports are available just as it would in their absence; otherwise, although capital imports would help in raising current standards of living, they would not fulfil the function of increasing the rate of investment and furthering the economy's development.

To prevent a possibly misleading impression, I should like to emphasize that capital imports — and the process of investment in physical assets — were by no means the only vehicle through which Israel's economy raised its standard of living. Although the rate of investment was sufficient to increase, over the period as a whole, the amount of fixed assets *per capita*, this could not in itself sufficiently explain the increase in *per capita* income. The other explanation was the one described vaguely as 'increases in productivity'. The difficulties involved in defining and measuring changes in productivity are only too well known. Nevertheless, it should probably be mentioned that available estimates of these changes in Israel come to the conclusion that from 30 to 40 per cent of the total change in the economy's GNP during the decade could be explained by rising productivity.[3] What is of particular interest, however, is the fact that productivity not only failed to rise, but even declined during the first few years of the decade. These were the years when the rate of capital imports and the rate of investment in the economy were particularly high — apparently too high to be consistent with a stable degree of efficiency in the use of resources. This may illuminate a well-known argument: that the desired rate of investment, and of foreign assistance to the country, is conditioned, *inter alia*, by the capacity of the economy to 'absorb' investment — namely, to use it efficiently. Israel was indeed fortunate, due to the special circumstances described at the outset, in being able to absorb efficiently most of the time the large amount of capital imports which it was able to secure.

Finally, it is worth asking whether an economy, once it becomes dependent on outside sources for its development, could become self-dependent again. I doubt whether any answer of general validity could be offered to this question. For whatever it is worth, however, Israel's experience in this matter should be pointed out. It appears that although even by the end of the decade Israel was still dependent to a large extent on capital from the outside world, the degree of this dependence was much lower than during the country's earlier years. In 1950–51 the size of the import surplus was about 30 per cent of the total resources used by the economy (that is, of the GNP combined with the import surplus(; in 1959–60 this proportion declined by a half, that is, to about 15 per cent. At the same time, the rate of increase of *per capita* income was not lower at the end of the period than it had been at the beginning; on the contrary, it was even slightly higher. In the case of Israel, thus, a tentative answer to the question posed would be that despite an extremely heavy dependence on capital imports for its development at the early stage of its emergence, the country has been able to reduce this dependence gradually; and that it probably could be able to continue its growth even should it be gradually cut out of all, or most, foreign assistance sources still available to the economy.

[3] These estimates were made by Don Patinkin, *The Israel Economy: The First Decade* (Jerusalem: Falk Project for Economic Research in Israel, 1960); and A. L. Gaathon, *Capital Stock, Employment and Output in Israel 1950–1959* (Jerusalem: Bank of Israel Special Studies, 1961).

3. The Experiment in Planning

Planning is a very familiar term in Israel. As in other underdeveloped countries — and in some of the more developed — 'planning' was supposed by many to be the 'Open Sesame', the magic trick by which the economy may somehow prosper and progress while avoiding sacrifices. Actual attempts of planning in Israel were, however, less comprehensive than, say, in India, Norway or Netherlands. As early as 1950 a four-year development plan was prepared by the office of the Prime Minister. It was, in effect, a statement of targets expressed in a national-accounts system, which did not go into physical planning. The plan did not commit the government, however, in its actual conduct of policy, and was thus not much more than an attempt of predicting the general course of the country's development, conditioned on certain assumptions of behaviour some of which did not materialize. Since then, there were a few programmes of physical planning, mainly in the areas of agriculture and manufacturing. From 1957 on, the government has presented to the Knesset (Israel's parliament) annual national budget estimates, along with the government's own budget. These, again, were primarily predictions, but the government's budget was supposed to conform to and be consistent with the prediction. Only at the beginning of the present year — 1962 — was a Planning Authority established by the government. Its function is mainly to prepare a long-range development programme, by which the government should abide. The programme should both state general targets and establish criteria by which the merits of each specific investment project should be decided. Policy measures adopted by the government should conform to this programme.

The lessons drawn from Israel's experiment in planning by various observers are sometimes diametrically opposite; here, therefore, even more than in my earlier remarks, my conclusions should be taken merely as reflecting my own judgement (and probably my own prejudices). Likewise, it would not be feasible to support my analysis by careful documentation in the scope of these remarks.

Looking back upon the past decade, a glaring contradiction appears between what economists had thought at the emergence of the country about the future prospects of the economy, and the actual course the process of development has taken. At the time, Israel seemed to be the economist's despair. It is a rather poor country so far as agriculture is concerned: most of the country's area is desert, steep hills, or otherwise uncultivable land; moreover, the cultivable parts require most often a considerable amount of irrigation in order to be profitably put to crops, while the total amount of available water is very limited and their transportation from source to destination quite expensive. Climatically, the country seemed suitable primarily for one export crop — citrus fruits. So far as mineral raw materials are concerned the country is not in an enviable position either. The chief source of raw materials is the Dead Sea, from which mainly potassium is extracted; but the extractive process is quite expensive, due to geographical and political reasons. Prospects for indus- trial development looked more bright, due to the availability of skilled labour. But even here, the skills were primarily not those required in industrial manufacturing, and there was a general lack of industrial tradition. To reverse the well-known boast, there was a general feeling that 'anything we can do, others can do better'. On top of it, trans - portation of import and export goods to and from the country is particularly expensive since Israel has no trade relations. due to political hostilities, with any of the countries with which it directly borders.

Yet, as could be gathered from the national income figures, the economy progressed rapidly — and, indeed, on all fronts. Many new industries have emerged, some of which even to the degree of having a substantial export capacity. Israel's exports, which at the early period of the state consisted overwhelmingly of citrus fruits, are now quite diversi- fied (beside increasing more than fivefold during the decade) — only less than 30 per cent of total exports consist now of citrus fruits, while most of the rest are manufactures. And there is little doubt that the actual direction development took could not, by and large, be — and had not in effect been — foreseen by the planners of, say, 1950. Moreover, when one looks at sub-branches of certain industries, it is seen that some have progressed fast, while others have stagnated — and which sub-branch would fall in each category could by no means have been predicted by the economist. He could not have foreseen that, say, the export of raincoats would rise rapidly, while that of men's suits would not — as the case has actually been; or that Israel should develop a rather profitable export of rubber tyres, as it actually did.

My conclusion on this score is, thus, that economists should not be asked to state what industries ought to be developed. They could provide only a very general outline, such as, for instance, that the country has a comparative advantage in manufacturing rather than in agriculture; but they should not be expected to go much further than that. Physical planning, that is, the planning of specific projects and industries, cannot efficiently be initiated from above, namely, from some centralized authority. The answer as to what specific industries, sub-industries and plants should be established must be provided by the initiative and calcula- tions of multitudes of individuals, each familiar with his particular line of trade and profession. These individuals need not necessarily be private entrepreneurs. They may be employees of the government or of some semi-public institution, such as the 'Histadrut' in Israel, just as they may be local capitalists or foreign investors. But they are not economists located in some centralized planning authority. An exception which should be mentioned is that of infrastructure investment, mainly in public utilities, such as railways, harbours or electric power. Here it is indeed the function of the planner to calculate the needs of the economy for the services of the industry and to determine the rate and timing of its development.

What, then, is the place of the economist in planning? It is, to my mind, the provision of certain rules, certain criteria, by which the schedule of preference of projects submitted by that multitude of individuals could be determined. In other words, while the economist cannot be expected to initiate projects, he should be able to make the selection of the most profitable to the economy, among those submitted for his consideration. And here, it appears that economists in Israel have fulfilled their function rather well. In particular, experience has shown most often that whenever projects were established despite a negative verdict from the economist, the result to the economy was detrimental, as a rule, and the investment was wasteful. Cases in point are numerous, but I should like to mention specifically only one, that of a steel plant, because investment in steel seems to look attractive to many underdeveloped countries — partly, at least, for misconceived reasons of national prestige.[4] The steel plant has been the largest single investment yet, in manufacturing, amounting to some 30 million dollars, and it was undertaken in spite of the economists' protests. At present, after a few years of operation, the *current* variable cost of producing steel in that plant is still higher than the world price of steel.

The argument of 'infant industries' deserves a particular attention here. Very often industries have been established because, it was claimed, they would become profitable with time, after experience is acquired. From Israel's recent history it seems that only if an industry is fairly close to being profitable at the time of its establishment, could it be hoped that investment in that industry may look justified in the long run. A high rate of loss in the short run does not, as a rule, disappear even after a long span of time. An argument that could still be maintained, of course, is that the loss of a particular industry in which investment is undertaken is more than offset by benefits accrued to other industries by this investment. This argument, which could rarely be substantiated nor refuted by measurement, tends always to leave the economist frustrated.

[4] This may not be entirely their own fault. I recall a not atypical conversation with a professor of business administration at a highly reputable university in a highly developed country. Asked to specify the precise content of the phrase 'rate of development', his response was: 'Why, of course the rate of increase of steel production; could you suggest any better criterion?'

To summarize this discussion, my lesson from Israel's experience would be that the planning body should not attempt to initiate investment projects. Instead, it should determine overall targets for the economy's growth and, in accordance with these, criteria for the selection of investment projects — and ensure that the same criteria are applied in all investment decisions. Indeed, as has been mentioned before, this is approximately the direction followed by the newly established Planning Authority in Israel.

One other point should not be overlooked. The feeling in the earlier years of the state that anything could be done better — or rather cheaper — by others, was not entirely unjustified. At the rate of foreign exchange maintained at that time, this feeling was generally true. The establishment of new profitable industries has required an increase of the relative prices of export and import goods over other prices. This was achieved by a gradual rise of the rate of exchange (that is, of the price of foreign exchange): from 1950 to the present, the rate of foreign exchange more than doubled, relatively to the increase in domestic prices.[5] It is obvious that without this increase, most of Israel's newly founded industries would have proven definitely unprofitable. This is another lesson which, to my mind, is applicable to many other emerging economies: much as currency devaluation is an unpopular and unattractive policy measure, it is probably indispensable when substantial development efforts are pursued by the country, requiring the establishment of industries progressively lower on its list of comparative advantage.

Moreover, to borrow the wise saying about justice, the correct rate of exchange should not only exist — it should also be seen. And the same goes for similar prices. I refer here to the possibility of using 'shadow (accounting) prices' instead of those existing in the market. Although devaluation was carried out in Israel a few times, the government was always reluctant to do it, and took this step only in large intervals and after the need and pressure for it became more than obvious. Likewise, as was explained earlier, the government maintained a relatively low rate of interest on its development loans. The planners realized only too well that the rate of interest and, very often, the rate of exchange were below their equilibrium levels. In judging the merits of proposed investment projects, they used higher 'shadow' rates. This, indeed, was preferable to the use of the prevailing rates; but the planners' use of correct rates cannot fully replace the actual implementation of these rates in the market. The reason for it is that, as was emphasized earlier, the initiative in suggesting investment projects does not — and cannot — come from the planners. It comes from that multitude of individual entrepreneurs, who inevitably

---

[5] Between 1950 and 1962 the rate of exchange changed from IL0.357 to IL3 per U.S. dollar, that is, it increased about 8.4 times; the index of consumer prices increased at the same period about 3.8 times.

base their calculations on prices as *they* see them. It is thus likely, as has often been the case in Israel, that the planners have to make their selection of projects out of a rather poor list — poor not because those who originate the projects lack insight or because they are weak in their profit and loss accounting, but because they do not use the correct prices; while potentially profitable investments, from the economy's viewpoint, never come to light — for they cannot even be conceived.

SWEDEN—A CASE STUDY OF ECONOMIC DEVELOPMENT

BY TORSTEN GÅRDLUND

Stockholm School of Economics

Let me, by way of introduction, say a few words on my choice of subject matter. When, some months ago, I suggested a variation on the question which was put to me, my choice had been made mainly through a process of elimination. Having no experience of conditions in this part of Africa, I felt unable to contribute much to a specific discussion of development problems of a country like Nyasaland. I had, on the other hand, worked in two or three of the other new nations of Africa long enough to come to doubt the value of a general formula and the possibility of a general strategy of economic development put forward by some of my constructive and brilliant fellow economists.

The position I have come to take is much closer to the more modest one expounded by Simon Kuznets in two recent books, *Economic Change* (1952) and *Economic Growth* (1959). In his lecture on 'International Differences in Income Levels', reprinted in the first of these books, Kuznets stresses the fact that economic development of the type that is now sought by the new nations spread from a centre of innovation in Western Europe (mainly England and Belgium) during the nineteenth century. It penetrated only to such countries which 'by a shift in the general outlook of ever growing proportions of the population toward an acceptance of rational calculation' had been made ready for 'a widespread application of science'.

In his more recent book Kuznets furthermore underlines that in the long period since the Industrial Revolution in Great Britain at the end of the eighteenth century the industrial system has spread only to a limited part of the world, still including only about a quarter of the world population. Its technological and social impact has not advanced the economic performance of the rest of the world to levels anywhere near those for the developed countries of Western Europe and North America. As a starting point for further research Kuznets also makes the statement that the science-based industrial system, wherever it appears, seems to require a minimum of social concomitants: a minimum level of literacy and skill in the population, a shift from a personal and family organization of society to an impersonal and bureaucratic organization, a minimum of political independence and of efficiency in the structure of state.

It so happens that the history of Sweden's transformation from an underdeveloped position around 1850 to the prosperity of modern times conforms extremely well with this statement. My motive for telling you some of the story of Sweden's industrialization has thus been to try to meet, in some degree, the demands for more specific research put forward by a fellow economist to whose insight and judgement I would like to pay homage.

During the first half of the nineteenth century the most burning social and economic issue in Swedish society was the care of the poor — the destitutes and vagrants from a growing landless proletariat. Sweden's population had increased from 1,781,000 in 1750 to 2,347,000 in 1800 and 3,483,000 in 1850, that is by 32 per cent in the first fifty year period and 48 per cent in the second. The inability to find enough new land for a growing population had increased the landless part of the rural population. Whereas in 1775 as much as 66 per cent of the rural population had consisted of landowning farmers (and only 34 per cent of such landless categories as cottagers, crofters and farm labourers), the proportion of landowning farmers had decreased to 60 per cent in 1800 and to 52 per cent in 1870.

'Cottagers made an extremely precarious livelihood' writes the American sociologist Dorothy Thomas in her penetrating study of Swedish population movements 1750–1933, 'and their small plots furnished a bare subsistence through potato culture. The demand for their labour in agriculture was uncertain and fluctuating, but they were tied to the land to an extent that made it difficult to seek employment in such industry as existed. Crofters were often bound to contracts which were exploitative, and while they were relatively secure in their right to the land, they felt the pressure of the need for cash as the old selfsufficient household type of economy gradually gave place to a more differentiated economic structure.'

The population growth in Sweden during the nineteenth century had much the same causes as in the underdeveloped world of today. It was due, said a famous Swedish poet and bishop Esaias Tegner in a statement on a report on the Poor Laws of 1837, to the lowering effects on the death-rate of 'peace, vaccines and potatoes'.

The economic development which set in about 1850 — in the form of industrialization, railway building and agrarian development — absorbed the greater part of the vast underemployment as well as the continued increase in population, and it also made possible a continually improved standard of living. There was, however, also another factor that contributed to the solution of the problems of underemployment and poverty. Between 1850 and 1910 Sweden had a net migration to foreign countries of about a million people, most of whom went to the United States.

During the 1880's the emigration reached its peak level, when it amounted yearly to 7 per 1,000 of the population, the increase of which thus was limited to 10 per 1,000. Without emigration, the increase of the Swedish population during the 1880's would obviously have reached the level of 17 per 1,000, which would have been close to the level now prevalent in the underdeveloped world. To give another indication of the economic importance of our nineteenth century emigration: between 1870 and 1900 the number of men between 15 and 65 years of age in Sweden increased by 390,000; during the same period 360,000 men in this same age group emigrated. Emigration during this period thus accounted for almost half of the increase in the productive male population.

There is clear evidence that nineteenth century Swedish emigration mainly had economic motives, and it is also obvious that most of the emigrants improved their lot by moving to the United States. Nevertheless they generally paid a certain price for what they gained, in the difficulties of adjustment to a new environment.

The reorganization of agriculture, which greatly contributed to the increase in the standard of living, involved a transition to a more productive system of crop rotation, changes in the types of crops themselves, an increased importance of animal over vegetable production and improvement in all aspects of the agricultural techniques: draining and cultivation of land, supplying of chemical fertilizers, harvesting, etc. As the following table shows, the total grain crops increased both through an extension of the cultivated area and increased production per hectare. The increase in production per hectare from 1·2 to 1·6 tons, or 30 per cent, took place during the forty years before World War I.

Cultivated area and crops in grain production

Yearly	Area in hectare	Crop in metric tons	Tons per hectare
1866–70	1,261,000	1,549,000	1·23
1906–10	1,690,000	2,709,000	1·60
1951–55	1,571,000	2,877,000	1·96

A special and very important factor in this connexion were the changes in distribution and size of holdings, which followed the repartitioning and the removal of legal restrictions on disposal of real property. Land reform was a precondition for the change-over to more productive agricultural methods. The enclosure movement started already in the late eighteenth century and culminated during the three or four decades after the Enclosure Act of 1827. The number of official land surveyors reached a level of 300 to 400 already in the late eighteenth century and still remains at this level.

The enclosure movement meant that land which had been either partitioned in very small holdings — strips often not more than a few yards wide — or used collectively by the villagers was regrouped in individual farms on which the owners, now unfettered by a restrictive village organization, became free to use more modern methods. The removal of legal restrictions on disposal of real property meant that land which was formerly regarded as belonging to the family and thus withdrawn from impersonal market transactions could now be acquired by individual farmers capable of putting it to better use through modern agricultural methods.

It goes without saying that these reforms — repartition of land as well as its commercialization — were of an almost revolutionary nature. They were directed against old traditions, the abolishment of which must have been very painful to a rural population with settled ideas. Going back to the parliamentary debates of the time one gets the impression that the 'psychic price' of development paid by the old generation of farmers must have been considerable — as were the material rewards won by succeeding generations.

Through the reorganization of agriculture the Swedish population, a considerable part of which had been undernourished in the early days of the nineteenth century, had at the end of the century by and large reached a fairly adequate nutritional standard. Even if the diet was still lacking in animal products, the earlier deficiency in calories had, at any rate, been overcome by the increased output of grains and potatoes. At the end of the nineteenth century the Swedish workers thus already had reached a food standard roughly corresponding to the one which today, half a century later, is found in Soviet Russia and Eastern Europe.

The development of agriculture was of importance also in that it created an expanding market for many of the new industries. When the farming population received more cash for their increasing crops, it could turn an effective demand towards many of the new factory-made products: chinaware, glass, cutlery, yarn and cloth, ovens and other cast-iron products. At the same time the farmers had more and more to give up their home production of such consumer goods, to be able to concentrate their work on more demanding agricultural techniques.

A dynamic relationship between agricultural and industrial progress applied also the production side of agriculture. The tool manufacturing and mechanical industries had considerable markets among farmers and lumberers for spades, axes, and all sorts of implements and machines. On the other hand the new factory-made tools and implements made work in the fields and the forests much more efficient. Through its contribution to increased production in agriculture and forestry, industry helped to create important markets for its own products. Swedish economic history thus clearly bears out a fact, which may well be of general importance, that effective national demand, without which general industrialization cannot make much progress, can be created only by a parallel economic growth in the agricultural sectors of the economy.

Although agricultural development was of great importance for the solution of the burning problem of poverty, industrialization became more and more the leading force in the creation of wealth. The modern sector of the economy — industry, commerce and transport — had already at the time of World War I almost the same share of total employment as agriculture, but its share of the national income was, of course, far greater.

Population by industry (in per cent) 1870–1950

Year	Agriculture, forestry, fishing	Mining, manufacturing, commerce	General administration, professions	Total
1870	72·4	19·8	7·8	100·0
1910	48·4	45·4	5·8	100·0
1950	24·6	65·3	10·1	100·0

From the table above the continued increase in the modern sector also stands out. By 1950 it included almost two-thirds of the employed population, whereas agriculture, which eighty years earlier had given work to almost three-quarters of the population had decreased its share to one-quarter.

Number of workers in Swedish industry 1875 and 1912
(For 1875 partly estimates)

Industry	1875	1912
Iron, steel and mining	30,000	32,000
Metal manufacturing and engineering	15,000	66,000
Saw-mill and wood-working	20,000	53,000
Wood-pulp and paper	4,000	26,000
Textiles	16,000	44,000
Food products	7,000	34,000
Stone, clay and glass	7,000	43,000
Other	11,000	44,000
	110,000	342,000

As can be seen from the table above, the expansion of employment was greatest in the industries based on the traditional raw materials, iron adn wood. To the former a modern branch, the mechanical industry, was grafted in the middle of the nineteenth century, and the old saw-mill industry was further enlarged with wood-working and paper-pulp industries. Together these two groups of industries had about two-thirds of total industrial employment in 1875 and half of total industrial employment in 1912. Beside the metal and wood groups the only important industry to develop already around 1850 was the textile industry, which produced cotton and woollen goods from imported raw material with mainly imported machines.

The industries of the earlier period of industrialization had mostly produced semi-finished products, consumer goods still being almost totally made either by artisans or in the home. At the very end of the century industrialization began to spread also to the final stages, with factory production of shoes, clothes, canned food-stuffs, tobacco, beer, etc. The capital goods industries, which mainly worked for export markets, also gradually increased their degree of manufacturing and processing. The iron and steel industry turned more and more to such products as nails, screws, chains, tools and cutlery and the mechanical industry to specialized machinery. The saw-mills began to fabricate their products more and more; a new wood-working industry for the production of furniture and other joinery products came into being. At the turn of the century the pulp and paper industry went through an extremely rapid development which soon made it the largest branch of the forestry group.

The increase in the standard of living during these decades was very impressive. Between 1861 and 1913 industrial wages increased by 300 per cent; taking the increasing cost of living into consideration the rise in real wages was still about 250 per cent. At the same time the working day became shorter. During the 1870's the average effective working day had been ten to eleven hours. Including rests this meant twelve to thirteen hours a day and there were many factories which worked longer hours than the average. By 1910, when the trade unions had become a power, the working time had been reduced to ten hours *including rests* in most of the bigger industries.

In concrete terms the increased standard of living meant that ordinary people were now much better fed, clothed and housed and were even able to afford some luxury goods like tobacco, beer and spirits. The new products were partly produced by national industries, partly imported through the proceeds of an increasingly productive export industry. For the ordinary people work had also been made easier both by more efficient tools and by machines. Even if the new factory techniques had introduced some dangers and inconveniences, fairly efficient legislation — on working hours for women and young people, on sanitary conditions and protection against accidents — had already been enacted at the turn of the century.

It seems to be a fact that Sweden nowadays has reached a higher national income per inhabitant than most other European countries. Taking one of the comparative tables of Kuznets' study of 1959, we find that of twelve countries in Western Europe, Sweden had the second place in average *per capita* production during the early 1950's. The figure quoted for Switzerland was 1,010 US dollars, for Sweden 950 dollars, for Great Britain 780 dollars, for France 740 dollars and for Germany 510 dollars. The rate of increase each decade in *per capita* production averaged for Sweden 27·6 per cent between the 1860's and the early 1950's. This meant that Sweden had one of the leading places in a group of six countries in the world, on which Kuznets makes the comment that their cumulated rises in *per capita* production over a century 'stagger the imagination'.

It is interesting to ask whether this position can be explained by favours of natural endowment, that is by extraordinary natural gifts in climate and supply of energy and raw materials. Knowing that Sweden was one of the poorer European countries only a century ago, we would obviously not expect the answer to be in the affirmative without qualifications. But it could, nevertheless, be possible that the later generations of Swedes had, when for some reason they decided to develop their country, found at their disposal extraordinary although previously dormant natural riches.

I do not quite think that the Swedish entrepreneurs in agriculture, trade and industry, and technicians and office personnel and workmen, who between themselves created the economic revolution of the late nineteenth century, did it all by force of character. But, although I want to be modest when speaking about my own country, I cannot, on the other hand, see that they were to any great degree favoured by Nature, compared with the natural endowment of most of the other nations of Western Europe. As you may know, Sweden, like Norway and Finland, and for that matter Russia, suffers from a severe climate. The growing season is short, which means only one yearly crop from the fields and slow growth of the forests. The costs of warming the houses and keeping land and water traffic going during the long, cold winters are quite high. Reckoned per year rainfall is satisfactory, with an average of 500 to 600 mm, but its distribution over the seasons are decidedly unsatisfactory in most parts of the country, with springs too dry and the harvesting season too wet. The quality of the soil is, by European standards, nothing to be very happy about. Of the three main productive ingredients, potassium presents no problem on the dominantly clay soils. The large northern regions are, on the other hand, poor in nitrates, the low temperature inhibiting the work of nitrate-producing bacteria. And most of the soils are also lacking in phosphates. The high yields of Swedish agriculture are, in fact, dependent on very considerable imports of fertilizers. Of late, fertilizers have also been applied to the forests, in order to overcome their growth handicaps in comparison with Continental Europe.

Industrial raw materials are ample in certain fields. It was on a high quality iron ore, and on good ore supplies for other metals like copper, that the earlier Swedish industries had been built. The main energy base is nowadays electricity generated by water power. But it was only at the turn of the last century that electric power came into being. During the decades of industrial take-off, water-wheels were used for motive power in rural industries and steam-engines in urban industries. Charcoal was used for the smelting and refining of iron. Neither water-wheels nor charcoal was a very economic source of energy, and the coal to fire the steam-engines had to be imported.

If Sweden's natural endowment is, as I believe, rather below the European average, we must turn to other factors when trying to explain its high rate of economic growth during the last century. Of primary importance seems to have been the factor which Kuznets indicated by the expression 'efficiency in the structure of state'. Sweden had, as you may remember from European history classes, begun to emerge as a national state already in the Middle Ages. A centralized administration gradually took form during the thirteenth, fourteenth and fifteenth centuries, and by that time the country had also begun to take its place in the European community: trading with Europe, sharing its religious and social outlook, striving for national aims and trying to defend them before European opinion. At the end of the sixteenth century national selfconsciousness had reached such heights that the Swedish king, Erik XIV, who was not only well versed in European culture and politics but also, it must be conceded, a little mad, had sent an envoy to ask for the hand of the queen of England!

There was also a period during the seventeenth and early eighteenth century when Sweden had become one of the major powers of Europe, trying to enlarge her influence and territory far beyond the Baltic sea by waging large-scale wars against Russia, Poland, Denmark and certain Germanic states. This was a costly business and it did not do much to increase the general welfare of the country. Yet it all had its importance for later economic development.

When, after the Napoleonic wars, Sweden had lost all remnants of its position as a great power, and had even lost the Finnish territory acquired in the Middle Ages, she had a well developed national structure obtained through many centuries of history as a continuous state. She was used to striving for common goals; she had a political machinery for decision-making on national issues; she had a fairly efficient administrative system to implement a national policy. In this respect the Sweden of the middle nineteenth century differed not only from most of the new nations of today which still have to develop their state machinery but also from several European countries of the time, which had yet to win their independence and national cohesion.

There were indeed many decisions needed to make the country ready for the industrial system. In the older society economic life had been rigidly regulated by the State to ensure stability and the rights of status. Handicrafts and internal trade were the privileges of the town guilds; external trade and industry were regulated according to monopolistic principles believed to be in the interest of the nation. Already in the early part of the nineteenth century it was noticed by such Swedes as followed European events that countries like England were able to press forward economically under a new system of natural liberty. When this notion had developed into political conviction — had developed into a creed of economic liberalism — it had its chance of success in a political environment permitting basic social and economic change. Beginning in the 1840's a whole series of political decisions were taken to make the country ready for far-reaching economic transformation. In practice the 'new system of natural liberty' came to mean, of course, that the State still was very active, although in other fields and by other methods than before.

In 1840 an administrative reform was passed, introducing a number of new ministries and giving further political independence to civil servants. In 1842 a law on compulsory education was introduced, giving at least one primary school for every parish (half of them had previously been without). In 1846 the guild-system was abolished as were most of the special regulations governing internal trade and the iron industry. In 1847 a reform of secondary education was instituted whereby science was given an increased influence at the expense of the study of religion and classical languages.

Between 1821 and 1848 a number of technical schools were founded: one for each of the professions of veterinary surgeons, forestry technicians and agronomists, two schools for metallurgists and three schools for a general technical education. During the first decades of their existence almost all of these schools were of a rather elementary, not to say primitive nature. The really surprising thing is, however, that they were founded at all at this early time when the demand for a rational technology was still at its very beginning. I think these early initiatives in technical training give quite good proof of my thesis: that the Swedish State really was up and doing, carefully preparing the scene for the Industrial Revolution.

I could certainly give several more indications of the importance of the 'efficiency in the structure of state' for the economic development of my ex-underdeveloped country — but let me for practical reasons assume that you are already convinced. If this factor implies a certain political maturity and rationality in outlook and perhaps also some other laudable traits, there was another growth factor of a general nature which could not possibly be put to the credit of the enterprising generations of the 1850's, the 1870's and 1890's: that they were allowed to spend their energy in developing certain basic industries in which their fathers and forefathers had already done a good job. I think it was of great help to the early industrialization of Sweden that its basic vocation had already been decided.

The leading export industry had for centuries been the iron industry, which sold on the European market a high quality of wrought iron which was both smelted in blast furnaces and refined in forges by charcoal. In the early part of the nineteenth century European demand for iron had increased through the beginning industrialization of such countries as England, Belgium and France. But at the same time the cheaper methods of smelting and puddling iron with coke, which were invented in England at the end of the eighteenth century, had begun to threaten Sweden's position as one of the main suppliers of the international market. The Swedish iron masters had an organization, 'Jernkontoret', whose purpose was not only to work for a common monopolistic sales policy but also to obtain productivity gains through technical research. When sales started to fall in the 1820's they sent their metallurgists to England to study the new technique hoping to be able to adapt it for the Swedish charcoal process. This was the initiative behind the spectacular increase of iron production mentioned before, whereby the output per hearth increased about 400 per cent during the forty years around 1850. Once the iron industry had been revived by this extensive technical reform, the further innovations introducing mass-production of steel (the Bessemer, Martin and Siemens methods) followed much easier. In fact Swedish metallurgists were in the forefront in developing one of the new methods in the late 1850's, the Bessemer technique, and they were also among the leading nations in developing such mechanical processes as steel-rolling.

In the saw-mill industry a similar technical revolution was going on. In order to meet the enlarged foreign demand, mainly due to the industrialization of Great Britain as well as the gradual lowering of British import duties between 1821 and 1866, a structural reform within the Swedish saw-mill industry was needed. It consisted of the migration of the industry from the western parts of the country, where the older water-driven saw-mills had during the previous century consumed most of the forests, to the northern parts, where enormous virgin forests could now be exploited with the help of powerful steam-driven saw-mills. The new mills were located at the convenient points where the timber, floated down the rivers, reached the Baltic coast, to be sawn and loaded into ships for export. This structural change started as early as the 1850's, and, after the initial success, a further expansion of the industry, including planing and other manufacturing of boards came without great difficulties.

The decisive technical progress in the largest of the traditional Swedish industries, the iron and steel industry, came, as we have seen, through impulses from abroad. The iron masters were, in fact, well informed of foreign innovations through a voluminous journal of theirs which since its beginning in 1817 had published long technical reports: on the use of fine cast-iron for the production of household products, on the use of new forges for iron fining which in Sweden came to be called the Lancashire method, on mining, smelting and rolling techniques and so forth. In the iron industry the foreign technique was usually studied by Swedish metallurgists travelling abroad, primarily in England but also in Belgium, France and, later, the United States and Germany.

The other traditional industry, the saw-mill industry, had already since the eighteenth century a well developed technique in water-driven sawing frames. The change-over to steam-driven frames — and simultaneously to thinner and less timber-consuming saw-blades — was partly due to national innovations, partly to a borrowing of techniques from the British wood-working industries (the most advanced of which were the London Navy yards run by Jeremy Bentham's brother). The foreign impulses in sawing techniques reached Sweden both by the travels of Swedish mechanics and by imports of British machinery (which had to be smuggled into the country, until Great Britain generously decided to put its technical advance at the disposal of foreign countries by the repeal of the prohibition on exports of machinery in 1843).

For the newer industries, the textile and machine industries, the modern technology was also to a large degree learned by young Swedish workmen and engineers travelling and often working for long periods of time abroad. Abroad, nine times out of ten, meant Great Britain during the early and middle part of the nineteenth century, the United States and Germany at the turn of the century and later. But in the textile and machine industries, neither of which used techniques traditional to Sweden, a large number of foreign technicians and skilled workers were brought to the country to set up factories and instruct a labour force. Quite often these foreign experts stayed in the country founding their own manufacturing firms. In the machine industry all of the larger factories in the middle of the nineteenth century were led either by Swedish mechanics who had worked for many years in British workshops or by British 'millwrights' working in Sweden on fairly long contracts.

One of these last, Samuel Owen, who came to Sweden in the early years of the century to set up some steam-engines delivered by Boulton & Watt, stayed on to found his own business. He later ran into financial trouble, and when the Swedish Parliament was asked to come to his rescue, it was pointed out that he had lost a lot of money doing what we nowadays call 'technical assistance'. 'As he continuously has had to use rude, churlish and in all respects ignorant workmen in his factory, he has never had time to impart any high degree of professional skill to them before they were snapped away by other factories and iron works, whereupon he has been forced to fill the vacancies with a new lot of ignorant workers.' Towards the end of his life Owen wrote an autobiographical sketch, in which he refers to his technical assistance activities: 'When I first started my foundry in Stockholm, there was not one man who had even *seen* iron being smelted. In those days it was not easy to start a machine factory, but now, when several hundred skilled workers have been trained in my works, it is less difficult.'

In Simon Kuznets's book *Economic Growth*, to which I have so often referred for the simple reason that my views so closely coincide with his, it is stated 'Without the emergence and development of science and science-based technology, neither economic production nor population could have grown at the high rates indicated for the last century to century and a half in the developed countries.' I would like to make my contribution by stressing that 'science-based technology' not only implies technology in the limited sense of the 'great inventions'. I would like to add that without a readiness on the part of all personnel to submit to the rules of rational organization of work — or, rather, without a willingness on their part to enter freely into the spirit of these organizational rules — economic development would never have had a chance, no matter how many great inventions had been made by the great inventors.

The whole period from, let us say, the 1830's to the time of World War I was in Sweden one long training operation, whereby a people, the great majority of whom were nothing but 'rude, churlish and in all respects ignorant', was moulded into a disciplined and skilful working force. To this educational process contributions came from many quarters. The schools — general and technical — certainly laid the foundations. The popular organizations — trade-unions, temperance lodges, consumer co-operatives, educational branches of the political parties — made very important contributions. (No Swedish trade-union has, to give one example, ever defended a member who has been disciplined or fired by the employer for turning up at work under the influence of alcohol.)

The main contributions were, of course, given by the business leaders, the engineers and the foremen themselves. The factory and the office were the most important class-rooms for the educational process I am speaking of. There is in this connexion a somewhat special document which I want to quote because I believe its implication to be general. There was, during the years 1813–39, at one of the leading iron works an office manager by the name of Muhr, who taught his young apprentices a series of rules of conduct to be remembered when they went out into the industry one day to become managers themselves. These rules were first copied by hand and widely distributed among the young employees of the industry, but at the end of the nineteenth century they were printed in several editions under the name of 'Muhr's Catechism for the Iron Industry'. This booklet contains something that could be called the ethics of industrial work.

Its values of personal conduct are simplicity, moderation, economy, punctuality, foresight and, perhaps more than anything else, care and conservation of any tool, machine and raw material that have been entrusted to a man. Sound advice is also given in what we call personnel management: 'Never give an order which cannot be obeyed, over which control cannot be applied, or which may be regarded as unfair or difficult . . . Never write or say anything which you do not fully understand but look first for the necessary information.' A warning was given against one of the not uncommon mental characteristics of underdevelopment, the 'leave-it-to-tomorrow' attitude: 'Give support to your memory by diligently making notes, and do not permit a postponement until tomorrow of what can be done today.' And the first principle of all bureaucracy, the need for written documents, was clearly stated. All transactions with workmen, purveyors and customers should be noted in the books, and all contracts should if possible be made in writing.

All this is, of course, in the best Puritan and Quaker tradition, and I think it is in this perspective one has to see the impulses that the new Swedish industries received from Britain and the United States during the nineteenth century. The British 'mill-wrights' brought new standards of orderliness, punctuality, care and discipline to the human riff-raff, which in Sweden was migrating from the rural proletariat to the towns. The reports and diaries of Swedish mechanics, who worked in the leading machine shops in Britain in the middle of the century, abound with impressions of a rational organization of factory work. These young men certainly studied, sketched and described many ingenious machines they first saw in Britain and later in the United States. But they were above all impressed by the high level of organization they found: by the 'beautifully organized' light forge in Joseph Bramah's establishment, by the way in which Henry Maudslay preserved his drawings and took care of his tools, by the order and tidiness they found at Sharp & Roberts, by the standardization of measures which Joseph Whitworth was developing.

The development of new methods of production, and of their social concomitants, was, of course, reflected in an increase in capital formation. According to the National Accounts study published by Stockholm University gross investment rose from just under 5 per cent of GNP during the 1860's to about 15 per cent at the turn of the century. The increase has since continued, even if there have been breaks for the two world wars. The present day ratio of gross investment to GNP is above 30 per cent. Although the statistical material may underrate the investment volume for the earlier decades of the period, when agricultural investment, difficult to assess, was prominent, there can be little doubt that the investment ratio increased considerably — perhaps doubled or even trebled — during the half century before World War I. Of the investment volume roughly two-thirds went into building and construction, one-third into machinery and other equipment.

I made, some years ago, a study of the financing of a certain number of Swedish industrial firms — in the iron, machinery, sawmill and textile industries — during the half century before World War I. As research material I used the individual accounts of these firms. For sixteen of the firms I could get back as far as 1856, for six other firms I could find comparable figures only from the early 1880's. The following table gives the aggregated balance sheets of the sixteen and twenty-two firms in million crowns for two periods: 1856–84 and 1884–1913.

Assets	16 firms			22 firms		
	1856	1884	Increase	1884	1913	Increase
Liquid assets	3·4	7·1	3·7	10·4	31·6	21·2
Stock	6·8	18·0	11·2	20·3	47·5	27·2
Fixed assets	11·4	33·4	22·0	41·6	134·5	92·9
	21·6	58·5	36·9	72·3	213·6	141·3
Liabilities						
Short-term debts	1·5	3·8	2·3	4·3	23·7	19·4
Long-term debts	7·0	23·6	16·6	24·5	98·4	73·9
Capital	13·1	31·1	18·0	43·5	91·5	48·0
New shares	—	—	—	(27·6)	(45·2)	(17·6)
Funds and profits	—	—	—	(15·9)	(46·3)	(30·4)
	21·6	58·5	36·9	72·3	213·6	141·3

As you can see from the table, a lot of capital had to be found for the expansion of these firms. The group of sixteen increased the value of stock by 11·2 millions and of fixed assets by 22·0 millions, and the somewhat larger group needed 27·2 millions more for stock and as much as 92·9 millions for fixed assets during the second period. Most of the new fixed investment could be financed by equity capital: 18·0 out of the 22·0 millions needed during the first period, and 48·0 out of the 92·9 millions needed during the second period.

Of the expanded equity capital by far the largest part was found within the financial framework of the firms: through the ploughing back of profits. For the first period this does not appear from the table, as all of the sixteen firms did not have company form at this time. But for the nine firms which were registered companies the accounts show that out of a total increase of equity capital of 11·0 millions, only 2·9 millions were had by issues of new shares and the rest by a ploughing back of profits. And for the second period you can see from the table that only 17·6 millions came from issues of new shares and not less than 30·7 millions from profits ploughed back. If you could look closer into the accounts you would, moreover, find that for both periods a large part of the 'new shares' really emanated from profits previously distributed by the firms. The reason for this is that the new shares were generally bought by the very limited group of original share-holders, who had made a large part of their fortunes through earlier dividends from the company in question.

If my results can be regarded as representative of Swedish conditions in general — even if my material does not comprise a great *number* of industrial firms, it does, by including the biggest firms, take in a large part of the production value of each of the industries — they throw some light on the problem of industrialization and capital formation. It appears that a very large part of the fixed investment was created out of profits within the firms themselves. In this light, capital formation appears mainly as an aspect of a more general process of technological change and market expansion. The capital formation needed for an important although gradual technical development was perhaps not so much a *pre-condition* of economic expansion as a productive element *coming forward during and through this expansion.*

But, critical of any unfounded generalization as I presume you are, you will probably say that, especially during the latter part of the period studied, a considerable part of the total capital needed *was* found either in the form of short-term credits, presumably granted by creditor firms, or in the form of long-term credits, presumably given by commercial banks and bond-holders. That is true. Of a total capital need of 141·3 millions during the second period, increased short-term indebtedness accounted for 19·4 millions; and long-term debts, mainly to banks and bond-holders, for not less than 73·9 millions.

To speak only of the increase in long-term indebtedness, it can, however, to a certain extent be included in the formula I just spoke of. The share-owners of the commercial banks as well as the depositors of these banks were generally individuals or institutions saving out of such profits as had been generated by the industrial expansion. Still, an increasing part of the supply of saving did come from social groups not directly connected with industrial and commercial ownership. The growing influence of the commercial banks towards the end of the century — as suppliers of credit themselves and as middlemen placing bonds on the market — was no doubt a sign of the increased importance of general saving for industrial capital formation. And although the earlier industrial expansion — between, say, 1850 and 1890 — could be financed with rather limited capital resources and without much help from a national credit market, the more capital-intensive expansion which set in during the 1890's (mass production of steel, specialized machine industry, electrical industry, pulp and paper industry) — had to be financed in the wider context of a banking system based on a growing national supply of saving.

Against a background of the development problems of our time you may wonder to what extent the borrowed part of industrial capital came from foreign sources. Towards the end of the century foreign lending did account for as much as half of Swedish domestic net capital formation. (The loans were paid back during the ten or fifteen years after 1910 and Sweden thereafter in a modest way became a creditor country.) The foreign credits, which played a certain role during the period 1860–1910, were taken up by the State, the larger townships and some of the semi-public mortgage institutions, which were able to place bond loans on foreign markets — mainly the French — where the interest rates were considerably lower than at home. The private industrial companies, which anyway started to use bonds for their long-term financing only at the turn of the century, were not in a position to find long-term credits abroad.

It is true that the iron and steel and saw-mill industries received some short-term commercial credits from or through their foreign agents, but even if these credits might have been of importance at especially critical times, they generally did not amount to much if the *total* capital needs of the firms are taken into consideration. For Swedish industry the import of capital was thus mainly of indirect importance in the sense that, once the public sector's capital needs for construction and housing had been filled from foreign sources, a large part of domestic saving could be put at the disposal of the expanding Swedish industry and trade.

The generating factors during the industrialization of Sweden seem to have been the *exports* of iron and steel, iron ore, specialized machinery, sawn wood, pulp and paper and the *investment* in plant and machinery, farms, city property, transportation and other public utilities. Of secondary importance, in the sense that their growth was determined mainly by the generating factors just mentioned, were *imports* and the *home-market industries*.

The expansion of exports was to a large extent determined by the demand created in the countries which had begun to be industrialized earlier than Sweden. In Britain, to mention the largest market for Swedish exports, industrialization created a strong demand for timber used for building of cities, pit-props for the mines, sleepers for the railways, iron and steel for machines and cutlery, wood-pulp and paper for the newspaper and printing trades.

In the early days of the Industrial Revolution the expansion of exports was a rather automatic affair, and there are many amusing stories about how little the Swedish producers knew of their foreign markets. Gradually, however, the export trade became more complex. The exporting industries found it more and more to their advantage to build up their own selling organizations rather than to rely on the merchant houses which often demanded high commissions without making very particular selling efforts. By the end of the nineteenth century some of the more ambitious industrial firms had begun to organize their own export departments. Punctual deliveries, fairness towards the customers in cases of complaints, and, above all, a promise of high and uniform quality of the product became the principles consciously striven for in Swedish exporting firms. It took specialized export departments with direct contacts with the customer to build up this kind of selective sales policy.

I have, thus far, dwelt on the more technical aspects of the selling activities, when rather recently the industrial firms themselves became more active in the export field. There is, however, a more important point to make about the role of the merchants in the economic development of the country. Even if the technicians made extremely important contributions to industrial progress — and, perhaps, were even the most important group in the founding of new firms in such branches as the machine, the cutlery and the wood-working industries — the merchants were the dominant founders of modern Swedish industry.

In the leaders of the exporting and importing merchant houses, Sweden had its most competent entrepreneurial class. Many of the big traders were, by the way, foreigners. Of the twenty large merchant houses registered in Stockholm in 1798 fifteen had been founded by foreigners: eight by Germans, three by Englishmen, two by Dutchmen, one by a

Frenchman and one by an Italian. During the early years of the nineteenth century foreign merchants arrived in increasing numbers. In Gothenburg, on the Swedish west coast, English and Scottish merchants established themselves and often also went into industrial undertakings — in the iron, saw-mill and textile trades—and German and Norwegian merchants played an important role in the development of the northern saw-mill industry.

It stands to reason that the big merchants had invaluable contributions to make to industrial progress. They were in contact with economic and technical events in foreign countries, they had capital resources from the proceeds of their trading activities and, perhaps the most important factor, they knew something that seems to be hard to acquire by technical people and public servants: how to run a business on sound economic principles.

There was a fairly long tradition of accountancy in the iron industry, but it seems that its cost calculation was better developed than the branches of accountancy centred on financing and other matters of management control. Already in the 1850's one begins to notice a spirit of reform in the basic accounting valuation of Swedish industry, and it often seems attributable to the commercial influence in industrial life. There are accounting instructions for the iron industry in the late 1850's stating the principle of valuation of goods in stock at 'the lowest value', to avoid fictitious profits due to a rise in prices. In the largest of the machine-producing firms (Motala), the auditors in their report for 1849 extensively discussed the appropriate rates of depreciation on fixed assets, and four years later they recommended a new and more cautious policy for the valuation of stock. During the following decades more rational and cautious accounting principles were introduced in most of the larger companies, so in their case the new Companies Act of 1910 meant only a codification of an existing practice.

These tendencies gathered strength at the change of the century, when the commercial banks began to use a critical study of company balance sheets as a basis for granting credits. It was the Enskilda Banken of Stockholm which first (in 1900) built up a department for the study of creditworthiness. It was modelled on Credit Lyonnais' department for 'études financières'. In the early days of the commercial banks, that is during the second half of the nineteenth century, it had been common for a firm to have debts with two or three — or even four, five or six — different banks, never disclosing its total financial obligations to any of them. With the new Companies Act, which made it obligatory to set up balance sheet and profit and loss account in a prescribed form and submit them to the authorities, and with the new banking practice just referred to, an era of closer co-operation between borrower and lender and greater openness in company life had started.

In this brief survey of the Swedish process of industrialization certain fundamental factors have appeared: the importance of agricultural development, the role of earlier industrial traditions, the importance of exports as a prime generating factor, the influence of the merchants as founders of new industries and, above all, the need for the basic reorganization of education, work habits and economic attitudes. I would, of course, never dream of pointing to the Swedish experience as something that could be copied by the developing countries in the very different world of today. But I thought the facts I have stated may still have a certain interest. It should be possible to throw light on some of the current development problems by discussing which of the factors, fundamental to Sweden's development, still remain fundamental in the world of today and which of these factors must be treated as accidental occurrences of only historical importance.

POLITICAL IMPLICATIONS OF ECONOMIC DEVELOPMENT AND PITFALLS TO BE AVOIDED

BY DR. EUGENE STALEY

Centre for Cultural and Technical Interchange between East and West, Honolulu, Hawaii

Participation in this symposium is a novel and welcome experience. It is novel because questions have been posed by leaders of one of the young governments of Africa, designed to throw light on problems that the Africans themselves consider to be knotty, and because we participants are asked to look at these problems from the angle of the Africans. It is welcome because the problems of emerging African nations are extremely important today in the never-ending upward struggle of humanity. Also, we who have been invited from outside welcome the opportunity to deepen our acquaintance with African problems by some first-hand observation and by discussions with African leaders.

My own direct observations of developing countries has been mainly in other parts of the world. It is with great humility, therefore, that I shall respond to the two questions put to me, trying to look at them, as requested, from the African angle. Please assume that after each of the statements in this paper there is a series of question marks. Is this applicable to African conditions as you know them? How important is it? What, if anything, can the leaders of newly emerging African nations do about it? In the discussions at Blantyre those of you who know so much more about the specific problems of Africa will, I hope, weigh and correct my remarks.

The two questions assigned me are:

What are the political implications of economic development?
What pitfalls must be avoided by political leaders in developing countries?

'Political' I take to mean issues which must concern leaders of governments and parties. 'Economic development' can be defined as increase of the output of goods and services per person and all the things necessary to bring this about. 'Political implications' of economic development will be interpreted to include both the political requisites and the political consequences of economic development.

When you ask me, in the second question, to discuss 'pitfalls' to be avoided by political leaders in developing countries, you are in effect inviting me to give advice. And the advice will concern countries not my own, whose particular problems I have not had opportunity to study in detail. To attempt to give such advice might seem presumptuous on my part, except that you have asked for it. I accept the assignment with diffidence, reminding you that what I can contribute must be based more on study of developing countries in general and on my experience in other newly developing countries, mainly in Asia and Latin America, than on knowledge of your specific African problems.

I. POLITICAL IMPLICATIONS OF ECONOMIC DEVELOPMENT — INTERNAL

A.   The Human Factor in Development.—Few political leaders in history have faced tasks more delicate and demanding than those that confront the leaders of new nations in Africa. In order to bring rapid economic development, so that their peoples can have better food, clothing, shelter, health services, and educational opportunities, they must lead the way from a traditional economy and society to a modern type of economy and society. The human problems of such a transition are immense and they are full of political difficulties.

Economic development is a complex of many related changes. There must be a steady increase in capital equipment — new roads, harbours, machines for factories and farms, school buildings, and power stations. There must be new applications of science and technology. There must be changes in the forms of association by which men live and work — growth of cities, new governmental practices, new types of business organization, readjustments in land tenure, and changes in family ties, in tribal authority, even in religion. Millions of individuals must learn new skills and new habits of thought — reading and writing, how to drive a truck, new respect for scientific method, and the revolutionary idea that progress is possible.

If we must simplify, we are least likely to go wrong when we think of economic development in terms of changes in human beings and social institutions and only secondarily in terms of material capital or equipment. If the human skills, motivation, and organization are present, then capital funds with which to buy equipment become very important in determining the speed with which development can proceed; but in the absence of the human and social requisites for development, capital funds can do little. As evidence that availability of capital does not guarantee development, or even seem to be the key factor, note that the oil-rich countries like Iran, Saudi Arabia, Iraq, Indonesia, and Venezuela have not notably outdistanced other countries that started at similar levels of development. On the other hand, where the human factors of motivation, skill, organization, and willingness to work together are favourable, the absence of initial capital, while a handicap, is a handicap that can be overcome, as the experience of many countries shows.

The real key to development is the human factor. And this is the realm of the political leader, together with the educator and the business organizer.

Especially in Africa, where the gap between existing traditional ways of life and those required in a modern economy are very great, the human factor is the key to everything else. The problem of the African leader who wants economic development for his country can most usefully be viewed, I suggest, as a massive problem in human education and social readjustment. Economic development requires a host of skills in engineering, agriculture, teaching, prevention and treatment of disease, and many other fields. It is people who have to be motivated to learn these skills and to apply them effectively. Their efforts have to be organized and directed along consistent and well chosen lines, so that what they do fits together and adds up to national progress. They have to be taught, persuaded, induced, sometimes even forced, to co-operate in reasonably harmonious relations with their fellows for the general good. These are some of the great tasks of political leadership.

The modern system of production in agriculture and industry which has made high standards of living possible in the more developed countries is not like a piece of machinery which can be imported, uncrated, and simply set going. Tractors can, of course, be shipped in, and from the purely mechanical point of view they can be made to work. But to use them effectively to advance the well-being of the people requires a revolution in thinking and a number of institutional changes as well as the learning of mechanical skills. The economic productivity of the tractor depends upon having a large market for the crops it helps to produce, and this in turn demands drastic departures from the traditional system of local trading. In some regions, tractors may be quite impracticable, pending new social arrangements, because land is owned in tiny, separate patches. In other regions, tractors may give large land-holders the incentive and the economic power to displace small proprietors and tenants, thus disrupting traditional ways of livelihood in villages before people are able or willing to find new employment and adopt new ways of living in the growing towns and cities. There are many political implications, clearly, in the introduction of such an apparently simple machine as the farm tractor.

The notion that old social institutions can be kept unchanged while only the mechanical side of modern industrialization is adopted may lead to complete frustration. Or it could lead to a social monstrosity, dangerous to the people of a country and to their neighbours. It cannot bring solid, healthy, economic and social development. On the other hand, the variety of ways in which the political, social, and economic organization for modern production can be set up and be made to operate with reasonable effectiveness is probably larger than most of us suspect.

Every newly developing country in Africa will have to solve certain fundamental problems in institution-building. For example, each will have to strive to develop good public administration under a government responsive to the needs of the people, to make educational opportunity widely available, to stimulate individual and group initiative, and to harness this initiative to the advancement of the general good. But in the *manner* of solving these problems there would seem to be room for almost infinite variation in detail. Today's highly developed countries have not all met them in the same ways. In the very different settings of the new African nations the most appropriate institutional forms will be different from any now existing in the more developed countries. African leaders will, of course, continue to get many useful ideas from abroad. But they will need to scrutinize them carefully and add innovations of their own. A good motto might be, 'Do not *adopt*, but *adapt*.'

B.   *Some Political Requisites of Economic Development.*—Suppose we try to list the main human or social factors requisite for rapid economic development — an agenda for political leaders of newly developing countries. I would suggest:

1. Order
2. The will to develop (motivation)
3. A well considered programme of development
4. Development of human resources (education)
5. Institution building

A modern economy, much more than an economy of the traditional type, depends on specialization, exchange of products, long-range plans, long range investments, and continuous flow of production and distribution. The price of a more productive society is a more interdependent society. Violence and threats of violence, chronic insecurity of life and property, are poisons to which the modern economy is very vulnerable. Order is essential. This is not to recommend a police state as the foundation for modern economic growth. On the contrary, the highest talent of the political leader is to obtain order by persuasion, consensus and compromise rather than by repression.

Encouraging the will to develop — motivating people to undertake new things — is another great task of political leadership in a newly developing country. It is not enough to want the fruits of development, such as plenty of food, bicycles, motor cars, and medicines. People must be led to see that it is futile to will the ends without willing the essential means, which include hard work and sacrifice and, perhaps most difficult of all, willingness to adopt new habits and customs, replacing others which have given great satisfaction in the traditional society but do not fit the modern one. Here, as in so many other things, the political leader must be a teacher.

In the public service, he must try to imbue his aides and civil servants with a developmental 'can do' spirit instead of the traditionally safe adherence to routine. In relation to the private sector, he must encourage the spirit of entrepreneurship, carefully considered but sufficiently bold and path breaking new business ventures, and willingness to save and invest.

A well-considered programme of development is necessary because the fabric of development must be woven of many different threads. The intention is to bring about many changes, and to bring them about rapidly. These changes must be in reasonable sequence and relation with each other. Investment in new factories must be kept in step with the training of men to run them. The output of new goods must be parallel to the growth of markets. Transport and power must not be allowed to become bottlenecks because of failure to anticipate future needs. Overall commitments for new investment and for imports must be adjusted to the country's ability to finance them. Priorities must be given to the most urgent purposes. Some of the problems of constructing a development programme are technical, and political leaders will need the best planning technicians they can find. But the weighting of one purpose against another, the determination that this course of action is feasible and that one not, and the persuasion of all important groups in the country that they should co-operate for the execution of the development programme are political tasks demanding the highest skills of judgement and leadership.

Investment in education, to make better use of human resources, is the crucial investment for the future development of African nations. Whatever the natural resource endowment of a country and its capital supply, these resources will be put to use only through the skills, motivation, and organization of the human factor. Education of children and young people is, of course, highly important, as is well recognized. But where rapid change is the order of the day, adult education in various forms should, I suggest, be given much more attention than has usually been the case. Investment of effort and funds in adult education, if well done, brings quicker returns, raises the national income more immediately, and increases the capacity to support more education and other developmental investment. Adult education also helps to mitigate the socially undesirable tendency for an immense gap to arise between the knowledge possessed by parents and by their children. Skilled and dedicated leadership is required to adapt educational ideas, both for children and for adults, to African needs. New techniques of education will have to be invented so as to cope more effectively with the dilemma of enormous educational needs and very limited resources. To stimulate educational investment and educational innovation is another of the great developmental tasks of African political leadership.

Finally, the political leader who wants to hasten economic development must build, or encourage others to build, a multitude of new institutions. Motivations and skills are not enough. There must also be organization, so that people can work together and apply themselves effectively. The most immediate task is building effective governmental institutions, to reflect the attitudes and hopes of the important social groups in the country, to take decisions, and to carry out these decisions. A well trained, adequately compensated and well motivated civil service is important, and the creative political leader will need to devote considerable thought to this aspect of his task. Educational institutions will, of course, require a large share of creative effort. It will also be important to build up research institutions, so that African nations will be able to draw selectively upon the vast world store of scientific and technological knowledge and to apply this knowledge with suitable adaptation to African conditions. The political leader must also concern himself with the encouragement, either directly or indirectly, of modern business institutions, including banks and other financial organizations of both public and private character, and modern types of commercial and industrial organizations.

C. *Some Political Consequences of Economic Development.*—Already millions of Africans, especially those who have moved to the rapidly growing cities, have been caught up by the forces of modernity. But the great majority living outside the cities have only begun to feel the impact of these forces. In the next decade or two, if economic development proceeds, more and more people will find their way of life profoundly affected. Urbanism, industrialism, transport facilities that permit a new freedom of movement, communication facilities transmitting new ideas, factory products that create new wants and also compete with the products of traditional craftsmen — these are some of the accompaniments of economic development which produce a new way of life. On the positive side, they offer new freedoms, new opportunities, and a rising material standard of living. On the negative side, they weaken family ties, undermine respect for traditional authority, and substitute a rootless, anonymous, and often jobless existence in cities for the close personal relations and assured status of the village and tribe.

These transformations in the way of life are bound to go much further as economic development proceeds. It will be the task of the creative political leader to understand them, to help guide them along lines as constructive as possible, and to try to reconcile the oft-times conflicting interests of groups that are affected in diverse ways by the processes of development.

Political leaders in the newly developing countries will find a host of old and new problems pressing upon them. Here, for example, are just a few indications of what to expect:

Urban problems.—These will continue to rise in importance. What is to be done about city government, planning and control of city growth, and the huge investments needed for city utilities? What can be done to cope with unemployment, crime, delinquency, dependency, and other social maladjustments which take new forms and demand new methods of treatment in the cities?

Population problems.—Economic development and improved health measures will bring death rates down more and more. Birth rates will probably continue for a considerable time at or near the high levels that were formerly necessary to reproduce the race under the conditions of the old, traditional society, for the customs that affect birth rates change relatively slowly. The resulting 'explosion' of population growth will give political importance to questions of population policy. Should family planning and spread of birth control information be encouraged? If not, the increase in numbers may seriously counteract the effects of investment in education, industry, agriculture, health, and other fields, with the result that living levels are kept from rising at the hoped-for rate.

National unity versus sectionalism.—As communication and transport facilities improve and trade increases, groups formerly isolated from each other will come into contact more and more frequently. Interdependence will grow, and in field after field national rather than sectional approaches to problems will be necessary. The need for national action and national unity will repeatedly conflict with strong survivals of sectionalism. Language questions, for example, represent one such conflict. Political leaders will find these issues extremely difficult, demanding their best talents of persuasion and reconciliation.

Decline of old crafts and rise of new.—As modern forms of production develop, some traditional occupations become obsolete, and this creates political problems. For example, what is to be done about the traditional artisans who find themselves unable to make a living in competition with factory goods? To be sure, the new, emerging, modern economy with its higher levels of living and more complex methods of work will probably need more artisans than were formerly needed in the traditional economy. But most of them will be needed in new crafts and at different locations. Instead of potters, hand-weavers, and blacksmiths, the new economy will require electricians, plumbers, photographers, and radio service-men. The political problems connected with this type of change in the economy are not easy to handle. Some people find their livelihood slipping away as a result of the very developments that bring better livelihood to the country as a whole. Many of the people adversely affected, especially the older people, are not able to shift into the new and advancing occupations.

Security for the individual.—Traditional systems of social security by which the family, the village, and the tribe care for individual members in time of misfortune will become less and less applicable as economic development brings greater mobility of persons, new kinds of employment, movement to cities, and the scattering of kinship groups. The resulting social necessity will produce political demands for new types of security against the hazards of illness, accident, unemployment, and dependent old age. Political leaders will have to seek solutions through such instrumentalities as the state, the factories, the trade unions, the co-operative societies. A particularly difficult political problem connected with this shift to types of social security that fit the modern economy will be the problem of keeping legislative promises in realistic relation to the country's capacity to fulfil them. It is desirable to build up modern social security systems in step with the progress in economic development. But there will be political pressures to promise more at a given stage than the country can afford — that is, more than its productive capacity can provide without seriously neglecting other needs, especially investment for future growth.

D. Broadening the Base of Political Power.—Economic development will also bring shifts in the relative political power of different groups. The realistic political leader must, of course, be alert to these changes.

No doubt the partisans of the 'new' will rise in influence as compared to the partisans of the 'old', but — judging from experience in other parts of the world — there will from time to time be powerful movements, even fanatical movements, for return to old ways.

The numbers, wealth, education, and political influence of city people will rise, but — again, if experience in some other countries is a guide — the rural influence in political matters for a long time will be felt to an extent out of proportion to its declining relative position in the economy.

The influence of organized labour and of organized commercial, industrial, and agricultural groups will grow. Their demands will sometimes be based on rather short-sighted self-interest, posing problems for the political leader who has at heart his country's overall advancement.

Political leaders can to some extent hasten, retard, or redirect the course of these shifts in political power, within limits set by the circumstances in their countries and by their own conceptions of leadership. One of the great opportunities and tasks of political leadership in newly developing countries, it seems to me, is that of deliberately broadening the base of political power so as to build truly democratic, responsible, and effective self-governing societies. Broadening the base of political power means enabling more people to take part in shaping decisions that affect them. This is brought about by the spread of education, by better nutrition and health (which means that the common people have more energy, are more alert), by experience for more people in group leadership and in management of public or private business, and by the creation of conditions under which more people can attain to some degree of economic independence (as contrasted with being dependent on a landowner, or on any one employer, whether private or governmental). Economic independence can be promoted by widening the distribution of land ownership where it is now excessively concentrated, by encouraging the modernization and healthy growth of small and medium-sized enterprises, and by stimulating economic growth that creates a variety of opportunities for those who seek employment and for the self-employed, including the politically very important category of professional people.

Broadening the base of political power implies, at the same time, training people in responsible use of their new power. It is relatively easy to install the *forms* of democratic government. It is much harder to achieve the *substance* which can make the forms work well. Without the substance of a broad diffusion of economic, social, and political opportunity and competence, the forms of democratic self-government could prove worse than useless. These dangers are particularly acute in the half-way stages of political maturity, where the masses have learned to read and to understand simple slogans but are still unfit for the heavy tasks of responsible citizenship in a complex society. The saying that 'A little learning is a dangerous thing' is very true in the transitional steps to a democratic society. The political leader who would perform a truly constructive role must make himself a teacher of his people, teaching them to participate responsibly in public affairs.

II. Some External (International) Implications of Economic Development

There are external as well as internal political requisites for satisfactory economic progress in the new African nations.

The most important, of course, is peace. Peace among the African nations themselves is essential. Quarrels and wars or threats of wars would divert the attention of leaders and divert much needed resources from the great tasks of raising living levels.

Peace between the great world power blocs headed by the United States and the Soviet Union is likewise extremely important to Africa. War between the great power blocs would risk touching off a nuclear holocaust that would be disastrous for all peoples. In fact, the harmful radiation that might be let loose in a large-scale nuclear war would spread far from the immediate target areas and could conceivably end all human life on this planet. Even short of the disaster of nuclear war, however, violent skirmishes between the great power blocs and a mounting threat of unbridled force could seriously interfere with the aspirations of African people for development. In such a situation the rights of small states and newly independent nations would be in great peril. For when great powers are at each others' throats, they are not inclined to be too tolerant of the rights and interests of others. Furthermore, though great power rivalries sometimes produce competing offers of help to newly developing nations, offers motivated by an acute struggle for power are likely to have undesirable political strings attached. If the world power struggle should move closer and closer to large-scale military conflict, the chances are that capital and other resources would be channelled in still larger amounts into military preparations and that less would be available to assist economic development. It is, therefore, very much in the interest of the new African nations to do what they can to calm a very troubled world and to try to promote a live-and-let-live attitude between the great power blocs.

Does it perhaps seem futile to point out that the new African nations have a strong interest in influencing the great powers? It may be thought that this is something about which they can do nothing. But, in fact, African statesmen do already have a moral influence in the councils of nations, especially through the forum provided by the United Nations. And one of the political consequences of economic development of African nations will be a gradual increase in their influence, adding to the moral weight of people who obviously have a great stake in peace the weight of increasingly developed material resources and increasingly educated people.

The rise in power and influence which will come with economic development carries with it increasing responsibility. If I may express a hope, it is that the new African nations will constantly advocate in the United Nations and in their dealings with other countries what might be called the world community point of view. This is a point of view which starts from the proposition that there are certain problems such as peace and war and the development of underdeveloped countries, that can only be satisfactorily dealt with by an approach that looks first to the interest of the whole interdependent community of mankind rather than to the interest of one power bloc or the other. With regard to development, this approach suggests more emphasis on multilateral, especially United Nations, aid for newly developing countries. It suggests pressure on the two great power blocs to get them to agree to take the question of aid to newly developing countries right out of the cold war. This could be done by channelling such aid increasingly through agencies so constituted as to represent the world community interest rather than any single power or bloc — that is, through United Nations agencies in which donor nations and assisted nations, non-Communist nations and Communist nations, have a voice but do not dominate.

I believe that this world community approach is in the interest of the new African nations and also in the interest of my own country, the United States. I have written a book addressed primarily to Americans in which I say this, with particular reference to international development aid. Opinion and policy in my country have been moving somewhat in this direction, and there is a good chance that this movement will continue. If you leaders of African nations will keep nudging us, that will help. You must also not forget to nudge the Soviet Union in the same direction.

Another political implication of African economic development relates to race relations. The status and respect accorded to African people and to people of African origin throughout the world will rise, if and when development moves successfully ahead in the new nations of Africa. Already, I hope, the day is past when a third-rate white man, merely because of skin colour, could lord it over even a first-rate black man. Economic progress in African nations, including, as it must, a revolution in educational opportunities, will help to end discrimination wherever found and will help to hasten the day when skin colours will no longer be important and men can co-operate on the basis of a common humanity.

III. Pitfalls to be Avoided

You have also asked me to consider pitfalls which political leaders in newly developing countries should avoid. The political-economic forest is full of pitfalls, but I shall be brief and point to only three: the 'anti' pitfall; the pitfall of ideology; and the pitfall of excessive nationalism.

The 'Anti' Pitfall.—Political leaders in many African states have come to power after years of struggle against a system of foreign rule. Sometimes they went to jail in their defiance of authority. Now they are in the government. The problem is no longer to tear down an old system but to construct a new one. Therefore, the old slogans, the old tactics, the old objectives, and the old ways of thinking no longer serve. But habits of political behaviour may persist after the occasion for them has passed. Political leaders in government and in opposition now must seek to find a basis for national consensus, working together to attain positive national goals.

Internationally, the political situation has also changed to the point where some of the old slogans and tactics are becoming inapplicable. At any rate, they require new thinking and a new, more positive content. This is true, I suggest, of 'anti-imperialism' and 'anti-colonialism'. Do not misunderstand; I am not advocating imperialism and colonialism. But the battle against imperialism and colonialism in the old forms is nearly won — not quite, but nearly. The danger now is that the old slogans will become pitfalls for the unwary and will actually be used to disguise new forms of imperialism and colonialism: to put it bluntly, the propaganda of the Soviet and Chinese communists labels as 'imperialist' or as serving the 'imperialists' any opposition to their own efforts to extend a new form of rule over other people.

Perhaps the best way to avoid the 'anti' pitfall is to accentuate the positive. Is it not a prime task of political leaders in these times to state positively what they are for and not merely what they are against? For example, the positive side of anti-imperialism might be expressed as independence and self-government of nations within a framework of a self-governing community of nations.

The Pitfall of Ideology.—A second pitfall is the temptation to accept a ready-made ideological formula, constructed to fit other times and places, as a guide to action in the new African nations. The formula most insistently offered these days is the Marxist-Communist formula. At the opposite pole there is the extreme 'leave-it-to-private-enterprise' formula. Neither, in my judgement, has much value for the guidance of development policy in the new African states. No rigid doctrine will fit their diverse and changing needs.

Experience in other newly developing countries suggests that leaders of new African states will be wise to think in terms of a 'mixed system'. They should adopt a deliberately experimental, flexible approach in which government takes the lead in planning and promoting development and executes essential projects that for one reason or another government can best do directly. But also they should encourage private initiative and private enterprise and many types of quasi-private, quasi-public associations and co-operatives. The exact 'mix' would vary from country to country and from stage to stage of development.

Can we not learn to think about the problems of political economy, and of development policy in particular, not in doctrinaire terms but in technological terms? I am speaking now of social technology, not of mechanical technology. Social technology refers to methods of administration, management, organization, education, and development policy and planning. If political leaders can agree upon broad national goals, then many (though not all) of the problems of attaining those goals can be viewed as technological in this sense. Economic and political techniques which have worked well in somewhat comparable situations abroad deserve to be carefully considered; usually they cannot be taken over intact, but must be modified and adapted to local circumstances. Not mere copying, but social invention is required.

The Pitfall of Excessive Nationalism.—Nationalism is a constructive force when it serves to unite people. People from different parts of the country and from different groups must be persuaded to work together willingly towards common goals. The new African states will for many years need to cultivate national unity.

But nationalism becomes a pitfall when it *divides* people who ought to work together, instead of uniting them. Many independent states today are too small for maximum effectiveness in economic development. There is urgent need for co-operation with neighbouring states and for the formation of larger political-economic groupings.

Also, of course, the national feeling which leads men to strive for national freedom and to unify their efforts to achieve national goals need not and must not interfere with the building of a sense of world community. The freedom and development of all nations, African nations included, demands a world order characterized by unity in diversity. Supplementing our national patriotism we must cultivate a world patriotism, a patriotism of mankind.

WHAT SOCIALISM SHOULD MEAN IN THE NEW COUNTRIES OF AFRICA

BY GEORGE THOMSON, M.P.

I think the question I have been asked to discuss is one of the most important arising out of the swift progress of African countries to independence. It is certainly one of the most formidable, and for a western Socialist who has been deeply interested in the winning of freedom from colonialism, one of the most fascinating.

Although there has been much Socialist study of the problems of ending colonialism there has been curiously little written about the forms of Socialism in the newly emancipated countries. Amongst the few studies in this field in the United Kingdom is Dr Rita Hinden's pamphlet, *Principles of Socialism — Africa and Asia* (Fabian Commonwealth Bureau, London, 1961). I am also much indebted to the same writer for the opportunity to read before publication a paper, 'Africa and Democracy' (*Encounter* Pamphlet 1963).

I ought to begin, I think, by indicating some of the personal principles and prejudices with which I approach the question.

First and foremost I come to this question as a working politician, a run-of-the-mill Parliamentarian. I am conscious that Mr Chisiza and I are the only politicians amongst so many experts and I am reminded in your beautiful but poor country of Dean Swift's remark that 'whoever could make two ears of corn or two blades of grass to grow upon a spot of ground where only one grew before would deserve better of mankind and do more essential service to his country than the whole race of politicians put together'.

Yet with due respect to the economists, I recommend Mr Chisiza to remain an unrepentant politician. For I have noted as one of the lessons of the recent troubled years in Nyasaland that when you had no representative politicians the agricultural experts found a distrust of new and desirable methods of cultivation. Now the very methods that were opposed because they were associated with colonial rule are being enthusiastically supported. It is only now when you have politicians who enjoy the consent of most (There have, of course, been a number of additions to this literature since this paper was delivered.)

of those who govern, that it is possible to get ahead with growing two ears of corn where only one grew before.

I speak not only as a politician, but as a Socialist politician. And I belong to the Fabian stream of British Socialism. This is no doubt partly a matter of personal temperament, of which you must take account when I try to apply myself to your problems. It is also, however, that I think the Fabian approach of undogmatically finding out the facts, and carrying through changes by persuasion and consent, has best fitted the realities of the British political situation. Sydney Webb, a great Fabian, once summed it up in a famous phrase — 'the inevitability of gradualism'.

But in Africa the reality is very different. An African Fabian would have to alter the slogan to something like 'the inevitability of rapidism'. There is a headlong rate of political change throughout the African continent. Here right at the start is an example of how very different from the political realities in Britain is the African framework within which Socialist attitudes must be shaped.

But how far is Socialism relevant to Africa at all? The question ought to be asked.

Socialism was born in Europe out of the agonies of the agricultural and industrial revolutions which uprooted the common people and degraded them from human persons to being so many hands helping to make private profits for the few. Either in its social democratic form or in its totalitarian communist form Socialism was the historic child of Europe. What does it mean in Africa?

At first sight a great deal. Most African nationalist parties profess also to be socialist in their outlook. But this applies equally to very nearly all African political groupings.

This vague and widespread claim to be Socialist has a familiar ring for us in the west. In 1895 the then Prince of Wales, later Edward VII, made a speech in which he said, 'We are all Socialists nowadays.' In India I found wealthy capitalists who had as much claim to left-wing leanings as Edward VII saying that they share the general national acceptance of Mr Nehru's socialistic planning.

The truth, of course, is that in the developed nations an important part of what we mean by Socialism is now common, uncontroversial ground accepted without thinking by the most confirmed Conservative. 'Do you mean to say you believe in Socialised medicine?' an aggressive American asked Earl Attlee during a recent lecture tour. 'Don't you believe in Socialised sewage?' replied Attlee. Yet early Fabians had great battles about municipal Socialism providing communal sewage systems.

In the underdeveloped world, acceptance of Socialist economic ideas is a commonplace for different reasons. So much of the development that did take place under colonial regimes had to be done by the Government. So British Conservative governments to whom nationalization was anathema, set up nationalized railway systems in dependent territories. Many of the things that were done by private capital in Europe, had in Africa to be done by public capital — or, as was too often the case, not done at all. And the new African nations, facing up to their legacy of chronic poverty and lack of local capital, again find as a matter of necessity and not of political doctrine, that economic progress is predominantly a matter of government initiative. As Lionel Elvin puts it:[1] 'Socialism may or may not be essential for Britain; it is indispensable for Africa.'

Or here is Lord Hailey, who cannot be accused of being a Socialist propagandist:[2]

> 'The conclusion which emerges from this consideration of the limitations on the flow of private capital into Africa is that the character of African development must largely depend upon the action of Governments.'

It is this 'dependence on the actions of Governments' which makes it inevitable that Africa is going to have a Socialistic economic framework in the future. But Socialism in Africa or elsewhere ought to go a good deal deeper than that.

For although public ownership and Government economic action are an essential part of Socialism, Socialism is much more than an economic system. Hitler called his brand of Fascism National Socialism, but although there was a strong element of Government planning in it, this was a great blasphemy. The Soviet Union calls its totalitarian society Socialism, and this is a great heresy. It is a heresy and not a blasphemy because the Communists are seeking the right ends in the wrong way. They are, in fact, seeking, as Socialists do, a society in which the spirit of service and fellowship dominates the pursuit of profit, what Marx called 'the kingdom of the free and the equal'. But the Communists have sought these ends in Russia, and now in China and other Communist countries, by tyrannical and ruthless means which are unjustified in themselves and distort and make impossible the ends which they seek.

This is the dividing line between democratic Socialists and Communists. The democratic Socialist in the west believes that public ownership and other economic devices of Socialism are not ends in themselves but merely means towards the real long-term aim of Socialism which is the humanist aim of the liberation of the individual personality.

Implicit in democratic Socialism is a view about the nature of man in

---

[1] *New Fabian Colonial Essays*, London, 1959.
[2] *An African Survey:* Revised 1956.

society. The democratic Socialist believes three interrelated things. First, that all human beings have an equal right to develop their personalities to the full. Second, that such fulfilment depends on the individual being free to exercise choice and responsibility. Third, that the individual cannot fulfil himself in isolation but only in fellowship that recognizes his obligations to the others in his community.

Democratic Socialists hold that these objects of *equality, liberty and fraternity* can only be achieved for the individual if the community commands power over what the late Aneurin Bevan called 'the commanding heights of the economy'.

Now these are ideals that have grown up — and are still being debated and discussed — in western Socialist movements. I recognize that they have been the product of history and experience very different from that of Africa.

But what I am anxious to argue is that 'control over the commanding heights of the economy' in Europe or in Africa, although an essential condition of achieving Socialism, is not enough by itself. It is an economic means to certain ethical ends, which may or may not be achieved, depending upon the will of the people. And I would assert the conviction that although the economic means towards Socialism may vary widely between Europe and Africa, the Socialist ends have a universal validity.

Keir Hardie, the father of British Socialism, put it this way:

> 'Socialism is at bottom an ethical or moral problem. It is concerned with what should be the relationship between a man and his fellows.'

And all Keir Hardie's utterances make it clear that the Socialist essence of that relationship between man and man is mutual self-respect.

It seemed to me that Dr Hastings Banda, the father of Nyasaland, put the same point in the words of his evidence to the Devlin Commission which have always stuck in my mind. The economic advantages of the Central African Federation were pointed out to him. He replied simply, 'I prefer poverty to slavery.' It was the same fundamental assertion of self-respect as Keir Hardie's — in this case national self-respect, the unwillingness to be ruled from outside.

This illuminates one of the essential differences between the approach to Socialism between Europe and Africa. In Europe, faced with the interconnected values of freedom, equality and fellowship, the Socialist has given priority to equality. He already enjoyed a considerable measure of political self-determination. What affronted his sense of human dignity were the glaring inequalities of uncontrolled capitalism.

In Africa, as in Asia, it has been freedom first — national freedom. It was impossible to assert human dignity and self-respect until the right to self-determination had been achieved. But in all but a few areas of Africa national freedom from colonial rule has been or is being achieved. The big question for the future is — after national freedom, what?

Many people of many differing points of view join together in national liberation movements. Many who struggle for national freedom are not Socialists, either consciously or unconsciously, and never will be, though you cannot be a Socialist in a colonial territory without struggling for national freedom. Nor will all who believe in freedom for the African nation from colonial rule then go on to believe in freedom for people to rule themselves, through some form of Parliamentary democracy.

The Communists, for example, would say that the next priority after national political freedom is national economic freedom, and that personal freedom comes a long way behind that, and indeed stands in the way of speedy economic progress. Socialists, on the other hand, will believe that there is no true Socialism without political freedom and democracy, and that although people may feel they are sacrificing their liberty only temporarily, history shows that once it is surrendered it is much more difficult to win back again.

But quite apart from the Communists there are many in Africa and Asia as well as in the west who will say that it is unreasonable to expect democracy to flourish in an emerging country. They point to the failure of democratic regimes in the developing world and to the fact that Europe which is inclined to lecture the underdeveloped world on its dictatorial leanings does not have such a fine record of flourishing democracies itself.

Moreover they argue that emerging countries have a special justification for dispensing with internal democracy. They face the massive task of accumulating out of their own poverty-stricken people the capital necessary to raise their living standards. If there is universal franchise and there are competing political parties the electorate will never be far-sighted enough to vote for reduced consumption today in order to assure a more stable prosperity for their children. The economic future will be sabotaged by unscrupulous politicians outbidding each other.

It is added that Britain accumulated the capital out of the sufferings and hardships of its people long before they had a vote — and had much longer to do it than the African nations who have to be in such a hurry. I have laid this argument out at some length because it has considerable plausibility. I believe, however, that it is wrong. I produce in evidence the experience of China which has chosen the Communist non-democratic way, and of India which has stuck to its democracy and is in fact the biggest Parliamentary system in the world with 200 million voters. I accept the fact than an authoritarian regime like China's may be able to force a faster pace. But what if it travels faster along the wrong road?

This is what appears to be happening in China where the ruthless drive for collectivized agriculture appears to have produced damaging results. In India, on the other hand, I saw the opposite method — a great Government-backed community development scheme with agricultural advisory services which seek to make the most of the labour power of tremendous numbers of under-employed people. It lacked the drama of the Chinese communes and it was slow. In one village I visited the school. A little boy with eyes bright as jewels said, 'I am the Minister of Agriculture. I make sure the school garden uses the new methods.' The civil servant with me told me that the children are already making the fathers change their ways and will soon take over from the older generation.

John Strachey in a recent pamphlet[3] tells of China and India in terms of Aesop's fable of the hare and the tortoise:

> 'China with the Government imposing its will through totali-
> tarian methods, including the forced collectivisation of agricul-
> ture, has had some spectacular achievements, but agriculture is
> already in difficulties; the hare which started off so triumphantly
> is in serious trouble. In the meantime the Indian tortoise, work-
> ing by democratic methods, by winning consent and experi-
> menting through trial and error, gains ground steadily.'

Professor Arthur Lewis in his book, *The Theory of Economic Growth*, adds some further evidence on this subject:

> 'The case against detailed central planning is that it is undemo-
> cratic, bureaucratic, inflexible, and subject to great error and con-
> fusion. It is also unnecessary. There is a much better case for
> piecemeal planning; that is to say, for concentrating on a few
> matters which it is particularly desired to influence, such as the
> level of exports, or of capital formation, or of industrial produc-
> tion, or of food production; and for leaving all the rest of the
> economy to adjust itself to demand and supply.'

So it seems really unnecessary to give up democracy in order to ensure economic growth. There is a good deal of evidence that democracy is perfectly compatible with wise economic planning in developing countries, and indeed a help to it.

But by democracy I do not mean a neat little imitation of Westminster with its opposing front benches, its Speaker with a wig and its gilt mace on the table. Our Westminster system is the peculiar result of our own peculiar history. By all means adapt some of its picturesque rituals if you feel inclined, though I am sure you have plenty of traditional ceremonials

[3] *Encounter* Pamphlet, London, 1962.

of your own to use. But do not confuse the shadow of Parliamentary procedure with the substance of democratic liberty. The institutions of democracy themselves are infinitely variable as one looks around. There are Westminster systems where the chief executive emerges from the majority party in Parliament. And there are presidential systems where he is separately elected. There are two-party systems and twenty-two-party systems and one-party systems democratically elected like that of the Tanganyika African National Union. There are problems about that, but then there are also problems of democratic liberty for minorities in the face of the highly disciplined Labour and Conservative parties in the House of Commons.

Julius Nyerere has defended the democratic nature of his one-party Parliament:[4]

> 'An organised opposition is *not* an essential element . . .' he has written. 'An organised opposition may arise, or it may not; but whether it does or not depends entirely upon the choice of the people themselves and makes little difference to free discussion and equality in freedom.'

M Andre Philip, the French writer, in a chapter on Socialism and the Underdeveloped Countries in a recent book,[5] puts this line of argument in a more extreme form. He draws a distinction between a totalitarian society where there is no freedom of discussion and authoritarian leadership which allows both freedom of discussion and a measure of independence for trade unions, co-operative societies and other groups separate from the Government:

> 'Moreover, when we look at the under-developed countries, we ought not to criticize them, crying out that they are dictatorships; they all of them have, inevitably, authoritarian regimes, because of the miserable poverty from which they are emerging, because of illiteracy, because of the general absence of economic and social maturity; but we should make the distinction between *authoritarianism*, inevitable in a transitional period, and *totalitarianism*, which indeed always leads, finally, to catastrophe.'

Some people have argued that democracy is in fact incompatible with African tribal traditions and the autocratic power of traditional rulers. This does not seem to me to be so. It is dangerous to generalize about Africa, but the selection of chiefs, though the candidates are drawn from a restricted group, is normally based on the consent of the members of the tribe and his power is limited by custom.

[4] Julius Nyerere : 'The African and Democracy,' in *Africa Speaks*, Princeton, N.J. 1961.
[5] *Le Socialisme Trahi*, Paris, 1959.

There is, however, no tradition of an organized, constitutional opposition.

Is an organized opposition a prerequisite of democracy? It is certainly desirable. It is much better that alternative policies should be argued publicly between parties than privately inside a party, however frank and democratic that inner party debate may be. But in a young country there are obvious dangers in division, and the overwhelming majority of the voters may prefer to vote for one party. Or an opposition may discredit the party system by refusing to accept that it, too, has obligations to recognize the rights of the majority and to conduct its campaign against the Government by constitutional means.

I would distinguish three essentials for democracy. First there must be a representative assembly freely elected. Although there may not be more than one party contesting the election, there should be no bar either by law or by other pressures against another party standing. And there should be freedom for members of the ruling party who have failed to obtain the official candidature to stand as independents and find out what public support they have.

Second, fundamental human rights should be respected, especially freedom to publish, to speak and to assemble.

Third, the Rule of Law and the independence of the judiciary should be preserved as a protection against arbitrary imprisonment.

Within these essentials there is room for a wide variety of experiments, and for a considerable degree of the strong rule necessary to get things done in a new country. But without these essentials it is impossible to say there is democracy. And without democracy there is no Socialism.

Neo-Colonialism.—But if Socialism means democratic control of the economy, is this possible in African states where so much of the economy is in foreign hands? This is the fear of neo-colonialism, and it represents formidable problems where a country is largely dependent on the exploitation of one or two commodities in foreign hands. Some Communist commentators have gone on to suggest that, therefore, political independence is a sham, because of continued economic dependence.

One has only to look at the changed economic pattern before and after independence in India to see that political independence has reality in economic terms. Socialism does not mean monolithic public ownership. A Socialist society and a mixed economy are perfectly compatible. A Socialist African Government will seek to attract foreign private investment and will give it the necessary security it requires, so long as it fits in with the needs of the national plan, and recognizes aspirations in terms of training and promotion.

Economic democracy.—So far I have discussed two of the attributes of a Socialist society — the Government having an overriding control of the economy, and the existence of political democracy. Africa seems certain to have the first, though the achievement of the second presents many more problems.

But there are other aspects of Socialism that have a special significance for Africa. There is an economic democracy to be created as well as a political democracy. The right to self-respect, to a control over one's conditions of life exists in the place of work — in field or in factory — as well as in Parliament. Trade unions and co-operatives therefore have an important role among the institutions of a society developing along Socialist lines. Co-operatives are particularly relevant to the problems of African Socialism. The great majority of the people of Africa live by agriculture conducted along traditional lines. Co-operative techniques of various kinds provide a means both of raising living standards and also of making easier the transition from a traditional society to a more modern one.

This brings me to that aspect of Socialism that I have not so far discussed directly — the nurturing of a sense of fellowship, a sense of brotherhood, a sense of sharing the common task of building a new nation. In this respect the colonial experience is leaving behind a mixed legacy. The British colonial administrators have handed on high standards of public service, of incorruptibility, often of dedication. But it has necessarily been a paternalistic system, and since it is the system with which African political leaders are most familiar, there is danger that having struggled against it, they end up by imitating it.

I notice that Mr Julius Nyerere has been at particular pains to avoid this happening in Tanganyika. He has repeatedly emphasized that official salaries and conditions for Tanganyikans in the public service should be related to Tanganyika's circumstances and resources, and not to middle-class salaries in affluent Britain or to the special arrangements to attract specialists from abroad. It is an inverted idea of racial equality in an independent African country to pay your own civil servants or teachers at an expatriate level. It is far more important for the civil servant that there should be a sense of equality with his fellow-citizens than with middle-class Englishmen. Otherwise there is danger of cynicism amongst the ordinary people, as well as an unnecessary economic burden of salaries on the country.

Lord Attlee once remarked sharply to British Socialists that we would make more converts to Socialism by behaving in a Socialist way to our neighbours than by our most eloquent speeches. It is these personal attitudes of fellowship — especially by those in positions of leadership —

that give the bare bones of Socialist economics flesh and blood and a heart.

The Socialist movement in Britain has always instinctively identified itself with creating the conditions of African independence precisely on this principle of brotherhood. When the British Labour Party recently restated its Socialist aims, it began by saying that 'its central ideal is the brotherhood of man'. It is interesting to note that it put as the first two of its twelve purposes:

1. The rejection of discrimination on grounds of race or colour. . . .
2. That since no nation, whatever its size or power, is justified in dictating to or ruling over other countries against their will, Socialism stands for the rights of all peoples to freedom, independence and self-government.

International Socialism.—There is one final aspect of African Socialism I wish to touch on and that is its relations with the developed world. If both economic growth and democracy are to be maintained in Africa, it must be on the basis of generous help from the wealthier nations. The first point is the adequacy of the aid; the point I wish to comment on is the way in which it is given. The essential Socialist value of self-respect is important here, too. I mention merely two points.

First, price stabilization agreements are useful because they enable emerging nations to earn the foreign exchange they need by their own efforts. In any case, from the economic point of view developing countries at present earn roughly five-sixths of their foreign exchange by trade and receive only one-sixth through aid.

Second, I would produce as an interesting example of a mutual aid scheme, the recent Commonwealth Education Plan. All countries rich and poor give scholarships according to their ability and receive them according to their need. Although the big flow of students is from Africa to the older Commonwealth, British and Australian students go to Makerere or Ibadan and Caribbean students to India. It is a two-way traffic and self-respect is protected as well as improved understanding between Africa and the West being facilitated.

All these concepts involve socialistic ideas of international economic planning and of international fellowship, though many of the participating countries would be embarrassed to have it so described. But in the international community as in Africa 'we're all Socialists now'.

CAPITALIST AND COMMUNIST METHODS OF ECONOMIC DEVELOPMENT—SIMILARITIES AND DIFFERENCES

BY V. K. R. V. RAO

Planning Commission, New Delhi

Before one embarks on the venturesome task of trying to determine the difference between the capitalist and communist methods of economic development, it is necessary to indicate what is meant by economic development and what its essential features are, irrespective of the politico-social framework under which it is undertaken.

Economic development involves such utilization of a country's national and human resources as will give its people the maximum possible income per head along with the capacity to maintain this income and ensure a reasonable rate of annual increase therein. This means not only economic growth from a given base to a predetermined target but also the inclusion in the economy of a built-in rate of further growth. It is recognized that the initial upward movement in income may involve the use of foreign aid; but foreign aid cannot be an indefinitely continuing feature of a country which has undergone economic development and can be listed under the developed countries. A further condition of economic development therefore is that within a reasonably short period, the maintenance of the higher level of income reached as a result of development as also the securing of a built-in rate of continuous growth does not require foreign aid. That is why economic development is identified not only with a significant rise in the national income per head but also with the establishment of what is termed a self-reliant, self-sustaining, and self-accelerating economy.

Economic development as described above requires for its implementation certain essential conditions which are independent of capitalist or communist ideology. These are summed up below in brief:

1. Increasing the current rate of investment and along with it the current rate of saving.
2. Directing and operating the increment in investment in such manner as to increase the output of consumer goods, of producers' goods and of skills.

3. Saving and investing a substantial portion of the increment in income resulting from the increase in investment.
4. Directing and operating the additional investment to increase the output of producer goods, consumer goods and skills.

The operational part of development is the increasing of investment, the pattern given to the increased investment, the efficiency with which the additional investment yields an increased output of goods and services, the extent to which the increased income is saved and invested, the pattern given to the additional investment, and so on till the circle is completed and starts again.

I now come to the more difficult part of the subject, namely, the difference between the capitalist and the communist methods of economic development. Before one can deal with this question, it is necessary to have a fairly clear idea of what is meant by capitalist economic development and communist economic development. There is no standard definition of capitalist economic development nor, I am afraid, is there a standard definition of communist economic development. Thus, e.g., the economic development of Great Britain has not followed the same pattern as that of the United States; and neither of them have followed the same pattern as that of Japan; and yet they are all capitalist economies. Similarly, there are significant differences in the pattern of development followed by the Soviet Union, Yugoslavia, Poland and China; and yet they all count as communist economies. All the same it is possible to indicate broadly the features which characterize capitalist development as distinguished from those which characterize communist development.

Capitalist economies leave to the individual entrepreneur the major role in economic development. The decisions which are taken regarding consumption and saving, the volume and pattern of investment, and the product-mix are all decisions taken by individuals. These decisions are taken in response to the stimuli offered by the market, which again is a compound of decisions regarding purchase and sales taken by individuals. Means of production are owned by individuals (or groups of individuals combined in partnerships or joint stock companies) and it is this ownership with which is linked the power to take the major economic decisions, viz. what to produce, how to produce, and how much to produce; while it is the individual recipient of income, whether from labour or property or from both, who decides what to buy, how much to buy and how much to save. The decisions regarding production are linked up with the ownership of property. The decisions regarding consumption are linked up with the ownership of income, which may be due either to labour or to property or to both, but in either case it is the individual who is the dominating figure. The individuals who own property or hire property are the persons who employ labour and it is they who take the economic decisions and determine the disposal of the economic surplus. Prices are given by the market and are determined by the forces of supply and demand, which in turn are determined by the pattern of income distribution, the schedule of wants, the state of knowledge and technology, and the dynamism and decision-making of entrepreneurs. Maximization of the difference between price and cost of production acts as the motive force, and profit becomes the determinant of allocation of resources. Private property in the means of production, freedom of individual enterprise, consumer sovereignty, and free play of market forces are the characteristics of a capitalist society and the entrepreneur is the key figure who operates the system. This in brief is a crude, but not incorrect, description of the capitalist economic system.

The communist system, on the other hand, gives to the community (operating through some person or groups of persons who function on behalf of the community) the authority to take the major economic decisions. There is no private property in the means of production nor is there wage labour hired by private individuals for purposes of production. The means of production are owned by the community; and it is the community which owns and determines the disposal of the economic surplus. The division of income between consumption and surplus is determined by the community. The decisions regarding the volume of investment, the pattern of investment, and the product-mix are all determined by the community. The free market does not exist, and prices are more the result of deliberate decision by the community rather than that of the spontaneous play of the forces of demand and supply. Similarly, the pattern of income distribution is more the result of deliberate decision by the community rather than that of market forces and property relations. Like the capitalist society, the communist society also has prices, incomes, wages and markets; but the forces that determine them are different in the two societies. Thus, in the communist society the means of production are owned by the community, the community takes on the entrepreneurial function, consumer sovereignty is diluted by the economic decision making of the community, and the market becomes an instrument for the implementation of this decision rather than a determinant of the volume and composition of the national product. This in brief is a crude, but I believe not incorrect, description of the communist economic system.

There are thus vast differences in the institutional framework and the social philosophy governing the working of the capitalist and communist system of society. What difference does this make to the methods they follow in the process of economic development?

We have already seen that economic development as such has certain features that are independent of the system under which it takes place. Accumulation of capital and human skills are both common to the capitalist and communist methods of economic development. The pain involved in the task of accumulation is common to both: and this is amply borne out by the history of development under both the systems. Under the capitalist system, the worker is denied that increment in consumption that he desires and the surplus gets channelled into investment via the entrepreneur who himself restrains his own consumption (at least in the earlier stages of development); while under the communist system, the same thing happens except that the surplus gets channelled into investment via the state.[1] Under both the systems, the exploitation of the worker becomes possible because of the absence of political and industrial democracy, in the initial stages of development; and it is only as development gets under way and the economy attains the required rate of saving and investment that freedom in the current western sense gets established in the institutional framework of the developed and developing society.[2] Non-voluntary participation by the working class in the process of capital accumulation is common to the earlier stages of development in both the capitalist and communist economies. In both, we find the same accumulation, the same exploitation, the same restraints on consumption, the same increase of that element in national income which corresponds to profit in the case of the capitalist countries, and to public revenues whether by way of tax surplus or net receipts of public enterprise in the case of the communist countries. Where peasants formed a major section of the community and agriculture contributed a major portion of the national income, as it normally did in the earlier stages of development, the process of capital accumulation also involved the exploitation of the agricultural classes. It was thus exploitation of labour, both industrial and agricultural, together with the application of new methods of production that enabled the required expansion of the economic surplus and, with it, the capital accumulation necessary for the take-off from pre-development to development. We may not all see this basic similarity in the real costs of development in both the capitalist and communist societies, but that is partly the result of the normal human tendency to overlook and slur over things

[1] For a more elaborate account of this process and its similarity under the capitalist and communist systems, see my article, 'Freedom and Development — the challenge with special reference to India', *Journal of the Australian Institute of International Affairs*, August, 1960.

[2] The word 'exploitation' is used in the sense of denial to the worker of the whole product of his labour. It is this exploitation that leads to the emergence of what Marx called 'surplus value'.

that happened in the distant past while simultaneously being shocked and appalled by the identical phenomenon if it happens within one's living experience.

Does this mean that there is no difference between the two systems from the point of view of the methods of economic development? No. Obviously not. The two systems have followed somewhat different techniques in the process of development; and it is this difference that is of absorbing interest to those of us who come from countries that have either just undertaken or are still to undertake the task of economic development.

To begin with, a communist society must have economic planning; and whether centralized or decentralized, it must be planning on a national scale and, in fundamentals, at the national level. This is the reason why so many people identify planning in common parlance with communism. There can be no doubt that one cannot have communism without planning. But this does not mean that you cannot have planning without communism. Even in a capitalist society, there is some economic planning in the sense of projections, targets, and economic decisions taken in advance of events. Thus farmers have their plans, industrialists have their plans, the big corporations have their plans. There is a great deal of perspective planning even in a capitalist society. Only these plans are individual or sectional. The decisions that emerge in a capitalist society are the result of the inter-play of the decisions taken by a larger number of individuals and of groups, even though these may be based on their own individual plans. Thus there is no one body taking the crucial economic decisions in a capitalist society. This is the vital difference between a capitalist and a communist society, not the absence of any kind of planning, but the absence of national planning in the former and its inevitable presence in the latter.

Moreover, the very fact that vital economic decisions are taken as a result of national planning gives them a greater measure of certainty in implementation than when they are the result of the interaction of a series of individual and group decisions even if these are based on some kind of economic planning. In a capitalist society, one individual's decision to save may be nullified by another's decision to dis-save; whereas in a communist society, this does not happen as the decision to save is taken by the community and not left to the individual. Similarly, one individual's decision to step up investment may be negatived by another individual outbidding him in the purchase of factors of production, for increasing consumption. There is no certainty in a capitalist society that anticipated savings will equal actual investment nor is it likely that demands will equal supplies at expected prices. In a communist society, on the other hand, there is a certain measure of certainty in the savings-consumption ratio, the pattern of investment, and the product-mix, provided, of course, the planning is effective and not just a façade of wishful thinking. Thus national planning and a certain measure of certainty in the collective implementation of desired economic decisions pertinent to economic growth distinguish the technique of economic development in a communist society from that in a capitalist society.

The second major difference between a capitalist and a communist society — and in some ways following as a consequence of the first distinction — is the higher rate of capital accumulation in a communist society. This is due to two factors, namely, a higher rate of saving, and a pattern of investment more oriented towards accelerating capital accumulation. These two factors act and react on each other and result in turn in giving a communist society a higher and a quicker rate of capital accumulation.

Let us take the rate of saving first. We have already seen that the source of saving in any society, whether capitalist or communist, is the economic surplus. It is the magnitude and disposal of the economic surplus that determines the rate of saving in any society. In a capitalist society, the magnitude of this surplus depends upon the rate of profits, the level of wages, and the property relations that determine the distribution of the proceeds of production. Historically speaking, these factors work in favour of a high rate of saving in the earlier stages of capitalist development, and it is this factor which led Marx to attribute a progressive bias to early capitalism in the task of capital accumulation. But it must not be forgotten that earlier capitalist development coincided in point of time with an un-free society, when the worker and peasant possessed neither political power nor class organization and it was therefore possible for exploitation to increase the surplus. It is also a fact that, during this early phase of capitalist development, the capitalist was a man with a mission who used himself almost as harshly as his workers and restrained his consumption in order to increase the economic surplus. Self-exploitation by the capitalist combined with exploitation of workers and peasants with the help of a state which the masses did not control, and a production mechanism based on property relationships, helped the early capitalist society to achieve a high rate of saving.[3] What is true of early capitalist development in the nineteenth century is, however, not true of early capitalist development in the later half of the twentieth century; and it is this latter period which is relevant for the discussion of methods of economic development to the underdeveloped countries of emerging Asia and Africa today. In the modern age, where the capitalist system has reached maturity in many parts of the world with consequential changes

[3] See V.K.R.V. Rao, op. cit.

in the behaviour pattern of the capitalist, the balance of political power, and the structure of property relations, early capitalist development in the underdeveloped countries suffers from handicaps in the context of increasing the economic surplus which its counterpart did not suffer from during the nineteenth century when capitalism itself was a new force on the social and political horizon. A capitalist society in a contemporary underdeveloped country cannot exert the same pressure on worker and peasant incomes which it could in the underdeveloped countries in the nineteenth century; and the rate of exploitation, on which depends the size of the economic surplus, cannot be equal to what it was then. Moreover, the capitalist in the contemporary underdeveloped world is of a different brand from his earlier counterpart in the nineteenth century. He is no longer the man of austerity who treats himself harshly and restrains his consumption in order to increase the economic surplus. When he comes from abroad in the form of private foreign capital from developed capitalist societies, he brings along with him the standard of life and the consumption pattern that certainly does not err on the side of austerity. And when he is a native and claims indigenous roots, he is subject to the demonstration effect exerted by his compeers abroad and foreign capitalists at home, and is therefore not interested in restraining his own consumption and playing that role in increasing the economic surplus that his counterparts did in capitalist societies in the nineteenth century. The result is that the capitalist system does not lead to a high rate of saving in the contemporary world of underdeveloped countries. In a communist society, on the other hand, there is no private ownership of the economic surplus; and therefore no scope for its utilization for the purpose of increasing consumption. Nor are peasant and worker organizations permitted to play that kind of role *vis-a-vis* their levels of earnings and consumption standards that they do in contemporary capitalist societies, whether in developed or underdeveloped countries. In a communist society, there is no capitalist, no owner of private property, no owner of private enterprise, no interest or rent or profit accruing to private individuals; and therefore the whole of the surplus becomes available for saving and investment. There is also no inroad on this surplus by pressure, either political or organizational, of the workers and peasants. Politically, the workers and peasants are led by the communist party, which has the same sense of mission and plays the same role in regard to capital accumulation as the capitalist entrepreneurs did during the early phases of capitalist development in the now developed capitalist societies. Organizationally the workers and peasants are led by the same communist party, whose emphasis all the time is on production and accumulation rather than on consumption and immediate inroads into the increased production for purposes of increasing consumption. The rate of saving in a communist society is therefore likely to be much higher than in a capitalist society in the contemporary underdeveloped world. Whether it is higher than that in the earlier capitalist phase of the contemporary developed capitalist countries is a subject on which not enough data is available for an objective assessment. In any case, it is irrelevant as far as the contemporary underdeveloped world is concerned, for their interest lies in the rate of saving and how it is likely to behave under the capitalist and communist methods *now* rather than in the past.

The second major factor responsible for a higher rate of capital accumulation in a communist society is the pattern of investment. I am not referring in this connexion to the somewhat futile controversy that takes place in the contemporary underdeveloped countries about the public *versus* private sector. A good deal of investment that is taking place in the case of a country like India, for example, is no more than the building up of economic and social overheads, the infrastructure without which economic development is not possible, whether on capitalist or communist or socialist or other lines. In both capitalist and communist societies, as well as other societies which operate what is called a mixed economy, government plays the crucial role in the building of the infrastructure which makes expansion of production profitable for private enterprise and possible for public enterprise. One should not therefore mix up governmental investment in infrastructure with the pattern of investment that is peculiar to a communist society as distinguished from a capitalist society. When I talk of the pattern of investment in a communist society as more oriented towards capital accumulation, I talk of investment as between production of consumption goods and production of producer goods, the latter in turn being classified as producer goods for consumption industries, and producer goods for producer industries. The theoretical basis for this can be traced to Marx and his famous classification of the departments of production; but its importance in contemporary thinking on the promotion of economic growth owes much more to Soviet experience and the pattern of investment they have adopted in their planned economic development of their country. In a communist society, the pattern of investment is deliberately planned by central decision; and its emphasis is on the Department of Producer Goods rather than on that of Consumption Goods; and in producer goods, on producer goods for making producer goods rather than on producer goods for making consumption goods. In operational terms, this means higher priority in terms of time to producer goods for producing producer goods over producer goods for producing consumption goods, and to producer goods for producing consumer goods over consumption goods. The emphasis is thus more on productivity than on production, more on growth than on current consumption, and more on the future than on the immediate present. The task accepted by the communist system is a high rate of economic growth and therefore the pattern of investment takes the form of a high proportion of capital goods or of capital accumulation in depth, which has a built-in factor for the automatic increase of capital accumulation. Let me quote from the most recent and up-to-date authority on Soviet economic planning.[4]

'As the principal branch in the sphere of material production, industry plays a leading and transforming part in building up the material and technical basis of socialism and communism. The leading branch of industry, heavy industry, comprises the foundation of the socialist economy, the technical basis for the continuous and intensive growth of the productive forces.'

This was the reason why the first Soviet Five Year Plan not only provided for an unprecedented rate of investment (between a quarter and a third of the national income) but also assigned to heavy industry about three-quarters of the amount invested in industry as a whole.[5] Moreover, in actual operation the rate of investment in heavy industry was considerably increased over the original estimates, mainly at the expense of light industry. The growth rate of capital goods in industrial output was permitted to decline over the subsequent five year plans, as can be seen from the following table, but nevertheless it continued to have priority over consumption goods and still continues to be the sheet-anchor of Soviet planning.[6]

In the case of a capitalist society, on the other hand, the emphasis is more on consumption goods and producer goods for producing consumption goods than on producer goods for producing producer goods. The pattern of investment is, in historical terms, rather more on capital accumulation in volume than in depth, more on horizontal than on vertical expansion; and, while reducing the strain caused by capital accumulation it inevitably prolongs the process and makes for a lower rate of capital accumulation and, to that extent, therefore leads to a lower rate of economic growth. It is not possible to be dogmatic about the system of priorities followed in the pattern of investment in capitalist development,

[4] I. A. Yevenko, *Planning in the U.S.S.R.*, p. 126. Also compare the latest resolution on the subject passed at the 21st (Extraordinary) Congress of the Communist Party of the Soviet Union held in Moscow in 1959: 'The Communist Party of the Soviet Union attaches paramount importance to the development of industry, particularly heavy industry, which is the foundation of foundations of socialist economy and of the might of the country. Moreover, it is the decisive factor in the development of the productive forces and in the growth of labour productivity in all branches of the national economy.'
[5] Yevenko, op. cit., pp. 108–9.
[6] See Maurice Dobb, *Soviet Economic Development since 1917*, Fourth Edition, p. 234.

TABLE 1

Average Annual Growth Rate of Gross Industrial Output in the Soviet Union

| | | Of which: | |
| | | | |
Period	Percentage for industry as a whole	Output of the means of production (Group A)	Output of articles of consumption (Group B)
First Five-Year Plan (last quarter of 1928–32)	19·2	28·5	11·7
Second Five-Year Plan (1933–37)	17·1	19·0	14·8
Three pre-war years of the Third Five-Year Plan (1938–40)	13·2	15·3	10·1
Fourth Five-Year Plan (1946–50)	13·6	12·8	15·7
Fifth Five-Year Plan (1951–55)	13·2	13·8	12·0
Seventh Year Plan (1959–65)	8·6	9·3	7·3

partly because we do not have enough data on the subject and partly because of difficulties of interpretation arising from the very nature of investment in a capitalist society which is the result of the inter-play of many and unco-ordinated individual decisions. But I believe I would be correct in saying that, by and large, the priorities in capitalist development have been more on consumption goods and producer goods that would lead to an immediate increase in consumption goods than on producer goods as such. This has been well illustrated by Hoffman's study of the growth of Industrial Economies, where he has shown that the proportion of consumption goods in their industrial output was very high during the earlier stages of industrial development in a number of capitalist societies and gradually declined with the growing maturity of these economies. He sums up in the following table the overall trend he found in industrial

TABLE 2

Net Output of Consumer and Capital Goods Industries as a Percentage of Total Net Industrial Output

| | Stage of Industrialization | | |
	First	Second	Third
Consumer — goods industries	83%	71%	50%
Capital — goods industries	18%	29%	50%

development by analysing the changes in the relationship between the net output of consumer goods and capital goods industries in a number of economically developed countries.[7]

In fact, the proportion of consumer goods in industrial output has

[7] W. G. Hoffman, *The Growth of Industrial Economies*, p. 97.

declined to about 30 per cent in recent years in the major economically developed countries such as the United States, the United Kingdom, Germany, Belgium, and Japan. Thus, there is no difference between the capitalist and the communist system in regard to the place occupied by capital goods industries in the economy; only, the process has taken a much longer period of time in the capitalist countries, as earlier priorities were on consumption goods; while in the case of the communist countries, the time taken has been shorter, as earlier priorities were given to capital goods and that, too, by deliberate and centralized decision.

The combined effect of extracting a larger investible surplus and following a pattern of investment that places more emphasis on producer goods industries has thus led to a higher rate of capital accumulation in the Soviet Union; and, in turn, this has led to a higher annual rate of economic growth in the Soviet Union than in the capitalist economies. This is well illustrated in the following table.[8]

TABLE 3

Annual Rates of Growth in Industrial Output 1860–1958 per cent (compounded)

Period	UK	USA	Germany	France	Italy	Sweden	Japan	USSR
1860–80	2·4	4·3	2·7	2·4	—	—	—	6·4
1880–1900	1·7	4·5	5·3	2·4	4·5	8·1	—	6·4
1900–13	2·2	5·2	4·4	3·7	5·6	3·5	3·8	4·8
1913–25–29	0·3	3·7	0·3	1·4	2·6	1·6	7·5	1·1
1925–29–38	3·1	−0·9	3·5	−0·7	1·7	5·4	6·5	17·2
1938–58	2·9	5·3	3·5	3·6	4·3	3·5	3·4	8·9

So far I have been dealing with differences between the capitalist and communist methods of economic development that have redounded to the advantage of the former. Now I turn to some other differences which work in the opposite direction and perhaps show the capitalist methods of economic development to better advantage.

Agri

A major difference between the capitalist and communist systems is the performance of agriculture in the national economy. The technical methods followed for the development of agricultural productivity and expansion of agricultural production have been the same in both communist and capitalist economies, namely, mechanization and modernization, increase in size of operational units, use of tractors and other farm machinery, and increasing inputs of chemical fertilizers, pesticides, etc. But communist agriculture has not shown the same results in terms of productivity and output as communist manufacturing industries. Nor has it given the same results as agriculture in the capitalist economies. The

[8] Surendra J. Patel, 'Rates of Industrial Growth', *Economic Development and Cultural Change* Chicago, April 1961.

numerous crises through which Soviet agriculture has passed beginning with the great Kulak-liquidation and collectivization started by Stalin, the changing role of the machine tractor stations, the continuing (and, in a way, gradually extending) existence of a private sector and a free market within the collective farms, the association between the rise of Khrushchev and his image as the one person taking agriculture the most seriously among Soviet leaders and determined to solve its problem, the recent decrees on an increase in the prices of Soviet farm products with its attempt to improve the terms of trade between Soviet agriculture and Soviet industry and between the rural and the urban sector — all these furnish ample evidence of the uneasy bed that the communist system has provided to agriculture in the Soviet Union. The comparative failure of the communist system to solve the problem of agriculture has been demonstrated even more clearly by the changes that have taken place in Yugoslav and Polish agriculture with their virtual repudiation of the basic Stalinist concept of Soviet agriculture. And the most recent addition to the testimony has come from communist China which has now officially proclaimed a policy of slowing-down and admitted the existence of a formidable agricultural problem, following the initial slogan of the 'great leap forward' and the universal establishment of agricultural communes. Thus, peasant-led communism of China seems to have shared with worker-led communism of the Soviet Union the same experience of stresses, strains and disappointments when it came to dealing with agricultural production on the basis of communist ideology. And all this has been in contrast with the experience of agriculture in the capitalist societies led by the United States, where the problem has been one of how to deal with increasing agricultural productivity and rising agricultural surpluses. This comparative failure of communist agriculture both as compared to communist industry and capitalist agriculture cannot be explained away in terms of differences in scientific knowledge and technical skills. I have no doubt in my mind that the explanation is to be found basically in the differences between the two systems in terms of (i) ideology or outlook, (ii) agrarian structure and (iii) investment policy and priorities.

I have the impression that communist ideology does not show any special favour to the peasant community. It is true that the party is called a Workers' and Peasants' Party, but the industrial worker, the urban resident, occupies the pride of place. By and large, communist theories, practice and slogans are linked with the worker who is identified with the proletariat; but workers meant in practice primarily industrial workers rather than even the poor peasants. The latter were regarded as socially less advanced and ideologically not fit to assume leadership because of

their continuing subjection to feudal ideas and complexes. In fact, one of
the acknowledged tasks of the communist society was to bring about a
transformation of the peasantry and make them approximate to the
industrial working class in their psychology, discipline, and capacity for
co-ordinated and collective action. Thus, in some sense, the peasant in the
communist society — and this has been so even in China in spite of the
peasant-base of its communist party and the declared peasant-bias of its
leadership in apparent contrast to that of the Soviet Union — felt himself
a second class citizen rather than one of the elect; and this must have had
some connection with the comparative failure of agriculture in communist
societies to keep pace with their industry in productive efficiency.

More important than this psychological impact was that caused by the
changes in agrarian structure which communism brought in its train.
Communist theory repudiates private property in the means of production and this applied to land as well. Private peasant agriculture therefore
was brought to an end, the Kulaks (or the more well-to-do and efficient
farmers who generally also employed hired labour to assist them in farm
operations) were liquidated, and collective farms became the ruling form
of the communist agrarian structure. There were two major difficulties
that appeared in their operation and were, in fact, inherent in the new
structure. One was the difficulty of linking the distribution of farm output
sufficiently with individual contribution to production on the farm, with a
consequential reduction in the individual incentive for maximization of
output. The other was the undeniably adverse effect that absence of
private property in land had on the farmer's incentive for maximizing
his effort. This was practically the universal experience of collectivized
agriculture, in both the older and the newer communist societies, and led
to the abrogation of collective farming and the virtual restoration of
private property in land in two at least of the communist countries,
namely, Poland and Yugoslavia. Even when it continued — as in the case
of the Soviet Union and some of the other East European communist
societies and now in communist China, the system was diluted by the
introduction of a certain element of private agriculture in the collective
farms and the opportunity given for the sale of its output on a legally
recognized free market. In spite of that, difficulties continued to exist in
the task of maximizing farm output and, as we have already stated,
communist agriculture failed to keep pace in efficiency either with that of
communist industry or capitalist agriculture as in the United States or
even peasant agriculture as in Japan. I am developing the thesis that there
is something about land and agriculture that gives private property a far
more positive role in the stimulation of productive capacity than appears
to be the case with machinery and manufacturing industries. My conten-

tion is supported not only by the experience of industry in the Soviet Union and other communist countries but even by the experience of capitalist economies in the field of industry. Thus, in capitalist economies, private property is far more actively associated with enterprise and decision making in agriculture than in the case of industry, where shareholders in giant corporations like Imperial Chemicals or Imperial Tobacco or Unilever, for example, play hardly any role in decision-making.

The third factor making for a lower record of efficiency of agriculture in the communist system is the smaller volume of investment directed to agriculture and the lower priority it is given in the overall pattern of communist investment. The reason for this differentiation between agriculture and industry in the communist pattern of investment is, in my opinion, directly linked with the communist ideological bias in favour of industry. I am, therefore, inclined to believe that the comparatively lower efficiency of agriculture in communist economies is integrally connected with the nature of communist ideology and is therefore a noticeable disadvantage of the communist as compared to the capitalist system.

The second major difference between the communist and capitalist method of economic development that shows the former at a disadvantage stems from its centralization of decision-making in economic affairs and the consequent growth of a vast and powerful bureaucracy. While such centralization is of undoubted help in the allocation of resources between investment and consumption, the pattern of investment, and the composition of the product-mix, there is also no denying the adverse effect it has on local initiative, utilization of individual enterprise and capacity for risk-taking, and maximization of individual economic effort in terms both of intensity and of quality. Under the capitalist system, with its competition, profit making and possibilities of unlimited individual reward, individuals with resources are stimulated to put in their best efforts in their own interest, Adam Smith's 'divine hand' performing the task of reconciling the results of such individual enterprise with collective requirements. Administrative decrees and bureaucratic guidance, even if backed by a strongly organized party and ideological enthusiasm, are no substitute for the direct involvement of the individual in his economic activity through his self-interest and his desire for recognition and emulation. The result of this bureaucratization of economic organization and economic decision reached at the top and getting translated into orders at the bottom is not only a reduction in individual efficiency, but also the emergence of numerous imbalances in detail. It also leads to an attempt at implementation of decrees through evasion of regulations by different units at the expense of one another rather than by an increase in total resources by invention and improvization. Communist administrators and

23

party officials have been conscious of the built-in dangers of bureaucracy that centralized planning involves; and no item has figured more in communist discussions and internal propaganda than the dangers of bureaucracy. In fact, over the years, communist economic administration has been evolving a system of norms of performance, incentives, piece-wages, socialist emulation, decentralization, and other measures aimed precisely at this defect I have pointed out and providing communist substitutes for the capitalist system of private enterprise, competition and the free market, in its effect on the release and maximum deployment of individuals with resources. The cardinal principle of economic stimulation is inducement. You can take a horse to the water trough but you can't force it to drink. What is true of the horse is even more true of man, especially when the activity desired is not just consumption, but active production. However communistically inclined a person may be, there is a limit beyond which he will not just do what he is told, even if it is by communist authority. Force, even when backed by idealism, fails beyond a point. Human beings have their own ways of resisting force under any system when it is used to evoke positive responses; and positive responses are an essential condition for economic growth. The carrot is stronger than the whip in a developing economy. And one can say that the outstanding trend in communist economic administration over the years has been the substitution of the whip by the carrot.

The other day I was in Warsaw to attend a seminar, then in Moscow to deliver some lectures. I went out visiting shops in both places. I would ask the sales girls or boys about their wages. They would say that so much was their wages. Then they would go on to add that they got something extra if they exceeded their allotted quota. For practically every economic activity, an attempt has been made to create a norm. Output or performance that reaches the norm gets the normal wage. Exceeding the norm results in extra payment and thus an incentive is provided for increasing the intensity and quality of output of effort by labour. It is also widely believed that the norm is usually kept a little low, so that almost every one gets a little extra payment for exceeding it and also gets the feeling that he is participating in the development of the economy. With all these changes, however, though they are tending to minimize the adverse effect on individual initiative and effort that accompany nationalization of economic decisions, it still remains true that the capitalist system has an edge over the communist system in the matter of work motivation and individual response; and to that extent the latter is at a disadvantage in terms of overall economic efficiency.

One more difference between the capitalist and communist methods of economic development needs to be mentioned before I come to the concluding section of the paper. A capitalist society is an open society in the sense that no restrictions are placed on the free entry of visitors, import of private capital is allowed, and citizens are free to travel abroad. Whereas the communist society is a closed society and is guarded by what has come to be known as the 'iron curtain'. I am not concerned here with the political aspects of the iron curtain or its relevance to civil liberties. But the iron curtain has certain important economic implications of considerable relevance to a developing economy. Economic development under the communist system aims at a rate of saving and investment that is not only high but also higher than what the people would go in for if they had a free choice. It becomes easier to do this if the people are not physically aware of the various consumption goods that people in the developed capitalist countries are having. After all, basic consumption goods, essential for existence, form a comparatively small proportion of family budgets in western countries. Much of the consumption is of a non-basic character and it is this which accounts for a lower rate of saving in the developed capitalist countries as also the higher preference for investment in consumption goods. If therefore non-basic consumption goods are kept out of the people's sight, it becomes easier to raise the rate of saving without causing stresses and strains among the people and without using batons and machine guns for dealing with the same. This is what the 'iron curtain' does for the communist countries and it certainly facilitates a larger mobilization of domestic resources for purposes of planned investment. In the case of the non-communist developing economies, the iron curtain does not exist and the field is left free for the demonstration effect of a higher level and larger variety of consumption goods that people in capitalist countries enjoy. Private foreign capital that comes in brings with it foreign capitalists and technicians with levels of consumption that have a big demonstration effect on the local *élite* and leaders. This effect is further reinforced by the experience of those citizens who go abroad and bring back with them taste for and tales of non-basic consumption goods that they have seen during their foreign soujourn. The result is that the upper classes in the non-communist developing economies seek a higher level of consumption and therefore save less; and this, in turn, has a demonstration effect on the common masses in their countries and makes it more difficult to get them to accept austerity during the period of development. To this extent, the iron curtain, which is so closely identified with a communist economy, helps it in having a higher rate of saving than that in the open societies characteristic of capitalist economies.

Now these are some of the major differences between the capitalist and communist methods of economic development. I have not talked about the political differences, about democracy, the police state, civil liberties, class differentiations, inequalities, and other factors that distinguish the two systems from one another. Not that they are not important nor that I have no views on them; only this paper is concerned solely with the economic aspect of their difference and is therefore strictly neutral between them on the political front.

Now I come to the concluding portion, namely, the advantages and disadvantages of the two systems. The answer is necessarily of the nature of a generalization and is therefore subject to all the qualifications that any generalization on the comparative merits and demerits of two societies are subject to.

I would begin by saying that, for bringing about capital accumulation, for efficiency in generating, mobilizing, and accumulating the economic surplus, the communist system is more efficient than the capitalist system. Or to put it in a different way, the capitalist system will take a much longer time to reach a given level of capital accumulation than what the communist system is able to do. To quote Joan Robinson:

> 'Compared to a purely feudal system capitalism was a great invention for promoting accumulation. It shifted the balance of power from property to enterprise and got going the process of accumulation. Compared to capitalism, socialism makes the transfer in a still more thoroughgoing way. Property ceases to exist, and the animal spirits of enterprise drive the whole economy to undertake unprecedented feats. Thus, so far as undeveloped economies are concerned, it seems that socialism is going to beat capitalism at its own game, and the reason that it will do so is that it is a far more powerful instrument for extracting the investible surplus from an economy.'

I am not going into the politics of this conclusion. If you want to go into its politics, I can give you a gruesome picture of what happened in England in its early industrial history and the place of child labour therein and so on, all of which makes really gruesome reading; only it happened more than a hundred years ago and so no one remembers it now. What happened a hundred years ago is history. What happens today is contemporary politics. And there is a great deal of difference between history and politics. But as far as extracting the investible surplus is concerned, I believe that the communist system is more efficient than the capitalist system. And, in so far as the size of the investible surplus is an important determinant of the rate of economic growth, the communist system is superior to the capitalist system in bringing about economic growth. That is my first proposition.

Then comes the question of the pattern of investment. Here again, I am afraid, the balance of advantage is on the side of the communist system, because the investment policy of the communist society is, as stated earlier, more geared to economic growth than that followed in capitalist society. That is my second proposition.

Now comes the third factor. It is not merely the size of the investible surplus or the manner in which you invest the investible surplus that determines economic growth. It is also the efficiency of the operation, the productivity of labour in industry, in agriculture, in transport, and in other sectors of the economy. Regarding this productivity of labour in general, I have been trying to suggest that the honours rest more with the capitalist system than with the communist systems. This is because, in the case of the capitalist system the individual is the basis and motivation is directed towards the individual; while, in the case of the communist system, the individual is not the basis and motivation is directed towards the community functioning through its individuals in a mystic way under the leadership of the party. After all, productivity is not merely the result of having good technical skills; or of having modern machinery; or of having a favourable environment in terms of natural resources. Productivity is also the result of that little something which is the interest of the man concerned in bringing about the maximum production, his freedom to experiment, his freedom to make losses, his urge to express himself, his personality, his dynamism, his drive, his go-gettingness, his 'animal spirits' if you want to use Joan Robinson's phrase, in terms of economic activity. I think that in the case of the capitalist system the individual gets motivated to a much larger extent than he does in the communist system. And that is one major reason why, though the rate of growth is higher in terms of investment goods in the communist system, productivity therein per unit of labour in agriculture and in industry even today cannot compare with that in the advanced and developed capitalist societies. This is my third proposition.

It should be clear by now that neither the capitalist nor the communist systems can claim to have all the advantages. Both have their good points; and both have their weaknesses. If one were to treat the two systems as students who have appeared at an examination, then an impartial examiner's verdict would be that they have both passed, though it would be also true to say that neither of them can be awarded first class marks. Neither of them is likely to replace the other and they have to reconcile themselves to each other's existence on a continuing basis. That is why the cold war appears so futile to a non-aligned observer who does not owe allegiance to either of these systems. Coexistence of the capitalist and communist systems thus gets its logical basis not only on the balance of military power and international alliances but also on the failure of either to hold the unique key to economic development. That is why one can find an admittedly socialist but also internationally recognized economist like Joan Robinson taking up an apparently ambivalent position in regard to the rival claims of the capitalist and communist methods of economic development. I quote:[9]

> 'First I argued that the socialist system is well suited to the need of developing economies. Now I am maintaining that capitalism, if it is managed with intelligence and good will, may continue to flourish in economies that are already developed. If my argument is correct, we have to look forward to a long period of co-existence of different economic systems.'

I would, however, go farther than Mrs. Robinson and question the very validity of maintaining a continuing clear-cut distinction between the capitalist and communist systems of economic development. Communist methods of economic development during their earlier stages have a great deal of resemblance to some of the basic features of the early stages of capitalist economic development. Capitalist economic development in its later stages, as in the last decade and even earlier, contains a number of features that have formed an essential part of the communist methods of economic development. And communist economic development in its later stages, as in the case of the Soviet Union in the post–Stalinist era, is increasingly incorporating features, that have formed an essential part of the capitalist methods of economic development. The capitalist system in the developed countries is going in for planning, diminished competition, concentration of decision-making on vital economic issues in fewer and fewer hands, and increasingly diminishing play of volition and individual choice in determining the rate of saving and the pattern of investment. The communist system in the developed and even developing countries is, on the other hand, increasingly going in for decentralization, motivation directed towards individuals, competition rephrased as emulation, less un-free markets, and increasing use of incentives, inducements and stimulation rather than force, ideology, and administrative decrees. The capitalist and the communist systems are drawing closer and are not showing any inhibition in taking from each other what they think will serve them better in the strategy of economic development and the promotion of economic growth; only they are not getting merged with each other. The lines are still separate but they are no longer at right angles to each other. It is true they are moving as parallel lines and hence the continuing coexistence of the two systems; but the two parallel lines are getting nearer each other and hence the coexistence will get easier as

[9] Joan Robinson, *Collected Economic Papers*, Vol. II, p. 106.

time passes. I feel therefore that, from a strictly economic point of view, there is something more academic than practical in setting the one system against the other, in viewing them as two watertight alternative means to economic development.

I cannot conclude this paper without some reference to the non-economic aspects of this question. Capitalist and communist methods of economic development are both historical facts; and they have both passed the historical test in the achievement of economic development. But, as I have said earlier, neither of them has passed with first class honours. There can be other ways of economic development that can take the good points of both and yet avoid the bad points of each. Such a system may be called a 'mixed economy' or 'a socialist pattern of society' or *'Sarvodaya'* or Arab socialism or African socialism or Indian socialism. It is not the names that are important. It is the integration of economic development with human and social values, the creation of a social and political democracy side by side with economic growth and development, the reconciling of human dignity and civil liberty with economic efficiency and conquest of the material world, what *Acharya* Vinoba Bhave calls the combining of science with spirituality, that the developing economies of emergent Africa and awakened Asia should seek. That freedom and development can coexist and combine as a method of economic development may sound somewhat idealistic. If that is so, I must confess myself an unashamed idealist. I would rather trudge along this path and even take the risk of failing to scale the heights of the highest materialistic mountain rather than ensure success by following methods of economic development, whether capitalist or communist, that have in them elements that offend my sense of human dignity, human equality, human liberty and human spirituality. When we in the developing countries of Asia and Africa seek economic growth, let us not be overawed by the authority claiming voice of the expert economist and his protégé, the economic man. Instead, I would ask my listeners to remember the wise words with which my favourite economist for this paper, Joan Robinson concluded her now famous lecture on 'Marx, Marshall and Keynes' which she delivered at Delhi in 1955 under my chairmanship.

> 'The purpose of studying economics is not to acquire a set of ready-made answers to economic questions, but to learn how to avoid being deceived by economists.'

So do not expect the economist to guide you in your choice of the method of economic development. By all means, listen to him, use his analysis, but fill up the gaps he so obviously leaves, ignore the irrelevancies he so unconsciously introduces, and make up your own minds as human beings in search of both material well-being and spiritual fulfilment.

APPENDICES

SPEECH BY HIS EXCELLENCY THE GOVERNOR OF NYASALAND, SIR GLYN JONES, AT THE OPENING OF THE ECONOMIC SYMPOSIUM ON 18th JULY, 1962

It is a great personal pleasure to me to give the opening address at this symposium and to welcome on behalf of the Government the participants and observers to Nyasaland. You who are our guests come, without exception I should say, from more sophisticated though perhaps not more lovely surroundings than are found in Nyasaland, and to you a meeting of this sort may not seem out of the ordinary. But I can assure you that this is an event of great significance to us. Gathered in this hall are economists of world wide reputation from Great Britain, the United States of America, Western Germany, India, Ireland and Sweden, who will read papers on a variety of subjects of economic importance. And we have many distinguished observers too.

Even one year ago it would have been hard to imagine a meeting of this kind taking place in Nyasaland and I should like to take you back in time so that you can appreciate the full significance of this event.

Our guests come from countries with long histories, but the recorded story of Nyasaland as we know it today goes back only a hundred years. It begins with David Livingstone, who first reached Lake Nyasa in 1859. Much of the early history of Nyasaland is influenced by the great explorer. The path he opened up was followed by the Universities Mission to Central Africa and by the Church of Scotland Mission: and after his death, and inspired by it, missions were established at Livingstonia on the northern lake shore and here in Blantyre, named after his Scottish birthplace.

At this period the missionaries found themselves obliged to trade in order to maintain themselves in the country, but to relieve them of the commercial side of their activities a number of businessmen formed in

1878 the African Lakes Corporation as a transport and trading concern. This was the beginning of legitimate trade in the area and might be said to be the first signs of a coherent economy.

Other Europeans followed — missionaries, traders, hunters and planters, and in 1883 a representative of the British Government was accredited to this territory. In 1891 a Protectorate was proclaimed.

Although Nyasaland's progress has, with the exception of the interruption of the two world wars, been fairly peaceful, her economy has not developed rapidly, partly on account of her land-locked position, combined with poor communications with her neighbours; partly because of her lack of mineral wealth; but principally because of a serious lack of capital and skills with which to develop her natural resources — material and human. Until recent years Nyasaland had a mainly subsistence economy. The cash economy depended in the main on the two principal exports of tea and tobacco. These, with cotton and groundnuts, still account for some 80 per cent of the total value of the Protectorate's exports. In the past decade the money economy has grown considerably and has become more diversified with the growth of manufacturing and construction industries.

In this process greater numbers of the indigenous population have been drawn into the money economy, but even so, over half of the gross domestic product relates to subsistence production.

There is no doubt, however, that the economy has made considerable strides in recent years and this is sometimes overlooked by many of those who are grappling with the current problems of this part of Africa. It is fashionable nowadays in certain circles in many of the dependencies of the United Kingdom to refer rather scathingly to the long years of neglect. I think it important on an occasion such as this to analyse this proposition and to put it into proper perspective as far as this country is concerned.

Nobody I think would deny nowadays that for very many years the colonial powers were generally content to leave it to those who had gone to settle in their dependencies to provide the wherewithal to run the scanty services which the local government was under a duty to provide. In those days, of course, lack of fast communications meant that those responsible for the formulation of policy in the metropolitan country rarely if ever visited the dependent territories and were therefore unable to get a first hand glimpse of the way of life of the peoples whom they were governing by remote control: and they had an inadequate knowledge, therefore, of the difficulties which faced both the local governments and the devoted band of expatriates who had the welfare of the inhabitants of the country at heart, but who had not the financial resources to do very much to better their lot. But it is all too frequently forgotten that in the years when colonial powers lacked dynamic policies in respect of their dependencies, there were other nations in the world whose interest in those dependencies was either meagre or non-existent. It was not until the Second World War that the wealthy nations of the world began to acknowledge an obligation to assist in the development of the under-privileged territories.

The United Kingdom was one of the first countries to recognize the reality of the situation, and to appreciate that it had a far greater responsi-bility in respect of its dependencies than merely to provide a framework of Government in which a small handful of British people were expected to provide the means and the skills for bettering the lot of the indigenous peoples. If any substantial impact was to be made on those peoples, a regular flow of capital in the public sector would have to be stimulated and grants and loans would have to be made available by the mother country. The enactment of the Colonial Development and Welfare Act in 1945 was a first step to these ends, and this was followed by the creation of aid-giving institutions such as the Colonial Development Corpora-tion.

This is not to say that the British Government was entirely oblivious to the needs of its dependencies before this point of time. In Nyasaland, for example, during the 30's it provided between two and three million pounds for railway development in this territory and for providing its link with the sea at the port of Beira. But while this was a large sum of money to be lent to a tiny country in those years of world depression, and while we undoubtedly benefited from it and still do, this injection of capital failed to achieve any notable economic development.

It has often been held, and it was certainly held at the time, that the mere introduction of sophisticated methods of transport is sufficient in itself to stimulate local economic activity. I think that the history of the northern extension of the railway in this country well disproves that theory. I have no doubt that the new railway was a great fascination to the people through whose lands it passed. But there can be no doubt whatever that the mere presence of two steel rails was not such as to stimulate them to go back and plant crops for export over those rails. If only the British Government of the day could have provided a further grant of money which the Nyasaland Government could have utilized for the improvement of the agricultural potential of the area served by the railway, the latter would more effectively have served its purpose, and indeed the company owning the railway might as a result not be in the marginal financial position in which it finds itself today. Thus we have to admit that while the British Government gave Nyasaland appreciable help for certain specific projects she was for a long time unable to provide capital to stimulate general economic development.

In fact, no substantial sums of money were made available for general development until after the end of the Second World War. I think one should point to the year 1948 as the year from which the economic history of this territory should be dated. In this year a post-war development plan was launched and there arrived in this territory a Governor with great practical knowledge of the requirements for economic development. I refer to the late Sir Geoffrey Colby.

During the short period since 1948 much has happened. In 1948 there were only five miles of tarmacadam road in this country — between Blantyre and Limbe: every drop of water had to be boiled and filtered before it could be drunk; electricity was to be found only in Blantyre, Limbe and Zomba; the same went for waterborne sanitation: our postal system was primitive, much of the mail being carried by hand: the tele-communications network was both meagre and unreliable; the marketing organization for African grown crops was rudimentary and there were no co-operatives at all: there were only two single stream secondary schools to serve the whole country; and no facilities to speak of for technical training. The only recognized aerodrome in the country was of grass and was unsafe for aircraft larger than a Rapide. Owing to an unfortunate catastrophe there was no proper passenger vessel on Lake Nyasa.

Much of this has changed. We have now a considerable network of main roads, nearly 300 miles of which are macadamized; a modern postal and telecommunications system; supplies of pure water in the principal centres of the country and waterborne sanitation at many others; modern power stations at Blantyre, Zomba and Lilongwe. We have planted over 20,000 acres of softwoods as an investment for the future. We have nine secondary school streams catering for 665 students. An important cement industry has been established with private capital, as also have a number of smaller industries catering for the local market. I will not weary you with a catalogue of the achievements of the last decade. You will be able to read about them for yourselves in chapter 5 of the Government's latest development plan.

The tangible achievements in the public sector during this decade were made possible by substantial free grants of money under the British Colonial Development and Welfare Acts and by virtue of a £2 million loan raised on the London Market in 1952, and market and other loans totalling about £9 million which have come to us since then from various sources including the London, Rhodesian and New York markets.

Since 1953 all loans have been raised on our behalf by the Federal

Government. While I know full well that the present constitutional arrangements whereby this territory is associated with its Rhodesian neighbours in a federation are strongly disliked by the majority of the inhabitants of this country; while I know that the majority party is pledged to break away from this association and that the British Government has acknowledged the fact; and while I know that at this very moment distinguished men are studying the effect on this country of such a breakaway, I must acknowledge the historical fact that the acceleration in the pace of development over the last decade is in some measure to be attributed to this association. For instance I think it doubtful if the value of loans raised for capital purposes during that period would have otherwise attained the figure to which I have referred.

All the projects of this last decade were conceived by an unrepresentative Government in the modern sense of the term.

They characterized a genuine attempt on the part of that Government to provide a strong economic basis for future development and to apportion the available funds to what it considered to be the most worthy projects. Such things were done by a Government composed of officials, nominated members and others elected on a restricted franchise. It was a paternalistic Government which, while it may have failed to gain the enthusiastic support of the majority of the people, nevertheless provided for the present more representative Government, a foundation upon which to build a more imaginative and appealing development programme.

I refer to our new Development Plan, designed to reflect the wishes of the people as interpreted by their representatives in the Government. It places emphasis upon the continuation of the building of a strong base for our economy, upon the development of human resources, upon the expansion of agricultural productivity, and upon the improvement of the economic climate for commerce and industry. I think it is a bold and progressive plan, and one that will greatly repay study by those of you who are about to read papers in answers to questions bearing upon the economic theories which should lie behind the development of underdeveloped territories.

But even if the approach to development may have changed to some extent with the arrival on the scene of the representatives of the people, the difficulties attendant upon paying for development are still with us. True the great nations of the western world are now adopting a more enlightened attitude to the problems of underdeveloped countries; and they are increasing their financial assistance to the 'have nots'. But at the same time, of course, more erstwhile dependent territories are achieving independence, and more representatives of the people are coming to the centre of affairs with their urgent demands for more of the material things of life. There is still an enormous gap to be filled between the resources and requirements of the African continent.

Not the least of our difficulties is the need to service the capital assets which we create. There is an understandable tendency on the part of the assisting powers to wish to see their contributions translated into bricks and mortar; and to leave it to the receiving country to find the money to run the institutions thus created. But this is just where our needs are greatest. I think that many of us would rather see contributions, whether in cash or kind, designed to create a viable project, and to keep it going, if necessary within a modest though adequate building.

This is particularly important in a country such as Nyasaland where future wealth must, as far as we can see, depend upon the extent to which the soil can be made to bear fruit. Alas, the time taken for such fructification tends to be lengthy. For the stimulation of agricultural productivity we require above all free grants of money, or the provision of free services, or at the very least access to long-term loans free of interest and with generous grace periods for the repayment of capital — the sort of loan indeed in which the International Development Association specializes.

This is but one example of the practical difficulties which confront us who bear the responsibility for the development of an underdeveloped country; and there are others too. There are, for example, great human problems. While therefore we all look forward with the greatest interest to what our eminent visitors will have to say to us, and while we must be made aware of and thoroughly understand the doctrines and theories which should guide the development effort, the Governments who bear the ultimate responsibility for that development must never allow themselves to be blinded by science. The development of an underdeveloped territory is a vast human problem and, just as it often happens that a patient displays an allergy to a drug specified by medical science, so we must expect the indigenous peoples of underdeveloped territories to react adversely at times to the specifics which are prescribed by the far less exact science of economics.

This Symposium is nevertheless designed to point the way; and what could be more encouraging than that it should take the form of a realistic determination to face the economic facts and to grapple with them in collaboration with some of the world's experts. The searching questions which have been set to the participants to answer and discuss are evidence enough that Nyasaland means business. They demonstrate that her leaders are making every effort to chart the channels before proceeding into unknown and possibly perilous waters.

I started by saying that it is a personal pleasure to me to give the opening address here today. I meant this sincerely as I have spent over thirty years in Central Africa and have been closely associated with its peoples. It gives me great satisfaction to participate in proceedings which have as their ultimate aim the betterment of the lot of those peoples.

A good deal of the value of this gathering together of friendly experts who will give us their advice on our difficulties will be derived from their contacts with us outside the conference room. The list of social engagements is imposing but it has been arranged partly with a view to giving our visitors time for even more informal contacts. I do hope that lasting friendships will be made here and that we on our side will be able to persuade our visitors that, though a small country, we have sufficient character to justify their taking a continued interest in us.

We are happy that we can receive you in an atmosphere of tranquillity which is in some contrast to the turbulence of our recent history. We are in process of forgetting the difficulties and misunderstandings of the past in the effort to present a united front to our enemies — which have been realistically described as ignorance, poverty and disease. This ideal we cannot achieve without goodwill on all sides. I think that goodwill is being generated though perhaps it is sometimes obscured by thoughtless words and gestures. I myself, however, have great faith that in a country such as this, where the principles of Christianity have been so well understood and widely accepted by the people, all the races will combine to work for the good of Nyasaland and its inhabitants. I would like you to know that this faith is shared by Nyasaland's national leader, Doctor the Honourable H. K. Banda. He will have opportunities of telling you this himself. All I would say is that at this present stage of Nyasaland's history it is vital that the majority of the people here, through their elected leader Dr Banda, and the British Government through its representative, should be on easy terms of realistic co-operation. That, ladies and gentlemen, at the present point of time is the state of affairs here and that is the reason why we can all meet here today at ease in the confidence that friendships of lasting duration are going to be made.

This Symposium is due to the inspiration of an African, Dunduza Chisiza. He presents his case with an embarrassing frankness and humility. He informs the participants that in this country underdevelopment will stare them in the face and they will renew their acquaintance with ignorance, poverty and disease. I hope that you will not be misled by this, however. You must not undervalue the qualities possessed by the Nyasaland peoples. When I first went to Northern Rhodesia thirty years ago many of the highest posts available to Africans were occupied by Nyasalanders. They have a natural intelligence, a vitality and a courage that should not be underestimated. They possess an independent spirit and a forceful method of expression that appeal to many. Above all they give a warm hearted response to anyone who accords to them the privilege of human understanding and sympathetic guidance.

In the past it has been possible for them to oppose and criticize a benevolent and paternalistic regime which was unable to take adequate stock of local desires and aspirations. Now, however, they have their own representatives in the Government in ample proportions. I am happy to detect a new approach born of the realisation that they will from now on bear a large and increasing part of the responsibility for the successes and the failures — of which I hope there will be few — of the Government. In short, you must not allow the reference to our trilogy of chronic maladies to blind you to the fact that greatness of character is often to be found among those who have been underprivileged and subjected to the privations of poverty.

Before I end I have two tributes to pay.

First, we are deeply grateful to the Ford Foundation for their generosity in meeting the travelling expenses of participants and for making the many arrangements necessary to bring them together here. Without such assistance this Symposium could not have taken its present form.

Secondly, I must pay tribute to Mr D. K. Chisiza, who not only inspired the idea of the symposium but also, with his small committee, personally carried through almost every detail of it in the midst of his many other commitments in a heavy Government programme. He will no doubt pay tribute himself to the assistance he has received from his committee and from members of the civil service.

We expect to learn from your forthcoming discussions much that will be of direct benefit to us. We hope that in return your visit to Nyasaland and the things you see and hear in this small part of Africa will not be without interest to you as an example of conditions and thought in an undeveloped territory.

I wish you success in your discussions and a pleasant stay in Nyasaland. I have much pleasure in declaring this Symposium open.

CLOSING ADDRESS BY DR H. K. BANDA

PRIME MINISTER OF NYASALAND

Mr Chairman, distinguished visitors, ministers, ladies and gentlemen. I do not know how to tell you how happy I am to be standing in front of you this afternoon to make the closing speech at this historic symposium. I say I do not know how happy I am because, so far as I know, this is the first time that famous economists have gathered anywhere in Africa as they have gathered here. Most of the conferences I have attended have been held in Geneva, Paris, London, New York and Washington, but never in a small town, in a small country like this. When Dunduzu Chisiza told me that economists in America were thinking of holding a symposium somewhere in Africa, and that he wanted my consent and blessing to hold it here, I was delighted. I was delighted for more reasons than one. First, I wanted economists to come here and tell us of their knowledge and experience gained in other countries and, if possible, advise us what to do and what not to do. Secondly, I have always wanted the world to know my country; in other words, I wanted to advertise my little Nyasaland to the outside world. Finally, I wanted to expose my people, the Africans of this country, to the gaze and even the critical, hostile glare of the world outside.

So far as I know this is the first time that experts on the economic development of underdeveloped countries have held a meeting, conference or symposium in the setting of a typically underdeveloped country. I make no bones about it, this is a typically underdeveloped country, a poor country. You participants and observers have been here now for ten days or so and you have already discovered among other things the typically agricultural nature of the economy of this country. You will have discovered the fact that commercial life in this country is in the hands of, and controlled by, people other than the Africans of this country because the Africans of this country are poor and have no money to engage in trade and commerce.

I have not been able to come here in person every day that you held your meetings, but I have received reports of practically every session, and I know what has been discussed. I must say at once that I admire the spirit in which most of you came here. You came here, as one of you put it the first day, in a spirit of humility. I think it was the gentleman from Sweden, who said that you did not come here to impose, yourself on us or to tell us what to do. To me that is very important, very sensible and very reasonable. I am told that every day in the discussions differences of opinion among the participants have been obvious. That to me is a very significant thing.

We have here economists from America, Britain, Germany, Sweden and India. I am particularly happy to welcome our two Indian guests, because it became quite clear to me from Dr Rao's discourse that whilst we in this country will definitely benefit from the experiences of economists in America, Britain and other highly industrialized countries, it is from countries like India — where economic conditions are in some respects not very far removed from those which obtain in this country — that we can learn to our immediate benefit.

As some of you have already discovered, this country is poor, underdeveloped and essentially agricultural in its economy. Therefore, when your discussions are published, as I hope they will be, I shall be most interested to read what you have had to say about the problems of agricultural development in a country like this. Because in my view, if we are to develop Nyasaland in the way it should be developed, we must think in the first place in terms of developing and modernizing agriculture, rather than in terms of developing industries such as those they have in the Pittsburg or Ruhr steel complexes.

You will find that in the Development plan we have thought of every phase of our agriculture, forestry, fisheries and of the food crop. It so happens that for the reason that agriculture is the most important single subject in this country, I took charge of it myself, in order that if there is any mess to be made, I shall make that mess myself. And I have made it a rule in my ministry that all my agricultural officers must come down to earth, go to the farmers, and make themselves part and parcel of the people they are supposed to be teaching. You cannot teach anyone by looking down on him; you have to be with him, sit with him and talk to him as a friend. But that is only part of the story; we have to have some other means of increasing the facilities for people to come in contact with these agricultural officers and of modernizing agriculture. This is what we are doing. We are establishing, to begin with, three farm institutes, one in each province, and after that, I hope to have one in every district, and after that, one in every area. Fortunately for me and my ministry, the people in Britain are interested in us. The Mayor and City of Bristol have offered to raise money for agriculture to the tune of £47,000 to finance at least one of our main farm institutes in Lilongwe in the Central Province. If the Africans of this country are to be taught modernization of farming, they have to come to a place like this, where they can come in contact with the agricultural officers in larger numbers. We hope to have these

24

farm institutes, set in ten to twenty acres, where we can train our people, not only in the traditional method of hoeing, but also in ploughing, first with ox-drawn ploughs and, later on, with tractor-drawn ploughs.

At the same time, I want to instil into the people of this country the spirit of co-operation and self-reliance. Therefore, alongside the farm institutes, I want to organize co-operative societies so that when enough farmers have learnt to handle tractors, they can buy them, not as individuals but on a co-operative basis.

I am going further than that. It is not enough to organize my people, or to teach them through farm institutes and by organizing them into co-operative societies. There has to be a campaign of mass education in this country, apart from the formal kind of education that we know. Therefore, I am organizing community development in such a way that no matter how old a man or woman may be, he or she can learn, not only to read and write, but also how to make a bridge, how to improve their own hut, how to make dams with the advice of officers that will be sent from my Ministry. Because I so strongly believe in this movement, I have charged Kanyama Chiume with the whole question of social development, including community development schemes, so that we can achieve practical as well as formal education in this country. You cannot talk of modernizing agriculture with an uneducated community. To have a modern system of agriculture, you have to have educated, intelligent farmers; and, therefore, in our Development Plan education is priority number one. When I say education I use the word in its broadest sense: primary education, secondary education, teacher training colleges, technical colleges and finally a university. I am not going into details; you can read all this in our Development Plan.

I have said that one of the things that led me to encourage Dunduzu Chisiza to hold this symposium was that I wanted to advertise my country to the outside world. It has always been my intention that this country should be known and seen by people outside, by the world outside, much more than it is known and seen now. My country is beautiful, there are hills and mountains for those who love hills and mountains to climb. We have valleys for those who want to walk and we have our beautiful lake, 360 miles long and ninety miles at its widest, for those who like to swim and bathe in that clear water. You see, I am interested in tourism, and I hope some of you after you have gone back home will talk about my beautiful country. I am only sorry that there has not been enough time for all of you to go to Fort Johnson, Salima, Nkhotakota, Nkhata Bay and Karonga, to enjoy the beauty of our lake, the beauty of our little country.

Again, I have said that I was glad Dunduzu Chisiza should ask you to come here because I wanted to expose my people, the Africans of this country, to the gaze and even the critical and hostile glare of the whole world. You see, ladies and gentlemen, certain papers and news agencies have presented myself, my party and my people as being xenophobic. They have accused me and my party of being anti-white, anti-Indian, anti-everything but Africa. I wanted you gentlemen to come here and meet my people, see my people, talk to my people and make your own decision as to whether or not my people are xenophobic. During the time that you have been here you have met my people at social functions and I hope you have spoken to them and even joined in their free loud laughter, which is the gift of Africa to the world.

When I returned to this country in 1958, I found here a system of Government which in my view was not the right one. It was a Government of civil servants controlled by civil servants, a Government that did not do what the people wanted, simply because the people had no means of changing that Government. The Government comprised a Legislative Council of twenty-three members and an Executive Council of nine. Of the twenty-three members of the Legislative Council, only five were Africans. Of the eighteen European members twelve were civil servants and the rest non-official. There were no African members of the Executive Council.

This to me was not the kind of Government wanted in this country, at this stage, in the twentieth century, so I demanded a Government of elected representatives of the people as opposed to the Government of civil servants which I found. And, of course, second to that I demanded secession from their stupid Federation. Because I wanted self-government for my people, secession from the Federation, I was accused of xeno-phobia, hatred of the white man and hatred of the Indian. My quarrel was not, and is not, with the Europeans, not even with the British; nor is it with the Asians or Indians. I am not against the Europeans, I am not against the Indians, I am not against the British, my quarrel was and is with domination: domination of one race by another, domination of the Africans, my people, by the Europeans. I hated domination, I hate it now, and I shall always hate it.

While I am on that, I might as well answer the question, what is the future of Europeans in this country? I repeat that there is a bright future here for Europeans, on condition that they accept the fact that this is Nyasaland, and that we the Africans are in the majority, and that being in the majority we must govern this country. As long as people of other races accept this most reasonable condition, they are welcome here; but the minute they demand special privileges and assert that because they are white, because they are rich, because they are educated, they must have this or that which the African must not — then, I say to them, pack up now and go! This is Nyasaland — Malawi as I prefer to call it — on the continent of Africa; and in this Nyasaland, in this Malawi, we have no intention of tolerating foreign lords and masters.

In his speech on the opening day of this symposium, Sir Glyn Jones, the respected and beloved Governor of Nyasaland, touched on federation and secession, and His Worship the Mayor of Blantyre, at the lunch which he gave, touched on it too, in a joking way, in a story. It is inevitable that Sir Glyn and the Mayor should have touched on federation and secession, because secession of Nyasaland from the Federation is a topical subject just now. As economists I know that most of you support the Federation, for economic reasons. You are accustomed to think in terms of larger political units, which in your view provide larger markets, and therefore ensure economic viability and prosperity for any political organization.

But what is this Federation in Central Africa of which we now form an unwilling part? In my view it is not true federation at all. A true federation, as I understand it, is a union of peoples — independent or about to become so — who have come together for the benefit of all. They voluntarily surrender some of their sovereign powers to a government which unites them. We know this was the case with the former North American colonies of Britain. The Canadian Provinces, later on, similarly decided to form a federal government. They agreed with one another as to what powers they would give to that government, and what powers they would keep for themselves. So, too, with Australia. More recent examples of true federal unions are those of Nigeria and Malaya: in either case the peoples concerned have agreed with each other on the formation of a single state out of many states.

Was this what happened with the so-called Federation of Rhodesia and Nyasaland? Not in the least. Persuaded by European settlers in Central Africa, the British Government imposed this Federation on us and on our fellow-Africans in the two Rhodesias. Why did the British Government do this? According to a White Paper prepared in 1951 by Mr (now Sir) Andrew Cohen, federation was desirable for reasons of economics, defence and communications. The need for partnership was a fourth reason adduced at the time: for partnership, that is, between the races. But were these the reasons why the settlers of Central Africa wanted federation? I saw no reason to think so at the time, and I have seen no reason since. For I am old enough, after all, to know the historical background of this whole question.

When in 1951 Sir Godfrey Huggins (now Lord Malvern) and Mr (now Sir) Roy Welensky and their colleagues demanded federation of the two Rhodesias and Nyasaland, it was not the first time that the idea of union, at least of the two Rhodesias, had been mooted. So far as I know, this idea of union was first proposed as long ago as 1916. At that time the British South Africa Company, which then administered both the Rhodesias, wanted them to be joined under one government; but the European settlers, both in Northern and in Southern Rhodesia, would not have it. They rejected the idea. Three years later there was another attempt to achieve this union, but again the Northern and Southern Rhodesia settlers threw it out. And four years after that, in 1923, the question of union was once more raised. Desiring an administrative change in the Rhodesias, the British Government offered the Southern Rhodesia settlers a choice by referendum of three alternatives: to join the Union of South Africa, to join with Northern Rhodesia, or to form their own state. The Southern Rhodesia settlers chose to go it alone, and formed their own state.

Three times, we see, a majority of settlers rejected the idea of union in Central Africa, but in 1931 they changed their minds. In that year the settlers of Southern and Northern Rhodesia, and even those of Nyasaland, began to press for union of the three territories. Why, you may wonder, in 1931? What happened in 1931 to cause this change of front among the settlers? I will tell you. Lord Passfield, who was then Secretary of State for the Colonies, issued a memorandum in that year. This memorandum laid it down that whenever the interests of immigrant communities should conflict with those of the African peoples of the countries concerned, the interest of the Africans must be paramount; and made it clear, moreover, that this doctrine of colonial rule applied in Central Africa, as well as in Kenya to which the Duke of Devonshire had applied it, theoretically at least, eight years earlier. This infuriated the Central African settlers, and they demanded amalgamation of the two Rhodesias.

What moved them to make this demand? It is easy to answer that. There were two so-called native policies in Central Africa. One was that of the Colonial Office, which held, at least in theory, that Britain was in Africa as a trustee, her object being to prepare the Africans for the day when they would be able to stand on their own feet. This was known as the Policy of Trusteeship and Native Paramountcy and was first enunciated by the Duke of Devonshire when Secretary of State for the Colonies in the Conservative Government in 1923. But Lord Passfield's restatement of this policy, coming as it did from a socialist, sounded much worse to the Central African settlers. They accordingly demanded amalgamation of Northern with Southern Rhodesia so as to rid themselves of Colonial Office control, threatening as this did to allow the Africans, eventually, to come into their own. The settlers' simple idea was to extend the so-called native policy of Southern Rhodesia to Northern Rhodesia. And what was their native policy? It was radically different in practice and intention from the Policy of Trusteeship. This other native policy in Central Africa was in fact the same kind of rule as the white domination which existed in the Union of South Africa, and which exists today in the republic of that name.

Some people have argued that Southern Rhodesia is different from South Africa. I do not agree; and I have lived in both. When the Southern Rhodesia settlers were given self-government in 1923 they in any case copied the rules and regulations of the Union of South Africa. They copied such measures of the Hertzog Government of 1924 as the Native Registration Act, the Native Urban Areas Act, the Industrial Conciliation Act. They modelled their land laws on the Union's Native Lands Act of 1913. Not only that; at least in the early days of Southern Rhodesian self-government, they even brought European officers from the Union to administer these laws.

Understanding the aims of the Southern Rhodesia settlers in pressing for amalgamation, the Colonial Office could not, of course, agree with any such proposal. But the settlers continued to press their demand with such vehemence that the British Government eventually decided to appoint a Royal Commission to enquire into the advisability of a closer association between the three territories. This came about in 1937. Under their chairman, Lord Bledisloe, the members of the Commission visited all three territories and took much evidence. In 1939 they reported adversely on the idea of amalgamation, pointing out that Southern Rhodesia's avowed policy of race segregation and the institution of a colour bar clearly stood in the way. Even then the settlers did not drop their demand.

Under the leadership of Sir Godfrey Huggins in Southern Rhodesia and of Mr (now Sir) Roy Welensky in Northern Rhodesia, they continued to agitate for amalgamation. The war interposed a kind of moratorium on the question, but it was raised again as soon as the war was over. Indeed, it was raised even sooner than that: for once the British had begun to chase the Germans and Italians out of North Africa, Sir Godfrey Huggins went to London with a fresh demand for amalgamation. I know this because I was in London at the time. After the war, though, the settlers' leaders were advised by their friends among the Conservatives to adopt a new approach: they should ask for federation, not amalgamation, and they should shift their emphasis from politics to reasons of economics, defence, communications and partnership. They did so, urging in London the mining advantages that would flow from federation, and pointing out at the same time how seriously anti-British the situation was becoming in South Africa. It so happened at that time Mr James Griffiths, then Colonial Secretary, had given the Gold Coast a measure of self-government under Dr Kwame Nkrumah. The Central African settlers' leaders tried to draw out of this an advantage for themselves. In effect they said: look, Malan is in the south and Nkrumah in the north, but we in the centre will create a British state; and in this state partnership will be our central policy — neither white extreme nationalism nor black extreme nationalism will be able to prevail against it. That went well with the leaders of the British parties, especially, I am sorry to say, with those of the Labour party.

But I was not deceived. Not at the time, and not later. I remembered what these same settlers' leaders had said in 1931. Then they had explained how they were in Central Africa as rulers, and that any talk of trusteeship, of preparing the Africans for self-government, was unthinkable nonsense. And indeed I and those who thought with me were proved to be right. The leopard had not changed his spots. Immediately they had achieved their Federation — *their* Federation, let me emphasize, not ours — they made it clear that the sort of partnership they had in mind was the partnership between the rider and the horse. And that is why I want secession from their Federation. That is why we all want secession from their Federation. That is why we can be satisfied with nothing less. Arguments about 'economic necessity' do not influence me. Even if we have to eat roots, as our ancestors did in times of famine, we will do that rather than not secede.

Professor Brown spoke on economic union. No sensible person would quarrel with the idea of economic union as such. But, ladies and gentlemen, when you talk about economic union, before you can be dogmatic about it certain problems, certain questions have to be settled and answered. Who is to decide the formation of these unions? Is it to be decided by the people themselves or by someone from outside or from above? Which countries are to go into the union? Who is to decide what this country will do? And who are to negotiate on its behalf? I am asking all these questions because, so far as we are concerned here, we must know who is to decide. If it means this union must be decided by the people themselves and that the people's recognized leaders must be the ones to negotiate, then I ask, since I am where I am now in this country politically, with what countries am I justified in joining Nyasaland into economic union? With what politicians am I justified in negotiating political union, and at what stage of political development in this country? If I want to enter into economic union with Southern Rhodesia or Northern Rhodesia, with whom am I to negotiate and at what stage of political development in these countries?

On this question of secession from the Federation, and its component question of alternative union, I want no one to be left in doubt whatsoever that we will secede. I am determined to pull Nyasaland out of the Federation.

Similarly, before anyone can talk of an alternative form of association, these basic questions must be settled: with which country should Nyasaland be associated, at what stage of political development and with which politician should negotiations be opened?

Before these questions are settled, there can be no question of Nyasaland entering into any economic union with any country as long as I occupy the place I occupy now in the Government of this country, in the Malawi Congress Party and, above all, in the hearts and minds of my people.

DATE DUE

JA 30'71			
GAYLORD			PRINTED IN U.S.A.